W9-CBE-901

Technical Analysis from A to Z

Technical Analysis from A to Z

**Covers Every Trading Tool . . .
from the Absolute Breadth Index to the Zig Zag**

Second Edition

Steven B. Achelis

McGraw-Hill

New York   San Francisco   Washington, D.C.   Auckland   Bogotá
Caracas   Lisbon   London   Madrid   Mexico City   Milan
Montreal   New Delhi   San Juan   Singapore
Sydney   Tokyo   Toronto

Library of Congress Cataloging-in-Publication Data

Achelis, Steven B.
    Technical analysis from A to Z / by Steven B. Achelis.—2nd ed.
        p. cm.
    Includes bibliographical references and index.
    ISBN 0-07-136348-3
    1. Investment analysis—Terminology.   2. Stock price forecasting—Terminology.
  3. Stocks—Prices—Charts, diagrams, etc. I. Title.

[HG4529 .A294   2000]
332.6—dc21
                                   00-040100

McGraw-Hill

A Division of The **McGraw-Hill** *Companies*

   3 4 5 6 7 8 9 0   AGM/AGM   0 9 8 7 6 5 4 3 2

ISBN 0-07-136348-3

This book was set in Giovanni by Carlisle Communications, Ltd.

Printed and bound by Quebecor World/Martinsburg.

This publication is designed to provide accurate and authoritative information in regard to the subject matter covered. It is sold with the understanding that neither the author nor the publisher is engaged in rendering legal, accounting, futures/securities trading, or other professional service. If legal advice or other expert assistance is required, the services of a competent professional person should be sought.

    —*From a Declaration of Principles jointly adopted by a Committee
    of the American Bar Association and a Committee of Publishers.*

McGraw-Hill books are available at special quantity discounts to use as premiums and sales promotions, or for use in corporate training programs. For more information, please write to the Director of Special Sales, Professional Publishing, McGraw-Hill, Two Penn Plaza, New York, NY 10121-2298. Or contact your local bookstore.

 This book is printed on recycled, acid-free paper containing a minimum of 50% recycled, de-inked fiber.

CONTENTS

PREFACE TO FIRST EDITION xiii

PREFACE TO SECOND EDITION xiv

ACKNOWLEDGMENTS xv

TERMINOLOGY xvi

CALCULATIONS xvii

    Rounding xvii

    A-to-Z Companion Spreadsheet xvii

TO LEARN MORE xviii

PART ONE: INTRODUCTION TO TECHNICAL ANALYSIS 1

TECHNICAL ANALYSIS 2

    Some History 2

    The Human Element 2

    Fundamental Analysis 3

    The Future Can Be Found in the Past 3

    The Weatherman 3

    The Roulette Wheel 4

    Computerized Trading 5

PRICE FIELDS 6

CHARTS 7

    Line Charts 8

    Bar Charts 8

    Semi-Log Verus Linear Scaling .9

Volume Bar Chart 11

Other Chart Types 11

PERIODICITY 12

THE TIME ELEMENT 13

SUPPORT AND RESISTANCE 14

Supply and Demand 18

Traders' Remorse 19

Resistance Becomes Support 23

Review 25

TRENDS 25

MOVING AVERAGES 27

Time Periods in Moving Averages 29

Merits 30

Traders' Remorse 30

INDICATORS 31

Moving Average Convergence/Divergence (MACD) 31

Leading Versus Lagging Indicators 33

Trending Prices Versus Trading Prices 35

Divergences 36

MARKET INDICATORS 37

Categories of Market Indicators .38

LINE STUDIES 41

A SAMPLE APPROACH 41

CONCLUSION 43

PART TWO: REFERENCE 45

ABSOLUTE BREADTH INDEX 46

ACCUMULATION/DISTRIBUTION LINE 48

ACCUMULATION SWING INDEX 51

ADVANCE/DECLINE LINE 52

ADVANCE/DECLINE RATIO 55

ADVANCING-DECLINING ISSUES .56

ADVANCING, DECLINING, UNCHANGED VOLUME 58

ANDREWS'S PITCHFORK 60

ARMS INDEX (TRIN) 61

AROON 64

AVERAGE TRUE RANGE 68

BOLLINGER BANDS 71

BREADTH THRUST 74

BULL/BEAR RATIO 78

CANDLESTICKS, JAPANESE 79

CANSLIM 90

CHAIKIN MONEY FLOW 93

CHAIKIN OSCILLATOR 96

CHANDE MOMENTUM OSCILLATOR 100

COMMODITY CHANNEL INDEX .103

COMMODITY SELECTION INDEX 106

CORRELATION ANALYSIS 108

CUMULATIVE VOLUME INDEX .110

CYCLES 112

DEMAND INDEX 116

DETRENDED PRICE OSCILLATOR 117

DIRECTIONAL MOVEMENT 119

DOUBLE EXPONENTIAL MOVING AVERAGE 121

DOW THEORY 123

DYNAMIC MOMENTUM INDEX .128

EASE OF MOVEMENT 130

EFFICIENT MARKET THEORY 133

ELLIOTT WAVE THEORY 134

ENVELOPES (TRADING BANDS) 137

EQUIVOLUME 138

FIBONACCI STUDIES 141

FORECAST OSCILLATOR 145

FOUR PERCENT MODEL 147

FOURIER TRANSFORM 149

FUNDAMENTAL ANALYSIS 151

GANN ANGLES 153

HERRICK PAYOFF INDEX 156

INERTIA 157

INTEREST RATES 158

INTRADAY MOMENTUM INDEX 161

KAGI 164

KLINGER OSCILLATOR 167

LARGE BLOCK RATIO 171

LINEAR REGRESSION INDICATOR 172

LINEAR REGRESSION SLOPE 174

LINEAR REGRESSION TRENDLINES 176

MARKET FACILITATION INDEX 178

MASS INDEX 181

McCLELLAN OSCILLATOR 183

McCLELLAN SUMMATION INDEX 187

MEDIAN PRICE 190

MEMBER SHORT RATIO 192

MESA SINE WAVE .193

MOMENTUM 195

MONEY FLOW INDEX .197

MOVING AVERAGE CONVERGENCE/DIVERGENCE 199

MOVING AVERAGES 203

    Calculation, Simple Moving Average .207

    Calculation, Exponential Moving Average 208

    Calculation, Time Series Moving Average 210

    Calculation, Triangular Moving Average 210

    Calculation, Variable Moving Average 210

    Calculation, Volume-Adjusted Moving Average 212

    Calculation, Weighted Moving Average 212

NEGATIVE VOLUME INDEX 214

NEW HIGHS-LOWS CUMULATIVE 217

NEW HIGHS/LOWS RATIO 218

NEW HIGHS-NEW LOWS 220

ODD LOT BALANCE INDEX 222

ODD LOT PURCHASES/SALES 224

ODD LOT SHORT RATIO 225

ODDS PROBABILITY CONES 227

ON BALANCE VOLUME 229

OPEN INTEREST .232

OPEN-10 TRIN .233

OPTION ANALYSIS .236

OVERBOUGHT/OVERSOLD 240

PARABOLIC SAR .242

PATTERNS .245

PERCENT RETRACEMENT 250

PERFORMANCE 251

POINT AND FIGURE 253

POLARIZED FRACTAL EFFICIENCY 256

POSITIVE VOLUME INDEX 257

PRICE AND VOLUME TREND 261

PRICE CHANNEL 263

PRICE OSCILLATOR 265

PRICE RATE-OF-CHANGE 267

PROJECTION BANDS 270

PROJECTION OSCILLATOR 271

PUBLIC SHORT RATIO 274

PUTS/CALLS RATIO 276

QSTICK 278

QUADRANT LINES 280

R-SQUARED 282

RAFF REGRESSION CHANNEL 284

RANDOM WALK INDEX 285

RANGE INDICATOR 287

RECTANGLE 290

RELATIVE MOMENTUM INDEX 291

RELATIVE STRENGTH, COMPARATIVE 294

RELATIVE STRENGTH INDEX 297

RELATIVE VOLATILITY INDEX 300

RENKO 302

SPEED RESISTANCE LINES 305

SPREADS 306

STANDARD DEVIATION 308

STANDARD DEVIATION CHANNEL 310

STANDARD ERROR 311

STANDARD ERROR BANDS 313

STANDARD ERROR CHANNEL 315

STIX 316

STOCHASTIC MOMENTUM INDEX 318

STOCHASTIC OSCILLATOR 321

SWING INDEX 326

TEMA 328

THREE LINE BREAK 330

TIME SERIES FORECAST 333

TIRONE LEVELS 335

TOTAL SHORT RATIO 336

TRADE VOLUME INDEX 338

TRENDLINES 341

TRIX 342

TYPICAL PRICE 344

ULTIMATE OSCILLATOR 346

UPSIDE/DOWNSIDE RATIO 348

UPSIDE/DOWNSIDE VOLUME .350

VERTICAL HORIZONTAL FILTER 351

VOLATILITY, CHAIKIN'S 354

VOLUME 356

VOLUME OSCILLATOR 358

VOLUME RATE-OF-CHANGE 360

WEIGHTED CLOSE 362

WILDER'S SMOOTHING 364

WILLIAMS'S ACCUMULATION/DISTRIBUTION 366

WILLIAMS'S %R 369

ZIG ZAG 372

INDEX 375

PREFACE TO FIRST EDITION

Over the last decade I have met many of the top technical analysis "gurus" as well as shared experiences with thousands of newcomers. The common element I've discovered among investors who use technical analysis, regardless of their expertise, is the desire to learn more.

No single book, nor any collection of books, can provide a complete explanation of technical analysis. Not only is the field too massive, covering everything from Federal Reserve reports to Fibonacci arcs, but it is also evolving so quickly that anything written today becomes incomplete (but not obsolete) tomorrow.

Armed with the above knowledge and well aware of the myriad of technical analysis books that are already available, I feel there is a genuine need for a concise reference book on technical analysis that serves the needs of both the novice and veteran investor. That is what I have strived to create.

The first half of this book is for the newcomer. It is an introduction to technical analysis that presents basic concepts and terminology. The second half is a reference that is designed for anyone using technical analysis. It contains concise explanations of numerous technical analysis tools in a reference format.

When my father began using technical analysis 30 years ago, many people considered technical analysis just another 1960s adventure into the occult. Today, technical analysis is accepted as a viable analytical approach by most universities and brokerage firms. Rarely are large investments made without reviewing the technical climate. Yet even with its acceptance, the number of people who actually perform technical analysis remains relatively small. It is my hope that this book will increase the awareness and use of technical analysis, and in turn, improve the results of those who practice it.

PREFACE TO SECOND EDITION

This second edition of *Technical Analysis from A to Z* greatly expands on the original book by adding all new illustrations, over 30 new indicators, and detailed step-by-step calculations on more than 80 indicators.

While the changes in this book are significant, the changes that have taken place in the markets have been truly momentous: Web trading and the Internet, the e-Economy, and the extreme market valuations given to companies with few customers and fewer earnings. Yet one truth has remained constant during this period of change: the prices of securities are based on investor expectations and emotions. In a period where a company's fundamentals (i.e., earnings) seem to be ignored by the market, technical analysis is more viable than ever!

ACKNOWLEDGMENTS

The truth that no man is an island certainly holds true here. This book would not be possible without the help of thousands of analysts who have studied the markets and shared their results. To those from whom I have compiled this information, thank you.

There are two people who deserve enormous credit for the creation of this book: John Slauson and Jon DeBry. These two friends and colleagues spent countless hours buried in time-consuming editorial and research tasks. Without their help, this book would not exist.

TERMINOLOGY

For brevity, I use the term "security" when referring to any tradable financial instrument. This includes stocks, bonds, commodities, futures, indices, mutual funds, options, etc. While I may imply a specific investment product (for example, I may say "shares," which implies an equity), the investment concepts I present will work with any publicly traded financial instrument for which an open market exists.

> *Words are like money; there is nothing so useless, unless when in actual use.*
>
> *-Samuel Butler, 1902*

Similarly, I intermix the terms "investing" and "trading." Typically, an investor takes a long-term position, while a trader takes a much shorter-term position. In either case, the basic concepts and techniques presented in this book are equally applicable.

CALCULATIONS

Numerous formulas and tables explaining indicator calculations are presented throughout this book. If you are only interested in profiting from indicators, you can simply skip these complex details. If you are interested in the calculations, there are a few things you should know.

ROUNDING

As in a computer spreadsheet, the values in the following tables are often rounded to conserve space. For example, the value 9.87654321 might be displayed as 9.877. As in a spreadsheet, the calculations use the full values (not the truncated values displayed in the table).

A-TO-Z COMPANION SPREADSHEET

I have done my utmost to present the full indicator calculations in this book whenever practical. However, due to space limitations and/or complexity, some of the calculations are not presented.

To help you better understand the calculations, I have developed a computer spreadsheet that contains the calculations of more than a hundred of the indicators presented in this book. Each calculation is contained on its own page within the spreadsheet. The A-to-Z Companion Spreadsheet can be purchased at AtoZbook.com.

TO LEARN MORE

Investors share a common desire—they want to learn more. To learn more about technical analysis and charting, visit www.equis.com. Equis has an unparalleled selection of technical analysis books, software, and training materials.

This second edition was produced with the assistance of Jon DeBry. Jon was a senior computer programmer on the MetaStock investment analysis software project at Equis. He is now an independent money manager and investment software developer. Visit www.debry.com or email jdebry@debry.com to learn more about his services.

Steve Achelis

A companion spreadsheet, corrections, suggested books, and other supplemental information can be found at AtoZbook.com.

PART ONE

INTRODUCTION TO
TECHNICAL ANALYSIS

Part One was written for investors who are new to technical analysis. The chapters present the basic technical analysis concepts and terminology in a concise manner. If you are familiar with technical analysis, you will probably find Part Two (see page 45) to be the appropriate starting point.

TECHNICAL ANALYSIS

Should I buy today? What will prices be tomorrow, next week, or next year? Wouldn't investing be easy if we knew the answers to these seemingly simple questions? Alas, if you are reading this book in the hope that technical analysis offers the answers to these questions, I'm afraid I have to disappoint you early—it doesn't. However, if you are reading this book with the hope that technical analysis will improve your investing, I have good news—it will!

Some History

The term "technical analysis" is a complicated-sounding name for a very basic approach to investing. Simply put, technical analysis is the study of prices to make better investments, with charts being the primary tool.

The roots of modern-day technical analysis stem from the Dow Theory, developed around 1900 by Charles Dow. Stemming either directly or indirectly from the Dow Theory, these roots include such principles as the trending nature of prices, prices discounting all known information, confirmation and divergence, volume mirroring changes in price, and support/resistance. Of course, the widely followed Dow Jones Industrial Average is an important component of the Dow Theory.

Charles Dow's contribution to modern-day technical analysis cannot be understated. His focus on the basics of security price movement gave rise to a completely new method of analysis.

The Human Element

The price of a security represents a consensus. It is the price at which one person agrees to buy and another agrees to sell. The price at which an investor is willing to buy or sell depends primarily on his expectations. If he expects the security's price to rise, he will buy it; if he expects the price to fall, he will sell it. These simple statements are the cause of a major challenge in forecasting security prices, because they refer to *human* expectations. As we all know firsthand, humans are neither easily quantifiable nor predictable. This fact alone will keep any mechanical trading system from working consistently.

Because humans are involved, I am sure that many of the world's investment decisions are based on irrelevant criteria. Our relationships with our family, our neighbors, our employer, the traffic, our income, and our previous successes and failures all influence our confidence, expectations, and decisions.

Security prices are determined by money managers and home managers, students and strikers, doctors and dog catchers, lawyers and landscapers, and the wealthy and the wanting. This breadth of market participants guarantees an element of unpredictability and excitement as investor expectations swing from exuberance to terror.

Fundamental Analysis

If we were all totally logical and could separate our emotions from our investment decisions, then fundamental analysis, the determination of price based on future earnings (see page 151), would work magnificently. And since we would all have the same completely logical expectations, prices would change only when quarterly reports or relevant news were released. Investors would seek "overlooked" fundamental data in an effort to find undervalued securities.

The hotly debated "efficient market theory" (see page 133) states that a security's price represents everything that is known about the security at a given moment. This theory concludes that it is impossible to forecast prices, since prices already reflect everything that is currently known about a security.

The Future Can Be Found in the Past

> *"The big variable in a security's price is the premium or discount investors add to the "correct" price.*

> *I believe the future is only the past again, entered through another gate.*
> —*Sir Arthur Wing Pinero, 1893*

If prices are based on investor expectations, then knowing what a security *should* sell for (i.e., fundamental analysis) becomes less important than knowing what other investors *expect* it to sell for. That's not to say that knowing what a security should sell for isn't important—it is! But there is usually a fairly strong consensus about a stock's future earnings that the average investor cannot disprove. The big variable in a security's price is the premium or discount investors add to the "correct" price.

Technical analysis is the process of analyzing a security's historical prices in an effort to determine probable future prices. This is done by comparing current price action (i.e., current expectations) with comparable historical price action to predict a reasonable outcome. The devout technician might define this process with the cliché "History repeats itself," while others would say that we should learn from the past.

The Weatherman

Just as a weatherman uses past and current weather trends to forecast the weather, investors use technical analysis to forecast prices.

By studying the current and historical jet stream, pressure systems, temperatures, and precipitation, a meteorologist can make a reasonably accurate forecast for the near future. Certainly this approach isn't flawless because weather patterns can and do shift unexpectedly, but the approach greatly increases the accuracy of the forecast.

It is difficult to forecast the weather if you are sitting in your home with the blinds drawn. Yet armed with a satellite photo and a clear window, even a layperson can make a reasonable forecast of the next day's weather.

Likewise, attempting to invest without understanding current and historical price action is difficult, if not impossible. However, by looking at such basic charting information as the current trend, historical high and low prices, support and resistance levels, and the volume associated with changes in prices, a reasonable forecast can be made.

> *Technical analysis is the process of analyzing a security's historical prices in an effort to determine probable future prices.*

As with weather forecasting, technical analysis is not flawless, but the information contained in a chart is a critical aid in the investing process.

The Roulette Wheel

In my experience, only a tiny minority of technicians can determine future prices consistently and accurately. However, even if you are unable to forecast prices accurately, you can use technical analysis to consistently reduce your risks and improve your profits.

Another analogy about how technical analysis can help you improve your investing is a roulette wheel. I use this analogy with reservation, as gamblers have very little control over the odds when compared to investors—although considering the actions of many investors, gambling may be a very appropriate analogy.

A casino makes money with a roulette wheel not by knowing what number will come up next but by *slightly* improving its odds with the addition of 0 and 00 (i.e., "aught" and "double-aught").

> *There are two times in a man's life when he should not speculate; when he can't afford it, and when he can.*
> —Mark Twain, 1897

Similarly, when an investor purchases a security, she doesn't know that its price will rise. However, if she buys a stock in a rising trend, after a minor sell-off, and when interest rates are falling, she will have improved her odds for making a profit. That's not gambling—it's intelligence. Yet many investors buy securities without ever attempting to control the odds!

Contrary to popular belief, you do not need to know what a security's price will be in the future to make money. Your goal should be simply to improve the odds of making profitable trades. Even if your analysis is as simple as determining the short-, intermediate-, and long-term trends of the security,

FIGURE 1

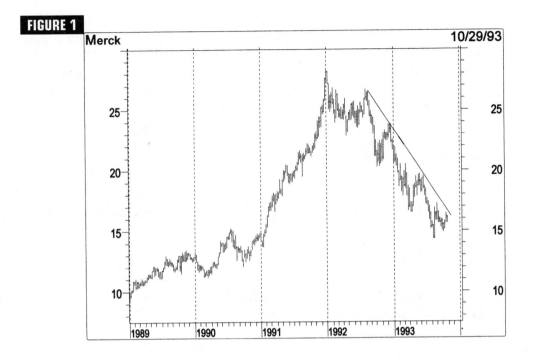

Merck — 10/29/93

you will have gained an edge that you would not have without technical analysis.

Consider the chart of Merck in Figure 1, where the trend is obviously down and there is no sign of a reversal. While the company may have great earnings prospects and fundamentals, it just doesn't make sense to buy the security until there is some technical evidence in the price that this trend is changing.

Computerized Trading

If we accept the fact that human emotions and expectations play a significant role in security pricing, we should also admit that our emotions play a significant role in our decision making. Many investors try to remove their emotions from their investing by using computers to make decisions for them. The concept of an intelligent computer making decisions for you, like "Hal" in *2001: A Space Odyssey*, is appealing.

Yes, mechanical trading systems can help us separate our emotions from our decisions. For example, the popular investment analysis software, Meta-Stock (which was used to generate all of the charts in this book), can run a "system test" in which you specify the buy/sell rules, commission rates, and interest rate you earn when not in a trade and the software quickly calculates every trade and determines how much you would have made or lost. The software can also "optimize" your buy/sell rules by automatically changing various parameters to enhance their profitability.

Yet since we are analyzing a less than logical subject (human emotions and expectations), we must be careful that our mechanical systems do not mislead us into thinking that we are analyzing a logical entity.

That is not to say that computers aren't wonderful technical analysis tools—they are indispensable. In my *totally biased* opinion, technical analysis software has done more to level the playing field for the average investor than any other non-regulatory event. However, as a former developer of technical analysis tools, I caution you not to let the software lull you into believing markets are as logical and predictable as the computer you use.

Likewise, the flow of news and information on the Internet is seductive. Knowing more about the companies, the industries, and the environment in which you invest is important, but the overwhelming flow of information and rumors often leads to more confusion, whereas a simple chart cuts through the noise and reveals the true value of a security.

PRICE FIELDS

Technical analysis is based almost entirely on the analysis of price and volume. The fields that define a security's price and volume are explained below.

Open—This is the price of the first trade for the period (e.g., the first trade of the day). When analyzing daily data, the open is especially important as it is the consensus price after all interested parties were able to "sleep on it."

High—This is the highest price that the security traded during the period. It is the point at which there were more sellers than buyers (i.e., there are always sellers willing to sell at higher prices, but the high represents the highest price that buyers were willing to pay).

Low—This is the lowest price that the security traded during the period. It is the point at which there were more buyers than sellers (i.e., there are always buyers willing to buy at lower prices, but the low represents the lowest price sellers were willing to accept).

Close—This is the last price that the security traded during the period. Due to its availability, the close is the price used most often for analysis. The relationship between the open (the first price) and the close (the last price) is considered significant by most technicians. This relationship is emphasized in candlestick charts (see page 79).

Volume—This is the number of shares (or contracts) that were traded during the period. The relationship between prices and volume (e.g., increasing prices accompanied by increasing volume) is important.

Open Interest—This is the total number of outstanding contracts (i.e., those that have not been exercised, closed, or expired) of a future or option. Open interest is often used as an indicator (see page 232).

Bid—This is the price a market maker is willing to pay for a security (i.e., the price you will receive if you sell).

Ask—This is the price a market maker is willing to accept (i.e., the price you will pay to buy the security).

These simple price fields are used to create literally hundreds of technical tools that study price relationships, trends, patterns, etc. Not all of these price fields are available for all security types, and many quote providers publish only a subset of these. Table 1 shows the typical fields that are reported for several security types.

TABLE 1

Price Field	Futures	Mutual Funds	Stocks	Options
Open	Yes	No	Often	Yes
High	Yes	Closed end	Yes	Yes
Low	Yes	Closed end	Yes	Yes
Close	Yes	Yes (*NAV)	Yes	Yes
Volume	Yes	Closed end	Yes	Yes
Open Int.	Yes	N/A	N/A	Often
Bid	Intraday	Closed end	Intraday	Intraday
Ask	Intraday	Closed end	Intraday	Intraday

*Net Asset Value.

CHARTS

The foundation of technical analysis is the chart. In this case, a picture *is* truly worth a thousand words.

FIGURE 2

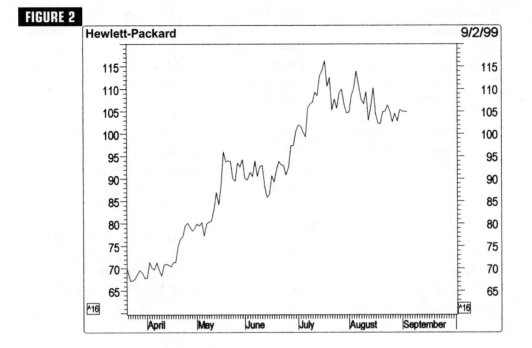

Line Charts

A line chart is the simplest type of chart. As shown in the chart of Hewlett-Packard in Figure 2, the single line represents the security's closing price on each day. Dates are displayed along the bottom of the chart and prices are displayed on the side(s).

A line chart's strength comes from its simplicity. It provides an uncluttered, easy-to-understand view of a security's price. Line charts are typically displayed using a security's closing prices.

Bar Charts

A bar chart displays a security's open (if available), high, low, and closing prices. Bar charts are the most popular type of security chart.

As illustrated in the bar chart in Figure 3, the top of each vertical bar represents the highest price that the security traded during the period, and the bottom of the bar represents the lowest price that it traded. A closing "tick" is displayed on the right side of the bar to designate the last price that the security traded. If opening prices are available, they are signified by a tick on the left side of the bar.

FIGURE 3

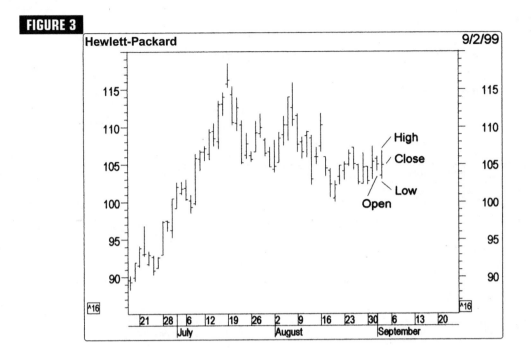

Semi-Log Versus Linear Scaling

The vertical scale on a price chart can be displayed using one of two methods. On a linear scale, the distance between each point is the same regardless of its value. For example, the distance between 1.0 and 2.0 is the same as the distance between 98.0 and 99.0. Linear scaling is sometimes referred to as arithmetic scaling.

On a semi-log scale, the distance between each point depends on its value. For example, the distance between 10 and 20 (a 10-point and 100-percent increase) is the same as the distance between 50 and 100 (a 50-point increase, yet still a 100-percent increase). Semi-log scaling is sometimes referred to as logarithmic or ratio scaling.

Figure 4 shows charts of the Dow Jones Industrial Average from 1900 through 1999. The chart on the top uses linear scaling while the chart on the bottom uses semi-log scaling. Note that prices look much "higher" on the linearly scaled chart, whereas the chart on the bottom probably shows a more realistic, yet still very high, perspective. The difference between linear and semi-log scaling is most apparent when the price has a significant price change from near zero.

FIGURE 4

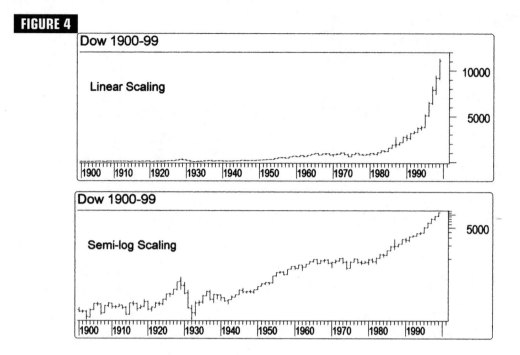

FIGURE 5

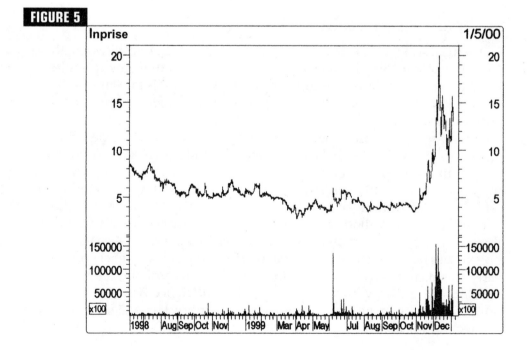

Volume Bar Chart

Volume is often displayed as a bar graph at the bottom of the chart. In Figure 5, note how volume increased as Inprise's price soared.

Figure 5 displays "zero-based" volume. This means the bottom of each volume bar represents the value of zero. However, most analysts prefer to see volume that is "relative-adjusted" rather than zero-based. This is done by subtracting the lowest volume that occurred during the period displayed from all of the volume bars. Relative-adjusted volume bars make it easier to see trends in volume by ignoring the minimum daily volume.

Figure 6 displays two charts of the same volume information. The upper chart contains zero-based volume, whereas the lower chart displays relative-adjusted volume. You can see that the lower chart emphasizes changes in volume.

Other Chart Types

Security prices can also be displayed using other types of charts, such as Candlestick, Equivolume, Kagi, Point and Figure, etc. For brevity's sake, explanations of these charting methods appear only in Part Two (see page 45).

FIGURE 6

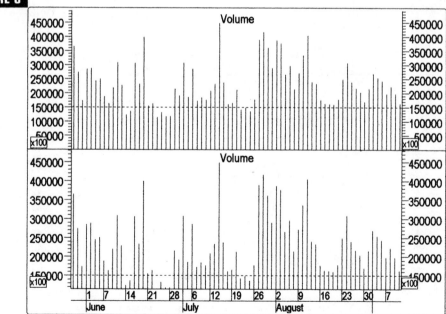

PERIODICITY

Regardless of the "periodicity" of the data in your charts (i.e., hourly, daily, weekly, monthly, etc.), the basic principles of technical analysis endure. Consider the charts of Boeing shown in Figures 7, 8, and 9. Although the periodicities range from 5-minute to weekly bars, the basic price movements are very similar.

> *While we stop and think, we often miss our opportunity.*
>
> —*Publius Syrus, 1st century* B.C.

Typically, the shorter the periodicity, the more difficult it is to predict and profit from changes in prices. The difficulty associated with shorter periodicities is compounded by the fact that you have less time to make your decisions.

FIGURE 7

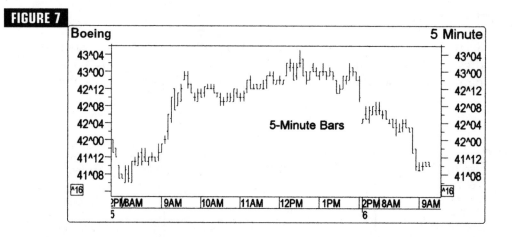

FIGURE 8

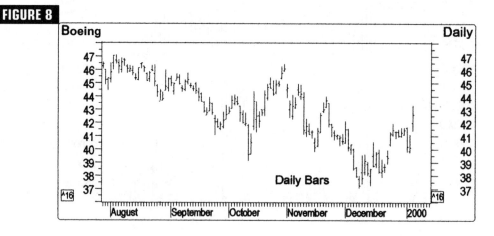

FIGURE 9

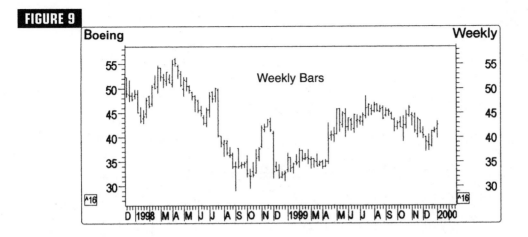

Opportunities exist in any time frame, but I have rarely met a successful short-term trader who wasn't also a successful long-term investor. Also, I have met many investors who get caught by the grass-is-greener syndrome, believing that using shorter and shorter time periods is the secret to making money. It isn't.

As you shorten the periodicity, the quality and timeliness of the data become more important. For example, daily data arriving an hour late is no big deal, but a tick that arrives 5 minutes late can be devastating. Unfortunately, many of the "real-time" quotes (i.e., those that are updated instantly) on the Internet are anything but real-time. Most of the delays on the Internet have less to do with the Internet itself than with data suppliers who don't seem to understand the importance of timely data.

The indicator interpretations and calculations in this book often refer to daily data. For example, I might say, "If the closing price is greater than the previous day's closing price." However, you can substitute any time frame for the term "day." For example, when looking at an hourly chart, the preceding phrase could be restated, "If the closing price is greater than the previous hour's closing price."

THE TIME ELEMENT

The discussion that began on page 6 explained the open, high, low, and closing *price* fields. This section presents the *time* element, because much of technical analysis focuses on changes in prices over time.

FIGURE 10

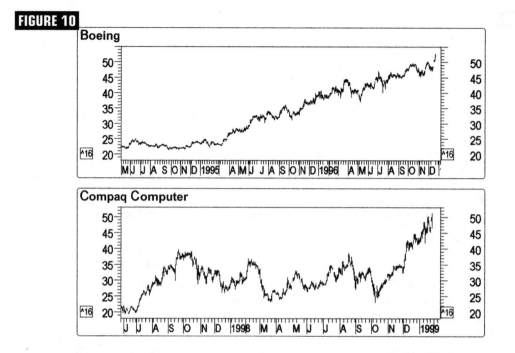

Figure 10 shows charts of Boeing and Compaq, both having increased from near $20.00 to more than $50.00 over a 20-month period. Note how Boeing's price increased consistently over the 20 months as investors' expectations for Boeing improved gradually, whereas Compaq moved sideways in a trading range for 16 months and then shot up rapidly over the final 4 months.

An interesting aspect of point-and-figure charts (see page 253) is that they totally disregard the passage of time and only display changes in price.

SUPPORT AND RESISTANCE

Think of security prices as the result of a head-to-head battle between a bull (the buyer) and a bear (the seller). The bulls push prices higher, and the bears push prices lower. The direction prices actually move reveals who is winning the battle.

Using this analogy, consider the chart of Compaq in Figure 11. During the period shown, note how each time prices fell to near 14⅜ the bulls (i.e., the buyers) took control and prevented prices from falling further. That means that at the price of 14⅜, buyers felt that investing in Compaq was worthwhile (and sellers were not willing to sell for less than 14⅜). This type of price action is referred to as support, because buyers are supporting the price.

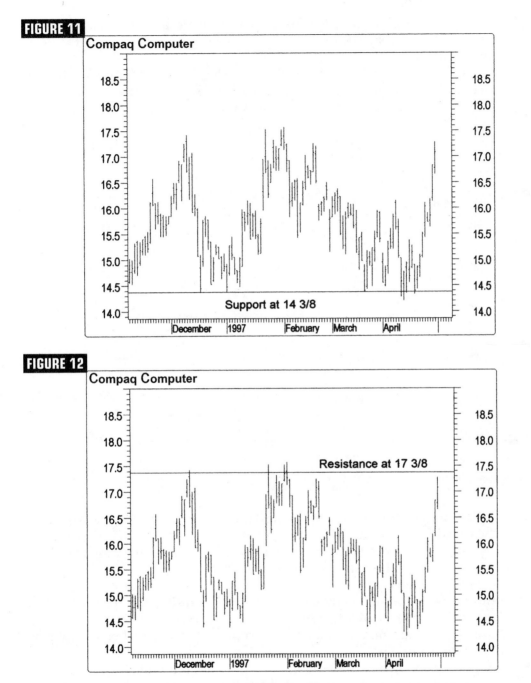

FIGURE 11

Compaq Computer

Support at 14 3/8

FIGURE 12

Compaq Computer

Resistance at 17 3/8

Similar to support, a resistance level is the point at which sellers take control of prices and prevent them from rising higher. Consider Figure 12. Note how each time prices neared the level of 17⅜, sellers outnumbered buyers and prevented the price from rising.

The price at which a trade takes place is the price at which a bull and bear agree to do business. The bulls think prices will move higher, and the bears think prices will move lower.

Support levels indicate the price where the majority of investors believe prices will move higher, and resistance levels indicate the price at which a majority of investors feel prices will move lower.

However, *investor expectations change with time!* Although investors did not expect Compaq to rise above 17⅜ (as shown in Figure 12), only 5 months later investors were willing to buy Compaq at $40 (Figure 13).

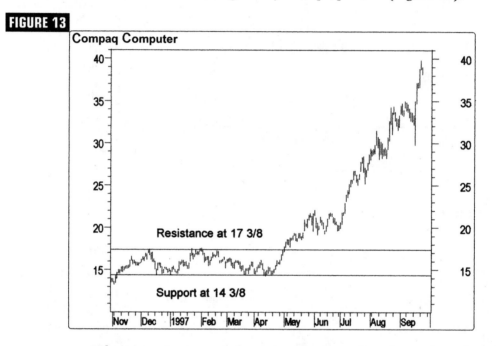

When investor expectations change, they often do so abruptly. Note how when Harley-Davidson's prices rose above the resistance level in Figure 14, they did so decisively. Note, too, that the breakout above the resistance level was accompanied by a significant increase in volume.

Once investors accepted that Harley-Davidson could trade above 14, more investors were willing to buy it at higher levels (causing both prices and volume to increase). Similarly, sellers who would previously have sold when prices approached 14 also began to expect prices to move higher and were no longer willing to sell.

The development of support and resistance levels is probably the most noticeable and recurring event on price charts. The penetration of support and resistance levels can be triggered by fundamental changes that are above or below investor expectations (e.g., changes in earnings, management, competition, etc.) or by self-fulfilling prophecies (investors buy as they see prices rise). The cause is not as significant as the effect: new expectations lead to new price levels.

FIGURE 14

FIGURE 15

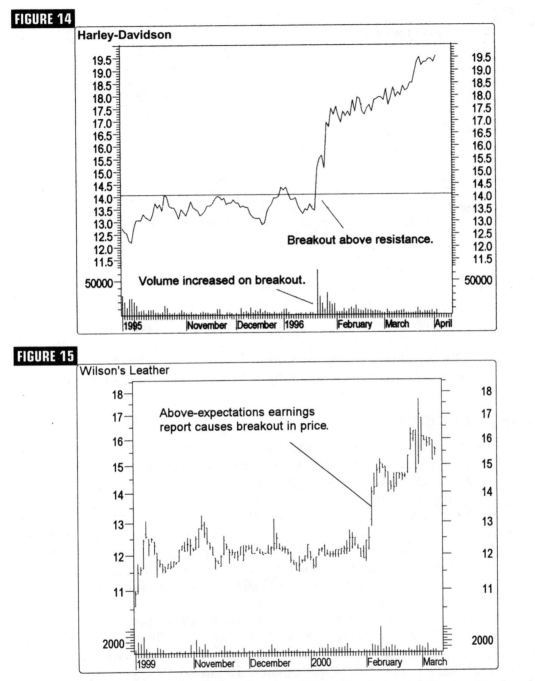

Figure 15 shows a breakout caused by fundamental factors. The breakout occurred when Wilson's Leather released a higher-than-expected earnings report. We know it was higher than expectations by the resulting change in prices following the report.

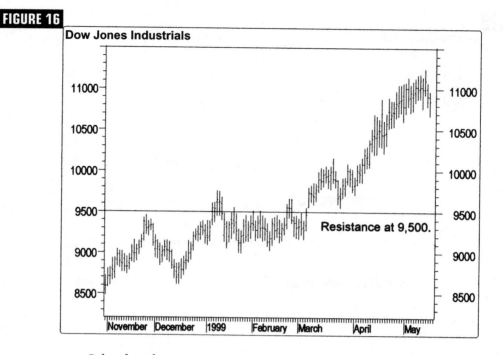

FIGURE 16

Dow Jones Industrials

Resistance at 9,500.

Other breakouts are more emotional. For example, the Dow had a tough time changing investor expectations when it neared 9,500 (see Figure 16).

Supply and Demand

There is nothing mysterious about support and resistance—it is classic supply and demand. Remember Economics 101: supply/demand lines show what the supply and demand will be at a given price.

In Figure 17 the supply line shows the quantity (i.e., the number of shares) that sellers are willing to supply at a given price. Supply lines always slope upward because as prices increase, the number of sellers also increases (i.e., more people are willing to sell at higher prices).

The demand line shows the number of shares that buyers are willing to buy at a given price. Demand lines always slope downward because as prices decrease, the number of buyers increases.

Of course, buyers and sellers can't simply pick the price at which to buy and sell. They must pick a price at which a buyer is willing to buy and a seller is willing to sell. This point, the equilibrium point, occurs where the supply and demand lines cross (approximately 37½ in Figure 17).

At any given price, a supply/demand chart shows the number of buyers and sellers. For example, Figure 17 shows that at the price of 42½, there will be 10 buyers and 25 sellers.

FIGURE 17

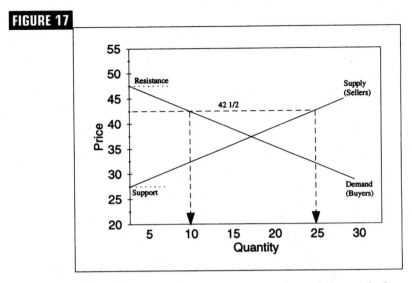

Support occurs at the price where the supply line touches the left side of the chart (e.g., 27½ in Figure 17). Prices can't fall below this amount because no sellers are willing to sell for less than 27½. Resistance occurs at the price where the demand line touches the left side of the chart (e.g., 47½). Prices can't rise above this amount because there are no buyers willing to buy for more than 47½.

In a free market, these lines are continually changing. As investor expectations change, so do the prices buyers and sellers find acceptable. A breakout above a resistance level is evidence of an upward shift in the demand line as more buyers become willing to buy at higher prices. Similarly, the failure of a support level shows that the supply line has shifted downward.

The foundation of most technical analysis tools, and the pricing of most goods and services, are rooted in the concept of supply and demand. Charts of security prices give us a superb view of these forces in action.

Traders' Remorse

Following the penetration of a support/resistance level, it is common for traders to question the new price level. For example, after a breakout above a resistance level, buyers and sellers may both question the validity of the new higher price and may decide to sell. This creates a phenomenon I refer to as traders' remorse, when prices temporarily return to a support/resistance level following a price breakout.

Consider the breakout of Questar in Figure 18. Note how the breakout was followed by two corrections in the price, where prices returned to the resistance level.

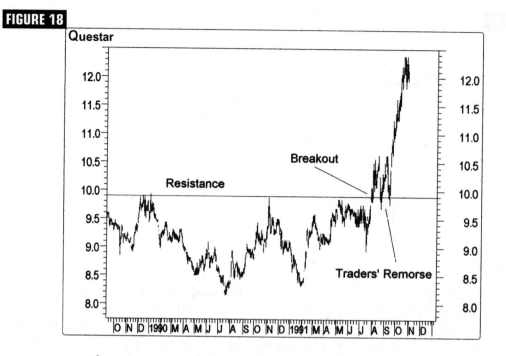

FIGURE 18

The price action following this remorseful period is crucial. One of two things can happen. Either the consensus of expectations will be that the new price is not warranted, in which case prices will move back to their previous levels, or investors will accept the new price, in which case prices will continue to move in the direction of the penetration.

If, following traders' remorse, the consensus of expectations is that a new higher price is not warranted, a classic bull trap (or false breakout) is created. Figure 19 shows prices penetrating the resistance level near 33 (luring in a herd of bulls who expected prices to move higher) and then dropping back to below the resistance level, leaving the bulls holding overpriced stock.

Similar sentiment creates a bear trap. Figure 20 shows AlliedSignal testing its support near 16½ several times. The support failed as prices fell lower, but only long enough to get the bears to sell (or sell short). Prices then returned to the support level, yet rather than retreating, they continued higher, leaving the bears out of the market. Ouch!

Another trend that can happen following traders' remorse is that investors' expectations may change, causing the new price to be accepted. In this case, prices will continue to move in the direction of the penetration (i.e., up if a resistance level was penetrated or down if a support level failed). Figure 21 shows a breakout above the support level of $35.00, two "remorseful" periods where bulls and bears questioned the new price, followed by a solid change in expectations as prices moved up strongly.

FIGURE 19

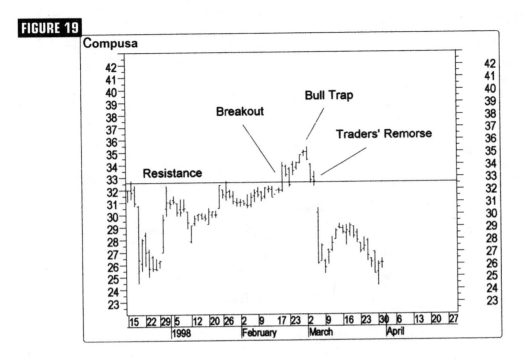

FIGURE 20

FIGURE 21

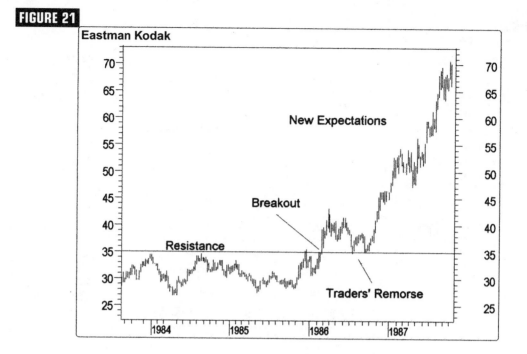

FIGURE 22

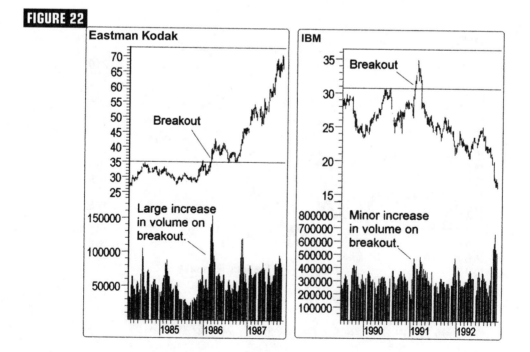

A good way to quantify expectations following a price breakout is with the volume associated with the breakout. If prices break through the support/resistance level with a large increase in volume, it implies that the new expectations will rule. This is especially true if the volume decreases during the remorseful period (a minority of investors are remorseful).

Conversely, if the breakout is on moderate volume, it implies that very few investor expectations have changed and a return to the original expectations (i.e., original prices) is warranted.

Consider Figure 22, which shows two securities that penetrated their resistance levels. When Eastman Kodak penetrated its resistance level, it was on significantly increased volume. During the subsequent remorseful period, volume decreased. Both of these were signs that the breakout was real and that prices would increase. Conversely, when IBM penetrated its resistance level, volume was about average. This indicated that expectations hadn't changed and that the new prices wouldn't last.

Resistance Becomes Support

When a resistance level is successfully penetrated, that level usually becomes a new support level. Similarly, when a support level fails, that level usually becomes a new resistance level. This is an important concept.

An example of resistance changing to support is shown in Figure 23. After prices broke above the resistance level near 10, the level of 10 became the new support level.

This happens because a new generation of bulls who didn't buy when prices were less than 10 (they didn't have bullish expectations then) are now anxious to buy anytime prices approach 10.

You can see that the support/resistance level in Figure 23 is not precise—prices occasionally cross the line. This "level" is really a range between approximately 9½ and 10. This is typical. The purpose of support/resistance levels isn't to provide an absolute value but rather to foster understanding that when expectations change dramatically (as shown by the breakout in Figure 23) prices will behave much differently from that point forward.

Similarly, when prices drop below a support level, that level often becomes a resistance level that prices have difficulty penetrating. When prices approach the previous support level, investors attempt to limit their losses by selling. Figure 24 shows how Boeing's prices encountered support *and* resistance at 21.

This phenomena—in which a resistance level becomes a support level (and vice versa)—is extremely common. In fact, the first thing I look for on a chart is the historical support/resistance levels; using the weatherman analogy (see page 3), this is like asking "How has the weather been?" Before I'm going to consider buying or selling, I need to know the general climate—I need to know if I am in Texas during the summer or Montana in the winter.

FIGURE 24

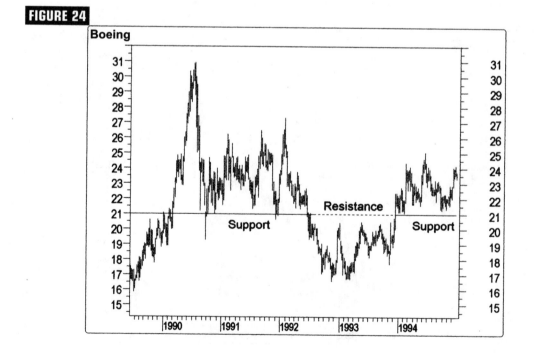

Review

The preceding discussions of price action, investor expectations, and support/resistance are as concise as possible. However, I am thoroughly convinced that most investors could significantly improve their performance if they would pay more attention to the underlying causes affecting security prices: investor expectations and supply/demand.

The following is a brief review of the support/resistance concepts discussed in this section.

1. A security's price represents the fair market value as agreed to by buyers (bulls) and sellers (bears).
2. Changes in price are the result of changes in investor expectations of the security's future price.
3. Support levels occur when the consensus is that the price will not move lower.
4. Resistance levels occur when the consensus is that the price will not move higher.
5. The penetration of a support or resistance level indicates a change in investor expectations and a shift in the supply/demand lines.
6. Volume is useful in determining the real strength of the change in investor expectations.
7. Traders' remorse often follows the penetration of a support or resistance level as prices retreat to the penetrated level.
8. Once penetrated, support levels often provide price resistance and vice versa.

TRENDS

In the preceding pages, we explored how support and resistance levels can be penetrated by a change in investor expectations, which results in shifts of the supply/demand lines. This type of change is often abrupt and "news-based."

In this section, we'll explore trends. A trend represents a consistent change in prices (i.e., changes in investor expectations). Trends differ from support/resistance levels in that trends represent change, whereas support/resistance levels represent barriers to change.

As shown in Figure 25, a rising trend is defined by successively higher *low* prices. A rising trend can be thought of as a rising support level—the bulls are in control and are pushing prices higher.

FIGURE 25

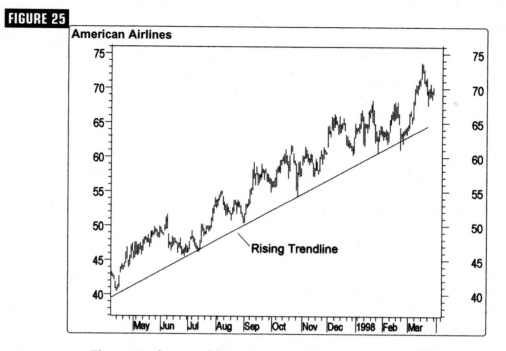

Figure 26 shows a falling trend. A falling trend is defined by successively lower *high* prices. A falling trend can be thought of as a falling resistance level—the bears are in control and are pushing prices lower.

FIGURE 26

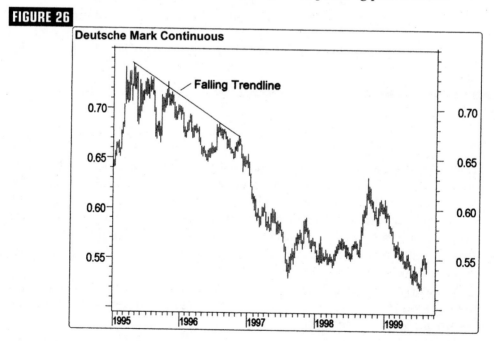

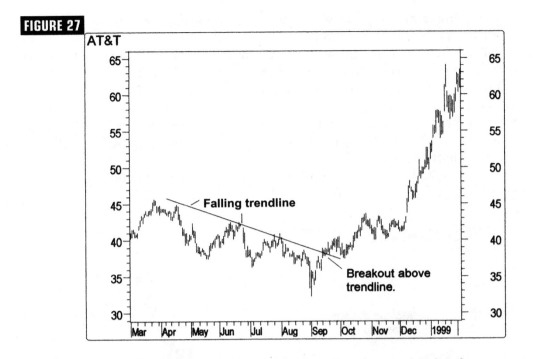

FIGURE 27

AT&T — Falling trendline; Breakout above trendline.

Just as prices penetrate support and resistance levels when expectations change, prices can penetrate rising and falling trendlines. Figure 27 shows the penetration of AT&T's falling trendline as investors no longer expected lower prices.

As with support and resistance levels, it is common to have traders' remorse following the failure of the trendline. In Figure 27 prices broke out above the falling trendline; the bears temporarily regained control and pulled prices back to the trendline (traders' remorse), and then prices advanced dramatically.

MOVING AVERAGES

The moving average is one of the oldest and most popular technical analysis tools. The following pages contains descriptions of the basic calculation and interpretation of moving averages. Full details on moving averages are provided in Part Two (see page 203).

A moving average is the average price of a security at a given time. When calculating a moving average, one specifies the time span for calculating the average price (e.g., 25 days).

A simple moving average is calculated by adding the security's prices for the most recent time periods ("n") and then dividing by "n." For example, to calculate a 25-day moving average, add the closing prices of a security for the most recent 25 days and then divide by 25. The result is the security's average price over the last 25 days. This calculation is done for each period (e.g., day) in the chart.

A moving average cannot be calculated until you have "n" time periods of data. For example, you cannot display a 25-day moving average until you can include the twenty-fifth day in a chart.

Figure 28 shows a 25-day simple moving average of Crude Oil.

FIGURE 28

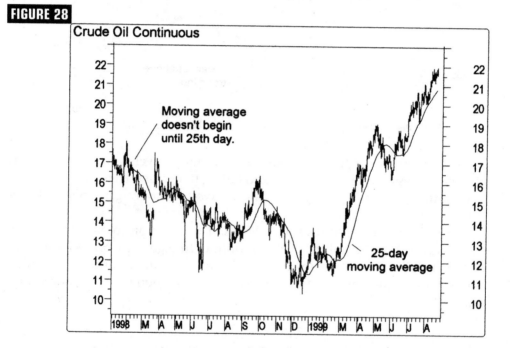

Since the moving average in this chart is the average price of Crude Oil over the last 25 days, it represents the consensus of investor expectations over the last 25 days. If a security's price is above its moving average, it shows that investors' current expectations (i.e., the current price) are higher than their average expectations over the last 25 days and that investors are becoming increasingly bullish on the security. Conversely, if today's price is below its moving average, it shows that current expectations are below the average expectations over the last 25 days.

Traditionally, moving averages denote changes in prices and as such are used to observe such changes. When prices rise above their moving average, it indicates that investors are becoming more bullish, and it is usually a good time to buy. Conversely, when prices fall below their moving average, it indicates that investors are becoming more bearish, and it is usually a good time to sell.

"Buy" arrows were drawn on the chart in Figure 29 to show when Ford's price rose above its 25-week moving average; "sell" arrows were drawn when Ford's price fell below its 25-week moving average.

FIGURE 29

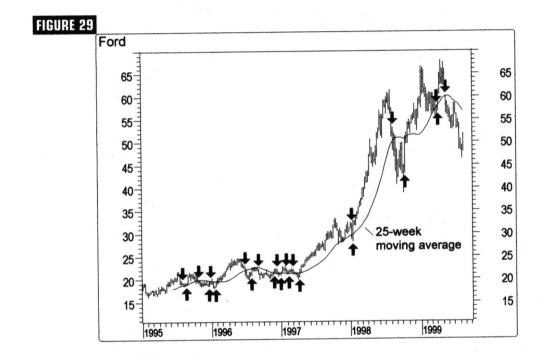

You can see that the moving average does a good job of keeping investors on the "right" side of the market during major moves, but it tends to give "whipsaw" signals when prices move sideways.

You can also use moving averages to smooth erratic data. The chart in Figure 30 shows the number of stocks making new highs (upper graph) and a 10-week moving average of this value (lower graph). Note how the moving average makes it easier to view the true trend of the data.

Time Periods in Moving Averages

Long-term trends can be isolated using a 200-day moving average. Ignoring commissions, higher profits are usually found using shorter moving averages (i.e., fewer time periods). You can use computer software (see page 5) to

FIGURE 30

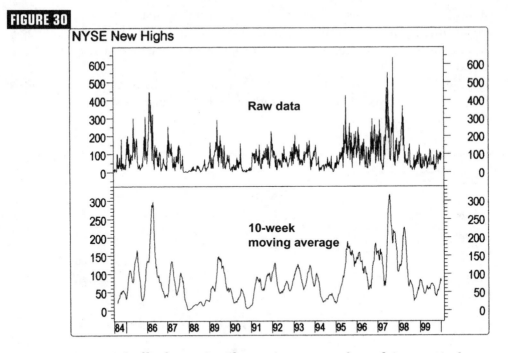

NYSE New Highs

automatically determine the optimum number of time periods to use in the moving average. For example, the buy/sell arrows in Figure 29 were automatically displayed using MetaStock.

Merits

The merit of this type of moving average system (i.e., buying and selling when prices penetrate their moving average) is that you will always be on the "right" side of the market—prices cannot rise very much without the price rising above its average price, which generates a buy signal, nor can they fall very far without falling below the moving average and generating a sell signal.

The disadvantage of this type of moving average system is that you will always buy and sell late. Also, if the trend doesn't last for a significant period of time (typically twice the length of the moving average), you'll lose money. For example, in Figure 29 the sideways periods during 1996 and early 1997 generated many false signals.

Traders' Remorse

Moving averages often demonstrate traders' remorse (see page 19). Figure 31 shows that it is very common for a security to penetrate its long-term moving average and then return to the average before continuing on its way.

FIGURE 31

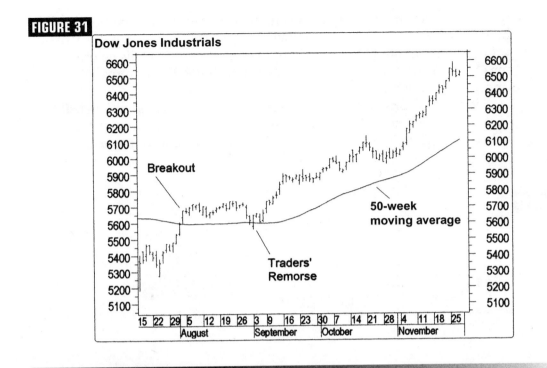

Dow Jones Industrials

INDICATORS

An indicator is a mathematical calculation that is applied to a security's price and/or volume fields. The result is a value that is used to anticipate changes in prices.

A moving average fits this definition of an indicator: it is a calculation that is performed on a security's price to yield a value that is used to anticipate changes in prices.

Part Two (see page 45) contains numerous examples of indicators. Let's briefly review one simple indicator here, the Moving Average Convergence Divergence (MACD).

Moving Average Convergence Divergence (MACD)

The MACD is calculated by subtracting a 26-day moving average of a security's price from a 12-day moving average of its price. The result is an indicator that oscillates above and below zero.

When the MACD is above zero, it means the 12-day moving average is higher than the 26-day moving average. This is bullish, since it shows that recent expectations (i.e., the 12-day moving average) are more bullish than previous expectations (i.e., the 26-day average). This implies a bullish, or upward, shift in the supply/demand lines. When the MACD falls below zero, it means that the 12-day moving average is below the 26-day moving average, implying a bearish shift in the supply/demand lines.

Figure 32 depicts Intuit and its MACD. The chart has been labeled with "buy" arrows when the MACD rose above zero and "sell" arrows when it fell below zero. The 12- and 26-day moving averages are also displayed on the price chart.

FIGURE 32

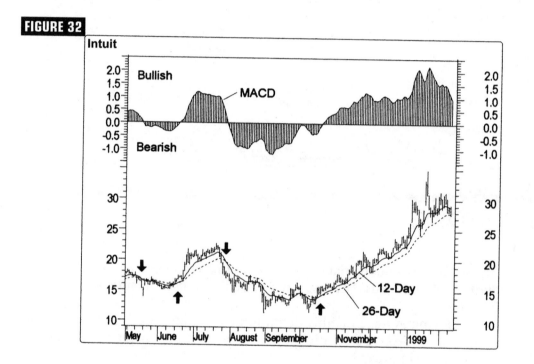

A 9-day moving average of the MACD (not of the security's price) is usually plotted on top of the MACD indicator. This line is referred to as the "signal" or "trigger" line. The signal line anticipates the convergence of the two moving averages (i.e., the movement of the MACD toward the zero line).

The chart in Figure 33 shows the MACD and its signal line (the dotted line). "Buy" arrows were drawn when the MACD rose above its signal line and "sell" arrows were drawn when the MACD fell below its signal line. You can see that this approach ensured that you stayed on the right side of the market, although it did generate several "whipsaw" signals.

FIGURE 33

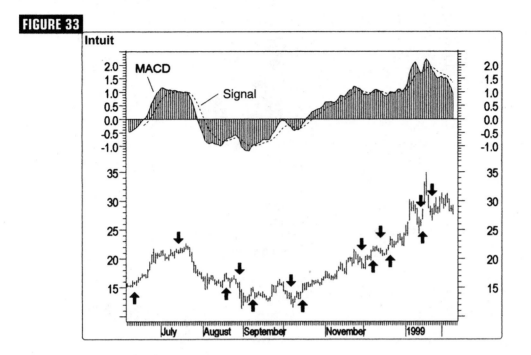

Let's consider the rationale behind this technique. The MACD is the difference between two moving averages of price. When the shorter-term moving average rises above the longer-term moving average (i.e., the MACD rises above zero), it means that investor expectations are becoming more bullish (i.e., there has been an upward shift in the supply/demand lines). By plotting a 9-day moving average of the MACD, we can see the changing of expectations (i.e., the shifting of the supply/demand lines) as they occur.

Leading Versus Lagging Indicators

Moving averages and the MACD are examples of trend-following, or "lagging," indicators (see Figure 34). You can see that the buy and sell signals in Figure 34 occurred late (i.e., "lagged"), but they did let you profit from the major trends. These indicators are superb when prices move in relatively long trends. They don't warn you of upcoming changes in prices; they simply tell you what prices are doing (i.e., rising or falling) so that you can invest accordingly. Trend-following indicators always have you buy and sell late and, in exchange for missing the early opportunities, they greatly reduce your risk by keeping you on the "right" side of the market.

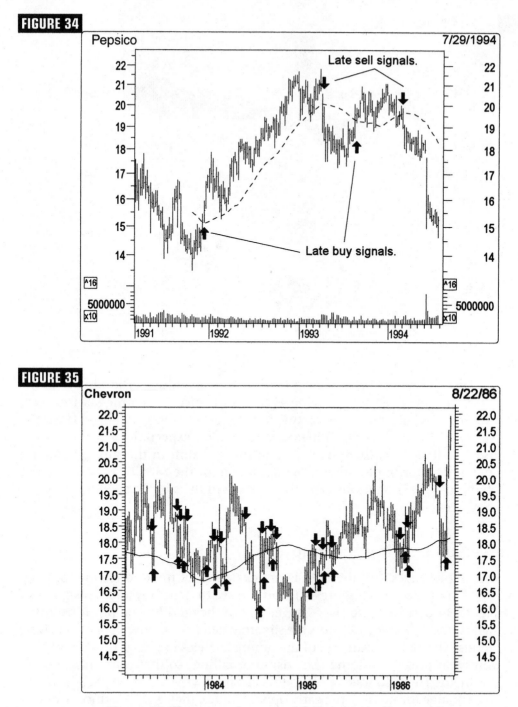

FIGURE 34

FIGURE 35

Figure 35 illustrates that trend-following indicators do not work well in sideways markets.

"Leading" indicators constitute another class of indicators. They help you profit by predicting what prices will do next. Leading indicators provide greater rewards at the expense of increased risk. They perform best in sideways "trading" markets.

Leading indicators typically work by measuring how "overbought" or "oversold" a security is. This is done with the assumption that a security that is "oversold" will bounce back. Figure 36 shows Chevron's weekly prices with its Stochastic Oscillator (see page 321). "Buy" arrows indicate when the Stochastic Oscillator peaked in overbought territory and "sell" arrows indicate when it bottomed out in oversold territory. You can see that these were early signs of price reversals.

FIGURE 36

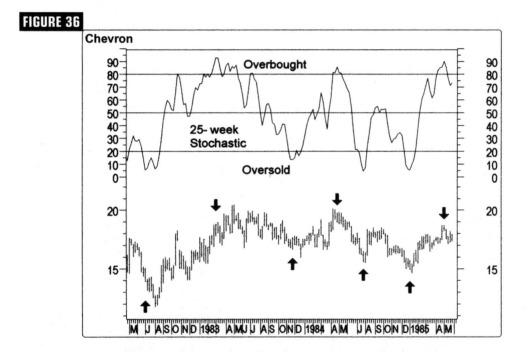

The type of indicator you use, leading or lagging, is a matter of personal preference. It has been my experience that most investors (including me) are better at following trends than predicting them. Thus, I personally prefer trend-following indicators. However, I have met many successful investors who prefer leading indicators.

Trending Prices Versus Trading Prices

Several trading systems and indicators have been developed that determine if prices are trending (i.e., moving strongly in one direction) or trading (i.e., moving sideways in a back-and-forth pattern). The intended approach is that you should use lagging indicators (see page 33) during trending markets and leading indicators during trading markets.

This approach is sound, with one caveat: although it is relatively easy to determine if prices are trending or trading, it is extremely difficult to know if prices *will* trend or trade in the future. Figure 37 shows *The Washington Post* in a 2-year trading range followed by 2 years in a trending pattern.

FIGURE 37

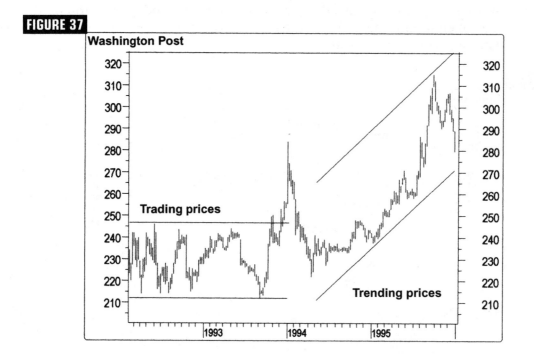

Indicators that help determine whether prices are trending or trading include Aroon (see page 64), Chande Momentum Oscillator (see page 100), Commodity Selection Index (see page 106), Directional Movement (see page 119), MESA Sine Wave (see page 193), Polarized Fractal Efficiency (see page 256), Random Walk Index (see page 285), Vertical Horizontal Filter (see page 351), and r-Squared (see page 282).

Divergences

A divergence occurs when the trend of a security's price doesn't agree with the trend of an indicator. Many of the examples in Section Two demonstrate divergences.

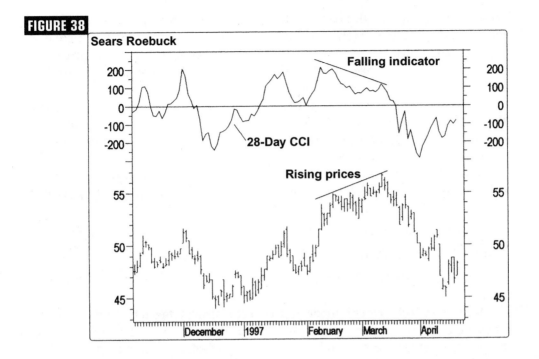

FIGURE 38

The chart in Figure 38 shows a divergence between Sears Roebuck and its 28-day CCI (Commodity Channel Index, see page 103). Sears' prices were making new highs while the CCI was failing to make them. When divergences do occur, prices usually change direction to confirm the trend of the indicator, as shown in Figure 38. This occurs because indicators are often better at gauging price trends than the prices themselves.

MARKET INDICATORS

All of the technical analysis tools discussed thus far were calculated using prices (e.g., open, high, low, close) and, possibly, volume. Another group of technical analysis tools is designed to help you gauge changes in *all* securities within a specific market. These indicators are usually referred to as "market indicators" because they gauge an entire market, not just an individual security. Market indicators typically analyze the stock market, although they can be used for other markets (e.g., futures).

While the data available for an individual security are limited to its open, high, low, close, volume (see page 6), and sparse financial reports, numerous data are available for the overall stock market, for example, the number of stocks that made new highs for the day, the number of stocks that increased in price, the volume associated with the stocks that increased in price, etc. Market indicators cannot be calculated for an individual security because the required data are not available.

Market indicators add significant depth to technical analysis because they contain much more information than price and volume. A typical approach is to use market indicators to determine where the overall market is headed and then use price/volume indicators to determine when to buy or sell an individual security. Based on the analogy "All boats rise in a rising tide," it is much less risky to own stocks when the overall stock market is rising.

Categories of Market Indicators

Market indicators typically fall into three categories: monetary, sentiment, and momentum.

Monetary indicators concentrate on economic data such as interest rates. They help investors determine the economic environment in which businesses operate. These external forces directly affect a business's profitability and share price.

Examples of monetary indicators are interest rates, the money supply, consumer and corporate debt, and inflation. Due to the vast quantity of monetary indicators, only a few of the basic monetary indicators are discussed in this book.

Sentiment indicators focus on investor expectations—often before those expectations are discernible in prices. With an individual security, prices are usually the only available measure of investor sentiment. However, for a large market such as the New York Stock Exchange, many more sentiment indicators are available. These include the number of odd lot sales (i.e., what are the smallest investors doing?), the puts/calls ratio (i.e., how many people are buying puts versus calls?), the premium on stock index futures, the ratio of bullish versus bearish investment advisors, etc.

"Contrarian" investors use sentiment indicators to determine what the majority of investors expect prices to do; they then do the opposite, their rationale being that if everybody agrees prices will rise, there probably aren't enough investors left to push prices much higher. This concept is well proven—almost everyone is bullish at market tops (when they should be selling) and almost everyone is bearish at market bottoms (when they should be buying).

> *The man who follows the crowd will never be followed by a crowd.*
>
> —*R. S. Donnell*

Momentum indicators show what prices are actually doing, but do so by looking deeper than price. Examples of market momentum indicators include all of the price/volume indicators applied to the various market indices (e.g., the MACD of the Dow Industrials), the number of stocks that made new highs versus the number of stocks that made new lows, the relationship between the number of stocks that advanced in price versus the number that declined, and the comparison of the volume associated with increasing prices versus the volume associated with decreasing prices.

These three types of market indicators provide insight into the following:

1. The external monetary conditions affecting security prices. This tells us what security prices should do.
2. The sentiment of various sectors of the investment community. This tells us what investors expect prices to do.
3. The current momentum of the market. This tells us what prices are actually doing.

Figure 39 shows the New York Stock Exchange (NYSE) Composite Index and the prime interest rate (a monetary indicator). The chart shows "thumbs-up" when interest rates were falling and "thumbs-down" when rates were rising. Although not perfect, prices certainly did better when rates were falling.

FIGURE 39

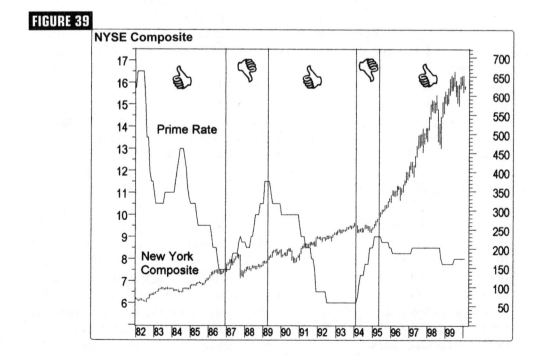

FIGURE 40

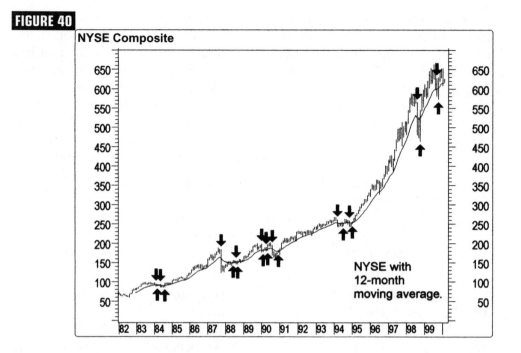

Figure 40 shows a 12-month moving average (a momentum indicator) of the New York Composite Index. "Buy" arrows indicate when the index rose above its 12-month moving average; "sell" arrows indicate when the index fell below its moving average. You can see how this momentum indicator caught every major market move, although in a market with such an upward bias, a buy-and-hold strategy would have worked well, too.

Figure 41 merges the preceding monetary and momentum concepts. "Thumbs-up" indicates when the prime rate was below its 10-month moving average (interest rates were falling) and when the New York Stock Exchange was above its 15-month moving average. The graph illustrates that prices always increased during these bullish periods and that by being out of the market when "thumbs" were not "up," investors could have avoided the major sell-offs that occurred in 1987, 1990, and 1998.

Figure 41 is a good example of the roulette and weather metaphors presented on pages 3 and 4. You don't need to know exactly where prices will be in the future—you simply need to improve your odds. At any given time during the period shown in this chart, I couldn't have told you where the market would be six months later. However, we know that the odds favor a rise in *stock* prices when interest rates are falling and when the NYSE is above its long-term moving average. By limiting long positions (i.e., buying) to periods when both of these indicators are bullish, you could dramatically reduce your risks and increase your chances of making a profit.

FIGURE 41

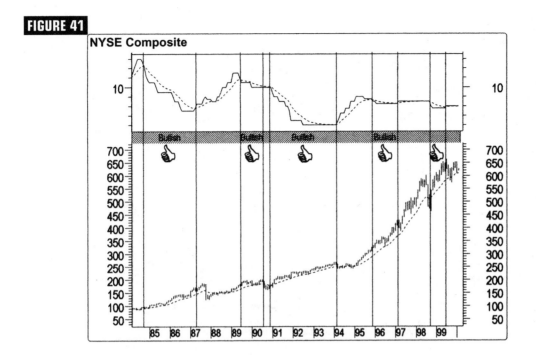

LINE STUDIES

Line studies are technical analysis tools that consist of lines drawn on top of a security's price and/or indicator. These include the support, resistance, and trendline concepts already presented.

Figure 42 illustrates several line studies. Part Two contains explanations of these, as well as numerous additional studies.

A SAMPLE APPROACH

Many technical analysis tools are described in this book. The most difficult part of technical analysis may be deciding which tools to use! The following is an approach you might try.

1. **Determine the overall market condition.** If you are trading equity-based securities (e.g., stocks), determine the trend in interest rates, the trend of the New York Stock Exchange, and the trend of investor

FIGURE 42

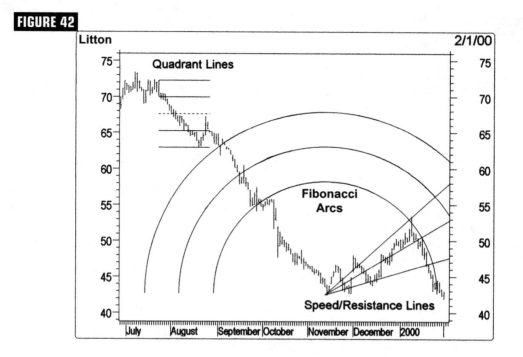

sentiment (e.g., read the newspaper). The object is to determine the trend of the overall market.

2. **Pick the securities.** I suggest that you pick the securities using either a company or industry you are familiar with, or the recommendation of a trusted analyst (possibly fundamental analysis, see page 151, to compliment your technical approach).

3. **Determine the overall trend of the security.** Plot a 200-day (or 39-week) moving average of the security's closing price. Only take long positions when the security is above the moving average (the best buying opportunities will occur when the security has just risen above this long-term moving average).

4. **Pick your entry points.** Buy and sell using your favorite indicator, only taking positions that agree with the trend of both the overall market and the individual.

> *A fool sees not the same tree that a wise man sees.*
>
> —*William Blake, 1790*

Much of your success in technical analysis will come from experience. The goal isn't to find the holy grail of technical analysis: rather, the goal is to reduce your risks (e.g., by trading with the overall trend) while capitalizing on opportunities (e.g., using your favorite indicator to time your trades). As you gain experience, you will make better, more informed, and more profitable investments.

CONCLUSION

This concludes the introduction to technical analysis. I suggest you refer to Section Two while you continue to explore this exciting and potentially profitable pursuit.

A fitting conclusion to an introduction to technical analysis is a list of lessons I have learned, both from others and the hard way:

> *Opportunities flit by while we sit regretting the chances we have lost.*
>
> —Jerome K. Jerome, 1889

- Don't compound your losses by averaging down (i.e., don't keep buying additional shares at lower prices). It is tempting to think that a loss "doesn't count" until the position is closed—but it does!
- Any time you own a security, ask yourself if you would buy it today. If you wouldn't buy it, you should probably sell it.
- Don't get distracted by others' investment prowess. Most investors only discuss their successes, threatening your focus and confidence.
- Wise investments aren't made with Ouija boards. They are made using logical approaches that minimize risks and maximize opportunities.
- Master the basics. Most investors spend their time looking for easy money (which is not an easy search) instead of learning the key factors to security prices—supply and demand.

A companion spreadsheet, corrections, suggested books, and other supplemental information can be found at AtoZbook.com.

PART TWO

REFERENCE

Part Two is a concise reference to a vast array of technical indicators and line studies.

The discussion of each tool includes an overview, an explanation of its interpretation, and an example of the indicator or line study in action. Most indicators also include step-by-step calculations.

Most of these techniques can be applied to any type of security, including stocks, bonds, options, futures, mutual funds, and indices.

ABSOLUTE BREADTH INDEX

Overview

The Absolute Breadth Index (ABI) is a market momentum indicator that was developed by Norman G. Fosback.

The ABI shows how much change (i.e., volatility) is taking place on the New York Stock Exchange. It measures the magnitude of the changes taking place while ignoring the direction of the change.

Interpretation

You can think of the ABI as an activity index. High readings indicate high market activity and change, while low readings indicate lack of change.

In *Stock Market Logic*, Fosback indicates that, historically, high values typically lead to higher prices 3 to 12 months later. Fosback found that a highly reliable variation of the ABI is to divide the weekly ABI by the total issues traded. He would then calculate a 10-week moving average of this value. Readings above 40 percent are very bullish, and readings below 15 percent are bearish.

The number of issues traded on the NYSE has steadily increased during the 1990s, making Fosback's 40 percent value achievable virtually every week. Thus, it is more appropriate to determine "high" ABI values relative to the ABI's recent history.

Example

Figure 43 shows the S&P 500 and a 5-week moving average of the ABI. Strong rallies occurred every time this moving average rose above 450.

Calculation

The ABI is calculated by taking the absolute value of the difference between the number of advancing issues and the number of declining issues on the New York Stock Exchange. (The term "absolute value" means "regardless of sign." For example, the absolute value of −3 is 3.)

$$ABS \ (Advancing \ Issues - Declining \ Issues)$$

FIGURE 43

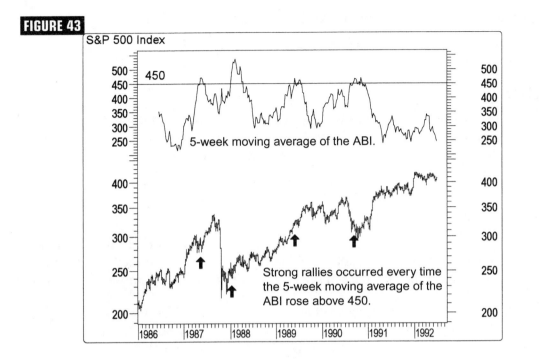

S&P 500 Index

5-week moving average of the ABI.

Strong rallies occurred every time the 5-week moving average of the ABI rose above 450.

Table 2 illustrates the calculation of the Absolute Breadth Index.

- Column D is the difference between the number of advancing issues and the number of declining issues (i.e., Column B minus Column C). Column E is the absolute value of Column D.

TABLE 2

| | | ABSOLUTE BREADTH INDEX | | |
A	B	C	D	E
Date	Advancing Issues	Declining Issues	Advancing minus Declining Issues	Absolute Value of Column D
04/25/97	789	1,662	−873	873
04/28/97	1,348	1,085	263	263
04/29/97	2,085	531	1,554	1,554
04/30/97	1,599	941	658	658
05/01/97	1,450	1,021	429	429
05/02/97	2,119	476	1,643	1,643

ACCUMULATION/DISTRIBUTION LINE

Overview

The Accumulation/Distribution Line is a momentum indicator that associates changes in price and volume. The indicator is based on the premise that the more volume that accompanies a price move, the more significant the price move.

Interpretation

The Accumulation/Distribution Line is really a variation of the more popular On Balance Volume indicator (see page 229). Both of these indicators attempt to confirm changes in prices by comparing the volume associated with prices.

When the Accumulation/Distribution Line moves up for a security, it indicates that the security is being accumulated (i.e., bought), as most of the volume is associated with upward price movement. When the indicator moves down, it shows that the security is being distributed (i.e., sold), as most of the volume is associated with downward price movement.

Divergences (see page 36) between the Accumulation/Distribution and the security's price imply a change is imminent. When a divergence does occur, prices usually change to confirm the Accumulation/Distribution. For example, if the indicator is moving up and the security's price is going down, prices will probably reverse.

Example

Figure 44 shows Battle Mountain Gold and its Accumulation/Distribution Line. You can see that Battle Mountain's price diverged from the Accumulation/Distribution Line as prices were reaching new highs in late July and early August, while the indicator fell significantly from its previous high. Prices then corrected to confirm the indicator's trend.

Calculation

The Accumulation/Distribution Line is calculated by adding or subtracting a portion of each day's volume from a cumulative total. The amount of volume to add or subtract is based on the relationship between the close and the

FIGURE 44

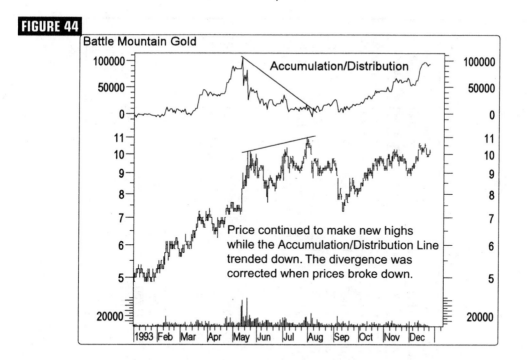

Battle Mountain Gold

Price continued to make new highs while the Accumulation/Distribution Line trended down. The divergence was corrected when prices broke down.

high-low range. The closer the close is to the high, the more volume is added to the cumulative total. Conversely, the closer the close is to the low, the more volume is subtracted from the cumulative total. If the close is exactly midway between the high and low prices, nothing is added to the cumulative total.

$$\sum \left[\frac{(close - low) - (high - close)}{(high - low)} * volume \right]$$

Table 3 illustrates the calculation of the Accumulation/ Distribution Line.

- Columns F, G, and H are straightforward calculations as explained in the column headings.
- Column I subtracts Column G from Column F. This is the numerator in the equation above.
- Column J divides Column I by Column H.
- Column K multiplies Column J by the volume (Column E).
- Column L is a cumulative total of Column K. This is the Accumulation/Distribution Line.

A

TABLE 3

A	B	C	D	E	F	G	H	I	J	K	L
					ACCUMULATION/DISTRIBUTION						
Date	High	Low	Close	Volume	Close minus Low	High minus Close	High minus Low	Col F minus Col G	Col I divided by Col H	Column J multiplied by Volume	Accumulation of Column K
05/14/93	8.625	8.250	8.625	19,194	0.375	0.000	0.375	0.375	1.000	19,194	19,194
05/17/93	8.875	8.375	8.375	10,768	0.000	0.500	0.500	-0.500	-1.000	-10,768	8,426
05/18/93	9.375	8.375	9.375	20,032	1.000	0.000	1.000	1.000	1.000	20,032	28,458
05/19/93	10.125	8.750	8.750	55,218	0.000	1.375	1.375	-1.375	-1.000	-55,218	-26,760
05/20/93	9.375	8.750	9.375	13,172	0.625	0.000	0.625	0.625	1.000	13,172	-13,588
05/21/93	10.125	9.250	9.875	22,245	0.625	0.250	0.875	0.375	0.429	9,534	-4,054
05/24/93	10.000	9.125	9.375	15,987	0.250	0.625	0.875	-0.375	-0.429	-6,852	-10,906
05/25/93	9.750	9.375	9.625	9,646	0.250	0.125	0.375	0.125	0.333	3,215	-7,691
05/26/93	9.500	9.000	9.125	10,848	0.125	0.375	0.500	-0.250	-0.500	-5,424	-13,115
05/27/93	9.625	8.875	9.250	14,470	0.375	0.375	0.750	0.000	0.000	0	-13,115
05/28/93	10.000	9.375	9.750	14,973	0.375	0.250	0.625	0.125	0.200	2,995	-10,120
06/01/93	9.750	8.750	8.875	15,799	0.125	0.875	1.000	-0.750	-0.750	-11,849	-21,969
06/02/93	9.125	8.750	8.875	16,860	0.125	0.250	0.375	-0.125	-0.333	-5,620	-27,589
06/03/93	9.250	9.125	9.125	6,568	0.000	0.125	0.125	-0.125	-1.000	-6,568	-34,157
06/04/93	9.375	9.250	9.375	8,312	0.125	0.000	0.125	0.125	1.000	8,312	-25,845
06/07/93	9.375	9.125	9.250	5,573	0.125	0.125	0.250	0.000	0.000	0	-25,845
06/08/93	9.375	8.625	8.625	11,480	0.000	0.750	0.750	-0.750	-1.000	-11,480	-37,325
06/09/93	8.625	8.250	8.500	6,366	0.250	0.125	0.375	0.125	0.333	2,122	-35,203
06/10/93	8.625	8.250	8.500	8,394	0.250	0.125	0.375	0.125	0.333	2,798	-32,405
06/11/93	8.625	7.875	7.875	12,616	0.000	0.750	0.750	-0.750	-1.000	-12,616	-45,021

ACCUMULATION SWING INDEX

Overview

The Accumulation Swing Index is a cumulative total of the Swing Index (see page 326). The Accumulation Swing Index was developed by Welles Wilder and presented in his book *New Concepts in Technical Trading Systems.*

Interpretation

In his book, Wilder quotes "one of the smartest technicians" he knows as saying, "Somewhere amidst the maze of Open, High, Low, and Close prices is a phantom line that is the *real* market." The Accumulation Swing Index attempts to show this phantom line. Since the Accumulation Swing Index attempts to show the "real market," it closely resembles prices themselves. This allows use of classic support/resistance analysis on the index itself. Typical analysis involves looking for breakouts, new highs and lows, and divergences.

Wilder notes the following characteristics of the Accumulation Swing Index:

- It provides a numerical value that quantifies price swings.
- It defines short-term swing points.
- It cuts through the maze of high, low, and close prices and indicates the real strength and direction of the market.

Example

Figure 45 shows corn and its Accumulation Swing Index. The breakouts of the price trendlines labeled A and B were confirmed by breakouts of the Accumulation Swing Index trendlines labeled A' and B'. This implied that the breakouts were valid and that prices would move higher.

Calculation

The Accumulation Swing Index is a cumulative total of the Swing Index (see page 326). The Accumulation Swing Index (and thus the Swing Index) requires opening prices.

Previous Accumulation Swing Index + Swing Index

FIGURE 45

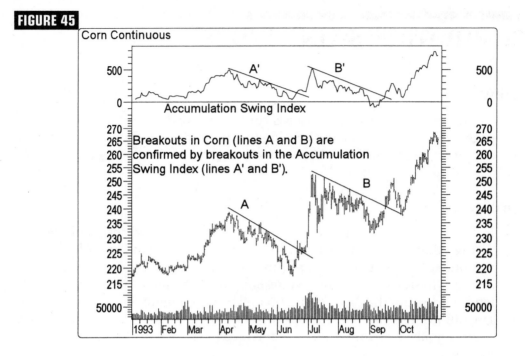

The Swing Index values Table 4 were calculated as explained on page 326.

TABLE 4

| | ACCUMULATION SWING INDEX | |
| A | B | C |
Date	Swing Index	Accumulation Swing Index
11/02/1999	−1.5918	−1.5918
11/03/1999	−9.3273	−10.9191
11/04/1999	−8.0592	−18.9783
11/05/1999	−3.7526	−22.7309
11/08/1999	15.3158	−7.4151

ADVANCE/DECLINE LINE

Overview

The Advance/Decline Line (A/D Line) is undoubtedly the most widely used measure of market breadth. When compared to the movement of a market index (e.g., Dow Jones Industrials, S&P 500), the A/D Line has proven to be an effective gauge of the stock market's strength.

Interpretation

The A/D Line is helpful when measuring overall market strength. When more stocks are advancing than declining, the A/D Line moves up (and vice versa).

Because the A/D Line always starts at zero, the numeric value of the A/D Line is of little importance. What is important is the slope and pattern of the A/D Line.

Many investors feel that the A/D Line shows market strength better than more commonly used indices such as the Dow Jones Industrial Average (DJIA) or the S&P 500 Index. By studying the trend of the A/D Line, you can see if the market is in a rising or falling trend, if the trend is still intact, and how long the current trend has prevailed.

Another way to use the A/D Line is to look for a divergence (see page 36) between the DJIA (or a similar index) and the A/D Line. Often, an end to a bull market can be forecast when the A/D Line begins to round over while the DJIA is still trying to make new highs. Historically, when a divergence develops between the DJIA and the A/D Line, the DJIA has corrected and gone the direction of the A/D Line.

A military analogy is often used when discussing the relationship between the A/D Line and the DJIA. The analogy is that trouble looms when the generals lead (e.g., the DJIA is making new highs) and the troops refuse to follow (e.g., the A/D Line fails to make new highs).

Example

Figure 46 shows the DJIA and the A/D Line. The DJIA was making new highs during the 12 months leading up to the 1987 crash. During this same period, the A/D Line was failing to reach new highs. This type of divergence, where the generals lead and the troops refuse to follow, usually results in the generals retreating in defeat, as happened in 1987.

Calculation

The Advance/Decline Line is calculated by subtracting the number of stocks that declined in price from the number of stocks that advanced, and then adding this value to a cumulative total.

Previous A/D Line + (Advancing − Declining Issues)

FIGURE 46

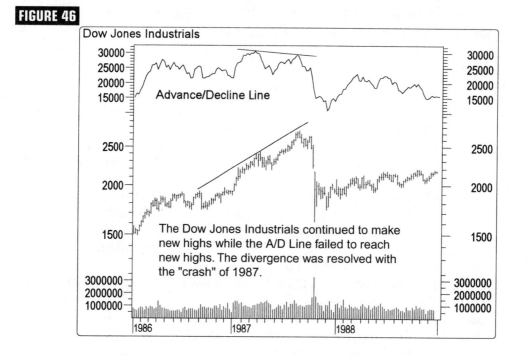

Table 5 illustrates the calculation of the Advance/Decline Line.

- Column D is the number of advancing issues minus the number of declining issues (i.e., Column B minus Column C).
- Column E is a cumulative total of Column D. This is the Advance/ Decline Line.

TABLE 5

	ADVANCE/DECLINE LINE			
A	**B**	**C**	**D**	**E**
Date	Advancing Issues	Declining Issues	Column B minus Column C	Accumulation of Column D
04/25/97	789	1,662	−873	−873
04/28/97	1,348	1,085	263	−610
04/29/97	2,085	531	1,554	944
04/30/97	1,599	941	658	1,602
05/01/97	1,450	1,021	429	2,031
05/02/97	2,119	476	1,643	3,674
05/05/97	1,958	677	1,281	4,955
05/06/97	1,258	1,270	−12	4,943
05/07/97	842	1,660	−818	4,125
05/08/97	1,398	1,097	301	4,426

ADVANCE/DECLINE RATIO

Overview

The Advance/Decline Ratio (A/D Ratio) shows the ratio of advancing issues to declining issues.

Interpretation

The A/D Ratio is similar to the Advancing-Declining Issues (see page 56) in that it displays market breadth. However, where the Advancing-Declining Issues subtracts the advancing-declining values, the A/D Ratio divides the values. The advantage of this ratio is that it remains constant regardless of the number of issues traded on the New York Stock Exchange (which has steadily increased).

Day-to-day fluctuations of the Advance/Decline Ratio can be reduced by smoothing the ratio with a moving average. For example, a moving average of the A/D Ratio makes an effective overbought/oversold indicator. The higher the value, the more excessive the rally and the more likely a correction. Likewise, low readings imply an oversold market and suggest a technical rally.

However, markets that appear to be extremely overbought or oversold may stay that way for some time. When investing using overbought and oversold indicators, it is wise to wait for the prices to confirm your belief that a change is due before placing your trades.

Example

Figure 47 shows the S&P 500 and a 15-day moving average of the A/D Ratio. Buy arrows indicate when the moving average rose above the oversold level of 0.9. Sell arrows indicate when the moving average fell below the overbought level of 1.25. You can see that the arrows were good indicators of upcoming changes in prices.

Calculation

The Advance/Decline Ratio is calculated by dividing the number of stocks that advanced in price by the number of stocks that declined.

$$\frac{Advancing\ Issues}{Declining\ Issues}$$

FIGURE 47

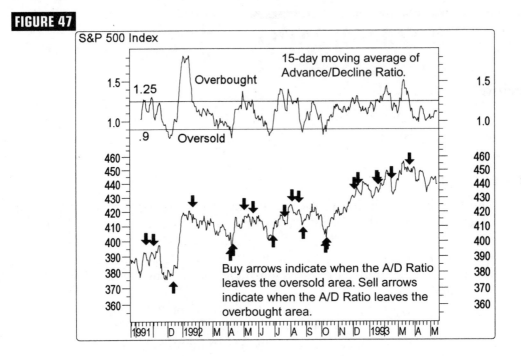

Table 6 illustrates the calculation of the Advance/Decline Ratio.

TABLE 6

| | ADVANCE/DECLINE RATIO | | |
| A | B | C | D |
Date	Advancing Issues	Declining Issues	Column B divided by Column C
04/25/97	789	1,662	0.47
04/28/97	1,348	1,085	1.24
04/29/97	2,085	531	3.93
04/30/97	1,599	941	1.70
05/01/97	1,450	1,021	1.42
05/02/97	2,119	476	4.45

ADVANCING-DECLINING ISSUES

Overview

Advancing-Declining Issues is a market momentum indicator that shows the difference between stocks listed on the New York Stock Exchange that advanced in price minus those that declined. As of this writing, more than 3,000 issues trade each day on the New York Stock Exchange.

The difference between the number of advancing and declining issues is the foundation of many market breadth indicators. These indicators include the Advance/Decline Line, Advance/Decline Ratio, Absolute Breadth Index, Breadth Thrust, McClellan Oscillator, and McClellan Summation Index. Indicators that use advancing and declining issues in their calculations are called "market breadth indicators."

Interpretation

The Advancing-Declining Issues indicator shows the difference between the number of advancing issues and the number of declining issues. Plotted by itself, this indicator helps to determine daily market strength. Strong up days generally show readings of more than +1,000. Very weak days have readings of less than −1,000.

I prefer to plot a 5-day to 40-day exponential moving average of the Advancing-Declining Issues rather than view the daily values themselves. The moving average creates an excellent short-term Overbought/Oversold indicator. Both the Overbought/Oversold indicator (see page 240) and the McClellan Oscillator (see page 183) are created using moving averages of advancing minus declining issues.

Example

Figure 48 shows the Dow Jones Industrial Average and a 40-day moving average of the Advancing-Declining Issues indicator. "Buy" arrows indicate when the moving average rose above the oversold level of −200 and "sell" arrows indicate when the moving average fell below the overbought level of 200. The increase in the number of issues traded on the New York Stock Exchange has caused this indicator to show more extreme (i.e., higher and lower) values over time.

Calculation

The Advancing-Declining Issues is calculated simply by subtracting the number of declining issues from the number of advancing issues.

Advancing Issues − Declining Issues

Table 7 illustrates the calculation of the Advancing-Declining Issues.

FIGURE 48

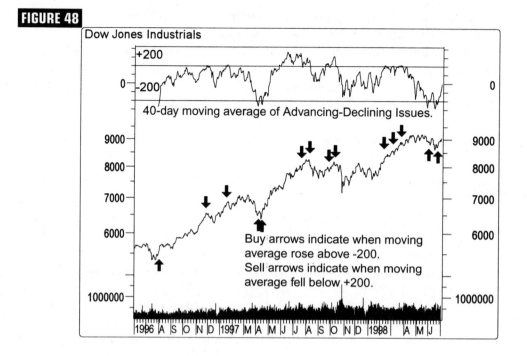

Dow Jones Industrials

40-day moving average of Advancing-Declining Issues.

Buy arrows indicate when moving average rose above -200.
Sell arrows indicate when moving average fell below +200.

TABLE 7

| A | ADVANCING-DECLINING ISSUES | | |
| | B | C | D |
Date	Advancing Issues	Declining Issues	Advancing Issues minus Declining Issues
04/25/97	789	1,662	−873
04/28/97	1,348	1,085	263
04/29/97	2,085	531	1,554
04/30/97	1,599	941	658
05/01/97	1,450	1,021	429
05/02/97	2,119	476	1,643

ADVANCING, DECLINING, UNCHANGED VOLUME

Overview

Advancing, declining, and unchanged volume are all market momentum indicators. They reflect movement on the New York Stock Exchange in millions of shares.

Advancing volume is the total volume for all securities that advanced in price. Declining volume is the total volume for all securities that declined in price. Similarly, unchanged volume is the total volume for all securities that were unchanged in price.

Interpretation

Numerous indicators have been developed using up and down volume indicators. These indicators include the Cumulative Volume Index (see page 110), Negative Volume Index (see page 214), Positive Volume Index (see page 257), and the Upside/Downside Ratio (see page 348). Charts of the advancing or declining volume can be used to look for volume divergences (where advancing volume increases but the market falls) to see if selling pressure is waning, to view daily trends, etc.

Due to the erratic fluctuations in advancing and declining volume, I suggest you smooth the indicators with a 3- to 10-period moving average.

Example

Figure 49 shows the NYSE Composite and a 10-day moving average of advancing volume. A bearish divergence developed as prices were making higher highs (trendline A) while the advancing volume was declining (trend-

FIGURE 49

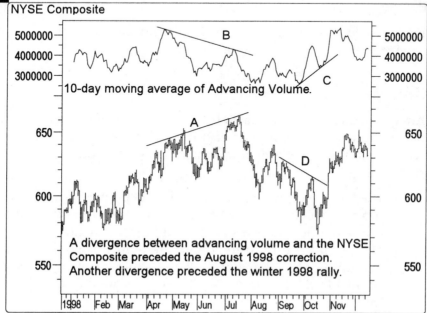

NYSE Composite

10-day moving average of Advancing Volume.

A divergence between advancing volume and the NYSE Composite preceded the August 1998 correction. Another divergence preceded the winter 1998 rally.

line B). If you only looked at the NYSE Composite, you might think the market was gaining strength. The advancing volume showed the true picture and prices were forced to correct.

Later, a bullish divergence emerged as advancing volume surged (trendline C) while prices were declining (trendline D). Again, the advancing volume showed the underlying market direction, as prices rallied.

ANDREWS'S PITCHFORK

Overview

Andrews's Pitchfork is a line study consisting of three parallel trendlines based on three points you select on a chart. This tool was developed by Dr. Alan Andrews.

Interpretation

The interpretation of a pitchfork is based on normal trendline support and resistance principles (see page 14).

Example

Figure 50 depicts an Andrews's Pitchfork for Gentner Communications. You can see how prices "walk" along the trendlines.

Calculation

An Andrews's Pitchfork is drawn by selecting three points on a chart. The first point selected is a major peak or trough near the left side of the chart. The second and third points denote a major peak and trough to the right of the first point.

- The first trendline begins at the leftmost point selected (either a major peak or trough). It is drawn so that it passes directly between the second and third points selected. This line is the "handle" of the pitchfork.
- The second and third trendlines are drawn beginning at the second and third points (a major peak and a major trough). They are drawn parallel to the first trendline. These lines are the "tines" of the pitchfork.

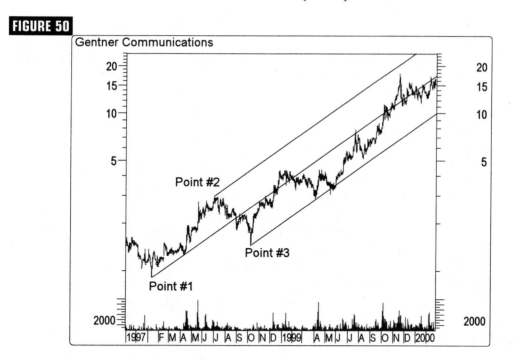

FIGURE 50

Gentner Communications

ARMS INDEX (TRIN)

Overview

The Arms Index is a market indicator that shows the relationship between the number of stocks that increase or decrease in price (advancing/declining issues) and the volume associated with stocks that increase or decrease in price (advancing/declining volume).

The Arms Index was developed by Richard W. Arms, Jr. in 1967. Over the years, the index has been referred to by a number of different names. When *Barron's* published the first article on the indicator in 1967, it was referred to as the Short-Term Trading Index. It has also been known as TRIN (an acronym for TRading INdex), MKDS, and STKS.

Interpretation

The Arms Index is primarily a short-term trading tool. It shows whether volume is flowing into advancing or declining stocks. If more volume is associated with advancing stocks than declining stocks, the Arms Index will be less than 1.0; if more volume is associated with declining stocks, the index will be greater than 1.0.

This index is usually smoothed with a moving average. I suggest using a 4-day moving average for short-term analysis, a 21-day moving average for intermediate-term analysis, and a 55-day moving average for longer-term analysis.

Normally, the Arms Index is considered bullish when it is below 1.0 and bearish when it is above 1.0. However, it seems to work most effectively as an overbought/oversold indicator. When the indicator drops to extremely over-bought levels, it foretells a selling opportunity. When it rises to extremely oversold levels, a buying opportunity is approaching.

Charts of the Arms Index feel a little upside down as oversold levels are associated with high Arms values and overbought levels are associated with low Arms values.

What constitutes an "extremely" overbought or oversold level depends on the length of the moving average used to smooth the indicator and on market conditions. Table 8 shows typical overbought and oversold levels.

TABLE 8

Moving Average	Overbought	Oversold
4-day	0.70	1.25
21-day	0.85	1.10
55-day	0.90	1.05

Example

Figure 51 on page 64 contains a 21-day moving average of the Arms Index and the New York Stock Exchange Index. Horizontal lines are drawn at the over-sold level of 1.1 and at the overbought level of 0.85. "Buy" arrows indicate when the Arms Index peaked above 1.1 and "sell" arrows indicate when it bottomed below 0.85. In most cases, significant changes in price occurred on, or 1 day before, the arrows.

Calculation

The Arms Index is calculated by first dividing the number of stocks that advanced in price by the number of stocks that declined in price to determine the Advance/Decline Ratio (see page 55). Next, the volume of advancing stocks is divided by the volume of declining stocks to determine the Upside/Downside Ratio (see page 348). Finally, the Advance/Decline Ratio is divided by the Upside/Downside Ratio.

TABLE 9

ARMS INDEX

A	B	C	D	E	F	G	H
Date	Advancing Issues	Declining Issues	Advancing Volume	Declining Volume	Column B divided by Column C	Column D divided by Column E	Column F divided by Column G
04/25/97	789	1,662	1,097,590	2,685,030	0.475	0.409	1.161
04/28/97	1,348	1,085	2,247,369	1,430,582	1.242	1.571	0.791
04/29/97	2,085	531	4,617,427	527,997	3.927	8.745	0.449
04/30/97	1,599	941	4,000,089	1,163,731	1.699	3.437	0.494
05/01/97	1,450	1,021	2,176,503	1,856,353	1.420	1.172	1.211
05/02/97	2,119	476	3,918,818	749,109	4.452	5.231	0.851
05/05/97	1,958	677	4,554,564	665,110	2.892	6.848	0.422
05/06/97	1,258	1,270	2,774,559	2,762,761	0.991	1.004	0.986
05/07/97	842	1,660	1,518,034	3,128,770	0.507	0.485	1.045
05/08/97	1,398	1,097	3,072,180	1,743,591	1.274	1.762	0.723
05/09/97	1,526	932	2,792,525	1,218,893	1.637	2.291	0.715
05/12/97	1,766	761	3,387,346	850,941	2.321	3.981	0.583
05/13/97	1,133	1,322	1,991,714	2,512,360	0.857	0.793	1.081
05/14/97	1,472	992	2,877,363	1,616,583	1.484	1.780	0.834
05/15/97	1,282	1,164	2,658,199	1,502,647	1.101	1.769	0.623
05/16/97	973	1,431	1,325,088	3,133,339	0.680	0.423	1.608
05/19/97	1,390	1,056	1,825,068	1,290,328	1.316	1.414	0.931
05/20/97	1,411	1,040	2,707,087	1,284,888	1.357	2.107	0.644

FIGURE 51

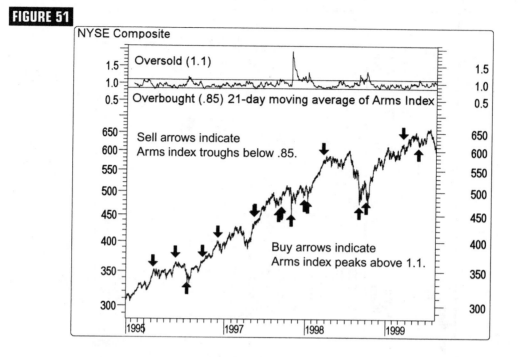

$$\frac{Advancing\ Issues\ /\ Declining\ Issues}{Advancing\ Volume\ /\ Declining\ Volume}$$

Table 9 on page 63 illustrates the calculation of the Arms Index.

- Column F is the number of advancing issues (Column B) divided by the number of declining issues (Column C).
- Column G is the advancing volume (Column D) divided by the declining volume (Column E).
- Column H is the value in Column F divided by the value in Column G. This is the Arms Index.

AROON

Overview

The Aroon indicator helps you to anticipate a change in security prices from trending to a trading range (and vise versa) by measuring the number of periods that have passed since prices reached recent high and low values. The Aroon indicator was developed by Tushar Chande.

Interpretation

The Aroon indicator displays as two plots: Aroon Up and Aroon Down.
Look for three conditions when interpreting the Aroon indicator:

1. Extremes at 0 and 100
2. Parallel movement between Aroon Up and Aroon Down
3. Crossovers between Aroon Up and Aroon Down

Extremes. When the Aroon Up line reaches 100, strength is indicated. If the Aroon Up remains persistently between 70 and 100, an uptrend is indicated. Likewise if the Aroon Down line reaches 0, potential weakness is indicated. If the Aroon Down remains persistently between 0 and 30, a downtrend is indicated.

If *both* Aroon Up and Aroon Down remain at extreme levels, rather than just one of the plots being at an extreme level, a stronger trend is indicated. Thus, a strong uptrend is indicated when the Aroon Up line persistently remains between 70 and 100 while the Aroon Down line persistently remains between 0 and 30. Conversely, a strong downtrend is indicated when the Aroon Down line persistently remains between 70 and 100 while the Aroon Up line persistently remains between 0 and 30.

Parallel Movement. Consolidation is indicated when the Aroon Up and Aroon Down lines move parallel with each other and are roughly at the same level. Expect further consolidation until a directional move is indicated by an extreme level or a crossover.

Crossovers. When the Aroon Down line crosses above the Aroon Up line, potential weakness is indicated. Expect prices to begin trending lower. When the Aroon Up line crosses above the Aroon Down line, potential strength is indicated. Expect prices to begin trending higher.

Example

Figure 52 shows Wal-Mart's 21-day Aroon Up and Aroon Down. When Aroon Up and Aroon Down were roughly parallel, Wal-Mart's price was consolidating. As the Aroon Up crossed above the Aroon Down and went to extreme readings, a strong uptrend developed.

Calculation

As with many indicators, you specify the number of time periods (e.g., days) to be used when calculating Aroon. This time period is referred to as "n" in the following equations.

FIGURE 52

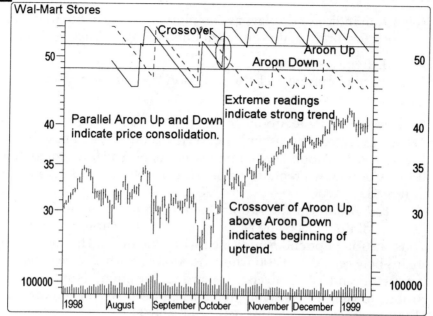

Aroon is calculated by subtracting the number of periods since prices reached a new high (or low) from "*n*," and then dividing by "*n*."

Aroon Up:

$$\frac{n - (\textit{Periods since highest high in "n + 1" periods})}{n} * 100$$

Aroon Down:

$$\frac{n - (\textit{Periods since lowest low in "n + 1" periods})}{n} * 100$$

Table 10 illustrates the calculation of the Aroon indicator. This table calculates a 5-period Aroon (i.e., "*n*" is 5).

- Column D contains the highest high in the previous 6 days (i.e., since "*n*" is 5 in this example, "*n* + 1" is 6). For example, on 10/12/98 the highest high over the preceding 6 days (i.e., 10/05/98 through 10/12/98) was 30.969.
- Column E is the number of time periods since the new high occurred. For example, on 10/12/98 this value is zero, because the highest high over the previous 6 days occurred *on* 10/12/98. Note that on 10/13/98 the value in Column E is 1, because it had been 1 day since

TABLE 10

AROON

A Date	B High	C Low	D Highest High in "n + 1" periods	E Periods Since Highest High in Column D	F "n" − Col E divided by "n" times 100 (Aroon Up)	G Lowest Low in "n + 1" periods	H Periods Since Lowest Low in Column G	I "n" − Col H divided by "n" times 100 (Aroon Down)
10/01/98	27.500	26.219						
10/02/98	28.125	26.313						
10/05/98	29.000	26.906						
10/06/98	30.313	29.188						
10/07/98	29.750	29.188						
10/08/98	28.563	26.594				26.219	5	0.000
10/09/98	29.813	27.875	30.313	2	60.000	26.313	5	0.000
10/12/98	30.969	30.250	30.313	3	40.000	26.594	2	60.000
10/13/98	30.594	29.750	30.969	0	100.000	26.594	3	40.000
10/14/98	31.125	29.813	30.969	1	80.000	26.594	4	20.000
10/15/98	32.500	30.406	31.125	0	100.000	26.594	5	0.000
10/16/98	33.844	32.844	32.500	0	100.000	27.875	5	0.000
10/19/98	34.469	33.813	33.844	0	100.000	29.750	4	20.000
10/20/98	34.719	32.688	34.469	0	100.000	29.750	5	0.000
10/21/98	33.031	32.281	34.719	1	80.000	29.813	5	0.000
10/22/98	33.625	32.281	34.719	2	60.000	30.406	5	0.000
10/23/98	34.000	32.938	34.719	3	40.000	32.281	1	80.000
10/26/98	33.813	32.688	34.719	4	20.000	32.281	2	60.000
10/27/98	33.156	31.500	34.719	5	0.000	31.500	0	100.000
10/28/98	32.969	31.375	34.000	3	40.000	31.375	0	100.000
10/29/98	33.813	32.656	34.000	4	20.000	31.375	1	80.000

the highest high occurred. The value in Column E will never exceed the number of time periods used to calculate the indicator (i.e., "*n*").

- Column F is the number of periods in the indicator (i.e., "*n*") minus the value in Column E, divided by "*n*," multiplied by 100. For example, on 10/08/98, this is $((5 - 2) / 5) * 100$, or 60.
- Columns G, H, and I are calculated in a manner similar to how Columns D, E, and F are calculated, except they deal with the lowest lows during the time period.

AVERAGE TRUE RANGE

Overview

The Average True Range (ATR) is a measure of volatility. Welles Wilder introduced it in his book *New Concepts in Technical Trading Systems,* and it has since been used as a component of many indicators and trading systems.

Interpretation

Wilder found that high ATR values often occur at market bottoms following a "panic" sell-off. Low ATR values are often found during extended sideways periods, such as those found at tops and after consolidation periods.

The ATR can be interpreted using the same techniques used with other volatility indicators. Refer to the discussion on Standard Deviation (page 308) for additional information on volatility interpretation.

Example

Figure 53 shows McDonald's and its ATR. This is a good example of high volatility when prices bottomed (vertical line labeled A) and low volatility as prices consolidated before a breakout (vertical line labeled B).

Calculation

The True Range indicator is the greatest of the following:

- The distance from today's high to today's low
- The distance from yesterday's close to today's high
- The distance from yesterday's close to today's low

FIGURE 53

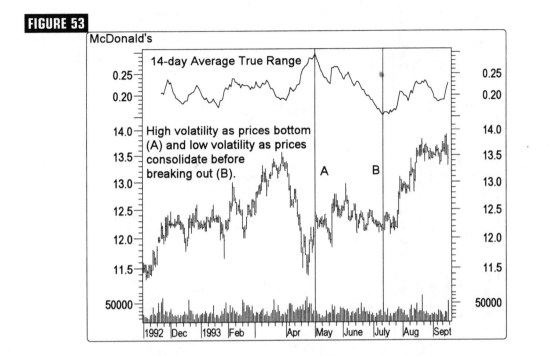

McDonald's

14-day Average True Range

High volatility as prices bottom (A) and low volatility as prices consolidate before breaking out (B).

The *Average* True Range is a moving average (typically 14 days) of the True Ranges. Note that the method used to calculate the moving average is unique—it appears Wilder used this method to simplify manual calculations.

Table 11 illustrates the calculation of the ATR indicator. This table calculates a 4-period ATR (i.e., the number of periods, "n," is 4).

- Columns E, F, and G are straightforward calculations as explained in the column headings.
- Column H is the maximum of Columns E, F, and G. This is the True Range. The remaining columns smooth the value of Column H.
- Column I subtracts the *previous* period's ATR (the previous Column K) from the current True Range (Column H). Note that Column K is initially seeded (on day 4) with the average of the preceding 4 values in Column H.
- Column J multiplies the value in Column I by "$1/n$." For example, when calculating a 4-period ATR, as in this example, you multiply the value in Column E by 1/4 (i.e., 0.25).
- Column K adds the *previous* period's ATR (i.e., the previous Column K) to the value in Column J. This is the ATR.

TABLE 11

AVERAGE TRUE RANGE

A	B	C	D	E	F	G	H	I	J	K
Date	High	Low	Close	High minus Low	High minus Previous Close	Previous Close minus Low	Maximum of Columns E, F, and G	True Range minus Previous ATR	Column I multiplied by "1/n"	Average True Range
01/04/93	12.3125	12.1875	12.2500	0.1250			0.1250			
01/05/93	12.2500	12.1562	12.1875	0.0938	0.0000	0.0938	0.0938			
01/06/93	12.3125	12.1875	12.2500	0.1250	0.1250	0.0000	0.1250			
01/07/93	12.2812	r12.1250	12.1875	0.1562	0.0312	0.1250	0.1562			0.1250
01/08/93	12.3750	12.1250	12.3750	0.2500	0.1875	0.0625	0.2500	0.1250	0.0313	0.1563
01/11/93	12.3750	12.2812	12.3125	0.0938	0.0000	0.0938	0.0938	-0.0625	-0.0156	0.1406
01/12/93	12.3125	12.1875	12.2188	0.1250	0.0000	0.1250	0.1250	-0.0156	-0.0039	0.1367
01/13/93	12.3750	12.1875	12.3438	0.1875	0.1562	0.0313	0.1875	0.0508	0.0127	0.1494
01/14/93	12.5000	12.2812	12.5000	0.2188	0.1562	0.0626	0.2188	0.0694	0.0173	0.1668
01/15/93	12.5938	12.3125	12.3750	0.2813	0.0938	0.1875	0.2813	0.1145	0.0286	0.1954
01/18/93	12.3438	12.2812	12.3438	0.0626	-0.0312	0.0938	0.0938	-0.1016	-0.0254	0.1700
01/19/93	12.4062	12.2812	12.3438	0.1250	0.0624	0.0626	0.1250	-0.0450	-0.0112	0.1587
01/20/93	12.3750	12.2812	12.2812	0.0938	0.0312	0.0626	0.0938	-0.0649	-0.0162	0.1425
01/21/93	12.4062	12.2812	12.3750	0.1250	0.1250	0.0000	0.1250	-0.0175	-0.0044	0.1381
01/22/93	12.3750	11.9688	12.0938	0.4062	0.0000	0.4062	0.4062	0.2681	0.0670	0.2052
01/25/93	12.2812	12.0938	12.1562	0.1874	0.1874	0.0000	0.1874	-0.0178	-0.0044	0.2007
01/26/93	12.2500	12.0000	12.0625	0.2500	0.0938	0.1562	0.2500	0.0493	0.0123	0.2130
01/27/93	12.0625	11.6562	11.9688	0.4063	0.0000	0.4063	0.4063	0.1933	0.0483	0.2614
01/28/93	12.3125	12.1562	12.1875	0.1563	0.3437	-0.1874	0.3437	0.0823	0.0206	0.2819
01/29/93	12.3125	12.1250	12.1562	0.1875	0.1250	0.0625	0.1875	-0.0944	-0.0236	0.2583

BOLLINGER BANDS

Overview

Bollinger Bands are similar to moving average envelopes (see page 137) and were created by John Bollinger.

The difference between Bollinger Bands and envelopes is that envelopes are plotted at a fixed percentage above and below a moving average, whereas Bollinger Bands are plotted at standard deviation levels (see page 308) above and below a moving average. Since standard deviation is a measure of volatility, the bands are self-adjusting, widening during volatile markets and contracting during calmer periods.

Interpretation

Bollinger Bands are usually displayed on top of security prices, but they can be displayed on an indicator. These comments refer to bands displayed on prices.

As with moving average envelopes, the basic interpretation of Bollinger Bands is that prices tend to stay within the upper and lower bands. The distinctive characteristic of Bollinger Bands is that the spacing between the bands varies based on the volatility of the prices. During periods of extreme price changes (i.e., high volatility), the bands widen to become more forgiving. During periods of stagnant pricing (i.e., low volatility), the bands narrow to contain prices.

Bollinger notes the following characteristics of Bollinger Bands:

- Sharp price changes tend to occur after the bands tighten, as volatility lessens.
- When prices move outside the bands, a continuation of the current trend is implied.
- Bottoms and tops made outside the bands followed by bottoms and tops made inside the bands call for reversals in the trend.
- A move that originates at one band tends to go all the way to the other band. This observation is useful when projecting price targets.

Example

Figure 54 shows Bollinger Bands on Exxon's prices. The bands were calculated using a 20-day exponential moving average and are spaced two deviations apart.

FIGURE 54

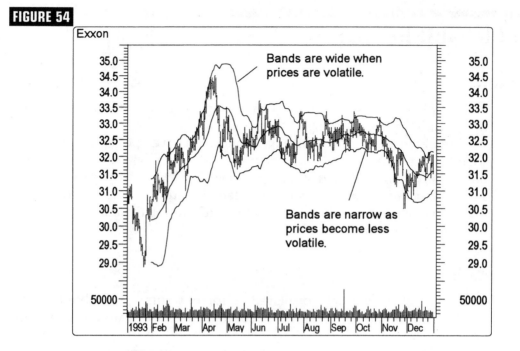

The bands were at their widest when prices were volatile during April. They narrowed when prices entered a consolidation period later in the year. The narrowing of the bands increases the probability of a sharp breakout in prices. The longer prices remain within the narrow bands the more likely a price breakout.

Bollinger recommends using 20 for the number of periods in the moving average, calculating the moving average using the "simple" method (as shown in the formula for the middle band), and using 2 standard deviations. He has also found that moving averages of less than 10 periods do not work very well.

Calculation

Bollinger Bands are displayed as three lines (bands).

The middle band is a simple moving average. In the following formula, "n" is the number of time periods in the moving average (e.g., 20 days).

$$Middle\ Band = \frac{\sum\limits_{j=1}^{n} Close_j}{n}$$

TABLE 12

BOLLINGER BANDS

A	B	C	D	E	F	G
Date	Close	5-day SMA (Middle Band)	One Standard Deviation	Column D multiplied by 2	Column C plus Column E	Column C minus Column E
01/03/94	31.8750					
01/04/94	32.1250					
01/05/94	32.3125					
01/06/94	32.1250					
01/07/94	31.8750	32.0625	0.1677	0.3354	32.3979	31.7271
01/10/94	32.3125	32.1500	0.1611	0.3221	32.4721	31.8279
01/11/94	32.2500	32.1750	0.1649	0.3298	32.5048	31.8452
01/12/94	32.4375	32.2000	0.1912	0.3824	32.5824	31.8176
01/13/94	32.8125	32.3375	0.3026	0.6052	32.9427	31.7323
01/14/94	32.3750	32.4375	0.1976	0.3953	32.8328	32.0422
01/17/94	32.5000	32.4750	0.1879	0.3758	32.8508	32.0992
01/18/94	32.4375	32.5125	0.1551	0.3102	32.8227	32.2023
01/19/94	32.7500	32.5750	0.1741	0.3482	32.9232	32.2268
01/20/94	33.1875	32.6500	0.2974	0.5948	33.2448	32.0552
01/21/94	33.0625	32.7875	0.2974	0.5948	33.3823	32.1927
01/24/94	33.0625	32.9000	0.2727	0.5454	33.4454	32.3546
01/25/94	33.1250	33.0375	0.1510	0.3021	33.3396	32.7354
01/26/94	33.0625	33.1000	0.0500	0.1000	33.2000	33.0000
01/27/94	32.8125	33.0250	0.1090	0.2179	33.2429	32.8071
01/28/94	32.8750	32.9875	0.1212	0.2424	33.2299	32.7451
01/31/94	33.2500	33.0250	0.1611	0.3221	33.3471	32.7029
02/01/94	33.1250	33.0250	0.1611	0.3221	33.3471	32.7029

The upper band is the same as the middle band, but it is shifted up by the number of standard deviations (e.g., 2 deviations). In this next formula, "D" is the number of standard deviations.

$$Upper\ Band = Middle\ band + \left[D * \sqrt{\frac{\sum_{j=1}^{n} (Close_j - Middle\ Band)^2}{n}} \right]$$

The lower band is the moving average shifted down by the same number of standard deviations (i.e., "D").

$$Lower\ Band = Middle\ band - \left[D * \sqrt{\frac{\sum_{j=1}^{n} (Close_j - Middle\ Band)^2}{n}} \right]$$

Table 12 on page 73 illustrates the calculation of Bollinger Bands. This table calculates a 5-period moving average with 2 deviation bands.

- Column C is a 5-period simple moving average of the close. It is calculated by adding the closing price for the preceding 5 days and dividing by 5. This is the middle band.
- Column D calculates the standard deviation of the closing prices over the preceding 5 days. In this table it was calculated using the *stdevp()* spreadsheet function. See page 309 for more information on calculating the standard deviation.
- Column E is the distance between the bands. Since we are calculating 2-deviation bands, this is the standard deviation (Column D) multiplied by 2.
- Column F is the middle band (Column C) plus the 2 deviations (Column E). This is the upper band.
- Column G is the middle band (Column C) minus the 2 deviations (Column E). This is the lower band.

BREADTH THRUST

Overview

The Breadth Thrust indicator is a market momentum indicator developed by Dr. Martin Zweig. A Breadth Thrust occurs when, during a 10-day period, the Breadth Thrust indicator rises from below 40 percent to above 61.5 percent.

Interpretation

A "Thrust" indicates that the stock market has rapidly changed from an over-sold condition to one of strength but has not yet become overbought.

There have only been 14 Breadth Thrusts between 1945 and 2000. The average gain following these 14 Thrusts was 24.6 percent in an average time frame of 11 months. Zweig points out that most bull markets begin with a Breadth Thrust.

As of this writing, the last Breadth Thrust was in 1984. In late 1998 the indicator came within 2 percent of a Breadth Thrust. This was followed by a very strong rally.

Example

Figure 55 shows the S&P 500 and the Breadth Thrust indicator. Horizontal lines are drawn on the Breadth Thrust indicator at 40.0 percent and 61.5 percent. Remember that a Thrust occurs when the indicator moves from below 40 percent to above 61.5 percent during a 10-day period. The two Breadth Thrusts that have occurred since 1980 are marked with arrows.

On December 18, 1984, I wrote (in a software manual) the following comment regarding the Breadth Thrust indicator: "At the time this discussion

FIGURE 55

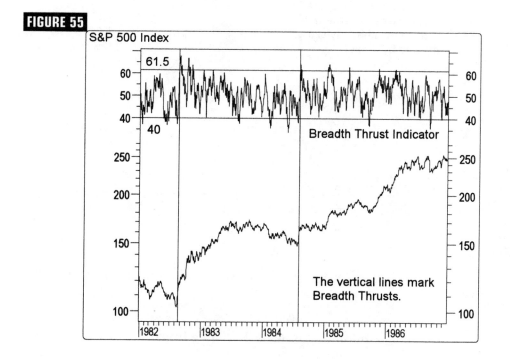

S&P 500 Index
Breadth Thrust Indicator
The vertical lines mark Breadth Thrusts.

on the Breadth Thrust is being written (12/18/84), the NYSE has gained only 1.6 percent since the 'Thrust.' If the market fails to go higher in the next 6 to 12 months, it will be the first false signal generated by the Breadth Thrust indicator in 39 years! With historical average gains of almost 25 percent, we feel the odds are in our favor when we go with the Thrust."

As shown in the example, the NYSE did in fact go higher in the ensuing months. Twelve months after the thrust occurred, the NYSE was up 21.6 percent. Twenty-one months after the thrust occurred, the NYSE was up a whopping 51 percent. Trust the next Thrust.

On October 20, 1998, the indicator came within 2 points of another Thrust, climbing from 37.3 to 59.4 in 8 days (see Figure 56). This was followed by an extremely strong rally.

FIGURE 56

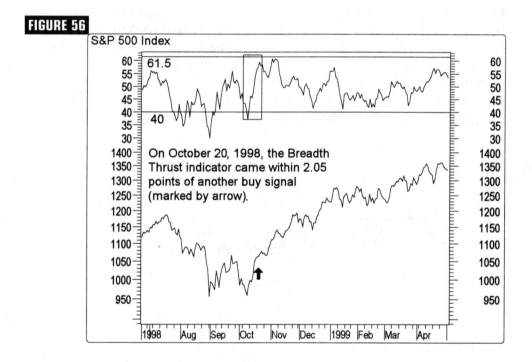

S&P 500 Index

On October 20, 1998, the Breadth Thrust indicator came within 2.05 points of another buy signal (marked by arrow).

Calculation

The Breadth Thrust indicator is a 10-day exponential moving average of the following ratio:

$$\frac{Advancing\ Issues}{Advancing\ Issues\ +\ Declining\ Issues}$$

Table 13 illustrates the calculation of the Breadth Thrust indicator.

- Column D is Column B plus Column C (i.e., the sum of the number of advancing issues and the number of declining issues).
- Column E is Column B (i.e., the number of advancing issues) divided by the sum of advancing issues and declining issues (Column D).
- Column F is the Breadth Thrust indicator. It is a 10-day exponential moving average of Column E. (See page 208 for detailed information on calculating exponential moving averages.) Briefly, the first row of Column F is seeded with the first value in Column E (i.e., 0.3219). Subsequent rows in Column F are calculated by multiplying the value in Column E by 0.1818..., then multiplying the previous day's value in Column F by 0.8181..., and finally adding these two values together. (The values 0.1818... and 0.8181... are the exponential percentages for a 10-period moving average as explained on page 208.) Note that this 10-period moving average is not valid until the tenth day (05/08/97).

TABLE 13

| | | | BREADTH THRUST | | |
A	B	C	D	E	F
Date	Advancing Issues	Declining Issues	Advancing Issues plus Declining Issues	Advancing Issues divided by Column D	10-day EMA of Column E
04/25/97	789	1,662	2,451	0.322	0.3219
04/28/97	1,348	1,085	2,433	0.554	0.3641
04/29/97	2,085	531	2,616	0.797	0.4428
04/30/97	1,599	941	2,540	0.630	0.4768
05/01/97	1,450	1,021	2,471	0.587	0.4968
05/02/97	2,119	476	2,595	0.817	0.5549
05/05/97	1,958	677	2,635	0.743	0.5891
05/06/97	1,258	1,270	2,528	0.498	0.5725
05/07/97	842	1,660	2,502	0.337	0.5296
05/08/97	1,398	1,097	2,495	0.560	0.5352
05/09/97	1,526	932	2,458	0.621	0.5508
05/12/97	1,766	761	2,527	0.699	0.5777
05/13/97	1,133	1,322	2,455	0.462	0.5566
05/14/97	1,472	992	2,464	0.597	0.5640
05/15/97	1,282	1,164	2,446	0.524	0.5567

BULL/BEAR RATIO

Overview

Each week a poll of investment advisors is taken and published by Investor's Intelligence of New Rochelle, New York. Investment advisors are tracked as to whether they are bullish, bearish, or expecting a correction (those expecting a correction are basically bullish but are looking for some sort of short-term weakness). The Bull/Bear Ratio shows the relationship between the bullish and bearish advisors.

Interpretation

The Bull/Bear Ratio is a market sentiment indicator. Dr. Martin Zweig sums up sentiment indicators in his book *Winning on Wall Street* by saying, "Beware of the crowd when the crowd is too one-sided." Extreme optimism on the part of the public and even professionals almost always coincides with market tops. Extreme pessimism almost always coincides with market bottoms.

High readings of the Bull/Bear Ratio are bearish (there are too many bulls), and low readings are bullish (there are not enough bulls). In almost every case, extremely high or low readings have coincided with market tops or bottoms. Historically, readings above 60 percent have indicated extreme optimism (which is bearish for the market) and readings below 40 percent have indicated extreme pessimism (which is bullish for the market).

Example

Figure 57 shows the Bull/Bear Ratio and the S&P 500. Advisors were extremely optimistic at point A, a market top, and extremely pessimistic at point B, a market bottom.

Calculation

The Bull/Bear Ratio is calculated by dividing the number of bullish advisors by the number of bullish plus bearish advisors (as shown in the following equation and Table 14). The number of neutral advisors is ignored.

$$\frac{Bullish\ Advisors}{Bullish\ Advisors\ +\ Bearish\ Advisors} * 100$$

FIGURE 57

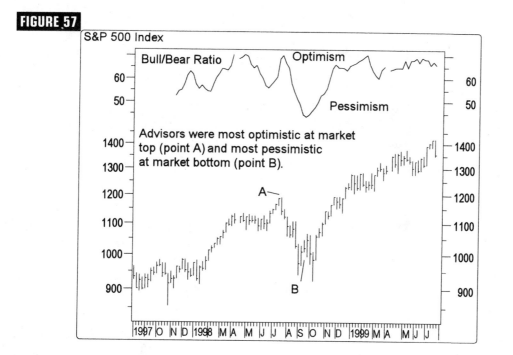

S&P 500 Index

Bull/Bear Ratio Optimism

Pessimism

Advisors were most optimistic at market
top (point A) and most pessimistic
at market bottom (point B).

A

B

1997 O N D 1998 M A M J J A S O N D 1999 M A M J J

TABLE 14

A	B	C	D	E
	BULL/BEAR RATIO			
Date	Bullish Advisors	Bearish Advisors	Column B plus Column C	Col B / Col D multiplied by 100
07/02/98	44.90	31.40	76.30	58.85
07/10/98	47.10	30.60	77.70	60.62
07/17/98	52.00	24.00	76.00	68.42
07/24/98	54.30	23.30	77.60	69.97
07/31/98	52.50	26.30	78.80	66.62
08/07/98	50.00	27.60	77.60	64.43

CANDLESTICKS, JAPANESE

Overview

In the 1600s, the Japanese developed a method of technical analysis to analyze the price of rice contracts. This technique is called "Candlestick Charting." Steven Nison is credited with popularizing it and has become recognized as the leading expert on the interpretation of Candlestick Charts.

C

FIGURE 58

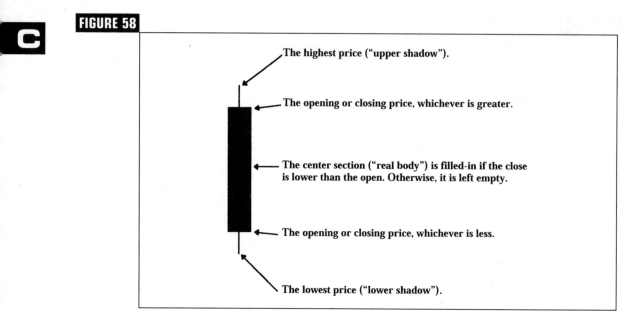

The highest price ("upper shadow").

The opening or closing price, whichever is greater.

The center section ("real body") is filled-in if the close is lower than the open. Otherwise, it is left empty.

The opening or closing price, whichever is less.

The lowest price ("lower shadow").

Candlestick Charts display the open, high, low, and closing prices in a format similar to a modern-day bar chart, but in a manner that extenuates the relationship between the opening and closing prices. Candlestick Charts are simply a new way of looking at prices; they don't involve any calculations.

Each Candlestick represents one period (e.g., day) of data. Figure 58 displays the elements of a candle.

Interpretation

I have met investors who are attracted to candlestick charts by their mystique—maybe they are the "long-forgotten Asian secret" to investment analysis. Other investors are turned off by this mystique—they are only charts, right? Regardless of your feelings about the heritage of candlestick charting, I strongly encourage you to explore their use. Candlestick charts dramatically illustrate changes in the underlying supply/demand lines.

Because candlesticks display the relationship between the open, high, low, and closing prices, they cannot be displayed on securities that only have closing prices, nor were they intended to be displayed on securities that lack opening prices. If you want to display a candlestick chart on a security that does not have opening prices, I suggest you use the previous day's closing price in place of the opening price. This technique can create candlestick lines and patterns that are unusual, but they are still valid.

The interpretation of candlestick charts is based primarily on patterns. The most popular patterns are explained on the following pages.

Candlestick Patterns

3 Method Formations 82
    Bearish 3 Method Formation 82
    Bullish 3 Method Formation 82
Big Candles 83
    Big Black Candle 83
    Big White Candle 83
Bodies 83
    Black Body 83
    White Body 83
Doji's 83
    Doji 83
    Double Doji 83
    Dragonfly Doji 84
    Gravestone Doji 84
    Long-Legged Doji 84
Engulfing Lines 84
    Bearish Engulfing Lines 84
    Bullish Engulfing Lines 84
Hammers 84
    Hammer 84
    Inverted Hammer 84
    Inverted Black Hammer 85
Harami's 85
    Bearish Harami 85
    Bullish Harami 85
    Harami Cross 85
    Bullish Harami Cross 85
Long Shadows 85
    Long Lower Shadow 85
    Long Upper Shadow 86
Separating Lines 86
Shaven Bottom/Head 86
    Shaven Bottom 86
    Shaven Head 86

Stars 86
    Doji Star 86
    Evening Star 87
    Evening Doji Star 87
    Morning Star 87
    Morning Doji Star 87
    Shooting Star 87
Threesomes 88
    Three Black Crows 88
    Three White Soldiers 88
Tweezers 88
    Tweezer Bottoms 88
    Tweezer Tops 88
Windows 88
    Falling Window 88
    Rising Window 89
Other Patterns 89
    Dark Cloud Cover 89
    Hanging Man 89
    On Neck-Line 89
    Piercing Line 89
    Spinning Top 90

Bearish 3 Method Formation

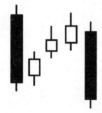

A long black body followed by three small, usually white, bodies and another long black body. The three white bodies are contained within the first black body's range.

This pattern indicates a continuation of a bearish trend. Prices were falling (the long black body), made three weak attempts at a rally (the three small white lines), and the decline continued (the long black body).

Bullish 3 Method Formation

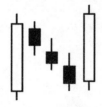

A long white body followed by three small, usually black, bodies and another long white body. The three black bodies are contained within the first white body's range.

This pattern indicates a continuation of a bullish trend. A strong up move, three soft days, and a strong continuation of the bullish trend.

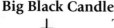

Big Candles

Big Black Candle

This is a bearish line. It occurs when prices open near the high and close significantly lower near the period's low.

Big White Candle

This is a bullish line. It occurs when prices open near the low and close significantly higher near the period's high.

Bodies

Black Body

This is a candlestick formed when the closing price is lower than the opening price.

This is a bearish line. It has more significance when it is part of a pattern.

White Body

A candlestick formed when the closing price is higher than the opening price.

This is a bullish line. It has more significance when it is part of a pattern.

Doji's

Doji

In a Doji, the opening and closing prices are the same, which makes a cross (i.e., the body is neither black nor white).

The Doji implies indecision because the security opened and closed at the same price.

Doji lines appear in many important candlestick patterns.

Double Doji

This pattern implies that a forceful move will follow a breakout from the current indecision.

Dragonfly Doji

This line also signifies a turning point. It occurs when the open and close are the same (a Doji) and the low is significantly lower than the open, high, and closing prices.

Gravestone Doji

In this line the open and close are at the low of the period. The line implies a market top reversal signal. The longer the upper shadow, the more bearish the signal.

Long-Legged Doji

This is a Doji line with very long upper and lower shadows. This line often signifies a turning point.

Engulfing Lines

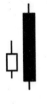

Bearish Engulfing Lines

This pattern occurs when a small white line is followed by, and contained within (engulfed), a large black line. This pattern is very bearish if it occurs after a significant uptrend.

Bullish Engulfing Lines

This pattern occurs when a small black line is followed by, and contained within (engulfed), a large white line. This pattern is very bullish if it occurs after a significant decline.

Hammers

Hammer

A Hammer is identified by a small real body (i.e., a small range between the open and closing prices) and a long lower shadow (i.e., the low is significantly lower than the open, high, and close). The body can be empty or filled.

This is a bullish line if it occurs after a significant downtrend. If the line occurs after a significant uptrend, it is called a Hanging Man (see page 89).

Inverted Hammer

This is an upside-down Hammer (white or black).

Inverted Black Hammer

This is an upside-down Hammer with a black body.

This implies a bottom reversal with expected confirmation on the next line.

Harami's

A Harami indicates a decrease in momentum. They occur when a line with a small body falls within the area of a larger body.

Bearish Harami

A small black body is contained within an unusually large white body. This implies a decrease in bullish momentum when it occurs in an uptrend.

Bullish Harami

A small white body is contained within an unusually large black body. This implies a decrease in bearish momentum when it occurs in a downtrend.

Harami Cross

This pattern is formed when the second line in a Harami is a Doji. As with other Harami patterns, the Harami Cross indicates a decrease in momentum. However, the Doji also signifies indecision.

Bullish Harami Cross

This is similar to a Bullish Harami (above), except a Doji is contained within a large black body. This is a bottom reversal signal.

Long Shadows

Long Lower Shadow

A candlestick (black or white) with a lower shadow that has a length 2/3 or more of the total range of the candlestick.

This is a bullish signal, particularly when around price support levels.

Long Upper Shadow

This candlestick (black or white) has an upper shadow with a length 2/3 or more of the total range of the candlestick.

It is a bearish signal, particularly around price resistance levels.

Separating Lines

In an uptrend, a black candlestick is followed by a white candlestick with the same opening price.

This is bullish as it indicates a strong resumption of the upward price trend following a brief decline.

In a downtrend, a white candlestick is followed by a black candlestick with the same opening price.

This is bearish as it indicates a resumption of the downward price trend following a brief rally.

Shaven Bottom/Head

Shaven Bottom

This candlestick (white or black) has no lower shadow.

Refer to the interpretation of the Inverted Hammer (see page 84).

Shaven Head

This candlestick (white or black) has no upper shadow.

Refer to the interpretation of the Hammer (see page 84) and Hanging Man (see page 89).

Stars

Stars indicate reversals. A star is a line with a small body that occurs after a line with a much larger body, where the bodies do not overlap. The shadows may overlap.

Doji Star

A "star" indicates a reversal and a Doji indicates indecision. Thus, this pattern usually indicates a reversal following an indecisive period. Wait for a confirmation (e.g., as in the Morning Star, page 87) before trading a Doji star. The first line can be empty or filled in.

C

Evening Star

This large white body is followed by a small body (white or black) with gaps above the white body (this is the star). The third candlestick is a black body that closes well into the white body.

This is a bearish pattern signifying a potential top. The Star indicates a possible reversal and the bearish (filled-in) line confirms this. The Star can be empty or filled in.

Evening Doji Star

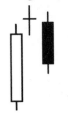

A large white body is followed by a Doji that gaps above the white body. The third candlestick is a black body that closes well into the white body.

This potential top signal is more bearish than the regular Evening Star pattern because of the Doji.

Morning Star

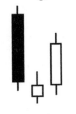

A large black body is followed by a small body (white or black) that gaps below the black body. The third candlestick is a white body that closes well into the black body.

This is a bullish pattern signifying a potential bottom. The Star indicates a possible reversal and the bullish (empty) line confirms this. The Star can be empty or filled in.

Morning Doji Star

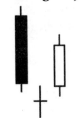

A large black body followed by a Doji that gaps below the black body. The third candlestick is a white body that closes well into the black body.

A bottom reversal signal that is more bullish than the regular Morning Star pattern because of the Doji.

Shooting Star

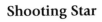

This candlestick (white or black) has a small body, a long upper shadow, and little or no lower shadow.

This pattern suggests a minor reversal when it appears after a rally. The star's body must appear near the low price and the line should have a long upper shadow.

Threesomes

Three Black Crows

Three long black candlesticks have consecutively lower closes that close near or at their low prices.

This is a bearish sign that indicates a reversal when it occurs during an uptrend or a continuation of a decline if it occurs during a downtrend.

Three White Soldiers

Three white candlesticks have consecutively higher closes that close near or at their high prices.

This is a bullish sign that indicates a reversal when it occurs during a downtrend or a continuation of an uptrend if it occurs during an uptrend.

Tweezers

Tweezer Bottoms

Two or more candlesticks have matching bottoms. The size or color of the candlestick does not matter. The candlesticks do not have to be consecutive.

This minor reversal signal is more important when the candlesticks form another pattern.

Tweezer Tops

Two or more candlesticks have matching tops.

This minor reversal signal is more important when the candlesticks form another pattern.

Windows

Falling Window

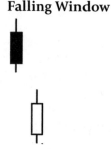

A window (i.e., gap) lies between the low of the first candlestick and the high of the second candlestick. This is a gap (see page 249) in a traditional bar chart.

A rally to close the window is likely. Prices should encounter resistance if they attempt to rise above the window.

Rising Window

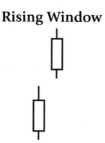

A window (i.e., a gap) lies between the high of the first candlestick and the low of the second candlestick. This is a gap (see page 249) in a traditional bar chart.

A decline to close the window is likely. Prices should encounter support if they attempt to fall below the window.

Other Patterns

Dark Cloud Cover

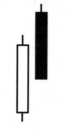

A long white candlestick is followed by a black candlestick. The black candlestick opens above the white candlestick's high and closes well into the white candlestick's body.

This is a bearish pattern when it occurs during an uptrend. The pattern is more significant if the second line's body is below the center of the previous line's body (as illustrated).

Hanging Man

A small body (white or black) is near the high, with a long lower shadow with little or no upper shadow. The lower shadow should be two or three times the height of the body.

These lines are bearish if they occur after a significant uptrend. If this pattern occurs after a significant downtrend, it is called a Hammer (see page 84).

On Neck-Line

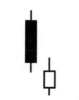

A black candlestick is in a downtrend followed by a small white candlestick with its close near the low of the black candlestick.

This is a bearish pattern where the security should move lower when the white candlestick's low is penetrated.

Piercing Line

This is a bullish pattern and the opposite of a dark cloud cover (above). The first line is a long black line and the second line is a long white line. The second line opens lower than the first line's low, but it closes more than halfway above the first line's real body.

C

Spinning Top

This candlestick (white or black) has a small body. The size of the shadows is not important.

These are neutral lines. They occur when the distance between the high and low, and the distance between the open and close, are relatively small.

Example

Figure 59 illustrates several Japanese candlestick patterns and principles.

You can see that advancing prices are usually accompanied by empty lines (prices opened low and closed higher) and that declines are accompanied by filled-in lines (prices opened high and closed lower).

Several bearish engulfing lines and bullish white lines have been labeled.

FIGURE 59

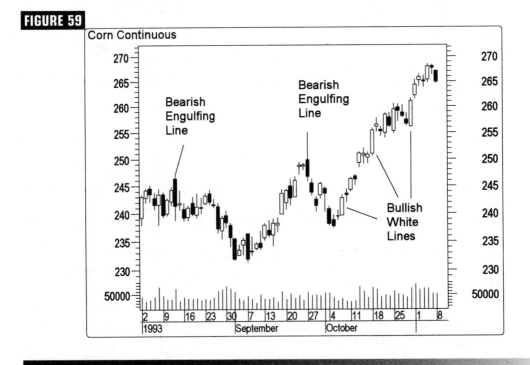

CANSLIM

Overview

CANSLIM is an acronym for a stock market investment method developed by William O'Neil. O'Neil is the founder and chairman of *Investor's Business Daily,* a national business newspaper. He also heads an investment research organization, William O'Neil & Company, Inc.

Drawing from his study of the greatest money-making stocks from 1953 to 1985, O'Neil developed a set of common characteristics that each of these stocks possessed. The key characteristics to focus on are captured in the acronym CANSLIM.

C urrent quarterly earnings per share

A nnual earnings growth

N ew products, new managements, new highs

S hares outstanding

L eading industry

I nstitutional sponsorship

M arket direction

Although not strictly a technical analysis tool, the CANSLIM approach combines worthy technical and fundamental concepts. It is covered in detail in O'Neil's *How to Make Money in Stocks*.

Interpretation

The following text summarizes each of the seven components of the CANSLIM method.

Current Quarterly Earnings.   Earnings per share (EPS) for the most recent quarter should be up at least 20 percent when compared to the same quarter for the previous year (e.g., first quarter of 1999 to the first quarter of 2000).

Annual Earnings Growth.   EPS over the last 5 years should be increasing at the rate of at least 15 percent per year. Preferably, the EPS should increase each year. However, a single-year setback is acceptable if the EPS quickly recovers and moves back into new high territory.

New Products, New Management, New Highs.   A dramatic increase in a stock's price typically coincides with something "new." This could be a new product or service, a new CEO, a new technology, or even new high stock prices.

One of O'Neil's most surprising conclusions from his research is contrary to what many investors feel to be prudent. Instead of adhering to the old stock market maxim, "Buy low and sell high," O'Neil would say, "Buy high and sell higher." O'Neil's research concluded that the ideal time to purchase a stock is when it breaks into new high territory after going through a 2- to 15-month consolidation period. Some of the most dramatic increases follow such a breakout, due possibly to the lack of resistance (i.e., sellers).

C

Shares Outstanding.   More than 95 percent of the stocks in O'Neil's study of the greatest stock market winners had fewer than 25 million shares outstanding. Using the simple principles of supply and demand (see page 18), restricting the shares outstanding forces the supply line to shift upward, which results in higher prices.

A huge amount of buying (i.e., demand) is required to move a stock with 400 million shares outstanding. However, only a moderate amount of buying is required to propel a stock with only 4 million to 5 million shares outstanding (particularly if a large amount is held by corporate insiders).

Leader.   Although there is never a "satisfaction guaranteed" label attached to a stock, O'Neil found that you could significantly increase your chances of a profitable investment if you purchase a leading stock in a leading industry.

He also found that winning stocks are usually outperforming the majority of stocks in the overall market as well.

Institutional Sponsorship.   The biggest source of supply and demand comes from institutional buyers (e.g., mutual funds, banks, insurance companies). A stock does not require a large number of institutional sponsors, but institutional sponsors certainly give the stock a vote of approval. As a rule of thumb, O'Neil looks for stocks that have at least 3 to 10 institutional sponsors with better-than-average performance records.

However, too much sponsorship can be harmful. Once a stock has become "institutionalized," it may be too late. If 70 to 80 percent of a stock's outstanding shares are owned by institutions, the well may have run dry. The result of excessive institutional ownership can translate into excessive selling if bad news strikes.

O'Neil feels the ideal time to purchase a stock is when it has just been discovered by several quality institutional sponsors and before it becomes so popular that it appears on every institution's hot list.

Market Direction.   This is the most important element in the formula. Even the best stocks can lose money if the general market goes into a slump. Approximately 75 percent of all stocks move with the general market. This means that you can pick stocks that meet all the other criteria perfectly, yet if you fail to determine the direction of the general market, your stocks will probably perform poorly.

Market indicators (see page 37) are designed to help you determine the conditions of the overall market. O'Neil says, "Learn to interpret a daily price and volume chart of the market averages. If you do, you can't get too far off the track. You really won't need much else unless you want to argue with the trend of the market."

CHAIKIN MONEY FLOW

Overview

The Chaikin Money Flow compares the closing price to the daily high-low range to determine how much volume is flowing into, or out of, a security, and then it compares this result to the total volume. It was developed by Marc Chaikin and is similar to the Chaikin Oscillator (see page 96).

Interpretation

The interpretation of the Chaikin Money Flow indicator is based on the assumption that market strength is usually accompanied by prices closing in the upper half of their daily high-low range with increasing volume. Likewise, market weakness is usually accompanied by prices closing in the lower half of their daily high-low range with increasing volume.

If prices consistently close in the upper half of their daily high-low range on increased volume, then the indicator will be positive. This indicates that the security is strong. Conversely, if prices consistently close in the lower half of their daily high-low range on increased volume, then the indicator will be negative. This indicates that the security is weak.

The Chaikin Money Flow indicator provides confirmation signals of trendline and support/resistance breakouts. For example, if a security's prices have recently risen above a downward sloping trendline (signaling a potential trend reversal), you may want to wait for further confirmation by waiting for the Chaikin Money Flow indicator to rise above the zero line. This may indicate an overall shift from a downtrend to a new uptrend.

A divergence between the Chaikin Money Flow indicator and prices is also significant. For example, if the most recent peak of the Chaikin Money Flow is lower than its prior peak, yet prices are continuing upward, this may indicate weakness.

Example

Figure 60 shows a 21-day Chaikin Money Flow of Airborne Freight. In the summer of 1992, prices diverged from the indicator (prices were trending down while the indicator was trending up). This divergence was resolved when the prices broke out of their downtrend and started a prolonged advance.

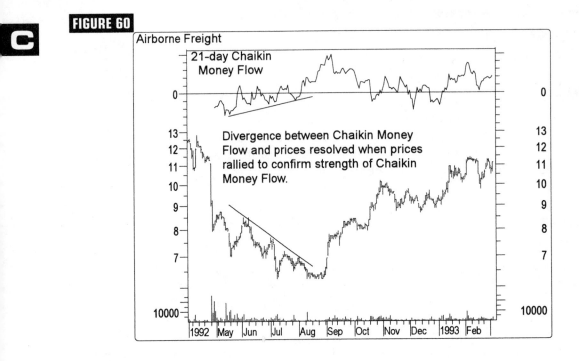

Calculation

The Chaikin Money Flow is calculated by summing the values of the Accumulation/Distribution Line (see page 48), then dividing by a summation of the volume. In the following equation, the numerator is the Accumulation/Distribution Line.

$$\frac{\sum_{1}^{n}\left[\frac{(close - low) - (high - close)}{(high - low)} * volume\right]}{\sum_{1}^{n} volume}$$

Table 15 illustrates the calculation of a 5-day Chaikin Money Flow indicator.

- Column F is the "(close − low) − (high − close) / (high − low)" portion of the numerator in the above equation.
- Column G is the value of Column F multiplied by volume (Column E).
- Column H is a 5-day summation of Column G.
- Column I is a 5-day summation of volume (Column E).
- Column J is the value of Column H divided by the value of Column F. This is the Chaikin Money Flow.

TABLE 15

CHAIKIN MONEY FLOW

Date	High	Low	Close	Volume	(Close — Low) minus (High — Close) divided by (High — Low)	Column F multiplied by Volume	5-day summation of Column G	5-day summation of Volume	Column H divided by Column I
	A	B	C	D	E	F	G	H	I	J
05/01/92	8.6250	8.3125	8.6250	4,494	1.0000	4,494.0000			
05/04/92	8.6250	8.4375	8.5000	2,090	−0.3333	−696.6667			
05/05/92	8.6250	8.4375	8.6250	1,306	1.0000	1,306.0000			
05/06/92	8.7500	8.6250	8.7500	4,242	1.0000	4,242.0000			
05/07/92	8.7500	8.4375	8.5000	2,874	−0.6000	−1,724.4000	7,620.9333	15,006	0.50786
05/08/92	8.5625	8.5000	8.5000	598	−1.0000	−598.0000	2,528.9333	11,110	0.22763
05/11/92	8.5000	8.1875	8.3125	2,668	−0.2000	−533.6000	2,692.0000	11,688	0.23032
05/12/92	8.3125	8.0000	8.0000	19,008	−1.0000	−19,008.0000	−17,622.0000	29,390	−0.59959
05/13/92	8.0625	8.0000	8.0625	6,712	1.0000	6,712.0000	−15,152.0000	31,860	−0.47558
05/14/92	8.0625	7.9375	8.0000	1,924	0.0000	0.0000	−13,427.6000	30,910	−0.43441

C

CHAIKIN OSCILLATOR

Overview

The Chaikin Oscillator is a moving-average oscillator based on the Accumulation/Distribution Line (see page 48). It was developed by Marc Chaikin to extend the work done by Joseph Granville and Larry Williams.

Interpretation

The following discussion of volume accumulation/distribution interpretation, written by Marc Chaikin, is reprinted here with his permission:

Technical analysis of both market averages and individual stocks must include volume studies in order to give the technician a true picture of the internal dynamics of a given market. Volume analysis helps in identifying internal strengths and weaknesses that exist under the cover of price action. Very often, volume divergences versus price movement are the only clues to an important reversal that is about to take place. While volume has always been mentioned by technicians as important, little effective volume work was done until Joseph Granville and Larry Williams began to look at volume versus price in the late 1960s in a more creative way.

For many years it had been accepted that volume and price normally rose and fell together, but when this relationship changed, the price action should be examined for a possible change of trend. The Granville OBV concept which views the total volume on an up day as accumulation and the total volume on a down day as distribution is a decent one, but much too simplistic to be of value. The reason is that there are too many important tops and bottoms, both short-term and intermediate-term, where OBV confirms the price extreme. However, when an OBV line gives a divergence signal versus a price extreme, it can be a valuable technical signal and usually triggers a reversal in price.

Larry Williams took the OBV concept and improved on it. In order to determine whether there was accumulation or distribution in the market or an individual stock on a given day, Granville compared the closing price to the previous close, whereas Williams compared the closing price to the opening price. He [Williams] created a cumulative line by adding a percentage of total volume to the line if the close was higher than the opening and subtracting a percentage of the total volume if the close was lower than its opening price. The Accumulation/Distribution Line improved results dramatically over the classic OBV approach to volume divergences.

C

Williams then took this one step further in analyzing the Dow Jones Industrials by creating an oscillator of the accumulation/distribution line for even better buy and sell signals. In the early 1970s, however, the opening price for stocks was eliminated from the daily newspaper and Williams's formula became difficult to compute without many daily calls to a stockbroker with a quote machine. Because of this void, I created the Chaikin Oscillator substituting the average price of the day for Williams's opening and took the approach one step further by applying the oscillator to stocks and commodities. The Chaikin Oscillator is an excellent tool for generating buy and sell signals when its action is compared to price movement. I believe it is a significant improvement over the work that preceded it.

The premise behind my oscillator is three-fold. The first premise is that if a stock or market average closes above its midpoint for the day (as defined by [high + low] / 2), then there was accumulation on that day. The closer a stock or average closes to its high, the more accumulation there was. Conversely, if a stock closes below its midpoint for the day, there was distribution on that day. The closer a stock closes to its low, the more distribution there was.

The second premise is that a healthy advance is accompanied by rising volume and a strong volume accumulation. Since volume is the fuel that powers rallies, it follows that lagging volume on rallies is a sign of less fuel available to move stocks higher.

Conversely, declines are usually accompanied by low volume, but end with panic-like liquidation on the part of institutional investors. Thus, we look for a pickup in volume and then lower-lows on reduced volume with some accumulation before a valid bottom can develop.

The third premise is that by using the Chaikin Oscillator, you can monitor the flow of volume into and out of the market. Comparing this flow to price action can help identify tops and bottoms, both short-term and intermediate-term.

Since no technical approach works all the time, I suggest using the oscillator along with other technical indicators to avoid problems. I favor using a price envelope (see page 137) around a 21-day moving average and an overbought/oversold oscillator together with the Chaikin Oscillator for the best short- and intermediate-term technical signals.

The most important signal generated by the Chaikin Oscillator occurs when prices reach a new high or new low for a swing, particularly at an overbought or oversold level, and the oscillator fails to exceed its previous extreme reading and then reverses direction.

1. Signals in the direction of the intermediate-term trend are more reliable than those against the trend.
2. A confirmed high or low does not imply any further price action in that direction. I view that as a non-event.

C

A second way to use the Chaikin Oscillator is to view a change of direction in the oscillator as a buy or sell signal, but only in the direction of the trend. For example, if we say that a stock that is above its 90-day moving average of price is in an uptrend, then an upturn of the oscillator while in negative territory would constitute a buy signal only if the stock were above its 90-day moving average—not below it.

"A downturn of the oscillator while in positive territory (above zero) would be a sell signal if the stock were below its 90-day moving average of closing prices."

Example

Figure 61 shows Eastman Kodak and the Chaikin Oscillator. Bearish divergences (where prices increased to new highs while the Oscillator was falling) occurred at points A and B. These divergences were warnings of the sell-offs that followed.

FIGURE 61

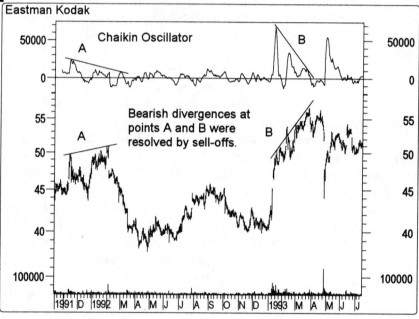

Calculation

The Chaikin Oscillator is created by subtracting a 10-period exponential moving average of the Accumulation/Distribution Line (see page 48) from a 3-period exponential moving average of the Accumulation/Distribution Line.

TABLE 16

CHAIKIN OSCILLATOR

A	B	C	D	E	F	G	H	I
Date	High	Low	Close	Volume	Accumulation/ Distribution	3-day EMA of Col F	10-day EMA of Col F	Column G minus Column H
05/14/93	8.625	8.250	8.625	19,194	19,194.00	19,194.00	19,194.00	
05/17/93	8.875	8.375	8.375	10,768	8,426.00	13,810.00	17,236.18	
05/18/93	9.375	8.375	9.375	20,032	28,458.00	21,134.00	19,276.51	
05/19/93	10.125	8.750	8.750	55,218	−26,760.00	−2,813.00	10,906.24	
05/20/93	9.375	8.750	9.375	13,172	−13,588.00	−8,200.50	6,452.74	
05/21/93	10.125	9.250	9.875	22,245	−4,054.43	−6,127.46	4,542.35	
05/24/93	10.000	9.125	9.375	15,987	−10,906.00	−8,516.73	1,733.56	
05/25/93	9.750	9.375	9.625	9,646	−7,690.67	−8,103.70	20.06	
05/26/93	9.500	9.000	9.125	10,848	−13,114.67	−10,609.18	−2,368.07	
05/27/93	9.625	8.875	9.250	14,470	−13,114.67	−11,861.92	−4,322.00	−7,539.93
05/28/93	10.000	9.375	9.750	14,973	−10,120.07	−10,991.00	−5,376.19	−5,614.80
06/01/93	9.750	8.750	8.875	15,799	−21,969.32	−16,480.16	−8,393.12	−8,087.03
06/02/93	9.125	8.750	8.875	16,860	−27,589.32	−22,034.74	−11,883.34	−10,151.40
06/03/93	9.250	9.125	9.125	6,568	−34,157.32	−28,096.03	−15,933.15	−12,162.87

Table 16 on page 99 illustrates the calculation of the Chaikin Oscillator.

- Column F is the Accumulation/Distribution Line as explained on page 49.
- Column G is a 3-day exponential moving average of Column F. See page 208 for details on calculating exponential moving averages. Briefly, the first row of Column G is seeded with the first value in Column F (i.e., 19,194). Subsequent rows in Column G are calculated by multiplying the value in Column F by 0.5, then multiplying the previous value in Column G by 0.5, and finally adding these two values together. (The values 0.5 and 0.5 are the exponential percentages for a 3-period moving average as explained on page 208.) This 3-period moving average is not valid until the third day (05/18/93).
- Column H is a 10-day exponential moving average of Column F. In this 10-day exponential moving average, Column F is multiplied by 0.1818..., the previous value in Column H is multiplied by 0.8182..., and the numbers are added together. This 10-period moving average is not valid until the tenth day (05/27/93).
- Column I is Column G minus Column H. This step isn't done until the tenth day (05/27/93) when both moving averages are valid.

CHANDE MOMENTUM OSCILLATOR

Overview

The Chande Momentum Oscillator (CMO) attempts to capture the "pure momentum" of a security. It differs from other momentum oscillators, such as RSI and Stochastics, in that it uses data for both up *and* down days in the numerator. It was developed by Tushar Chande.

Interpretation

Overbought/Oversold. The primary method of interpreting the CMO is looking for extreme overbought and oversold conditions. As a general rule, Chande quantifies an overbought level at +50 and the oversold level at −50. At +50, up-day momentum is 3 times the down-day momentum. Likewise, at −50, down-day momentum is 3 times the up-day momentum. These levels correspond to the 70/30 levels on the RSI indicator (see page 297).

You can also establish overbought/oversold entry and exit rules by plotting a moving average trigger line on the CMO. For example, if you are using a 20-period CMO, a 9-period moving average of the CMO may serve as a good trigger line. Buy when the CMO crosses above its 9-period trigger line; sell when it crosses below the trigger line.

Trendiness. The CMO can also be used to measure the degree to which a security is trending. The higher the absolute value of the CMO, the stronger the trend. Low absolute values of the CMO show a security in a sideways trading range.

You can use the CMO's ability to measure the trendiness of a security to enhance a trend following system. For example, only place trades based on trend-following indicators when the absolute value of the CMO is high and/or switch to a trading-range indicator when the absolute value of the CMO is low.

Example

Figure 62 shows Boeing and a 20-day CMO. Extremes in the oscillator above +50 and below −50 correspond fairly closely to extremes in the price action.

Calculation

The following is the calculation for the Chande Momentum Oscillator:

$$\frac{S_U - S_D}{S_U + S_D} * 100$$

FIGURE 62

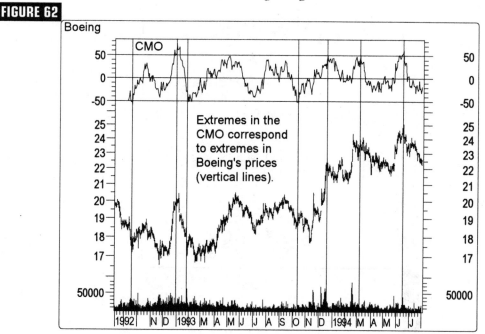

TABLE 17

CHANDE MOMENTUM OSCILLATOR

A	B	C	D	E	F	G	H	I	J
Date	Close	Change in Close	Change on Up Days	5-Day sum of Col D	Absolute Change on Down Days	5-Day sum of Col F	Col E minus Col G	Col E plus Col G	Col H / Col I multiplied by 100
03/03/97	51.0625								
03/04/97	50.1250	−0.9375	0.0		0.9375				
03/05/97	52.3125	2.1875	2.1875		0.0				
03/06/97	52.1875	−0.1250	0.0		0.1250				
03/07/97	53.1875	1.0000	1.0000		0.0				
03/10/97	53.0625	−0.1250	0.0	3.1875	0.1250	1.1875	2.0000	4.3750	45.7143
03/11/97	54.0625	1.0000	1.0000	4.1875	0.0	0.2500	3.9375	4.4375	88.7324
03/12/97	53.5000	−0.5625	0.0	2.0000	0.5625	0.8125	1.1875	2.8125	42.2222
03/13/97	51.5625	−1.9375	0.0	2.0000	1.9375	2.6250	−0.6250	4.6250	−13.5135
03/14/97	51.5000	−0.0625	0.0	1.0000	0.0625	2.6875	−1.6875	3.6875	−45.7627

Where:

- S_U is a summation of the difference between today's close and yesterday's close on up days.
- S_D is a summation of the absolute value of the difference between today's close and yesterday's close on down days. (The term "absolute value" means "regardless of sign." For example, the absolute value of -3 is 3.)

Up days are defined as days when today's close is greater than yesterday's close. Down days are defined as days when today's close is less than yesterday's close. Unchanged days are ignored.

Table 17 illustrates the calculation of a 5-day Chande Momentum Oscillator.

- Column C is the previous close minus the current close. This is the change in the closing price.
- Column D is the value in Column C, but only if Column C is greater than zero. If Column C is less than or equal to zero, then Column D is zero.
- Column E is the sum of the previous 5 days of Column D (because this is a 5-day CMO).
- Column F is the absolute value in Column C, but only if Column C is less than zero. If Column C is greater than or equal to zero, then Column F is zero.
- Column G is the sum of the previous 5 days of Column F (because this is a 5-day CMO).
- Column H is the value of Column E minus Column G.
- Column I is the value of Column E plus Column G.
- Column J is the value of Column H, divided by Column I, and multiplied by 100. This is the CMO.

COMMODITY CHANNEL INDEX

Overview

The Commodity Channel Index (CCI) measures the variation of a security's price from its statistical mean. High values show that prices are unusually high compared to average prices, whereas low values indicate that prices are unusually low.

Contrary to its name, the CCI can be used effectively on any type of security, not just commodities. It was developed by Donald Lambert.

Additional information on the CCI can be found in an article by Donald Lambert that appeared in the October 1980 issue of *Commodities* (now known as *Futures*) magazine.

Interpretation

There are two basic methods of interpreting the CCI: looking for divergences and as an overbought/oversold indicator.

- A divergence (see page 36) occurs when the security's prices are making new highs while the CCI is failing to surpass its previous highs. This classic divergence is usually followed by a correction in the security's price.
- The CCI typically oscillates between ±100. To use the CCI as an overbought/oversold indicator, readings above +100 imply an overbought condition (and a pending price correction) while readings below −100 imply an oversold condition (and a pending rally).

Example

Figure 63 shows Crude Oil and its 14-day CCI. A bullish divergence occurred in late 1998 (prices were declining as the CCI was advancing). Prices subsequently rallied. Note, too, that the divergence occurred at extreme levels (i.e., below −100), making it even more significant.

FIGURE 63

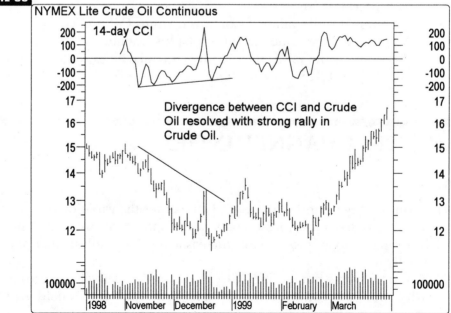

NYMEX Lite Crude Oil Continuous

14-day CCI

Divergence between CCI and Crude Oil resolved with strong rally in Crude Oil.

TABLE 18

COMMODITY CHANNEL INDEX

A	B	C	D	E	F	G	H	I	J	K
Date	High	Low	Close	Typical Price	5-day SMA of Column E	Today's Column F minus each of the 5 preceding Col E's (see text)	Column G divided by 5	Column H multiplied by 0.015	Column E minus Column F	Column J divided by Column I
10/12/98	15.1250	14.9360	14.9360	14.9990						
10/13/98	15.0520	14.6267	14.7520	14.8102						
10/14/98	14.8173	14.5557	14.5857	14.6529						
10/15/98	14.6900	14.4600	14.6000	14.5833						
10/16/98	14.7967	14.5483	14.6983	14.6811	14.7453					
10/19/98	14.7940	13.9347	13.9460	14.2249	14.5905					
10/20/98	14.0930	13.8223	13.9827	13.9660	14.4216					
10/21/98	14.7000	14.0200	14.4500	14.3900	14.3691					
10/22/98	14.5255	14.2652	14.3452	14.3786	14.3281	0.9307	0.1861	0.0028	0.0505	18.0890
10/23/98	14.6579	14.3773	14.4197	14.4850	14.2889	0.7738	0.1548	0.0023	0.1961	84.4605
10/26/98	14.7842	14.5527	14.5727	14.6365	14.3712	0.8105	0.1621	0.0024	0.2653	109.1186
10/27/98	14.8273	14.3309	14.4773	14.5452	14.4871	0.4152	0.0830	0.0012	0.0581	46.6540

Calculation

Table 18 on page 105 illustrates the calculation of the 5-day Commodity Channel Index.

- Column E is the sum of the high plus low plus close divided by three. This is the Typical Price.
- Column F is a 5-day simple moving average of the Typical Price calculated in Column E. It is calculated by adding the preceding 5 values in Column E and dividing by 5.
- Column G is rather complicated to explain. First, take the absolute value of today's Column F minus today's Column E. (The term "absolute value" means "regardless of sign." For example, the absolute value of -3 is 3.) This is then added to the absolute value of today's Column F minus yesterday's Column E. This process (i.e., taking the absolute value of the difference between today's Column F and a previous day's Column E) is repeated for 5 days.
- Column H is the value in Column G divided by 5.
- Column I is Column H multiplied by 0.015.
- Column J is Column E minus Column F.
- Column K is Column J divided by Column I. This is the CCI.

COMMODITY SELECTION INDEX

Overview

The Commodity Selection Index (CSI) is a momentum indicator. It is calculated using the ADXR component of the Directional Movement indicator (see page 119). Welles Wilder developed it and presents it in his book *New Concepts in Technical Trading Systems*.

Interpretation

The name of the index reflects its primary purpose: to help select commodities suitable for short-term trading.

A high CSI rating indicates that the commodity has strong trending and volatility characteristics. The trending characteristics are brought out by the Directional Movement factor (see page 119) in the calculation and the volatility characteristic is brought out by the Average True Range factor (see page 68).

Wilder's approach is to trade commodities with high CSI values (relative to other commodities). Because these commodities are highly volatile, they have the potential to make the "most money in the shortest period of time." High CSI values imply trending characteristics, which makes it easier to trade the security.

The CSI is designed for short-term traders who can handle the risks associated with highly volatile markets.

Example

Figure 64 shows Sugar and its 14-day CSI. Strong volatility and strong trends result in high CSI values at points A and B.

FIGURE 64

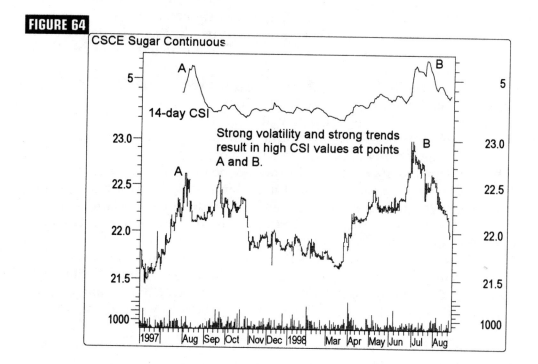

Calculation

The calculation of the CSI is beyond the scope of this book (it requires 21 columns of calculations). The A-to-Z Companion Spreadsheet (see page xvii) contains the full calculations.

CORRELATION ANALYSIS

Overview

Correlation analysis measures the relationship between two items, for example, a security's price and an indicator. The resulting value (called the "correlation coefficient") shows if changes in one item (e.g., an indicator) will result in changes in the other item (e.g., the security's price).

Interpretation

When comparing the correlation between two items, one item is called the "dependent" item and the other the "independent" item. The goal of correlation analysis is to see if a change in the independent item (which is usually an indicator) will result in a change in the dependent item (usually a security's price). This information helps you understand an indicator's predictive abilities.

The correlation coefficient can range between ±1.0 (plus or minus one). A coefficient of +1.0, a "perfect positive correlation," means that changes in the independent item will result in an identical change in the dependent item (e.g., a change in the indicator will result in an identical change in the security's price). A coefficient of −1.0, a "perfect negative correlation," means that changes in the independent item will result in an identical change in the dependent item, but the change will be in the opposite direction. A coefficient of zero means there is no relationship between the two items and that a change in the independent item will have no effect on the dependent item.

A low correlation coefficient (i.e., ±0.10) suggests that the relationship between two items is weak or nonexistent. A high correlation coefficient (i.e., outside of the ±0.10 range) indicates that the dependent variable (e.g., the security's price) will usually change when the independent variable (e.g., an indicator) changes.

The direction of the dependent variable's change depends on the sign of the coefficient. If the coefficient is a positive number, then the dependent variable will move in the same direction as the independent variable; if the coefficient is negative, then the dependent variable will move in the direction opposite the independent variable.

You can use correlation analysis in two basic ways: to determine the predictive ability of an indicator and to determine the correlation between two securities.

When comparing the correlation between an indicator and a security's price, a high positive coefficient (e.g., more than +0.70) tells you that a change in the indicator will usually predict a change in the security's price. A high negative correlation (e.g., less than −0.70) tells you that when the indicator changes, the security's price will usually move in the opposite direction. Remember, a low (e.g., close to zero) coefficient indicates that the relationship between the security's price and the indicator is not significant.

Correlation analysis is also valuable in gauging the relationship between two securities. Often, one security's price "leads" or predicts the price of another security. For example, the correlation coefficient of gold versus the dollar shows a strong negative relationship. This means that an increase in the dollar usually predicts a decrease in the price of gold.

Example

Figure 65 shows a 40-day correlation between corn and live hogs. The high correlation values show that, except during brief periods in January and June, there is a strong relationship between the prices of these items (i.e., when the price of corn changes, the price of live hogs also moves in the same direction).

FIGURE 65

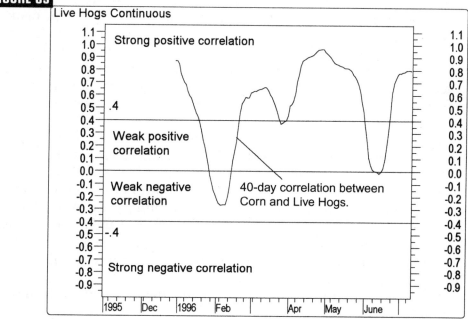

Calculation

The calculation for Correlation Analysis is beyond the scope of this book. It can be calculated in a spreadsheet using the *correl()* function. The A-to-Z Companion Spreadsheet (see page xvii) contains examples of both the brute force and the *correl()* method.

CUMULATIVE VOLUME INDEX

Overview

The Cumulative Volume Index (CVI) is a market momentum indicator that shows whether money is flowing into or out of the stock market. It is calculated by subtracting the volume of declining stocks from the volume of advancing stocks and then adding this value to a running total. Advancing, declining, and unchanged volume are discussed on page 58.

Interpretation

The CVI and OBV (On Balance Volume, see page 229) are quite similar. Many computer programs and investors incorrectly call the OBV the CVI. OBV, like the CVI, was designed to show if volume is flowing into or out of the market. However, because up-volume and down-volume are not available for individual stocks, OBV assumes that all volume is up-volume when the stock closes higher and that all volume is down-volume when the stock closes lower. The CVI does not have to make this large assumption, because it can use the actual up-volume and down-volume for the New York Stock Exchange.

Because the CVI always starts at zero, the numeric value of the CVI is of little importance. What is important is the slope and pattern of the CVI.

One useful method of interpreting the CVI is to look at its overall trend. The CVI shows whether there has been more up-volume or down-volume and how long the current volume trend has been in place. Also, look for divergences (see page 36) that develop between the CVI and a market index. For example, is the market index making a new high while the CVI fails to reach new highs? If so, it is probable that the market will correct to confirm the underlying story told by the CVI.

For additional information on interpreting the CVI, refer to the discussion on OBV (page 229).

C

Example

I wrote the following discussion on the CVI in a software manual on July 18, 1984.

"The trendline on the chart below shows that up-volume exceeded down-volume (on average) for all of 1983. When this rising trend was broken (in February of 1984), the market's weakness was confirmed.

"Since breaking down through its rising trendline, the CVI has begun to trend upward (and sideways) once again. While the market has been down, up-volume has exceeded or equaled down-volume (the CVI is trending upward again). There are two different ways to interpret this: Some investors feel that because the market has failed to go up (even though up-volume has exceeded, or at least kept pace with, down-volume) the overhead supply is too great. After all, if the market falls when there is more up-volume than down-volume, what is going to happen when there is more down-volume than up-volume? An opposing school of thought is that the CVI shows what the smart money is doing. Therefore, since money is flowing into the market on the up-side, the NYSE should soon correct the divergence and rise too."

Now that I have the advantage of retrospect, I can see that the CVI was in fact showing "what the smart money" was doing. As shown in Figure 66, shortly after the above commentary was written (in July, 1984), the market corrected the divergence and rose sharply.

FIGURE 66

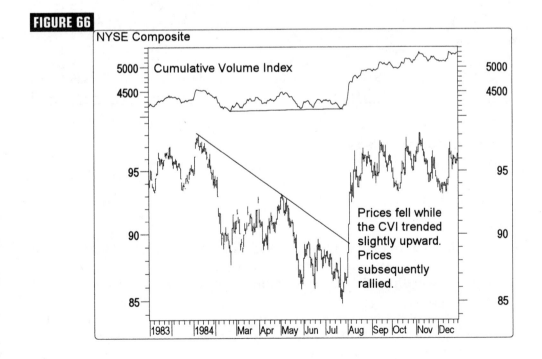

Calculation

C

The CVI is calculated by subtracting the volume of declining stocks from the volume of advancing stocks, and then adding this value to a cumulative total.

Yesterday's CVI + (Advancing Volume − Declining Volume)

Table 19 illustrates the calculation of the CVI:

- Column D is the advancing volume (Column B) minus the declining volume (Column C).
- Column E is a cumulative total of Column D (i.e., today's Column D plus yesterday's Column E).

TABLE 19

| | | CUMULATIVE VOLUME INDEX | | |
A	B	C	D	E
Date	Advancing Volume	Declining Volume	Column B minus Column C	Cumulative Total of Column D
04/25/97	1,097,590	2,685,030	−1,587,440	−1,587,440
04/28/97	2,247,369	1,430,582	816,787	−770,653
04/29/97	4,617,427	527,997	4,089,430	3,318,777
04/30/97	4,000,089	1,163,731	2,836,358	6,155,135
05/01/97	2,176,503	1,856,353	320,150	6,475,285
05/02/97	3,918,818	749,109	3,169,709	9,644,994
05/05/97	4,554,564	665,110	3,889,454	13,534,448
05/06/97	2,774,559	2,762,761	11,798	13,546,246
05/07/97	1,518,034	3,128,770	−1,610,736	11,935,511
05/08/97	3,072,180	1,743,591	1,328,589	13,264,100

CYCLES

Overview

Cycles allow us to accurately predict events in nature: bird migrations, the tides, planetary movements, and so on. Cycle analysis can also help us predict changes in financial markets, although not always with the accuracy found in nature.

The prices of many commodities reflect seasonal cycles. Due to the influence of agriculture on most commodities, these cycles are easily explained and understood. However, for some securities, the cyclical nature is more difficult to explain. Theories as to why certain securities exhibit cyclical patterns range from basic human psychology, to weather and sunspots, to planetary movement. I feel human psychology is responsible.

We know that prices are a consensus of human expectations. These expectations are always changing, shifting the supply/demand lines (see page 18), and causing prices to oscillate between overbought and oversold levels. Fluctuations in prices are a natural process of changing expectations and lead to cyclical patterns.

Many technical analysis indicators and tools were developed in an attempt to profit from the cyclical nature of prices. For example, overbought/oversold indicators (e.g., the Stochastic Oscillator and the Relative Strength Index) are designed to help you determine the excessive boundaries of a cycle.

Figure 67 shows the major components of a cycle.

FIGURE 67

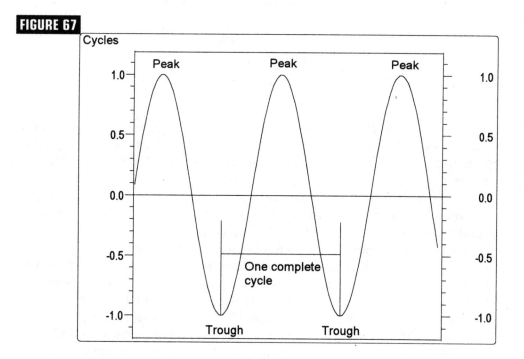

Interpretation

An entire book easily could be filled with a discussion of cycles and cycle analysis. In the following sections, I briefly explain some of the more popular cycles. A good starting point for learning more about cycles, and technical analysis in general, is Martin Pring's book *Technical Analysis Explained*.

Keep in mind that—in hindsight—you can find what appear to be patterns in anything. If you are to profit from cycle analysis, the cycle should have a strong track record and it should be used in conjunction with other trading tools.

Weekly Cycle. From 1900 through 1999, the strongest day of the week has been Friday, while the weakest day has been Monday (October 28, 1929, and October 19, 1987, are famous Monday spills). This trend has almost completely reversed in the 1990's, however, as Monday has become the strongest day and Friday has fallen to fourth place. See Table 20.

TABLE 20

	DOW JONES INDUSTRIALS			
	AVERAGE GAIN BY DAY OF WEEK			
Day of week	**1900 to 1999**		**1990 to 1999**	
Monday	−0.103%	5th	0.161%	1st
Tuesday	0.038%	3rd	0.065%	2nd
Wednesday	0.061%	2nd	0.058%	3rd
Thursday	0.030%	4th	−0.034%	5th
Friday	0.080%	1st	0.053%	4th

28-Day Trading Cycle. Research in the 1930s found a 28-day cycle in the wheat market. Some attribute this to the lunar cycle. Regardless of the cause, many markets, including stocks, do appear to have a 28-day cycle. (The 28-day cycle is *calendar* days. This is approximately 20 *trading* days.)

10 1/2-month Futures Cycle. Although individual commodities exhibit their own unique cycles, a cycle ranging between 9 and 12 months has been found in the Commodity Research Bureau (CRB) Index.

January Barometer. The stock market has shown an uncanny tendency to end the year higher if prices increased during the month of January, and to end the year lower if prices declined during January. The saying is "So goes January, so goes the rest of the year." Between 1950 and 1999, the January Barometer was correct 42 out of 50 times—an accuracy of 84 percent.

January Effect. After year-end tax-loss selling and window-dressing ends, the market tends to rally in January. As this effect has become common knowledge, the effect has moved to late in the previous year.

4-Year Cycle (Kitchin Wave). In 1923, Joseph Kitchin found that a 40-month cycle existed in a variety of financial items in both Great Britain and the United States between 1890 and 1922. The 4-year cycle was later found to have an extremely strong presence in the stock market between 1868 and 1945.

Although it is called a "4-year cycle," the cycle length has been found to vary between 40 and 53 months. This coincides with the typical 4-year economic business cycle.

Presidential Cycle. This cycle is based on the presidential election that occurs every 4 years in the United States. The concept is that stock prices will decline following the election as the newly elected president takes unpopular steps to make adjustments to the economy. At mid-term, stock prices will begin to rise in anticipation of a strong election-day economy.

9.2-Year Cycle (Juglar Wave). In 1860 Clemant Juglar found that a cycle lasting approximately 9 years existed in many areas of economic activity. Subsequent research found this cycle to have had a strong presence between 1840 and 1940.

54-Year Cycle (Kondratieff Wave). Named after a Russian economist, the Kondratieff Wave is a long-term, 54-year cycle identified in prices and economic activity. Since the cycle is extremely long-term, it has only repeated itself 3 times in the stock market.

The up-wave is characterized by rising prices, a growing economy, and mildly bullish stock markets. The plateau is characterized by stable prices, peak economic capacity, and strong bullish stock markets. The down-wave is characterized by falling prices, severe bear markets, and often by a major war.

Figure 68 of the Kondratieff Wave (from *The Media General Financial Weekly*, June 3, 1974) shows the Kondratieff Wave and U.S. wholesale prices.

FIGURE 68

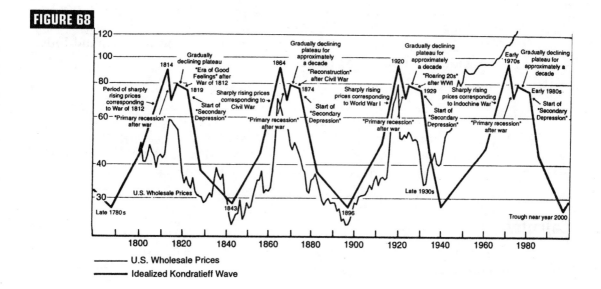

——— U.S. Wholesale Prices

▬▬▬ Idealized Kondratieff Wave

DEMAND INDEX

Overview

The Demand Index combines price and volume in such a way that it is often a leading indicator of price change. It was developed by James Sibbet.

Interpretation

Sibbet's original Demand Index plotted the indicator on a scale labeled "+0" at the top, "1" in the middle, and "−0" at the bottom. Most computer software makes a minor modification to the indicator so that it can be scaled on a normal scale.

Sibbet defined six "rules" for the Demand Index:

1. A divergence (see page 36) between the Demand Index and prices suggests an approaching weakness in price.
2. Prices often rally to new highs following an extreme peak in the Demand Index (the Index is performing as a leading indicator).
3. Higher prices with a lower Demand Index peak usually coincides with an important top (the Index is performing as a coincidental indicator).
4. The Demand Index penetrating the level of zero indicates a change in trend (the Index is performing as a lagging indicator).
5. When the Demand Index stays near the level of zero for any length of time, it usually indicates a weak price movement that will not last long.
6. A large long-term divergence between prices and the Demand Index indicates a major top or bottom.

Example

Figure 69 shows the Demand Index of AMP. A bearish divergence occurred in early 1990 as prices rose while the Demand Index fell. The divergence was resolved when prices corrected to the downside.

Calculation

The Demand Index calculations are beyond the scope of this book (they require 21 columns of data).

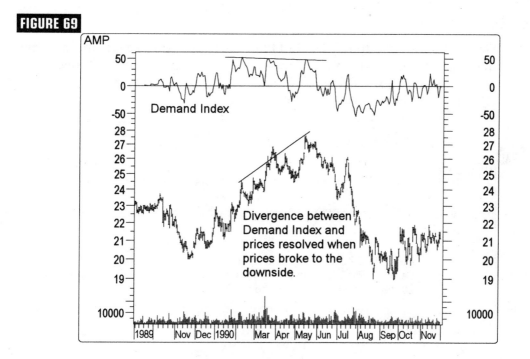

FIGURE 69

DETRENDED PRICE OSCILLATOR

Overview

The Detrended Price Oscillator (DPO) attempts to eliminate the trend in prices. Detrended prices allow you to identify cycles and overbought/oversold levels more easily.

Interpretation

Long-term cycles are made up of a series of short-term cycles. Analyzing these shorter-term components of the long-term cycles can be helpful in identifying major turning points in the longer-term cycle. The DPO helps you remove these longer-term cycles from prices.

To calculate the DPO, you specify a time period. Cycles longer than this time period are removed from prices, leaving the shorter-term cycles.

Example

Figure 70 shows the 20-day DPO of PMC-Sierra. You can see that minor peaks in the DPO coincided with minor peaks in PMC's price, but the longer-term price trend was not reflected in the DPO. This occurred because the 20-day DPO removes cycles of more than 20 days.

FIGURE 70

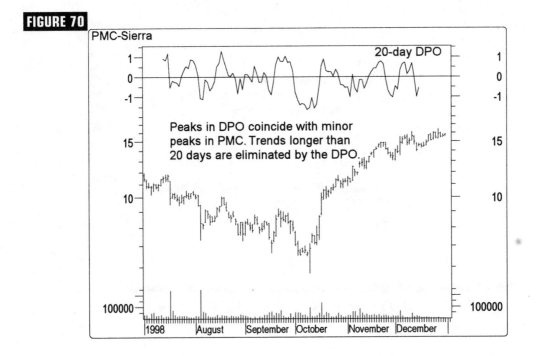

Calculation

To calculate the DPO, first create an *n*-period simple moving average (where "n" is the number of periods in the DPO).

Next, subtract the moving average "$(n/2) + 1$" days (in the future) from the closing price. This has the effect of shifting the DPO back "$(n/2) + 1$" periods. The shift is done to eliminate the trend in prices. The last "$(n/2) + 1$" periods of the DPO will have no value. (If the expression "$(n/2) + 1$" results in a fractional portion, the fractional portion is dropped.)

Table 21 illustrates the calculation of a 6-day Detrended Price Oscillator.

- Column C is a 6-period simple moving average of the close. It is calculated by adding the closing price for the preceding 6 days and dividing by 6.

TABLE 21

		DETRENDED PRICE OSCILLATOR		
A	**B**	**C**	**D**	**E**
Date	Close	6-day SMA	Column C 4 days hence	Column B minus Column D
02/01/93	21.6562			
02/02/93	21.6250		21.7083	−0.0833
02/03/93	21.5312		21.9063	−0.3751
02/04/93	22.0000		22.1458	−0.1458
02/05/93	21.5000		22.3594	−0.8594
02/08/93	21.9375	21.7083	22.5990	−0.6615
02/09/93	22.8438	21.9063	22.3386	0.5053
02/10/93	23.0625	22.1458	22.0938	0.9687
02/11/93	22.8125	22.3594	21.6302	1.1823
02/12/93	23.4375	22.5990	21.0781	2.3594
02/16/93	19.9375	22.3386		
02/17/93	20.4688	22.0938		
02/18/93	20.0625	21.6302		
02/19/93	19.7500	21.0781		

- Column D is the value of Column C 4 days hence. The "4" was calculated using the "$(n/2)+1$" formula (i.e., $6/2+1$ is 4).
- Column E is the closing price (Column B) minus Column D. This is the DPO. Note that the data for the last 4 days (i.e., 2/16/93 through 2/19/93) are blank.

DIRECTIONAL MOVEMENT

Overview

The Directional Movement system helps determine if a security is "trending." It was developed by Welles Wilder and is explained in his book *New Concepts in Technical Trading Systems*.

The Directional Movement system is composed of 5 different indicators:

- Plus Directional Indicator ("+DI")
- Minus Directional Indicator ("−DI")
- Directional Movement Index ("DX")
- Average Directional Movement Index ("ADX")
- Average Directional Movement Index Rating ("ADXR")

Interpretation

The basic Directional Movement trading system involves comparing the 14-day +DI ("Plus Directional Indicator") and the 14-day −DI ("Minus Directional Indicator"). This can be done either by plotting the two indicators on top of each other or by subtracting the +DI from the −DI. Wilder suggests buying when the +DI rises above the −DI and selling when the +DI falls below the −DI.

Wilder qualifies these simple trading rules with the "extreme point rule," which is designed to prevent whipsaws and reduce the number of trades. The extreme point rule requires that on the day that the +DI and −DI cross, you note the "extreme point." When the +DI rises above the −DI, the extreme price is the high price on the day the lines cross. When the +DI falls below the −DI, the extreme price is the low price on the day the lines cross.

The extreme point is then used as the point at which you should implement the trade. For example, after receiving a buy signal (the +DI rose above the −DI), you should wait until the security's price rises above the extreme point (the high price on the day that the +DI and −DI lines crossed) before buying. If the price fails to rise above the extreme point, you should ignore the signal.

In Wilder's book, he notes that this system works best on securities that have a high Average Directional Movement Index Rating ("ADXR"). He says, "As a rule of thumb, the system will be profitable on commodities that have an ADXR value above 25. When the ADXR drops below 20, then do not use a trend-following system."

Example

Figure 71 shows the +DI and −DI indicators for Texaco. The "buy" arrows indicate when the +DI rose above the −DI and "sell" arrows indicate when the +DI fell below the −DI. I only labeled the significant crossings and did not label the 3 short-term crossings.

Calculation

The calculations of the Directional Movement indicators are beyond the scope of this book (they require 21 columns of calculations). The A-to-Z Companion Spreadsheet (see page xvii) contains the full calculations.

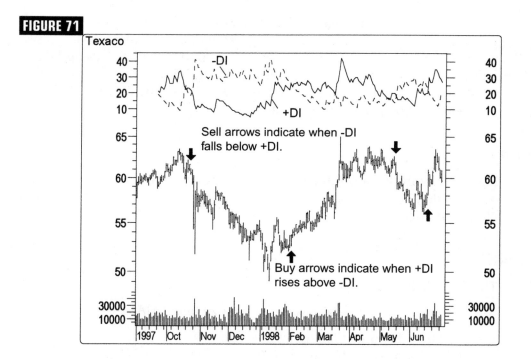

FIGURE 71

Texaco

Sell arrows indicate when -DI falls below +DI.

Buy arrows indicate when +DI rises above -DI.

DOUBLE EXPONENTIAL MOVING AVERAGE

Overview

The Double Exponential Moving Average (DEMA) is a composite of a single exponential moving average and a double exponential moving average that provides less lag time than either of the two individual moving averages. It is a unique calculation, however, *not* simply an exponential moving average of an exponential moving average.

DEMA was developed by Patrick Mulloy and presented in the January 1994 issue of *Technical Analysis of Stocks and Commodities.*

Interpretation

You can use DEMA in place of exponential moving averages (see page 203). You can also use it to smooth price data or other indicators.

Mulloy tested a DEMA-modified MACD and found it produced better results than the standard MACD (see page 199), which is based on an exponential moving average. I tested the traditional MACD system (buy/sell when the MACD penetrates a 9-day trigger) with a DEMA-based MACD system (where the MACD and the trigger were both calculated using DEMA rather than exponential moving averages). During the period from 1995 through 1999, the DEMA-based system was significantly better, although it also generated 60 percent more trades.

Example

Figure 72 contains a 50-day exponential moving average of AT&T and a 50-day DEMA. Notice how much more quickly the DEMA responds to a change in price.

Calculation

The formula for DEMA is:

$$(2 * n\text{-}day\ EMA) - (n\text{-}day\ EMA\ of\ EMA)$$

Where EMA = Exponential Moving Average
Table 22 illustrates the calculation of a 5-day DEMA:

- Column C is a 5-day exponential moving average of the close as described on page 208.

FIGURE 72

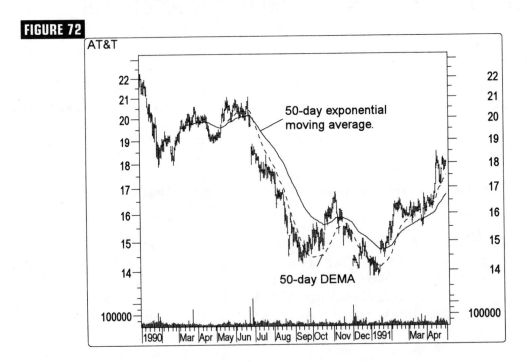

TABLE 22

		DEMA		
A	B	C	D	E
Date	Close	5-day EMA of Column B	5-day EMA of Column C	Column C * 2 minus Column D
12/02/99	122.906	122.9060		
12/03/99	126.500	124.1040		
12/06/99	140.406	129.5380		
12/07/99	174.000	144.3587		
12/08/99	159.812	149.5098	149.5098	
12/09/99	170.000	156.3399	151.7865	
12/10/99	176.750	163.1432	155.5721	
12/13/99	175.531	167.2725	159.4722	
12/14/99	166.562	167.0357	161.9934	172.0780
12/15/99	163.750	165.9404	163.3090	168.5718
12/16/99	170.500	167.4603	164.6928	170.2278
12/17/99	175.000	169.9735	166.4530	173.4940
12/20/99	184.750	174.8990	169.2684	180.5297
12/21/99	202.781	184.1930	174.2432	194.1428

- Column D is a 5-day exponential moving average of the exponential moving average calculated in Column C.
- Column E is Column C multiplied by 2, minus the value in Column D. Note that this 5-day DEMA is not valid until the ninth day.

DOW THEORY

Overview

In 1897, Charles Dow developed two broad market averages. The Industrial Average included 12 blue-chip stocks, and 20 railroad stocks comprised the Rail Average. These are now known as the Dow Jones Industrial Average and the Dow Jones Transportation Average.

The Dow Theory resulted from a series of articles published by Charles Dow in *The Wall Street Journal* between 1900 and 1902 and is the common ancestor to most principles of modern technical analysis.

Interestingly, the theory itself originally focused on using general stock market trends as a barometer for general business conditions. It was not originally intended to forecast stock prices. However, subsequent work has focused almost exclusively on this use of the theory.

Interpretation

The Dow Theory comprises six assumptions.

1. The Averages Discount Everything. An individual stock's price reflects everything that is known about the security. As new information arrives, market participants quickly disseminate the information and the price adjusts accordingly. Likewise, the market averages discount and reflect everything known by all stock market participants.

2. The Market Is Comprised of Three Trends. At any given time in the stock market, three forces are in effect: the Primary Trend, Secondary Trends, and Minor Trends.

The Primary Trend can either be a bullish (rising) market or a bearish (falling) market. The Primary Trend usually lasts more than 1 year and may last for several years. If the market is making successive higher highs and higher lows the primary trend is up. If the market is making successive lower highs and lower lows, the primary trend is down.

Secondary Trends are intermediate, corrective reactions to the Primary Trend. These reactions typically last from 1 to 3 months and retrace from one-third to two-thirds of the previous movement in the Primary Trend. Figure 73 shows a Primary Trend (Line A) and two Secondary Trends (B and C).

Minor trends are short-term movements lasting from 1 day to 3 weeks. Secondary Trends are typically comprised of a number of Minor Trends. The

FIGURE 73

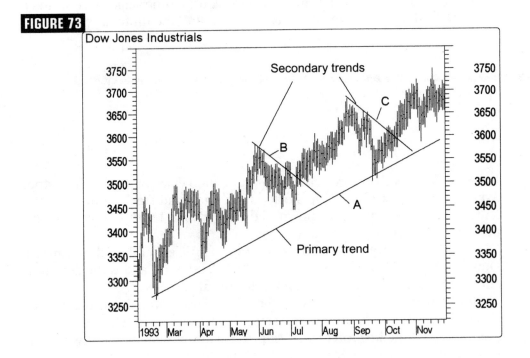

Dow Jones Industrials

Dow Theory holds that, since stock prices over the short term are subject to some degree of manipulation (Primary and Secondary Trends are not), Minor Trends are unimportant and can be misleading.

3. Primary Trends Have Three Phases. The Dow Theory says that the first phase is made up of aggressive buying by informed investors in anticipation of economic recovery and long-term growth. The general feeling among most investors during this phase is one of "gloom and doom" and "disgust." The informed investors, realizing that a turnaround is inevitable, aggressively buy from these distressed sellers.

The second phase is characterized by increasing corporate earnings and improved economic conditions. Investors will begin to accumulate stock as conditions improve.

The third phase is characterized by record corporate earnings and peak economic conditions. The general public (having had enough time to forget about its last "scathing") now feels comfortable participating in the stock market—fully convinced that the stock market is headed for the moon. Investors now buy even more stock, creating a buying frenzy. It is during this phase that those few investors who did the aggressive buying during the first phase begin to liquidate their holdings in anticipation of a downturn.

Figure 74 of the Dow Jones Industrials illustrates these three phases during the years leading up to the October 1987 crash. In anticipation of a

FIGURE 74

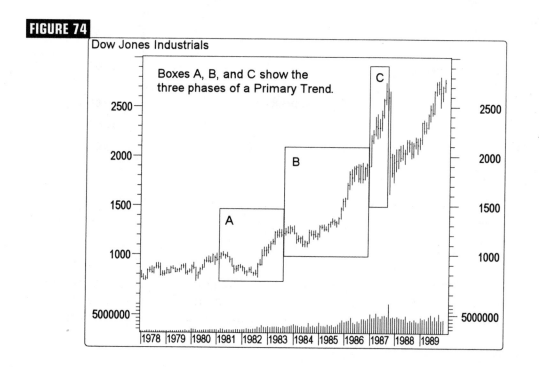

recovery from the recession, informed investors began to accumulate stock during the first phase (box A). A steady stream of improved earnings reports came in during the second phase (box B), causing more investors to buy stock. Euphoria set in during the third phase (box C), as the general public began to buy stock aggressively.

4. The Averages Must Confirm Each Other. The Industrials and Transports must confirm each other in order for a valid change of trend to occur. Both averages must extend beyond their previous secondary peak (or trough) in order for a change of trend to be confirmed.

Figure 75 shows the Dow Jones Industrials and the Dow Jones Transports at the beginning of the bull market in 1982. Confirmation of the change in trend occurred when both averages rose above their previous secondary peak.

FIGURE 75

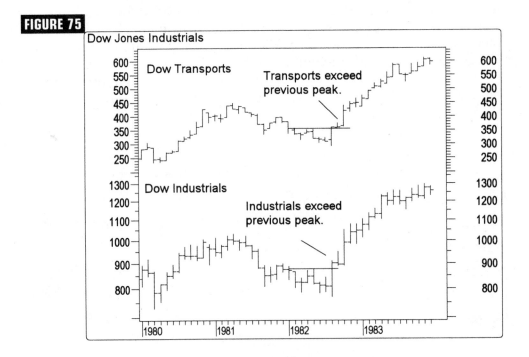

5. The Volume Confirms the Trend. The Dow Theory focuses primarily on price action. Volume is used only to confirm uncertain situations. Volume should expand in the direction of the primary trend. If the primary trend is down, volume should increase during market declines. If the primary trend is up, volume should increase during market advances.

Figure 76 shows expanding volume during an uptrend, confirming the primary trend.

D

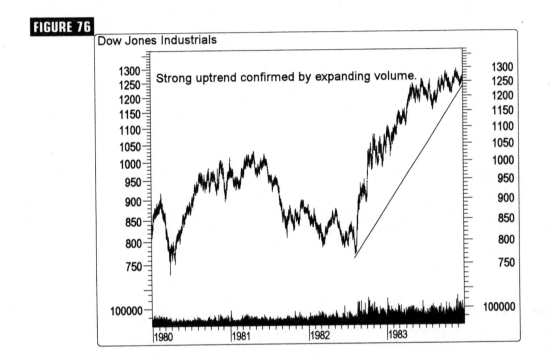

FIGURE 76

6. **A Trend Remains Intact Until It Gives a Definite Reversal Signal.** An uptrend is defined by a series of higher highs and higher lows. In order for an uptrend to reverse, prices must have at least one lower high and one lower low (the reverse is true of a downtrend). When a reversal in the primary trend is signaled by both the Industrials and the Transports, the odds of the new trend continuing are at their greatest. However, the longer a trend continues, the lower the odds of the trend remaining intact.

Figure 77 shows how the Dow Industrials registered a higher high (point A) and a higher low (point B), which identified a reversal of the downtrend (line C).

This simple theory, with the possible exception of the confirmation of the Industrials and the Transports, remains extremely sound and viable. Understanding these principles will help you understand the markets.

FIGURE 77

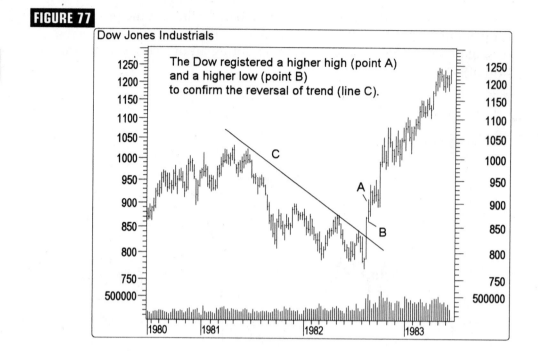

Dow Jones Industrials

The Dow registered a higher high (point A)
and a higher low (point B)
to confirm the reversal of trend (line C).

DYNAMIC MOMENTUM INDEX

Overview

The Dynamic Momentum Index (DMI) is identical to the Relative Strength Index (RSI, see page 297) except the number of periods is variable rather than fixed. The variability of the time periods used in the DMI is controlled by the recent volatility of prices. The more volatile the prices, the more sensitive the DMI is to price changes. In other words, the DMI will use more time periods during quiet markets and fewer during active markets. The maximum number of time periods the DMI can use is 30 and the minimum is 3.

The advantage of using a variable-length time period when calculating the DMI is that it overcomes the negative effects of smoothing, which often obscures short-term moves.

The DMI was developed by Tushar Chande and Stanley Kroll. For additional information, refer to Chande and Kroll's *The New Technical Trader*.

Interpretation

The DMI is interpreted much the same way as the RSI. However, because the DMI is more sensitive to market dynamics, it often leads the RSI into overbought/oversold territories by 1 or 2 days.

As in the RSI, look at the DMI for overbought (bearish) conditions above 70 and oversold (bullish) conditions below 30. However, before basing any trade on strict overbought/oversold levels using the DMI or any overbought/oversold indicator, Chande recommends that you first qualify the trendiness of the market using indicators such as r-Squared (see page 282) or the Chande Momentum Oscillator (see page 100). If these indicators suggest a non-trending market, then trades based on strict overbought/oversold levels should produce the best results. If a trending market is suggested, you can use the DMI to enter trades in the direction of the trend.

Also as in the RSI, look for specific chart formations, failure swings, support and resistance levels, and divergences (see page 297).

Example

Figure 78 shows AlliedSignal and the DMI. A bullish divergence occurred during August and September as prices were falling while the DMI was rising. Prices subsequently corrected and trended upward, confirming the DMI.

FIGURE 78

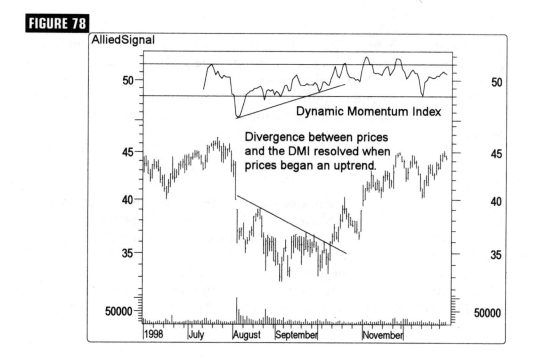

Calculation

Calculating the DMI is identical to calculating the RSI (see page 297), except the number of time periods used in the RSI calculation changes each day based on volatility. The following formula shows how the number of time periods is determined.

Time Periods = 14/Volatility Index (remove everything after the decimal)

Volatility Index = 5-day standard deviation of closing prices divided by a 10-day moving average of 5-day standard deviation of closing prices

Since the number of time periods used in the calculation changes each day, it isn't practical to show the calculations in a table (a separate table would be required for each day). The A-to-Z Companion Spreadsheet (see page xvii) contains a 15-column by 30-row spreadsheet illustrating the DMI for 1 day.

EASE OF MOVEMENT

Overview

The Ease of Movement indicator shows the relationship between volume and price change. As with Equivolume charting (page 138), this indicator shows how much volume is required to move prices.

The Ease of Movement indicator was developed by Richard W. Arms, Jr., the creator of Equivolume. It is described in his book *Volume Cycles and the Stock Market.*

Interpretation

High Ease of Movement values occur when prices are moving upward on light volume. Low Ease of Movement values occur when prices are moving downward on light volume. If prices are not moving, or if heavy volume is required to move prices, the indicator will also be near zero.

The Ease of Movement indicator produces a buy signal when it crosses above zero, indicating that prices are moving upward more easily; a sell signal is given when the indicator crosses below zero, indicating that prices are moving downward more easily.

Example

Figure 79 shows Compaq and a 14-day Ease of Movement indicator. A 9-day moving average was plotted on the Ease of Movement indicator. "Buy" and "sell" arrows indicate when the moving average crossed zero.

FIGURE 79

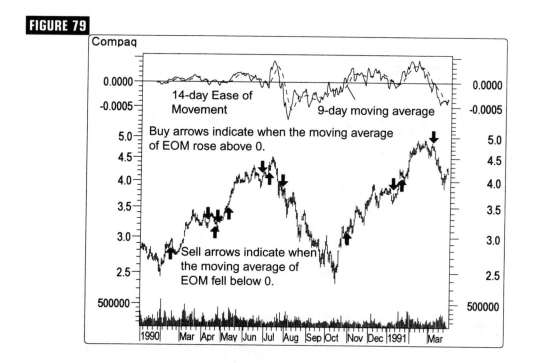

Calculation

In his book, Arms describes two methods of calculating the Ease of Movement indicator: the "exact method" as presented here and the "simplified method" where the "high + low" is expressed in eighths.

The first step in calculating the Ease of Movement indicator is to determine the Midpoint Move as shown below.

$$MM = \left(\frac{High + Low}{2}\right) - \left(\frac{Previous\ High + Previous\ Low}{2}\right)$$

Next, calculate the high-low Box Ratio.

$$Box\ Ratio = \frac{Volume\ (in\ 10,000s)}{High - Low}$$

TABLE 23

EASE OF MOVEMENT

A	B	C	D	E	F	G	H	I	J
Date	High	Low	Volume	High plus Low	Column E divided by 2	Column F minus Previous Column F	High minus Low	Col D / 10,000 divided by Column H	Column G divided by Column I
07/01/99	23.7500	23.0000	125,733	46.7500	23.3750	N/A	0.7500	16.7644	N/A
07/02/99	23.7500	23.1875	83,819	46.9375	23.4688	0.0938	0.5625	14.9012	0.0063
07/06/99	23.7500	23.2500	111,390	47.0000	23.5000	0.0313	0.5000	22.2780	0.0014
07/07/99	25.0625	23.5000	211,366	48.5625	24.2813	0.7813	1.5625	13.5274	0.0578
07/08/99	26.2500	25.0000	240,664	51.2500	25.6250	1.3438	1.2500	19.2531	0.0698
07/09/99	26.8750	25.8125	219,933	52.6875	26.3438	0.7188	1.0625	20.6996	0.0347
07/12/99	27.0000	25.8750	155,943	52.8750	26.4375	0.0938	1.1250	13.8616	0.0068
07/13/99	26.8750	25.7500	138,913	52.6250	26.3125	-0.1250	1.1250	12.3478	-0.0101
07/14/99	28.0000	26.3125	226,220	54.3125	27.1563	0.8438	1.6875	13.4056	0.0629
07/15/99	28.1875	27.3750	164,528	55.5625	27.7813	0.6250	0.8125	20.2496	0.0309
07/16/99	27.6875	27.1250	132,053	54.8125	27.4063	-0.3750	0.5625	23.4761	-0.0160
07/19/99	27.1875	26.0000	109,900	53.1875	26.5938	-0.8125	1.1875	9.2547	-0.0878
07/20/99	26.2500	25.1875	138,313	51.4375	25.7188	-0.8750	1.0625	13.0177	-0.0672
07/21/99	26.5000	25.3750	143,421	51.8750	25.9375	0.2188	1.1250	12.7485	0.0172
07/22/99	26.0000	24.8750	106,053	50.8750	25.4375	-0.5000	1.1250	9.4269	-0.0530
07/23/99	25.8750	24.3125	141,425	50.1875	25.0938	-0.3438	1.5625	9.0512	-0.0380
07/26/99	25.3750	24.2500	96,921	49.6250	24.8125	-0.2813	1.1250	8.6152	-0.0326
07/27/99	25.5000	24.7500	93,208	50.2500	25.1250	0.3125	0.7500	12.4277	0.0251

E

The Ease of Movement (EMV) indicator is then calculated from the Midpoint Move and Box Ratio.

$$EMV = \frac{Midpoint\ Move}{Box\ Ratio}$$

Table 23 illustrates the calculation of the Ease of Movement indicator.

- Column E is the sum of the high plus the low.
- Column F is the value in Column E divided by 2. This is the midpoint.
- Column G is calculated by subtracting Column F from the previous day's Column F.
- Column H is the value of the high minus the low.
- Column I is calculated by first dividing the volume by 10,000. Next, divide this result by Column H. This is the Box Ratio.
- Column J is Column G divided by Column I. This is the Ease of Movement.
- The raw Ease of Movement value is usually smoothed with a moving average.

EFFICIENT MARKET THEORY

Overview

The Efficient Market Theory says that security prices correctly and almost immediately reflect all information and expectations. It says that you cannot consistently outperform the stock market due to the random nature in which information arrives and the fact that prices react and adjust almost immediately to reflect the latest information. Therefore, it assumes that at any given time, the market correctly prices all securities. The result, or so the theory advocates, is that securities cannot be overpriced or underpriced for a long enough period of time to profit therefrom.

The theory holds that since prices reflect all available information, and since information arrives in a random fashion, there is little to be gained by any type of analysis, whether fundamental or technical. It assumes that every piece of information has been collected and processed by thousands of investors and this information (both old and new) is correctly reflected in the price. Returns cannot be increased by studying historical data, either fundamental or technical, since past data will have no effect on future prices.

E

The problem with both of these concepts is that *many* investors base their expectations on past prices (whether using technical indicators, fundamental track records, overbought/oversold conditions, industry trends, etc). Since investors' expectations control prices, it seems obvious that past prices do have a significant influence on future prices.

ELLIOTT WAVE THEORY

Overview

The Elliott Wave Theory is named after Ralph Nelson Elliott. Inspired by the Dow Theory (see page 123) and by observations found throughout nature, Elliott concluded that the movement of the stock market could be predicted by observing and identifying a repetitive pattern of waves. In fact, Elliott believed that all human activities, not just the stock market, were influenced by these identifiable series of waves.

With the help of C. J. Collins, Elliott's ideas received the attention of Wall Street in a series of articles published in 1939 in *Financial World* magazine. During the 1950s and 1960s (after Elliott's passing), his work was advanced by Hamilton Bolton. In 1960, Bolton wrote *Elliott Wave Principle: A Critical Appraisal*. This was the first significant work since Elliott's passing. In 1978, Robert Prechter and A. J. Frost collaborated to write *Elliott Wave Principle*.

Interpretation

The underlying forces behind the Elliott Wave Theory are those of building up and tearing down. The basic concepts of the Elliott Wave Theory are listed below.

1. Action is followed by reaction.
2. There are five waves in the direction of the main trend followed by three corrective waves (a "5-3" move).
3. A 5-3 move completes a cycle. This 5-3 move then becomes 2 subdivisions of the next higher 5-3 wave.
4. The underlying 5-3 pattern remains constant, though the time span of each may vary.

FIGURE 80

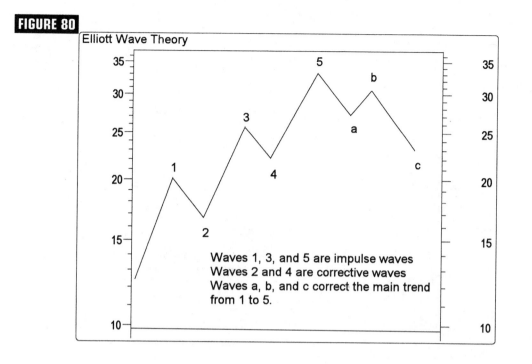

Elliott Wave Theory

Waves 1, 3, and 5 are impulse waves
Waves 2 and 4 are corrective waves
Waves a, b, and c correct the main trend
from 1 to 5.

The basic pattern is made up of 8 waves (5 up and 3 down) that are labeled 1, 2, 3, 4, 5, a, b, and c in Figure 80.

Waves 1, 3, and 5 are called "impulse waves." Waves 2 and 4 are called "corrective waves." Waves a, b, and c correct the main trend made by waves 1 through 5.

The main trend is established by waves 1 through 5 and can be either up or down. Waves a, b, and c always move in the opposite direction of waves 1 through 5.

Elliott Wave Theory holds that each wave within a wave count contains a complete 5-3 wave count of a smaller cycle. The longest wave count is called the "Grand Supercycle." Grand Supercycle waves are comprised of Supercycles, and Supercycles are comprised of Cycles. This process continues into Primary, Intermediate, Minute, Minuette, and Sub-minute waves.

Figure 81 shows how 5-3 waves are comprised of smaller cycles. This chart contains the identical pattern shown in the preceding chart (now displayed using dotted lines), but the smaller cycles are also displayed. For example, you can see that the impulse wave labeled "1" in the preceding chart is comprised of 5 smaller waves.

Fibonacci numbers (see page 141) provide the mathematical foundation for the Elliott Wave Theory. Briefly, the Fibonacci number sequence is made

FIGURE 81

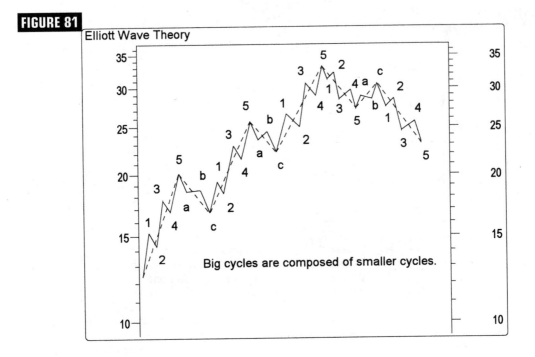

Big cycles are composed of smaller cycles.

simply by starting at 1 and adding the previous number to arrive at the new number (i.e., 0 + 1 = 1, 1 + 1 = 2, 2 + 1 = 3, 3 + 2 = 5, 5 + 3 = 8, 8 + 5 = 13, etc.). Each of the cycles that Elliott defined is comprised of a total wave count that falls within the Fibonacci number sequence. For example, Figure 81 shows 2 primary waves (an impulse wave and a corrective wave), 8 intermediate waves (the 5-3 sequence shown in the first chart), and 34 minute waves (as labeled). The numbers 2, 8, and 34 fall within the Fibonacci numbering sequence.

Elliott Wave practitioners use their determination of the wave count in combination with the Fibonacci numbers to predict the time span and magnitude of future market moves ranging from minutes and hours to years and decades.

Elliott Wave practitioners generally agree that the most recent Grand Supercycle began in 1932 and that the final fifth wave of this cycle began at the market bottom in 1982. However, much disparity has manifested since 1982. Many heralded the arrival of the October 1987 crash as the end of the cycle. The strong recovery that has since followed has caused them to reevaluate their wave counts. Herein lies the weakness of the Elliott Wave Theory—its predictive value is dependent on an accurate wave count. Determining where one wave starts and another wave ends can be extremely subjective.

ENVELOPES (TRADING BANDS)

Overview

An envelope is comprised of two moving averages (see page 203). One moving average is shifted upward and the second is shifted downward.

Interpretation

Envelopes define the upper and lower boundaries of a security's normal trading range. A sell signal is generated when the security reaches the upper band, whereas a buy signal is generated at the lower band. The optimum percentage shift depends on the volatility of the security—the more volatile, the larger the percentage.

The logic behind envelopes is that overzealous buyers and sellers push the price to the extremes (i.e., the upper and lower bands), at which point the prices often stabilize by moving to more realistic levels. This is similar to the interpretation of Bollinger Bands (see page 71).

Example

Figure 82 displays Alcoa with a 10-percent envelope of a 25-day exponential moving average. You can see how Alcoa's price tended to bounce off the bands rather than penetrate them.

FIGURE 82

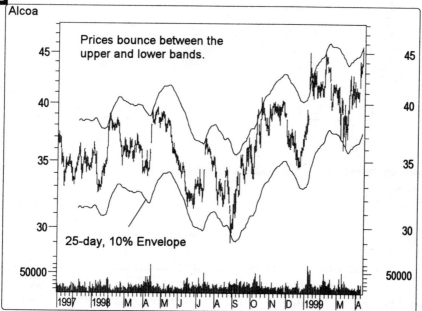

Calculation

Envelopes are calculated by plotting two moving averages that have been shifted up and down. For example, the upper band might be shifted up 3 percent and the lower band shifted down 3 percent.

Table 24 illustrates the calculation of Envelopes. In this example the Envelopes are calculated using a 5-week simple moving average with a 3-percent shift.

- Column C is a 5-period simple moving average of the close. It is calculated by adding the closing price for the preceding 5 periods and dividing by 5.
- Column D is the value of Column C multiplied by 1.03 (i.e., 100 percent plus a 3-percent shift). This is the upper band.
- Column E is the value of Column C multiplied by 0.97 (i.e., 100 percent minus a 3-percent shift). This is the lower band.

TABLE 24

| | | ENVELOPES | | |
A	B	C	D	E
Date	Close	5-week simple moving average	Column C multiplied by 1.03	Column C multiplied by 0.97
11/15/91	18.594			
11/22/91	18.656			
11/29/91	18.563			
12/06/91	19.563			
12/13/91	19.188	18.913	19.480	18.345
12/20/91	19.969	19.188	19.763	18.612
12/27/91	21.406	19.738	20.330	19.145
01/03/92	20.781	20.181	20.787	19.576
01/10/92	20.813	20.431	21.044	19.818

EQUIVOLUME

Overview

Equivolume displays prices in a way that emphasizes the relationship between price and volume. Equivolume was developed by Richard W. Arms, Jr. and is further explained in his book *Volume Cycles in the Stock Market*.

Instead of displaying volume as an afterthought on the lower margin of a chart, Equivolume combines price and volume in a two-dimensional box. As in a normal bar chart (see page 8), the top of the box is the high for the period and the bottom is the low for the period. However, the width of the box is the unique feature of Equivolume—it represents the volume for the period.

Figure 83 shows the components of an Equivolume box.

FIGURE 83

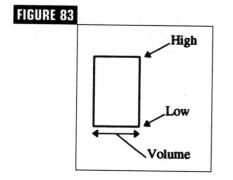

The spacing between periods on the bottom scale of an Equivolume chart is based on volume rather than on dates. This suggests that volume, rather than time, is the guiding influence of price change. To quote Arms, "If the market wore a wristwatch, it would be divided into shares, not hours."

Candlevolume. Candlevolume charts are a unique hybrid of Equivolume and Candlestick charts. Candlevolume charts possess the shadows and body characteristics of Candlestick charts (see page 79), plus the volume width attribute of Equivolume charts (i.e., their width is determined by volume). This combination gives you the unique ability to study Candlestick patterns in combination with their volume-related movements. Although this section explains Equivolume charts, this approach can also be applied to Candlevolume charts.

Interpretation

The shape of each Equivolume box provides a picture of the supply and demand for the security during a specific trading period. Short and wide boxes (heavy volume accompanied with small changes in price) tend to occur at turning points, while tall and narrow boxes (light volume accompanied with large changes in price) are more likely to occur in established trends.

Especially important are boxes that penetrate support or resistance levels, since volume confirms penetrations (see page 356). A "power box" is one in which both height and width increase substantially. Power boxes provide excellent confirmation of a breakout. A narrow box, due to light volume, puts the validity of a breakout in question.

Example

The Equivolume chart in Figure 84 shows McDonald's prices. Note the price consolidation from August to January with resistance around $7.60. The strong move above $7.60 in February produced with power boxes validated the breakout.

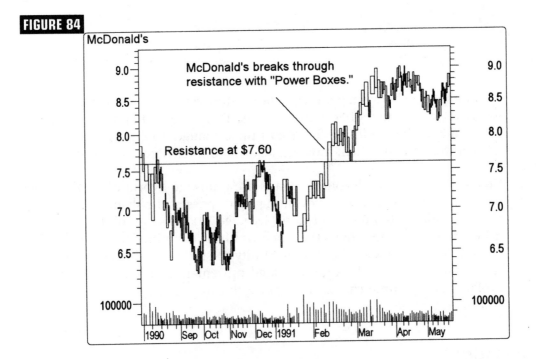

FIGURE 84

Figure 85 is a Candlevolume chart of Charles Schwab. You can see that this hybrid chart is similar to a Candlestick chart (see page 79), but the width of the bars varies based on volume.

FIGURE 85

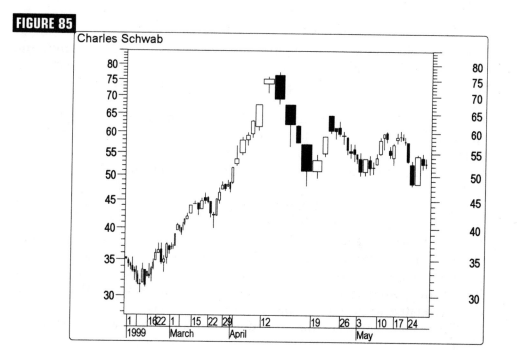

Charles Schwab

F

FIBONACCI STUDIES

Overview

Leonardo Fibonacci was a mathematician who was born in Italy around the year 1170. It is believed that Mr. Fibonacci discovered the relationship of what are now referred to as Fibonacci numbers while modeling population growth in rabbits.

Fibonacci numbers are a sequence of numbers in which each successive number is the sum of the two previous numbers:

1, 1, 2, 3, 5, 8, 13, 21, 34, 55, 89, 144, 233, etc.

These numbers possess an intriguing number of interrelationships, such as the fact that any given number is approximately 1.618 times the preceding number and any given number is approximately 0.618 times the following number. The booklet *Understanding Fibonacci Numbers* by Edward Dobson contains a good discussion of these interrelationships.

Interpretation

There are four popular Fibonacci studies: arcs, fan lines, retracements, and time zones. The interpretation of these studies involves anticipating changes in trends as prices near the lines created by the Fibonacci studies.

Fibonacci Arcs.   Fibonacci Arcs are displayed by first drawing a trendline between two extreme points, for example, a trough and an opposing peak. Three arcs are then drawn, centered on the second extreme point, so they intersect the trendline at the Fibonacci levels of 38.2 percent, 50.0 percent, and 61.8 percent.

The interpretation of Fibonacci Arcs involves anticipating support and resistance as prices approach the arcs. A common technique is to display both Fibonacci Arcs and Fibonacci Fan Lines and to anticipate support/resistance at the points where the Fibonacci studies cross.

Note that the points where the arcs cross the price data will vary depending on the scaling of the chart, because the arcs are drawn so that they are circular relative to the chart paper or computer screen.

Figure 86 illustrates MiniMed and how the arcs can provide support and resistance.

FIGURE 86

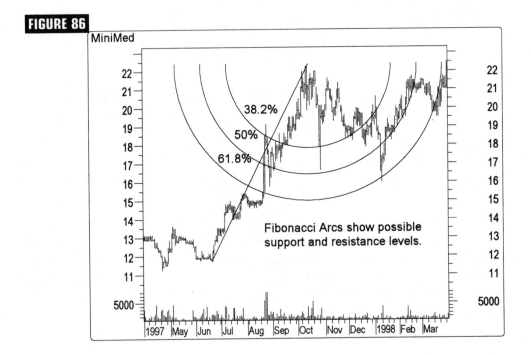

Fibonacci Fan Lines. Fibonacci Fan Lines are displayed by drawing a trend-line between two extreme points, for example, between a trough and an opposing peak. Then an "invisible" vertical line is drawn through the second extreme point. Three trendlines are then drawn from the first extreme point so that they pass through the invisible vertical line at the Fibonacci levels of 38.2 percent, 50.0 percent, and 61.8 percent. (This technique is similar to Speed Resistance Lines, page 305.)

Figure 87 shows how Texaco's prices found support at the Fan Lines. You can see that when prices encountered the top Fan Line (point A), they were unable to penetrate the line for several days. When prices did penetrate this line, they dropped quickly to the bottom Fan Line (points B and C) before finding support.

FIGURE 87

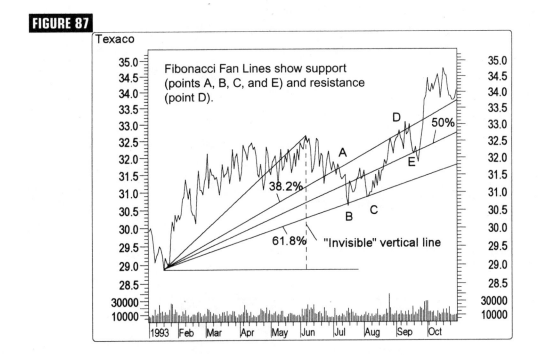

Also note that when prices bounced off the bottom line (point C), they rose freely to the top line (point D), where they again met resistance, fell to the middle line (point E), and rebounded.

Fibonacci Retracements. Fibonacci Retracements are displayed by first drawing a trendline between two extreme points, for example, between a trough and an opposing peak. A series of 9 horizontal lines are drawn intersecting the trendline at the Fibonacci levels of 0.0 percent, 23.6 percent, 38.2 percent, 50.0 percent, 61.8 percent, 100 percent, 161.8 percent, 261.8 percent, and 423.6 percent. (Some of the lines will probably not be visible because they will be off the scale.)

After a significant price move (either up or down), prices will often retrace a significant portion (if not all) of the original move. As prices retrace, support and resistance levels often occur at or near the Fibonacci Retracement levels.

In Figure 88 depicts Eastman Kodak and Fibonacci Retracement lines that were drawn between a major trough and peak. Support and resistance occurred near the Fibonacci levels of 23 and 38 percent.

FIGURE 88

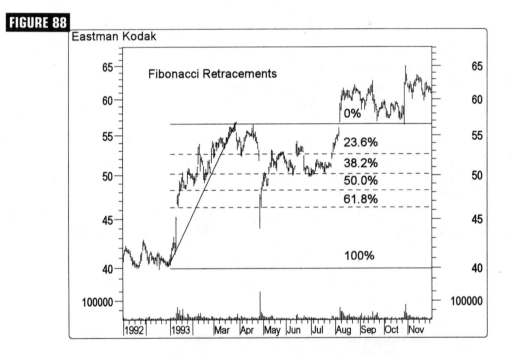

Fibonacci Time Zones. Fibonacci Time Zones are a series of vertical lines. They are spaced at the Fibonacci intervals of 1, 2, 3, 5, 8, 13, 21, 34, etc. The interpretation of Fibonacci Time Zones involves looking for significant changes in price near the vertical lines.

In Figure 89, Fibonacci Time Zones were drawn on the Dow Jones Industrials beginning at the market bottom in 1970. You can see that significant changes in the Industrials occurred on or near the Time Zone lines.

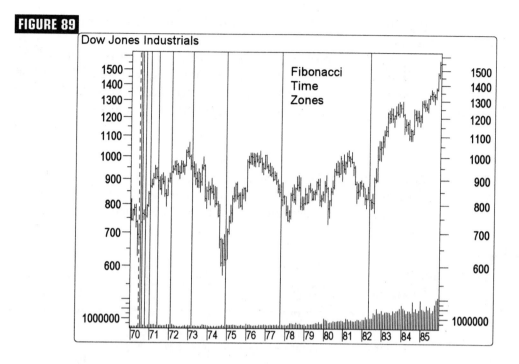

FIGURE 89

Dow Jones Industrials

Fibonacci
Time
Zones

FORECAST OSCILLATOR

Overview

The Forecast Oscillator is an extension of the linear regression-based indicators (see page 172). The Forecast Oscillator shows you, as a percentage, how the actual price compares to the price predicted by the Time Series Forecast Oscillator (see page 333). The oscillator is above zero when the actual price is greater than the forecast price. Conversely, it's less than zero when it's below. The Forecast Oscillator is zero when the forecast price matches the actual price.

The Forecast Oscillator was developed by Tushar Chande.

Interpretation

Actual prices that are persistently below the forecast price suggest lower prices ahead. Likewise, actual prices that are persistently above the forecast price suggest higher prices ahead. Short-term traders should use shorter time periods and perhaps more relaxed standards for the required length of time above or below the forecast price. Long-term traders should use longer time periods and perhaps stricter standards for the required length of time above or below the forecast price.

Chande also suggests plotting a 3-day moving average trigger line of the Forecast Oscillator to generate early warnings of changes in trend. When the Oscillator crosses below the trigger line, lower prices are suggested. When the Oscillator crosses above the trigger line, higher prices are suggested.

Example

Figure 90 shows a 50-day Forecast Oscillator of Southwest Airlines. I've drawn a rectangle around two periods where actual prices were persistently below the forecast price. Both periods were followed by lower prices.

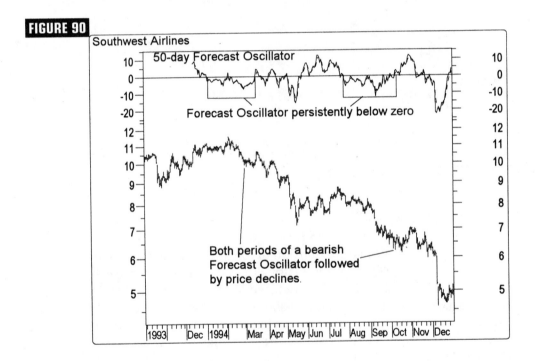

FIGURE 90

Calculation

The Forecast Oscillator is calculated using the Time Series Forecast (see page 333):

$$\left(\frac{Close - Previous\ Time\ Series\ Forecast}{Close}\right) * 100$$

Table 25 illustrates the calculation of a 5-day Forecast Oscillator.

- Column C is the Time Series Forecast indicator (see page 333).

TABLE 25

| | | FORECAST OSCILLATOR | | |
| A | B | C | D | E |
Date	Close	Time Series Forecast	Close minus Previous Col C	Col D / Col B multiplied by 100
01/18/94	16.4444			
01/19/94	16.3333			
01/20/94	16.3333			
01/21/94	16.4444			
01/24/94	16.4444	16.4333		
01/25/94	16.0556	16.1889	−0.3777	−2.3524
01/26/94	16.1667	16.0723	−0.0222	−0.1374
01/27/94	15.9444	15.8278	−0.1279	−0.8020
01/28/94	16.3889	16.1333	0.5611	3.4237
01/31/94	16.5556	16.5889	0.4223	2.5506
02/01/94	16.6111	16.7833	0.0222	0.1336

F

- Column D is the closing price (Column B) minus the previous period's Time Series Forecast (Column C).
- Column E is Column D divided by the close (Column B), multiplied by 100. This is the Forecast Oscillator.

FOUR PERCENT MODEL

Overview

The Four Percent Model is a stock-market timing tool based on the percent change of the weekly close of the (geometric) Value Line Composite Index. It is a trend-following tool designed to keep you in the market during major up moves and out (or short) during major down moves.

The Four Percent Model was developed by Ned Davis and popularized in Martin Zweig's book *Winning on Wall Street*.

Interpretation

A significant strength of the Four Percent Model is its simplicity. The model is easy to calculate and to analyze. In fact, only one piece of data is required—the weekly close of the Value Line Composite Index.

A buy signal is generated when the index rises at least 4 percent from a previous value. A sell signal is generated when the index falls at least 4 percent. For example, a buy signal would be generated if the weekly close of the Value Line rose from 200 to 208 (a 4-percent rise). If the index subsequently rallied to 250 and then dropped below 240 (a 4-percent drop), a sell signal would be generated.

From 1983 to 1998, a buy-and-hold approach on the Value Line Index would have returned 120 percent. Using the Four Percent Model (including shorts) during the same period would have returned 241 percent. (Neither return is adjusted for commissions, dividends, or taxes.) Interestingly, more than half of the signals generated would have resulted in a loss. However, the average gain was much larger than the average loss—an excellent example of the stock market maxim "Cut your losses short and let your profits run."

Example

Figure 91 shows the Zig Zag indicator (see page 372) plotted on top of the Value Line Composite Index, along with the buy and sell signals generated by the 4-percent rule. The Zig Zag indicator identifies changes in price that are at least 4 percent.

FIGURE 91

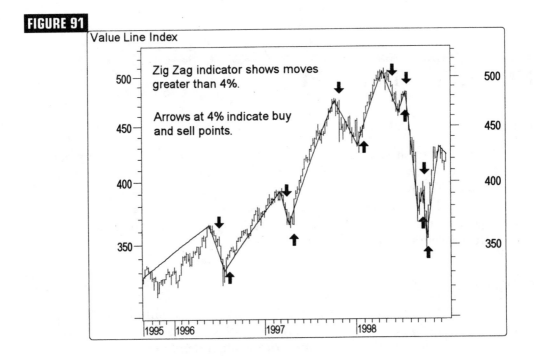

FOURIER TRANSFORM

Overview

Fourier Transforms were originally developed as an engineering tool for studying repetitious phenomena such as the vibration of a stringed musical instrument or an airplane wing during flight.

Fourier analysis is used in technical analysis to detect cyclical patterns within prices.

The complete Fourier analysis concept is called "spectral analysis." Fast Fourier Transform (FFT) is an abbreviated calculation that can be computed in a fraction of the time. FFT sacrifices phase relationships and concentrates only on cycle length and amplitude.

The benefit of FFT is its ability to extract the predominant cycle(s) from a series of data (e.g., an indicator or a security's price).

FFTs are based on the principle that any finite, time-ordered set of data can be approximated by decomposing the data into a set of sine waves. Each sine wave has a specific cycle length, amplitude, and phase relationship to the other sine waves.

A difficulty occurs when applying FFT analysis to security prices, because FFTs were designed to be applied to non-trending, periodic data. The fact that security prices are often trending is overcome by "detrending" the data, using either a linear-regression trendline or a moving average. To adjust for the fact that security data are not truly periodic since securities are not traded on weekends and some holidays, the prices are passed through a smoothing function called a "hamming window."

Interpretation

It is beyond the scope of this book to provide complete interpretation of FFT analysis. I focus my discussion on the "Interpreted" Fast Fourier Transforms found in the MetaStock computer program. This indicator shows the 3 predominant cycle lengths and the relative strength of each of these cycles.

Since the FFT algorithm *always* generates a result, even if there isn't enough data provided, results should be ignored if the time period of the dominant cycle is greater than the number of time periods, and it should be questioned if the predominant cycle is more than one-half of the data (e.g., if you have 500 days of data, question any cycle lengths greater than 250).

Figure 92 displays the Interpreted FFT of Becton Dickinson. The Interpreted FFT shows that predominant cycle lengths in Becton Dickinson are 93, 25, and 57 trading days.

FIGURE 92

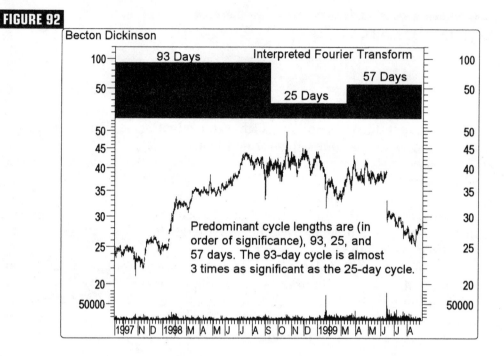

Becton Dickinson

The Interpreted FFT indicator in MetaStock always displays the most significant cycle (93 days in this example) on the left and the least significant cycle (57 days in this example) on the right. The length of each cycle is determined by the numeric value of the indicator (as read on the vertical scales on the sides of the chart).

The longer the indicator remains at a specific value, the more predominant the cycle in the data being analyzed. For example, in Figure 92, the 93-day cycle is almost three times as strong as the 25-day cycle, because the indicator was at 93 almost three times as long as it was at 25.

Once you know the predominant cycle length, you can use it as a parameter for other indicators. In this example, since Becton Dickinson has a predominant cycle of 93 days, you may want to plot a 46-day (half of the 93-day cycle) moving average or RSI on the security.

Calculation

It is beyond the scope of this book to provide a full explanation of Fourier analysis. Further information can be found in *Technical Analysis of Stocks and Commodities*, Vol. 1, Nos. 2, 4, and 7; Vol. 2, No. 4; Vol. 3, Nos. 2 and 7 ("Understanding Cycles"); Vol. 4, No. 6; Vol. 5, Nos. 3 ("In Search of the Cause of Cycles") and 5 ("Cycles and Chart Patterns"); and Vol. 6, No. 11 ("Cycles").

FUNDAMENTAL ANALYSIS

Overview

Fundamental analysis is the study of economic, industry, and company conditions to determine the value of a company's stock. Fundamental analysis typically focuses on key statistics in a company's financial statements to determine if the stock price is correctly valued.

Some people will find a discussion on *fundamental* analysis within a book on *technical* analysis peculiar, but the two theories are not as different as many people believe. It is quite popular to apply technical analysis to charts of fundamental data, for example, to compare trends in interest rates with changes in security prices. It is also popular to use fundamental analysis to select securities and then use technical analysis to time individual trades. Even die-hard technicians can benefit from an understanding of fundamental analysis.

Interpretation

Most fundamental information focuses on economic, industry, and company statistics. The typical approach to analyzing a company involves four basic steps:

1. Determine the condition of the general economy.
2. Determine the condition of the industry.
3. Determine the condition of the company.
4. Determine the value of the company's stock.

Economic Analysis. The economy is studied to determine if overall conditions are good for the stock market. Is inflation a concern? Are interest rates likely to rise or fall? Are consumers spending? Is the trade balance favorable? Is the money supply expanding or contracting? These are just some of the questions that the fundamental analyst would ask to determine if economic conditions are right for the stock market.

Industry Analysis. The company's industry obviously influences the outlook for the company. Even the best stocks can post mediocre returns if they are in an industry that is struggling. It is often said that a weak stock in a strong industry is preferable to a strong stock in a weak industry.

Company Analysis. After determining the economic and industry conditions, the company itself is analyzed to determine its financial health. This is usually done by studying the company's financial statements. From these statements a number of useful ratios can be calculated. The ratios fall into five main categories: profitability, price, liquidity, leverage, and efficiency. When performing ratio analysis on a company, the ratios should be compared to other companies within the same or similar industry to get a feel for what is considered "normal." At least one popular ratio from each category is shown below.

Net Profit Margin. A company's net profit margin is a profitability ratio calculated by dividing net income by total sales. This ratio indicates how much profit the company is able to squeeze out of each dollar of sales. For example, a net profit margin of 30 percent indicates that $0.30 of every $1.00 in sales is realized in profits.

P/E Ratio. The P/E ratio (i.e., Price/Earnings ratio) is a ratio calculated by dividing the security's current stock price by the previous four quarters of earnings per share (EPS).

The P/E ratio shows how much an investor must pay to "buy" $1 of the company's earnings. For example, if a stock's current price is $20 and the EPS for the last four quarters was $2, the P/E ratio is 10 (i.e., $20 / $2 = 10). This means that you must pay $10 to "buy" $1 of the company's earnings. Of course, investor expectations of a company's future performance play a heavy role in determining a company's current P/E ratio.

A common approach is to compare the P/E ratios of companies within the same industry. All else being equal, the company with the lower P/E ratio is the better value.

Book Value Per Share. A company's book value is a price ratio calculated by dividing total net assets (assets minus liabilities) by total shares outstanding. Depending on the accounting methods used and the age of the assets, book value can be helpful in determining if a security is overpriced or underpriced. If a security is selling at a price far below book value, it may be an indication that the security is underpriced.

Current Ratio. A company's current ratio is a liquidity ratio calculated by dividing current assets by current liabilities. This measures the company's ability to meet current debt obligations. The higher the ratio, the more liquid the company. For example, a current ratio of 3.0 means that the company's current assets, if liquidated, would be sufficient to pay for three times the company's current liabilities.

Debt Ratio. A company's debt ratio is a leverage ratio calculated by dividing total liabilities by total assets. This ratio measures the extent to which total assets have been financed with debt. For example, a debt ratio of 40 percent indicates that 40 percent of the company's assets have been financed with borrowed funds. Debt is a double-edged sword. During times of economic stress or rising interest rates, companies with a high debt ratio can experience financial problems. However, during good times, debt can enhance profitability by financing growth at a lower cost.

Inventory Turnover. A company's inventory turnover is an efficiency ratio calculated by dividing cost of goods sold by inventories. It reflects how effectively the company manages its inventories by showing the number of times per year inventories are turned over (replaced). This type of ratio is highly dependent on the industry. A grocery store chain will have a much higher turnover than a commercial airplane manufacturer. As stated previously, it is important to compare ratios with other companies in the same industry.

Stock Price Valuation.   After determining the condition and outlook of the economy, the industry, and the company, the fundamental analyst is prepared to determine if the company's stock is overvalued, undervalued, or correctly valued.

Several valuation models have been developed to help determine the value of a stock. These include dividend models, which focus on the present value of expected dividends; earnings models, which focus on the present value of expected earnings; and asset models, which focus on the value of the company's assets.

Fundamental factors no doubt play a major role in a stock's price. However, if you form your price expectations based on fundamental factors, it is important that you study the price history as well or you may end up owning an undervalued stock that remains undervalued.

GANN ANGLES

Overview

W. D. Gann (1878–1955) designed several unique techniques for studying price charts. Geometric angles in conjunction with time and price were central to Gann's techniques. Gann believed that specific geometric patterns and angles had unique characteristics that could be used to predict price action.

Interpretation

Gann angles are specified as two numbers separated by an "x." For example, in a "1 x 4" angle (referred to as a "one-by-four"), the first number is the amount the line rises and the second number is the time period in which the rise occurs (i.e., the "run"). That is, a "1 x 4" line rises 1 point for each 4 time periods (e.g., days). A "−1 x 4" line falls 1 point every 4 days.

Gann believed that the ideal balance between time and price exists when prices rise or fall at a 45-degree angle relative to the time axis. This is called a "1 x 1" angle (i.e., prices rise 1 price unit for each time unit).

All of Gann's techniques assumed that equal time and price intervals be used on the charts so that a rise/run of 1 x 1 will always equal a 45-degree angle. This means that the space between 1 time period (e.g., a day) must be the same as the space between each point (e.g., $1.00). Of course, this isn't very practical on a high-priced issue (such as the Dow at 10,000)! However, you can still use 1 x 1 lines and realize Gann would consider them 45 degrees (even if they don't appear at 45 degrees on your computer monitor).

Gann Angles are typically drawn between a significant bottom and top (or vice versa) at various angles. The 1 x 1 trendline, deemed the most important by Gann, signifies a bull market if prices are above the trendline or a bear market if below. Gann believed that a 1 x 1 trendline provides major support during an uptrend and that a major reversal in the trend is signified when the trendline is broken. Gann identified nine significant angles, with the 1 x 1 being the most important:

1 x 8, 82.5 degrees

1 x 4, 75 degrees

1 x 3, 71.25 degrees

1 x 2, 63.75 degrees

1 x 1, 45 degrees

2 x 1, 26.25 degrees

3 x 1, 18.75 degrees

4 x 1, 15 degrees

8 x 1, 7.5 degrees

Gann observed that each of the angles can provide support and resistance, depending on the trend. For example, during an uptrend the 1 x 1 angle tends to provide major support. A major reversal is signaled when prices fall below the 1 x 1 angled trendline. According to Gann, prices should then be expected to fall to the next trendline (i.e., the 2 x 1 angle). In other words, as one angle is penetrated, expect prices to move and consolidate at the next angle.

Gann developed several techniques for studying market action. These include Gann Angles, Gann Fans, Gann Grids, and Cardinal Squares.

Examples

A Gann Fan displays lines at each of the angles that Gann identified. Figure 93 shows a Gann Fan on the S&P 500. You can see that the S&P bounced off the 1 x 1 and 1 x 2 lines.

FIGURE 93

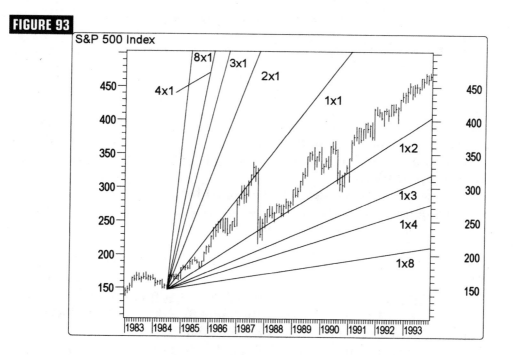

Figure 94 shows the same S&P 500 data with a Gann Grid. This is an 80 x 80 grid (each line on the grid slopes at 1 x 1 and the lines are spaced 80 weeks apart).

FIGURE 94

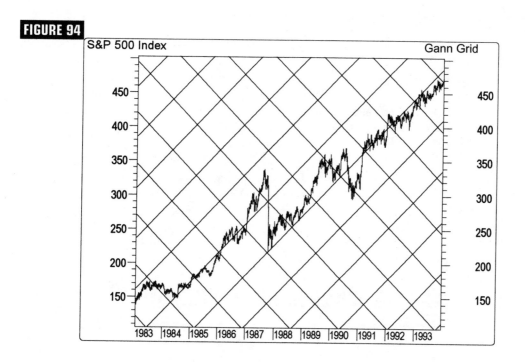

HERRICK PAYOFF INDEX

Overview

The Herrick Payoff Index (HPI) is designed to show the amount of money flowing into or out of a futures contract. The index uses open interest during its calculations; therefore, the security being analyzed must contain open interest (see page 6).

The Herrick Payoff Index was developed by John Herrick. The calculations are beyond the scope of this book. Refer to the March 1988 issue of *Technical Analysis of Stocks and Commodities.*

Interpretation

When the HPI is above zero, it shows that money is flowing into the futures contract (which is bullish). When the index is below zero, it shows that money is flowing out of the futures contract (which is bearish).

Interpreting the HPI involves looking for divergences (see page 36) between the index and prices.

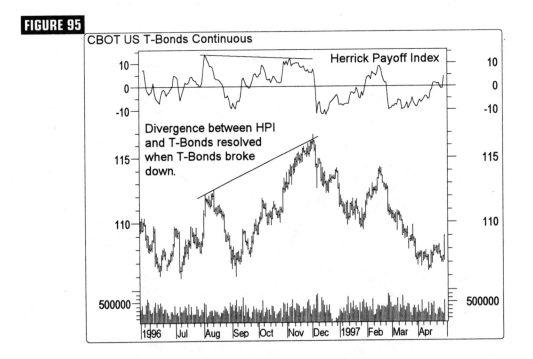

FIGURE 95

Example

Figure 95 shows U.S. Treasury Bonds and the HPI. The trendlines identify a bearish divergence where prices were making new highs while the HPI was failing to make new highs. As is typical with divergences, prices corrected to confirm the indicator.

INERTIA

Overview

The Inertia indicator, developed by Donald Dorsey, builds upon Dorsey's Relative Volatility Index (RVI) (see page 300).

Dorsey chose the name "Inertia" because of his definition of a trend. He asserts that a trend is simply the "outward result of inertia." It takes significantly more energy for a market to reverse direction than to continue along the same path. Therefore a trend is a measurement of market inertia.

In physics, Inertia is defined in terms of mass and direction of motion. Using technical analysis to analyze security prices, the direction of motion is easily defined. However, mass is not so easily defined. Dorsey asserts that "volatility" may be the simplest and most accurate measurement of inertia. This theory led him to use the RVI as the basis for a trend indicator.

Interpretation

When the Inertia indicator is above 50, positive inertia is indicated. The long-term trend is up and should remain up as long as the indicator stays above 50. When the Inertia indicator is below 50, negative inertia is indicated. The long-term trend is down and should remain down as long as the indicator stays below 50.

Example

Figure 96 shows a 20-day Inertia using a 14-day RVI of FileNet. The Inertia indicator fell below 50 in early December, giving investors an early warning sign that the stock had lost its momentum. The stock price finally followed suit in early January and broke to the downside.

FIGURE 96

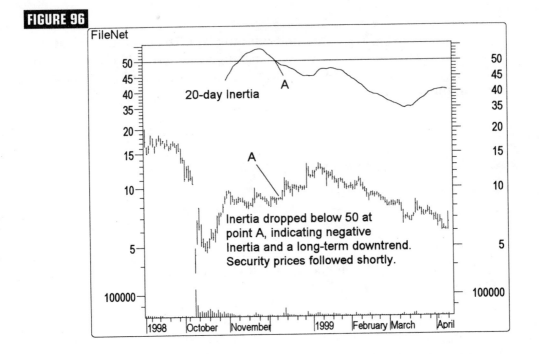

Calculation

The Inertia indicator is simply the RVI (see page 300) smoothed by the Linear Regression Indicator (see page 172).

INTEREST RATES

Overview

Interest rates play a key role in the general business cycle and the financial markets. When interest rates change, or interest rate expectations change, the effects are far-reaching. When rates rise, consumers spend less, which causes retail sales to slow, which leads to reduced corporate profits, a declining stock market, and higher unemployment.

The effect of declining corporate profits on the stock market is compounded by the fact that higher interest rates make interest-bearing investments more attractive, causing an exodus of money from the stock market.

FIGURE 97

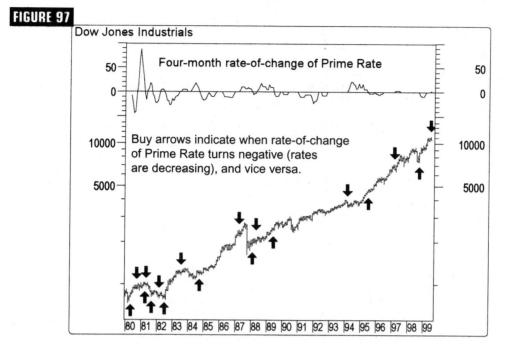

Dow Jones Industrials

Four-month rate-of-change of Prime Rate

Buy arrows indicate when rate-of-change
of Prime Rate turns negative (rates
are decreasing), and vice versa.

Interpretation

Historically, an increase in interest rates is bearish for the stock market, whereas a decrease is bullish.

Figure 97 shows the four-month rate-of-change of the prime rate and the Dow Industrials. "Buy" arrows indicate when interest rates were falling (the indicator was below zero) and "sell" arrows when rates were rising. Even in this strong bull market, you can see that all of the declines in the Dow occurred during periods of rising rates. These arrows show the strong correlation between interest rates and the stock market.

Corporate Bond Rates. Just as governments issue bonds to fund their activities, so do corporations. Corporate bonds are considered riskier than treasury bonds, and they compensate for their higher risk with higher yields. The yield of a specific corporate bond depends on numerous factors. The most important are the financial health of the corporation and prevailing interest rates. Several bond rating services provide investors with an evaluation to help judge the bond's quality.

The Confidence Index, developed by *Barron's* in 1932, uses corporate bond yields as one of its components. The Confidence Index attempts to measure the confidence that investors have in the economy by comparing high-grade bond yields to speculative-grade bond yields.

$$\frac{\textit{Average Yield of High Grade Corporate Bonds}}{\textit{Average Yield of Speculative Grade Corporate Bonds}}$$

If investors are optimistic about the economy, they are more likely to invest in speculative bonds, thereby driving speculative bond yields down and the Confidence Index up. On the other hand, if they are pessimistic about the economy, they are more likely to move their money from speculative-grade bonds to conservative high-grade bonds, thereby driving high-grade bond yields down and the Confidence Index down.

Discount Rate.   The discount rate is the interest rate that the Federal Reserve charges member banks for loans. Banks use the discount rate as the base for loans made to their customers. The discount rate is set by the Federal Reserve Board, which consists of seven members appointed by the president of the United States.

The discount rate does not fluctuate on a day-to-day basis like most other interest rates. Instead, it only changes when the Federal Reserve Board feels it is necessary to influence the economy. During recessionary times, the Fed will ease interest rates to promote borrowing and spending. During inflationary times, the Fed will raise interest rates to discourage borrowing and spending, thereby slowing the rise in prices.

Federal Funds.   Banks can lend their excess reserves to banks with deficient reserves at the Federal Funds Market. The interest rate charged for these short (often just overnight) loans is called the Fed Funds rate.

Prime Rate.   The prime rate is the interest rate U.S. banks charge their best corporate clients. Changes in the prime rate are almost always on the heels of a change in the discount rate.

Treasury Bond Rates.   An extremely important interest rate is the yield on 30-year treasury bonds ("long bonds"). The U.S. Treasury Department auctions these bonds every 6 months.

Long bonds are the most volatile of all government bonds because of the length of their maturities—a small change in interest rates causes an amplified change in the underlying bond price.

Treasury Bill Rates.   Treasury bills are short-term (13- and 26-week) money market instruments. They are auctioned by the U.S. Treasury Department weekly and are often used as a secure place to earn current market rates.

Example

Figure 98 shows several interest rates side by side.

FIGURE 98

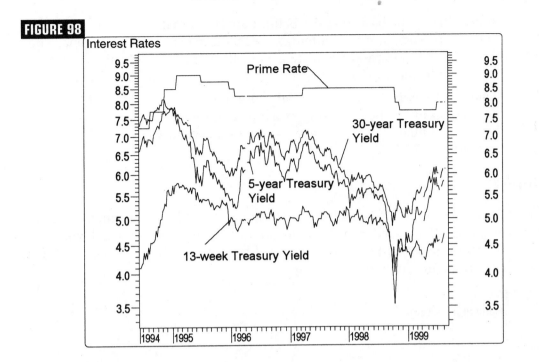

INTRADAY MOMENTUM INDEX

Overview

The Intraday Momentum Index (IMI) is a cross-breed between the Relative Strength Index (see page 297) and Candlestick analysis (see page 79). The IMI was developed by Tushar Chande.

Interpretation

Overbought/Oversold. IMI values above 70 indicate a potential overbought situation with lower prices ahead. Values below 30 indicate a potential oversold situation with higher prices ahead. As with all overbought/oversold indicators, you should first quantify the trendiness of the market before acting on the signals. Indicators like the Vertical Horizontal Filter (see page 351), the Chande Momentum Oscillator (see page 100), and r-Squared (see page 282) can be used to gauge the trendiness of the market.

Divergences.   The basic premise behind the IMI is that shifts in intraday momentum precede shifts in interday momentum. Look for divergences between the indicator and the price action. If the price trends higher and the IMI trends lower (or vice versa), a reversal may be imminent.

Candlestick Confirmation.   The IMI is useful in confirming Candlestick patterns. For example, before acting on a bullish Candlestick pattern, such as the Engulfing Bullish Lines (see page 84), you may want to confirm the bullishness with the IMI.

Example

Figure 99 shows a 14-day Intraday Momentum Index of Burlington Northern. The IMI diverged from prices in late 1994 (the prices trended down while the IMI trended up). This was followed by a reversal in the price trend that confirmed the strength of the IMI.

FIGURE 99

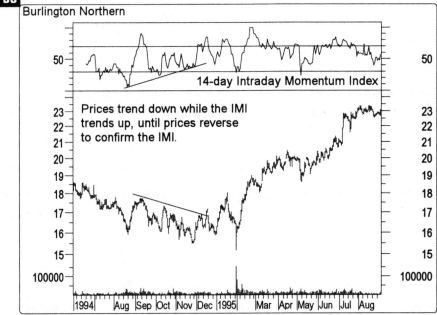

Calculation

The calculation of the IMI is very similar to that of the RSI, except it uses the relationship between the intraday opening and closing prices to determine whether the day is "up" or "down." If the close is above the open (i.e., a white Candlestick), it is an "up" day. If the close is below the open it (i.e., a black Candlestick), it is a "down" day.

TABLE 26

INTRADAY MOMENTUM INDEX

A	B	C	D	E	F	G	H	I	J
			Close minus Open	if Close > Open Column D Otherwise zero	7 day sum of Column E	if Close < Open Absolute value of Column D	7 day sum of Column G	Column F plus Column H	Col F / Col I multiplied by 100
Date	Open	Close							
06/01/94	18.5833	18.5000	-0.0833	0.0000		0.0833			
06/02/94	18.5417	18.4167	-0.1250	0.0000		0.1250			
06/03/94	18.4167	18.1667	-0.2500	0.0000		0.2500			
06/06/94	18.1667	18.1250	-0.0417	0.0000		0.0417			
06/07/94	18.1667	17.9583	-0.2084	0.0000		0.2084			
06/08/94	18.0417	18.0000	-0.0417	0.0000		0.0417			
06/09/94	18.0000	17.9583	-0.0417	0.0000	0.0000	0.0417	0.7918	0.7918	0.0000
06/10/94	17.9167	17.8333	-0.0834	0.0000	0.0000	0.0834	0.7919	0.7919	0.0000
06/13/94	17.7917	17.9583	0.1666	0.1666	0.1666	0.0000	0.6669	0.8335	19.9880
06/14/94	18.0417	18.5417	0.5000	0.5000	0.6666	0.0000	0.4169	1.0835	61.5228
06/15/94	18.5417	18.3333	-0.2084	0.0000	0.6666	0.2084	0.5836	1.2502	53.3195
06/16/94	18.3333	18.2917	-0.0416	0.0000	0.6666	0.0416	0.4168	1.0834	61.5285
06/17/94	18.2917	18.2917	0.0000	0.0000	0.6666	0.0000	0.3751	1.0417	63.9916
06/20/94	18.2083	18.3750	0.1667	0.1667	0.8333	0.0000	0.3334	1.1667	71.4237
06/21/94	18.3333	18.1667	-0.1666	0.0000	0.8333	0.1666	0.4166	1.2499	66.6693
06/22/94	18.1667	18.1250	-0.0417	0.0000	0.6667	0.0417	0.4583	1.1250	59.2622
06/23/94	18.1250	18.0833	-0.0417	0.0000	0.1667	0.0417	0.5000	0.6667	25.0037
06/24/94	18.0000	17.9167	-0.0833	0.0000	0.1667	0.0833	0.3749	0.5416	30.7792
06/27/94	17.8333	17.8750	0.0417	0.0417	0.2084	0.0000	0.3333	0.5417	38.4715

The IMI is calculated as follows:

$$IMI = \frac{IS_U}{IS_U + IS_D} * 100$$

Where:

- IS_U is a summation of the difference between the close and the open on days when the close was greater than the open,
- IS_D is a summation of the difference between the open and the close on days when the close was less than the open.

Table 26 on page 163 illustrates the calculation of a 7-day IMI.

- Column D is the close (Column C) minus the open (Column B).
- Column E is the value of Column D, but only if the close is greater than the open (i.e., only when Column D is greater than zero). If the close is less than or equal to the open, Column E is set to zero.
- Column F is the sum of the preceding 7 days of Column E (because we are calculating a 7-day IMI). This is "IS_U" in the above equation.
- Column G is the absolute value of Column D, but only if the close is less than the open (i.e., only when Column A is less than zero). If the close is greater than or equal to the open, Column G is set to zero. (The term "absolute value" means "regardless of sign." For example, the absolute value of -3 is 3.)
- Column H is the sum of the preceding 7 days of Column G. This is "IS_D" in the above equation.
- Column I is the sum of Column F (i.e., IS_U) plus Column G (i.e., IS_D).
- Column J is Column F (i.e., IS_U) divided by Column I (i.e., IS_U plus IS_D). This value is then multiplied by 100. This is the IMI.

KAGI

Overview

It is believed that Kagi charts were created around the time that the Japanese stock market began trading in the 1870s. Kagi charts display a series of connecting vertical lines where the thickness and direction of the lines are dependent on the price action. The charts ignore the passage of time. They were popularized in the United States by Steven Nison when he published the book *Beyond Candlesticks*.

Interpretation

Kagi charts illustrate the forces of supply and demand on a security:

- A series of thick lines shows that demand is exceeding supply (a rally).
- A series of thin lines shows that supply is exceeding demand (a decline).
- Alternating thick and thin lines shows that the market is in a state of equilibrium (i.e., supply equals demand).

The most basic trading technique related to Kagi charts is to buy when the Kagi line changes from thin to thick and to sell when the Kagi line changes from thick to thin.

A sequence of higher highs and higher lows on a Kagi chart shows that the underlying forces are bullish, whereas lower highs and lower lows indicate underlying weakness.

Example

Figures 100 and 101 show a 0.3-percent Kagi chart and a classic bar chart of the British pound. "Buy" arrows on the bar chart indicate when the Kagi lines changed from thin to thick, and "sell" arrows indicate when the lines changed from thick to thin.

FIGURE 100

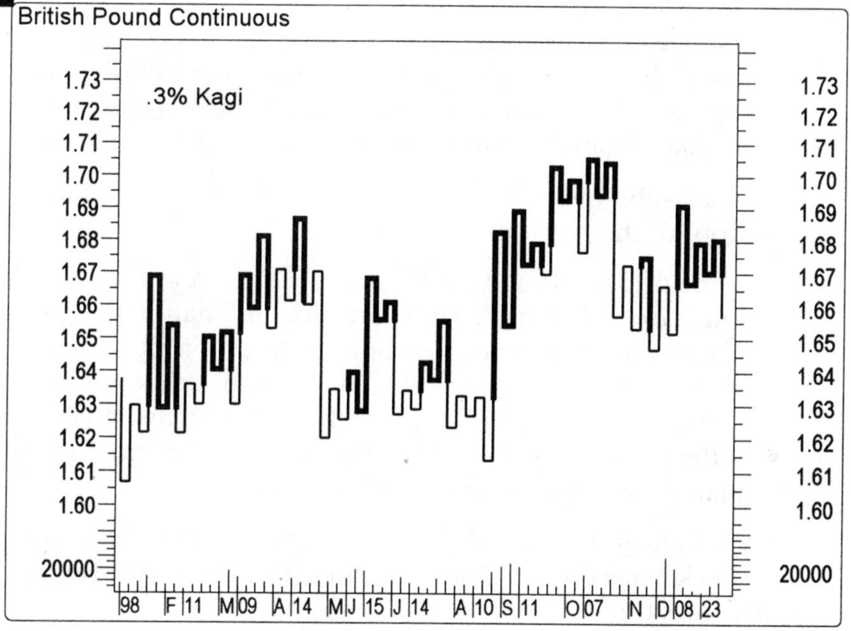

British Pound Continuous

.3% Kagi

FIGURE 101

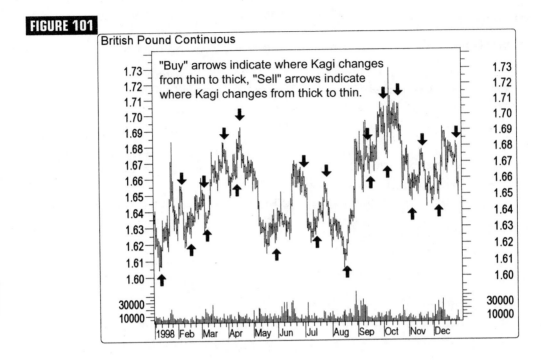

British Pound Continuous

"Buy" arrows indicate where Kagi changes from thin to thick, "Sell" arrows indicate where Kagi changes from thick to thin.

Calculation

The first closing price in a Kagi chart is the "starting price." To draw the first Kagi line, compare today's closing price to the starting price.

- If today's price is greater than or equal to the starting price, then a thick line is drawn from the starting price to today's closing price.
- If today's price is less than or equal to the starting price, then a thin line is drawn from the starting price to today's closing price.

To draw subsequent lines, compare the closing price to the tip (i.e. bottom or top) of the previous Kagi line:

- If the price continues in the same direction as the previous line, the line is extended in the same direction, no matter how small the move.
- If the price moves in the opposite direction by at least the reversal amount (this may take several days), a short horizontal line is drawn to the next column and a new vertical line is drawn to the closing price.
- If the price moves in direction opposite to the current column by less than the reversal amount, no lines are drawn.

If a thin Kagi line exceeds the prior high point on the chart, the line becomes thick. Likewise, if a thick Kagi line falls below the prior low point, the line becomes thin.

KLINGER OSCILLATOR

Overview

The Klinger Oscillator (KVO) is a volume-based indicator designed to measure both short- and long-term trends in the flow of money into and out of a security. The KVO was developed by Stephen J. Klinger and presented in the December 1997 issue of *Technical Analysis of Stocks and Commodities.*

Interpretation

The tenets of the KVO are as follows:

- Price range (i.e., High − Low) is a measure of movement. Volume is the force behind the movement. The sum of High + Low + Close, compared to the previous period's High + Low + Close, defines a trend.
- Accumulation occurs when the current period's sum is greater than the previous period's. Conversely, distribution occurs when the current period's sum is less than the previous period's. When the sums are equal, the existing trend is maintained.
- Volume produces continuous intraperiod changes in price, reflecting buying and selling pressure. The KVO quantifies the difference between the number of shares being accumulated and distributed each period as "volume force." A strong, rising volume force should accompany an uptrend and then gradually contract over time during the latter stages of the uptrend and the early stages of the following downtrend. This should be followed by a rising volume force reflecting some accumulation before a bottom develops.
- By converting the volume force into an oscillator representing the difference between a 34-period and 55-period exponential moving average with a 13-period trigger, the force of volume into and out of a security can easily be tracked. Comparing this force to price action can help identify divergences at tops and bottoms.

Trend. The most reliable signals occur in the direction of the prevailing trend. Strict stop guidelines (i.e., failure to penetrate the zero line or a violation of the trigger line) should remain in force.

Divergence. The most important signal occurs when the KVO diverges with the underlying price action, especially on new highs or new lows in overbought/oversold territory. For example, when a stock makes a new high or low for a cycle and the KVO fails to confirm this, the trend may be losing momentum and nearing completion.

Crossover. If the price is in an uptrend (i.e., above an 89-period exponential moving average), buy when the KVO drops to unusually low levels below zero, turns up, and crosses its trigger line. If the price is in a downtrend (i.e., below an 89-period exponential moving average), sell when the KVO rises to unusually high levels above zero, turns down, and crosses its trigger line.

While the KVO works well for timing trades in the direction of the trend, it is less effective against the trend. This can create problems for the trader trying to "scalp" a trade against the prevailing trend. However, when the KVO is used in conjunction with other technical indicators, better results can be achieved. Williams's %R (see page 369) is recommended for confirming an overbought/oversold price condition and Gerald Appel's MACD (see page 199) is recommended for confirming the short-term direction of price.

Example

Figure 102 shows Enron, the Klinger Oscillator, and a 13-day moving average of the Klinger Oscillator. Notice how the Oscillator diverges from Enron's price in September 1998, at which point the trend reverses and a long rally ensues.

Calculation

The Klinger Oscillator is a 34-day exponential moving average of volume force minus a 55-day exponential moving average of volume force.

The formula for volume force is shown below. Note that the vertical lines in the formula mean absolute value (i.e., disregard the sign of the expression contained within the bars).

$$Volume\ Force = V\left|\left(2\left(\frac{DM}{CM}\right) - 1\right)\right| * T * 100$$

Where:

- V = Volume
- T = The Trend (If today's "high plus low plus close" is greater than yesterday's, then the trend is +1, otherwise it is −1.)
- DM = Daily Measurement (This is the high minus the low.)
- CM = Cumulative Measurement (This is the sum of the Daily Measurements [DM] in the direction of the Trend.)

FIGURE 102

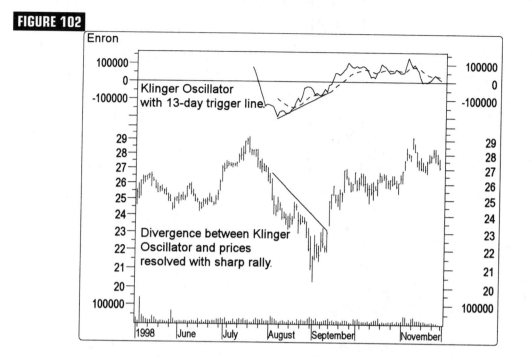

Enron

Klinger Oscillator
with 13-day trigger line.

Divergence between Klinger
Oscillator and prices
resolved with sharp rally.

1998 June July August September November

K

Table 27 illustrates the calculation of the KVO. Note that the KVO takes 55 days to come up to speed, but to conserve space I have only shown the first few periods.

- Column F is calculated by comparing the high plus the low plus the close of the current day with the high plus the low plus the close of the preceding day. If today's sum is greater, Column F is set to +1, otherwise it is set to −1. This is the Trend.
- Column G is the high minus the low. This is the Daily Measurement.
- Column H is the sum of Column G (the Daily Measurements) that are in the direction of the current Trend (Column F). Note that this is the sum of all the Daily Measurements (Column G) including *one record before* Column F changed. For example, when Column F changed from 1.0 to −1.0 on 11/11/99, Column H was the sum of Column G for both 11/10/99 and 11/11/99.
- Column I is calculated per the preceding volume force equation.
- Column J is a 34-day exponential moving average of the volume force (Column I).
- Column K is a 55-day exponential moving average of the volume force (Column I).
- Column L is calculated by subtracting Column K from the Column J. This is the Klinger Oscillator.

TABLE 27

KLINGER OSCILLATOR

A	B	C	D	E	F	G	H	I	J	K	L
Date	High	Low	Close	Volume	Direction of Trend	High minus Low	Cumulative Measurement (see text)	Volume Force (see text)	34-day EMA of Column I	55-day EMA of Column I	Col J minus Col K
11/02/99	181.500	176.875	178.000	40,530		4.625					
11/03/99	182.375	178.625	180.625	45,506	1.000	3.750	8.375	475,435.8	475,435.8	475,435.8	0.0
11/04/99	185.500	181.312	182.125	57,101	1.000	4.188	12.563	1,903,063.7	557,014.6	526,422.5	30,592.0
11/05/99	186.500	183.000	183.438	48,758	1.000	3.500	16.063	2,751,003.9	682,385.4	605,871.9	76,513.5
11/08/99	199.625	181.875	197.188	98,656	1.000	17.750	33.813	492,215.0	671,518.5	601,812.7	69,705.8
11/09/99	199.500	192.250	194.562	74,405	1.000	7.250	41.063	4,813,140.8	908,182.6	752,217.3	155,965.4
11/10/99	202.375	193.250	197.688	67,085	1.000	9.125	50.188	4,269,069.8	1,100,233.3	877,819.1	222,414.2
11/11/99	203.000	192.250	193.125	39,736	-1.000	10.750	19.875	-324,885.5	1,018,798.0	834,865.4	183,932.6
11/12/99	198.875	190.250	196.938	44,768	-1.000	8.625	28.500	-1,767,157.9	859,600.5	741,936.0	117,664.5
11/15/99	207.500	195.375	205.000	59,187	1.000	12.125	20.750	998,334.9	867,528.2	751,093.1	116,435.1
11/16/99	212.938	203.688	212.562	59,143	1.000	9.250	30.000	2,267,148.3	947,506.5	805,237.9	142,268.5
11/17/99	212.000	204.875	206.188	41,042	-1.000	7.125	16.375	-532,606.1	862,928.6	757,457.8	105,470.8
11/18/99	215.500	203.000	213.875	40,124	1.000	12.500	19.625	1,098,937.6	876,414.8	769,653.5	106,761.3
11/19/99	219.188	210.000	218.750	43,351	1.000	9.188	28.813	1,570,313.4	916,066.2	798,248.5	117,817.7

LARGE BLOCK RATIO

Overview

This market sentiment indicator shows the relationship between large block trades, which are trades of more than 10,000 shares, and the total volume on the New York Stock Exchange. The comparison of large block trades to total volume shows how active the large institutional traders are.

Interpretation

The higher the Large Block Ratio, the more institutional activity is taking place. To smooth out the day-to-day fluctuations, I recommend plotting a 20-day moving average of the Large Block Ratio.

A high number of Large Block trades in relation to total volume often coincides with market tops and bottoms. This occurs as institutions recognize the extreme overbought or oversold conditions of the market and place trades accordingly. Of course, this assumes the institutions know what they are doing!

Example

Figure 103 shows the New York Stock Exchange Composite and the Large Block Ratio smoothed by a 20-day moving average. Vertical lines indicate

FIGURE 103

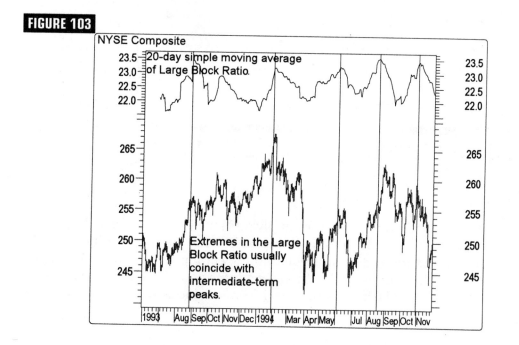

when the Large Block Ratio was relatively high. You can see that these points coincided with intermediate-term peaks.

Calculation

The Large Block Ratio is calculated by dividing the number of Large Block trades by the total volume on the New York Stock Exchange.

$$\frac{Number\ of\ Large\ Blocks}{Total\ NYSE\ Volume}$$

Table 28 illustrates the calculation of the Large Block Ratio.

- Column D is the number of large blocks (Column B) divided by the total New York Stock Exchange volume (Column C).

TABLE 28

| | LARGE BLOCK RATIO | | |
A	B	C	D
Date	Number of Large Blocks	Total NYSE Volume	Large Block Ratio
05/19/93	7,705.00	340	22.66
05/20/93	6,278.00	280	22.42
05/21/93	5,642.00	273	20.67
05/24/93	4,199.00	197	21.31
05/25/93	5,128.00	222	23.10
05/26/93	6,044.00	274	22.06
05/27/93	6,499.00	291	22.33
05/28/93	4,359.00	208	20.96

LINEAR REGRESSION INDICATOR

Overview

The Linear Regression Indicator simply plots the value of a Linear Regression Trendline (see page 176) for each period of data. Thus, any point along the Linear Regression Indicator is equal to the ending value of a Linear Regression Trendline. For example, the ending value of a Linear Regression Trendline that covers 10 periods will have the same value as a 10-period Linear Regression Indicator.

Interpretation

The Linear Regression Indicator shows where prices should be on a statistical basis. The interpretation of the Linear Regression Indicator is similar to a moving average (see page 203). However, the Linear Regression Indicator has two advantages over moving averages. Unlike a moving average, a Linear Regression Indicator does not exhibit as much "delay." Since the indicator is "fitting" a line to the data points rather than averaging them, the Linear Regression Indicator is more responsive to price changes. Any excessive deviation from the Linear Regression Indicator should be short-lived.

Example

Figure 104 shows a 14-day Linear Regression Indicator of American Express. When the price moved sharply away from the Linear Regression Indicator (marked with arrows), it tended to return to the price predicted by the indicator.

FIGURE 104

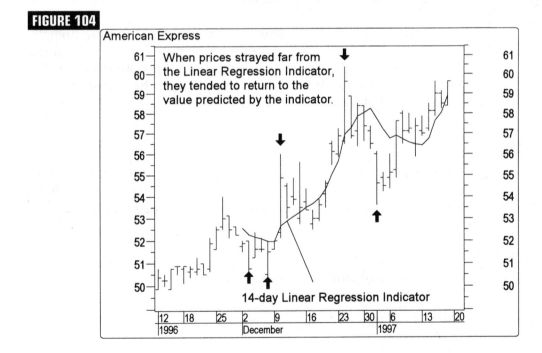

Calculation

Each point in the Linear Regression Indicator is simply the end-point of an *n*-period Linear Regression Trendline (see page 176). The Linear Regression Indicator can be calculated in a spreadsheet using the *forecast( )* function (as can the Time Series Forecast, see page 333).

LINEAR REGRESSION SLOPE

Overview

The Linear Regression Slope indicator is simply the slope of the Linear Regression Trendline (see page 176).

Interpretation

This indicator tells you how quickly a security is moving up or down. A positive value indicates that the trend is up, a negative value indicates that the trend is down. The more extreme the number, either positive or negative, the steeper the trend. When the indicator crosses zero, it shows a change in trend.

According to Tushar Chande, you should use the Linear Regression Slope in combination with r-Squared (see page 282). The slope gives you the direction and steepness of the trend, while the r-Squared tells you the strength of the trend. Chande recommends opening a long position when the slope first becomes significantly positive and opening a short position when the slope first becomes significantly negative. Positions can be closed or countertrends can be traded when the slope peaks or bottoms.

Example

Figure 105 shows a 14-day Linear Regression Slope of Walt Disney. In July 1996 the slope moved from strongly negative to positive territory. This indicated a change in trend from down to up, which continued for months.

Calculation

Following is the formula for Linear Regression Slope:

$$\frac{n\sum(xy) - (\sum x)(\sum y)}{n\sum x^2 - (\sum x)^2}$$

Where:

- x = The current time period
- y = The current price
- n = The total number of time periods

FIGURE 105

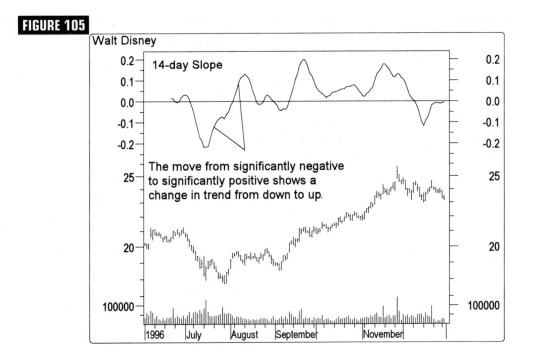

In simpler terms:

1. Subtract the starting value of an *n*-period Linear Regression Trendline from the ending value. This gives you the amount that the line increased/decreased during the period.
2. Divide the number in step 1 by n–1. This is the amount the line increased each day. (Note that "n–1" is used, because a trendline that starts on, for example, day 1 and ends on day 5 only spans 4 days.)

Adding this value to the Linear Regression Trendline (see page 176) or Linear Regression Indicator (see page 172) creates the Time Series Forecast (see page 333).

A table for the Linear Regression Trendline is beyond the scope of this book. The Linear Regression Trendline can be calculated in a spreadsheet using the *linest()* function. The A-to-Z Companion Spreadsheet (see page xvii) contains an example of the *linest()* method.

LINEAR REGRESSION TRENDLINES

Overview

Linear regression is a statistical tool used to predict future values from past values. In the case of security prices, it is commonly used to determine when prices are overextended.

A Linear Regression Trendline uses the "least squares fit" method to plot a straight line through prices so as to minimize the distances between the prices and the resulting trendline.

Interpretation

If you had to guess what a particular security's price would be tomorrow, a logical guess would be "fairly close to today's price." If prices are trending up, a better guess might be "fairly close to today's price with an upward bias." Linear regression analysis is the statistical confirmation of these logical assumptions.

A Linear Regression Trendline is simply a trendline drawn between two points using the least squares fit method. The trendline is displayed in the exact middle of the prices. If you think of this trendline as the "equilibrium" price, any move above or below the trendline indicates overzealous buyers or sellers.

A popular method of using the Linear Regression Trendline is to construct Raff Regression Channel lines (see page 284). A Linear Regression Trendline shows where equilibrium exists. Raff Regression Channels show the range in which prices can be expected to deviate from a Linear Regression Trendline.

The Linear Regression Indicator (see page 172) displays the same information as a Linear Regression Trendline. Any point along the Linear Regression Indicator is equal to the ending value of a Linear Regression Trendline. For example, the ending value of a Linear Regression Trendline that covers 10 days will have the same value as a 10-day Linear Regression Indicator.

Example

Figure 106 shows several Linear Regression Trendlines for Yahoo.

FIGURE 106

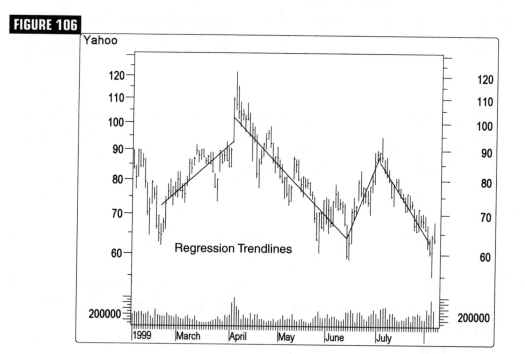

Calculation

The calculations for the Linear Regression Trendline are beyond the scope of this book. Following is the basic formula for calculating the Linear Regression Trendline:

$$a + bx$$

Where:

- $a = \dfrac{\Sigma y - b \Sigma x}{n}$

- $b = \dfrac{n \Sigma (xy) - (\Sigma x)(\Sigma y)}{n \Sigma x^2 - (\Sigma x)^2}$

- x = The current time period
- y = The data series (e.g., the closing prices)
- n = The total number of time periods

A Linear Regression Trendline can be calculated in a spreadsheet using the *trend()* function. The A-to-Z Companion Spreadsheet (see page xvii) contains examples of both the brute force and the *trend()* method.

MARKET FACILITATION INDEX

Overview

The Market Facilitation Index (MFI), created by Dr. Bill Williams, attempts to determine the efficiency of price movement by quantifying the price movement per unit of volume. This is done by taking the day's range (high minus low) and dividing it by the total volume.

Interpretation

As a stand-alone indicator, the MFI has little value. However, by comparing the current price bar's MFI and volume with the previous bar's MFI and volume, a tradable system emerges.

Williams defines the four possible combinations of MFI and volume with terms he coined: Green, Fade, Fake, and Squat. These combinations are shown in Table 29.

TABLE 29

Volume	MFI	Label
+	+	Green
−	−	Fade
−	+	Fake
+	−	Squat

A plus sign means the current bar's value is greater than the previous bar's value. A minus sign means the current bar's value is less than the previous bar's value.

Green. This bar shows an increase in volume and MFI relative to the previous bar. Hence, there is price movement, and the MFI is larger for this bar than for the previous bar. Further, more players are entering the market as signaled by the increase in volume. In addition, the price action is directional—that is, the market is moving in one direction due to the involvement of new traders putting on new positions. On a Green day, you would already want to have an open position in the same direction as the prevailing trend.

Fade. This bar shows a decrease in volume and MFI relative to the previous bar. The market has slowed and there is a minor amount of activity as indicated by the low volume. This type of day is called a Fade, as the traders' interest in the market by this point is fading. Often, this sort of day happens at the end of a trend. The market has simply reached a point where nobody is willing to establish new positions. At this point the market appears to be suffering from boredom. Keep in mind, however, that out of this market condition, a new trend can emerge.

Fake. This bar shows a decrease in volume but an increase in the MFI. This means that the increase in the high-low range outweighed the decrease in volume, resulting in a greater MFI. However, the decrease in volume is evidence that there is no new participation.

The price action may be driven by just the traders in the pit and not attracting new players from the outside. Williams has a hypothesis that the traders in the pit may be just strong enough to push the market to price levels where there are many stop orders resting in the hands of the brokers, hence faking out the off-floor traders.

Squat. This bar shows an increase in volume relative to the previous bar, but the MFI is lower. The increase in volume indicates heavy activity, but the decrease in the MFI indicates that the market is unable to make any real headway. Volume increased, the trend has stalled, and the price movement has stopped. This price action usually, but not always, occurs prior to an important move in the opposite direction. This type of bar is called a squat bar because the market appears to be squatting prior to a breakout. Often, the breakout of such a bar will indicate whether this Squat is a trend reversal Squat or a trend continuation Squat.

Example

Figure 107 shows an MFI of International Paper. Several fade bars appear as the price moves sideways, then two squat bars at the turning point, and finally several green bars start a rally.

Calculation

The calculation of the MFI is the high minus the low, divided by the volume.

$$\frac{High - Low}{Volume}$$

Table 30 illustrates the calculation of the MFI.

- Column E is the high (Column B) minus the low (Column C).
- Column F is Column E divided by the volume (Column D).

FIGURE 107

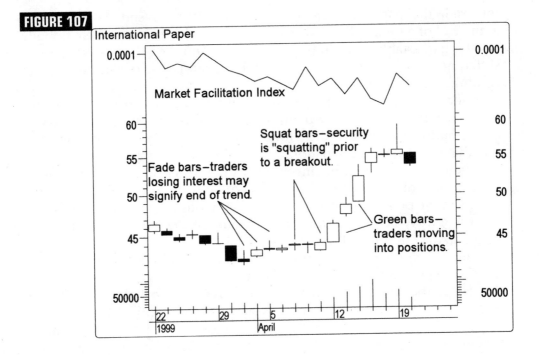

TABLE 30

		Market Facilitation Index			
A	B	C	D	E	F
				High minus Low	Column E divided by Column D
Date	High	Low	Volume		
03/24/99	45.3750	44.5000	10,365	0.8750	0.00008442
03/25/99	45.8125	44.8125	12,649	1.0000	0.00007906
03/26/99	45.1875	44.1250	10,666	1.0625	0.00009962
03/29/99	45.5000	44.1875	15,080	1.3125	0.00008704
03/30/99	44.0000	42.2500	23,699	1.7500	0.00007384
03/31/99	43.4375	41.8750	23,082	1.5625	0.00006769
04/01/99	43.8125	42.6875	19,517	1.1250	0.00005764
04/05/99	44.5000	43.3750	17,535	1.1250	0.00006416
04/06/99	44.0000	43.1875	14,794	0.8125	0.00005492
04/07/99	44.1875	43.3750	17,985	0.8125	0.00004518
04/08/99	44.2812	43.0625	15,746	1.2187	0.00007740
04/09/99	44.5625	43.3125	24,780	1.2500	0.00005044
04/12/99	46.7500	44.2500	40,875	2.5000	0.00006116

MASS INDEX

Overview

The Mass Index was designed by Donald Dorsey to identify trend reversals by measuring the narrowing and widening of the range between the high and low prices. As this range widens, the Mass Index increases; as the range narrows, the Mass Index decreases.

Interpretation

According to Dorsey, the most significant pattern to watch for is a "reversal bulge." A reversal bulge occurs when a 25-period Mass Index rises above 27.0 and subsequently falls below 26.5. A reversal in price is then likely. The overall price trend (i.e., trending or trading range) is unimportant.

A 9-period exponential moving average of prices is often used to determine whether the reversal bulge indicates a buy or sell signal. When the reversal bulge occurs, investors should buy if the moving average is trending down (in anticipation of the reversal) and sell if it is trending up.

Example

Figure 108 shows Litton and a 25-day Mass Index. A 9-day exponential moving average is plotted on top of Litton's prices. Arrows indicate when a reversal bulge occurred (i.e., the Mass Index rose above 27 and then fell below 26.5). If the 9-day moving average was falling, I drew a "buy" arrow. If the 9-day moving average was rising, I drew a "sell" arrow.

You can see that the signals generated by the Mass Index during this time period occurred a few days before the trend reversed.

Calculation

Following is the calculation of the Mass Index:

$$\sum_{1}^{n} \left[\frac{9\text{-}day\ EMA\ of\ (High - Low)}{9\text{-}day\ EMA\ of\ a\ 9\text{-}day\ EMA\ of\ (High - Low)} \right]$$

Note that the 9s in the above formula are constants, whereas the "n" is specified by the person calculating the Mass Index (e.g., 3 in the following example).

Table 31 illustrates the calculation of a 3-day Mass Index.

FIGURE 108

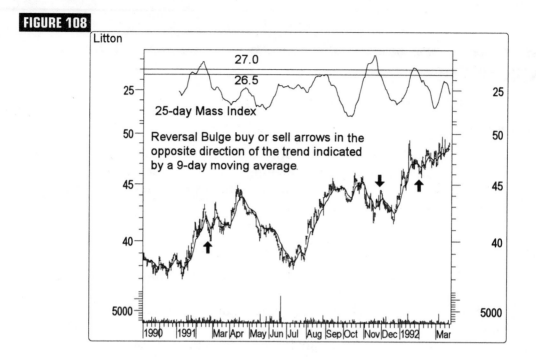

Litton

27.0

26.5

25-day Mass Index

Reversal Bulge buy or sell arrows in the
opposite direction of the trend indicated
by a 9-day moving average.

TABLE 31

M

			MASS INDEX				
A	B	C	D	E	F	G	H
Date	High	Low	High minus Low	9-day EMA of Col D	9-day EMA of Col E	Column E divided by Col F	3-day sum of Col G
02/01/90	38.1250	37.7500	0.3750	0.3750			
02/02/90	38.0000	37.7500	0.2500	0.3500			
02/05/90	37.9375	37.8125	0.1250	0.3050			
02/06/90	37.8750	37.6250	0.2500	0.2940			
02/07/90	38.1250	37.5000	0.6250	0.3602			
02/08/90	38.1250	37.5000	0.6250	0.4132			
02/09/90	37.7500	37.5000	0.2500	0.3805			
02/12/90	37.6250	37.4375	0.1875	0.3419			
02/13/90	37.6875	37.3750	0.3125	0.3360	0.3360		
02/14/90	37.5000	37.3750	0.1250	0.2938	0.3276		
02/15/90	37.5625	37.3750	0.1875	0.2726	0.3166		
02/16/90	37.6250	36.8125	0.8125	0.3806	0.3294		
02/20/90	36.6875	36.3125	0.3750	0.3794	0.3394		
02/21/90	36.8750	36.2500	0.6250	0.4286	0.3572		
02/22/90	36.9375	36.5000	0.4375	0.4303	0.3718		
02/23/90	36.5000	36.2500	0.2500	0.3943	0.3763		
02/26/90	36.9375	36.3125	0.6250	0.4404	0.3892	1.1317	
02/27/90	37.0000	36.6250	0.3750	0.4273	0.3968	1.0770	
02/28/90	36.8750	36.5625	0.3125	0.4044	0.3983	1.0152	3.2240
03/01/90	36.8125	36.3750	0.4375	0.4110	0.4008	1.0253	3.1175

- Column D is the high (Column B) minus the low (Column C).
- Column E is a 9-day exponential moving average of Column D. The first row of Column E is seeded with the first value in Column D (i.e., 0.375). Subsequent rows in Column E are calculated by multiplying the value in Column D by 0.2, then multiplying the previous day's value in Column E by 0.8, and finally adding these two values together. (The value 0.2 was calculated as "2 / (9 + 1)" as explained on page 208. The value 0.8 was calculated as "1 − 0.2" as explained on page 208.) Note that this 9-period moving average is not valid until the ninth day.
- Column F is a 9-period exponential moving average of Column E. The ninth row of Column F is seeded with the ninth value in Column E (i.e., 0.3360). The ninth value was used because it took 9 days for the 9-day moving average to become valid. Subsequent rows in Column F are calculated by multiplying the value in Column E by 0.2, then multiplying the previous day's value in Column F by 0.8, and finally adding these two values together.
- Column G is Column E divided by Column F. We don't begin this calculation until Column F is valid (i.e., it has 9 days of data).
- Column H is a 3-day sum of Column G. This is the Mass Index.

M

McCLELLAN OSCILLATOR

Overview

The McClellan Oscillator is a market breadth indicator that is based on the smoothed difference between the number of advancing and declining issues on the New York Stock Exchange.

It was developed by Sherman and Marian McClellan. Extensive coverage of the Oscillator is provided in their book *Patterns for Profit*.

Interpretation

Indicators that use advancing and declining issues to determine the amount of participation in the movement of the stock market are called "breadth" indicators. A healthy bull market is accompanied by a large number of stocks making moderate upward advances in price. A weakening bull market is characterized by a small number of stocks making large advances in price, giving the false appearance that all is well. This type of divergence often signals an end to the bull market. A similar interpretation applies to market bottoms, where the market index continues to decline while fewer stocks are declining.

The McClellan Oscillator is one of the most popular breadth indicators (another popular breadth indicator is the Advance/Decline Line, page 52). Buy signals are typically generated when the McClellan Oscillator falls into the oversold area of −70 to −100 and then turns up. Sell signals are generated when the McClellan Oscillator rises into the overbought area of +70 to +100 and then turns down.

If the McClellan Oscillator goes *beyond* these areas (i.e., rises above +100 or falls below −100), it is a sign of an extremely overbought or oversold condition. These extreme readings are usually a sign of a continuation of the current trend.

For example, if the McClellan Oscillator falls to −90 and turns up, a buy signal is generated. However, if it falls below −100, the market will probably trend lower during the next two or three weeks. You should postpone buying until the Oscillator makes a series of rising bottoms or the market regains strength.

Example

Figure 109 illustrates the five "trading zones" of the McClellan Oscillator (i.e., above +100, between +70 and +100, between +70 and −70, between −70 and −100, and below −100).

Figure 110 shows the McClellan Oscillator and the Dow Industrials. "Buy" arrows indicate when the McClellan Oscillator rose above −70 and

M

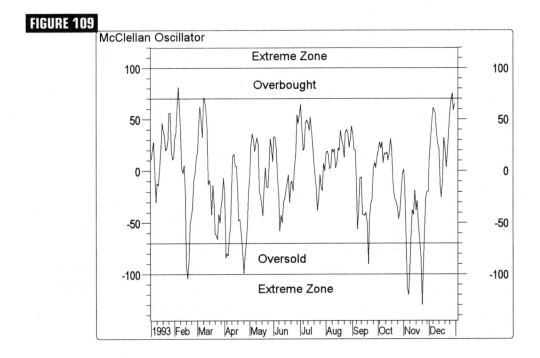

FIGURE 109

"sell" arrows indicate when it fell below +70. This indicator does an excellent job of timing entry and exit points.

Calculation

The McClellan Oscillator is the difference between 10 percent (approximately 19-day) and 5 percent (approximately 39-day) exponential moving averages of advancing minus declining issues.

(10% EMA of Advances-Declines) − (5% EMA of Advances-Declines)

Table 32 illustrates the calculation of the McClellan Oscillator.

- Column D is the number of advancing issues (Column B) minus the number of declining issues (Column C).
- Column E is a 10 percent exponential moving average of Column D. The first row of Column E is seeded with the first value in Column E (i.e., –873). Subsequent rows in Column E are calculated by multiplying the value in Column D by 0.1 (i.e., 10 percent), then multiplying the previous day's value in Column E by 0.9 (i.e., 90 percent), and finally adding these two values together. (The value 0.9 was calculated as "1.0 − 0.1" as explained on page 208.) Note that this "19-period" moving average is not valid until the nineteenth day.

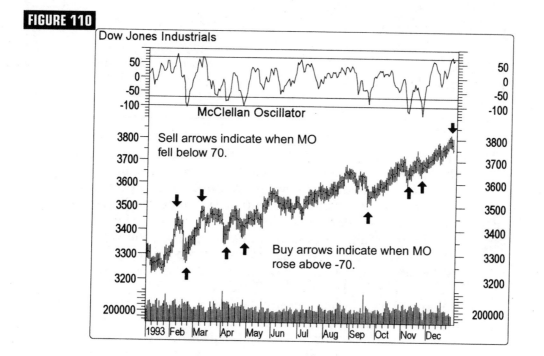

FIGURE 110

Dow Jones Industrials

McClellan Oscillator

Sell arrows indicate when MO fell below 70.

Buy arrows indicate when MO rose above -70.

1993 Feb Mar Apr May Jun Jul Aug Sep Oct Nov Dec

TABLE 32

			McClellan Oscillator			
A	**B**	**C**	**D**	**E**	**F**	**G**
Date	Advancing Issues	Declining Issues	Column B minus Column C	10% EMA of Column D	5% EMA of Column D	Column E minus Column F
04/25/97	789	1,662	−873	−873.0000	−873.0000	0.0000
04/28/97	1,348	1,085	263	−759.4000	−816.2000	56.8000
04/29/97	2,085	531	1,554	−528.0600	−697.6900	169.6300
04/30/97	1,599	941	658	−409.4540	−629.9055	220.4515
05/01/97	1,450	1,021	429	−325.6086	−576.9602	251.3516
05/02/97	2,119	476	1,643	−128.7477	−465.9622	337.2145
05/05/97	1,958	677	1,281	12.2270	−378.6141	390.8411
05/06/97	1,258	1,270	−12	9.8043	−360.2834	370.0877
05/07/97	842	1,660	−818	−72.9761	−383.1692	310.1931
05/08/97	1,398	1,097	301	−35.5785	−348.9608	313.3823
05/09/97	1,526	932	594	27.3794	−301.8127	329.1921
05/12/97	1,766	761	1,005	125.1414	−236.4721	361.6135
05/13/97	1,133	1,322	−189	93.7273	−234.0985	327.8258
05/14/97	1,472	992	480	132.3546	−198.3936	330.7481
05/15/97	1,282	1,164	118	130.9191	−182.5739	313.4930
05/16/97	973	1,431	−458	72.0272	−196.3452	268.3724
05/19/97	1,390	1,056	334	98.2245	−169.8279	268.0524
05/20/97	1,411	1,040	371	125.5020	−142.7865	268.2886
05/21/97	1,421	1,107	314	144.3518	−119.9472	264.2990
05/22/97	1,270	1,176	94	139.3166	−109.2498	248.5665
05/23/97	1,875	618	1257	251.0850	−40.9374	292.0223
05/27/97	1,221	1,299	−78	218.1765	−42.7905	260.9670
05/28/97	1,309	1,147	162	212.5588	−32.5510	245.1098
05/29/97	1,431	1,043	388	230.1029	−11.5234	241.6264
05/30/97	1,584	901	683	275.3927	23.2028	252.1899
06/02/97	1,530	963	567	304.5534	50.3926	254.1608

- Column F is a 5 percent exponential moving average of Column D. The first row of Column F is seeded with the first value in Column D (i.e., −873). Subsequent rows in Column F are calculated by multiplying the value in Column D by 0.05 (i.e., 5 percent), then multiplying the previous day's value in Column F by 0.95 (i.e., 95 percent), and finally adding these two values together. (The value 0.95 was calculated as "1.0 − 0.05" as explained on page 208.) Note that this "39-period" moving average is not valid until the thirty-ninth day (which is not displayed in this abbreviated table).
- Column G is Column E minus Column F. As with Column F, the values in Column D aren't value until the thirty-ninth day (which is not displayed in this abbreviated table). This is the McClellan Oscillator.

McCLELLAN SUMMATION INDEX

Overview

The McClellan Summation Index is a market breadth indicator based on the McClellan Oscillator (see page 183). It was developed by Sherman and Marian McClellan. Extensive coverage of the index is provided in their book *Patterns for Profit*.

Interpretation

The McClellan Summation Index is a long-term version of the McClellan Oscillator. Its interpretation is similar to that of the McClellan Oscillator except that it is more suited to major trend reversals.

As explained under calculation, below, there are two methods for calculating the McClellan Summation Index. The two calculation methods create indicators with identical appearances, but their numeric values differ. These interpretational comments refer to the "suggested" calculation method explained in the calculation section.

The McClellans suggest the following rules for use with the Summation Index:

- Look for major bottoms when the Summation Index falls below −1,300.
- Look for major tops to occur when a divergence (see page 36) with the market occurs above a Summation Index level of +1,600.

The beginning of a significant bull market is indicated when the Summation Index crosses above +1,900 after moving upward more than 3,600 points from its prior low (e.g., the index moves from −1,600 to +2,000).

Example

Figure 111 shows the McClellan Summation Index and the New York Stock Exchange Composite. At the point labeled A, the Summation Index fell below −1,300. This signified a major bottom. The point labeled B indicated the beginning of a significant bull market because the Summation Index rose above +1,900 after moving upward more than 3,600 points from its prior low.

Calculation

The McClellan Summation Index can be calculated using two different methods. This first method is the suggested method promoted by Mr. McClellan.

FIGURE 111

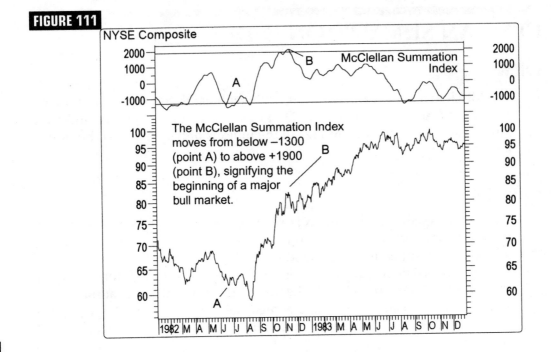

NYSE Composite

McClellan Summation Index

The McClellan Summation Index moves from below −1300 (point A) to above +1900 (point B), signifying the beginning of a major bull market.

It subtracts 10 percent (approximately 19-day) and 5 percent (approximately 39-day) exponential moving averages of advancing minus declining issues from the McClellan Oscillator.

McClellan Oscillator − ((10 * 10% trend) + (20 * 5% trend)) + 1000

Where:

- 5% trend = 5% EMA of (Advancing − Declining Issues)
- 10% trend = 10% EMA of (Advancing − Declining Issues)

The second method calculates a cumulative sum of the McClellan Oscillator values:

Yesterday's Summation Index + McClellan Oscillator

Table 33 illustrates the calculation of the McClellan Summation Index using the first method.

- Columns D, E, F, and G are identical to the McClellan Oscillator columns on page 186. These result in the McClellan Oscillator in Column G.
- Column H is the value in Column E multiplied by 10.

TABLE 33

McClellan Summation Index

A	B	C	D	E	F	G	H	I	J	K
Date	Advancing Issues	Declining Issues	Column B minus Column C	10% EMA of Column D	5% EMA of Column D	McClellan Oscillator	Column E multiplied by 10	Column F multiplied by 20	Column H plus Column I	Column G minus Column J plus 1,000
04/25/97	789	1,662	-873	-873.00	-873.00	0.00	-8,730.00	-17,460.00	-26,190.00	27,190.00
04/28/97	1,348	1,085	263	-759.40	-816.20	56.80	-7,594.00	-16,324.00	-23,918.00	24,974.80
04/29/97	2,085	531	1,554	-528.06	-697.69	169.63	-5,280.60	-13,953.80	-19,234.40	20,404.03
04/30/97	1,599	941	658	-409.45	-629.91	220.45	-4,094.54	-12,598.11	-16,692.65	17,913.10
05/01/97	1,450	1,021	429	-325.61	-576.96	251.35	-3,256.09	-11,539.20	-14,795.29	16,046.64
05/02/97	2,119	476	1,643	-128.75	-465.96	337.21	-1,287.48	-9,319.24	-10,606.72	11,943.94
05/05/97	1,958	677	1,281	12.23	-378.61	390.84	122.27	-7,572.28	-7,450.01	8,840.85
05/06/97	1,258	1,270	-12	9.80	-360.28	370.09	98.04	-7,205.67	-7,107.62	8,477.71
05/07/97	842	1,660	-818	-72.98	-383.17	310.19	-729.76	-7,663.38	-8,393.15	9,703.34
05/08/97	1,398	1,097	301	-35.58	-348.96	313.38	-355.78	-6,979.22	-7,335.00	8,648.38
05/09/97	1,526	932	594	27.38	-301.81	329.19	273.79	-6,036.25	-5,762.46	7,091.65
05/12/97	1,766	761	1,005	125.14	-236.47	361.61	1,251.41	-4,729.44	-3,478.03	4,839.64
05/13/97	1,133	1,322	-189	93.73	-234.10	327.83	937.27	-4,681.97	-3,744.70	5,072.52
05/14/97	1,472	992	480	132.35	-198.39	330.75	1,323.55	-3,967.87	-2,644.33	3,975.07
05/15/97	1,282	1,164	118	130.92	-182.57	313.49	1,309.19	-3,651.48	-2,342.29	3,655.78
05/16/97	973	1,431	-458	72.03	-196.35	268.37	720.27	-3,926.90	-3,206.63	4,475.00
05/19/97	1,390	1,056	334	98.22	-169.83	268.05	982.24	-3,396.56	-2,414.31	3,682.37
05/20/97	1,411	1,040	371	125.50	-142.79	268.29	1,255.02	-2,855.73	-1,600.71	2,869.00
05/21/97	1,421	1,107	314	144.35	-119.95	264.30	1,443.52	-2,398.94	-955.43	2,219.72
05/22/97	1,270	1,176	94	139.32	-109.25	248.57	1,393.17	-2,185.00	-791.83	2,040.40
05/23/97	1,875	618	1,257	251.08	-40.94	292.02	2,510.85	-818.75	1,692.10	-400.08
05/27/97	1,221	1,299	-78	218.18	-42.79	260.97	2,181.76	-855.81	1,325.96	-64.99
05/28/97	1,309	1,147	162	212.56	-32.55	245.11	2,125.59	-651.02	1,474.57	-229.46
05/29/97	1,431	1,043	388	230.10	-11.52	241.63	2,301.03	-230.47	2,070.56	-828.93
05/30/97	1,584	901	683	275.39	23.20	252.19	2,753.93	464.06	3,217.98	-1,965.79
06/02/97	1,530	963	567	304.55	50.39	254.16	3,045.53	1,007.85	4,053.39	-2,799.23

- Column I is the value in Column F multiplied by 20.
- Column J is the sum of Columns E and F.
- Column K is the value in Column G (i.e., the McClellan Oscillator) minus the value in Column J, plus 1,000. This is the McClellan Summation Index.

MEDIAN PRICE

Overview

The Median Price indicator is simply the midpoint of each day's price. The Typical Price (see page 344) and Weighted Close (see page 362) are similar indicators.

Interpretation

The Median Price indicator provides a simple, single-line chart of the day's "average price." This average price is useful when you want a simpler view of prices.

Example

Figure 112 shows the Median Price indicator (dotted line) on top a bar chart for Keycorp.

Calculation

The Median Price indicator is calculated by adding the high and low price together, and dividing by 2.

$$\frac{High\ +\ Low}{2}$$

Table 34 illustrates the calculation of the Median Price.

- Column D is the high price plus the low price.
- Column E is the value in Column D divided by 2.

FIGURE 112

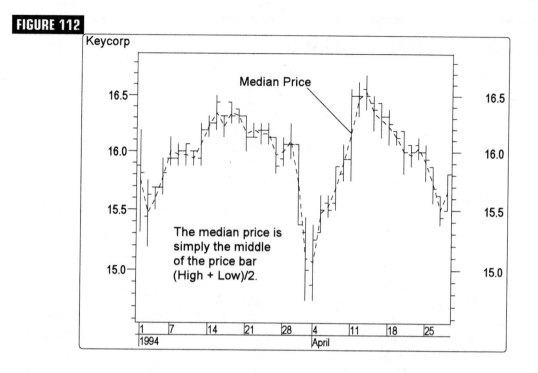

Keycorp

Median Price

The median price is simply the middle of the price bar (High + Low)/2.

M

TABLE 34

		MEDIAN PRICE		
A	B	C	D	E
			High plus Low	Column D divided by 2
Date	High	Low		
03/01/94	16.1875	15.3125	31.5000	15.7500
03/02/94	15.7500	15.1875	30.9375	15.4688
03/03/94	15.6875	15.5000	31.1875	15.5938
03/04/94	15.9375	15.6250	31.5625	15.7813
03/07/94	16.1250	15.8750	32.0000	16.0000
03/08/94	16.0625	15.8750	31.9375	15.9688
03/09/94	16.0625	15.8750	31.9375	15.9688
03/10/94	16.0000	15.8750	31.8750	15.9375
03/11/94	16.2500	15.8750	32.1250	16.0625
03/14/94	16.3125	16.1250	32.4375	16.2188

MEMBER SHORT RATIO

Overview

The Member Short Ratio (MSR) is a market sentiment indicator that measures the short-selling activity of members of the New York Stock Exchange. "Members" trade on the floor of the exchange, either for their own account or for their clients. Stocks are sold short in anticipation of the price falling.

Knowing what the "smart money" is doing (e.g., the Members) is often a good indication of the near-term market direction.

Interpretation

The MSR is the inverse of the Public Short Ratio (PSR) (see page 274). This is because there are only two players in the market, the Public and the Members (Members are further divided into Specialists and Others). When the PSR is 20 percent, the MSR must be 80 percent.

Because the MSR is the inverse of the PSR, interpretation of the MSR is the opposite of the PSR. When the members are short (a high MSR), you should be short, and when the members are long (a low MSR), you should be long. For more information on interpreting the MSR, refer to the discussion on the PSR.

Calculation

The MSR is calculated by dividing the number of Member shorts (defined as total short sales minus public short sales) by the total number of short sales. The resulting figure shows the percentage of shorts that were made by Members of the New York Stock Exchange.

$$\frac{Total\ Short\ Sales\ -\ Public\ Short\ Sales}{Total\ Short\ Sales} * 100$$

Table 35 illustrates the calculation of the Member Short Ratio.

- Column D is Total Short Sales (Column B) minus Total Public Short Sales (Column C). This is the Member Short Sales.
- Column E is the value in Column D divided by the Total Short Sales (Column B). This is then multiplied by 100. This is the Member Short Ratio.

TABLE 35

| | MEMBER SHORT RATIO | | | |
| A | B | C | D | E |
Date	Total Short Sales	Total Public Short Sales	Column B minus Column C	Col D / Col B multiplied by 100
01/02/98	195	74.5	120.5	61.795
01/09/98	310	154.7	155.3	50.097
01/16/98	324	142.4	181.6	56.049
01/23/98	263	114.1	148.9	56.616
01/30/98	337	137.6	199.4	59.169
02/06/98	398	162.7	235.3	59.121
02/13/98	350	149.3	200.7	57.343
02/20/98	256	110.8	145.2	56.719
02/27/98	312	128.8	183.2	58.718
03/06/98	340	153.6	186.4	54.824
03/13/98	338	148.8	189.2	55.976
03/20/98	343	149.3	193.7	56.472

M

MESA SINE WAVE

Overview

The MESA Sine Wave (MSW) indicator, developed by John Ehlers, determines whether a security is in a trending or cycling mode. If the security is in a cycling mode, the MSW will approximate a traditional sine wave. If the security is in a trending mode, the MSW will not resemble a traditional sine wave.

In technical terms, the MSW displays the sine of the measured phase angle over the specified time periods. A lead sine is also plotted, which is calculated on the phase angle advanced by 45 degrees. The phase angle tells how far along we are in the current cycle (e.g., if we are 25 percent of the way through the current cycle, the phase angle would be 90 degrees). The cycle is a user-specified value.

Interpretation

The MSW indicator consists of two plots: the sine and the lead sine. Together, the crossings of the sine and lead sine plots give advanced indication of cycle mode turning points.

When the MSW indicator resembles an actual sine wave, this suggests the market is in a cycle mode. A buy signal is given when the sine plot crosses above the lead sine plot. A sell signal is given when the sine plot crosses below the lead sine plot.

When the market is trending, the MSW indicator does not resemble a sine wave. In fact, the sine and lead sine plots typically languish in a sideways pattern around zero, running somewhat parallel and distant from each other. The correct trading strategy in the trend mode is to trade the trend. Basic moving-average crossovers are helpful for entering and exiting positions in this type of market.

Example

Figure 113 of Johnson & Johnson shows the 25-day sine and lead sine wave indicators. As the price moves out of a trading range, the indicators change from a sinelike appearance to a non-sinelike appearance.

Calculation

The calculation for the MSW is beyond the scope of this book. Refer to the November 1996 issue of *Technical Analysis of Stocks and Commodities.*

FIGURE 113

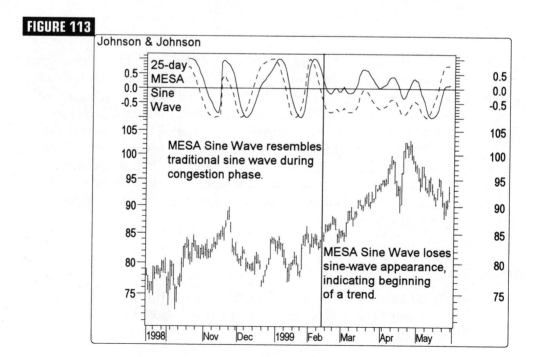

MOMENTUM

Overview

The Momentum indicator measures the amount that a security's price has changed over a given time span.

Interpretation

The interpretation of the Momentum indicator is identical to the interpretation of the Price ROC (see page 267). Both indicators display the rate of change of a security's price. However, the Price ROC indicator displays the rate of change as a percentage, whereas the Momentum indicator displays the rate of change as a ratio.

There are basically two ways to use the Momentum indicator:

- You can use the Momentum indicator as a trend-following oscillator similar to the MACD (this is the method I prefer) (see page 199). Buy when the indicator bottoms and turns up, and sell when the indicator peaks and turns down. As with the MACD, you may want to plot a short-term (e.g., 9-period) moving average of the indicator to determine when it is bottoming or peaking.

- If the Momentum indicator reaches extremely high or low values (relative to its historical values), you should assume a continuation of the current trend. For example, if the Momentum indicator reaches extremely high values and then turns down, you should assume prices will probably go still higher. In either case, trade only after prices confirm the signal generated by the indicator (e.g., if prices peak and turn down, wait for prices to begin to fall before selling). You can also use the Momentum indicator as a leading indicator. This method assumes that market tops are typically identified by a rapid price increase (when everyone expects prices to go higher) and that market bottoms typically end with rapid price declines (when everyone wants to get out). This is often the case, but it is also a broad generalization.

- As a market peaks, the Momentum indicator will climb sharply and then fall off—diverging from the continued upward or sideways movement of the price. Similarly, at a market bottom, Momentum will drop sharply and then begin to climb well ahead of prices. Both of these situations result in divergences (see page 36) between the indicator and prices.

Example

Figure 114 shows Integrated Circuits and a 12-day Momentum indicator. Divergences at points A and B provided leading indications of the reversals that followed.

Calculation

The Momentum indicator is the ratio of today's price compared to the price *n* periods ago.

$$\left(\frac{Close}{Close\ n\ periods\ ago}\right) * 100$$

Table 36 illustrates the calculation of the 12-day Momentum indicator.

- Column C is the closing price 12 days ago.
- Column D is the close (Column B) divided by Column C. This is then multiplied by 100. This is the Momentum indicator.

FIGURE 114

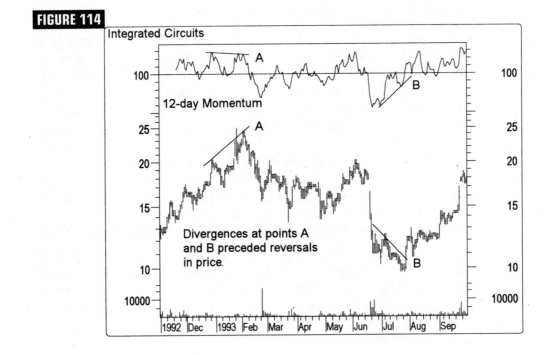

TABLE 36

	MOMENTUM		
A	B	C	D
Date	Close	Close 12 days ago	Col B / Col C multiplied by 100
11/02/92	13.0000		
11/03/92	12.6667		
11/04/92	12.6667		
11/05/92	12.6667		
11/06/92	13.0833		
11/09/92	14.0000		
11/10/92	14.1667		
11/11/92	15.3333		
11/12/92	15.2500		
11/13/92	14.1667		
11/16/92	14.1667		
11/17/92	14.0000		
11/18/92	13.8333	13.0000	106.4100
11/19/92	13.8333	12.6667	109.2100
11/20/92	14.3333	12.6667	113.1573
11/23/92	15.1667	12.6667	119.7368

M

MONEY FLOW INDEX

Overview

The Money Flow Index (MFI) is a momentum indicator that measures the strength of money flowing in and out of a security. It is related to the Relative Strength Index (RSI, see page 297), but whereas the RSI incorporates only prices, the MFI accounts for volume.

Interpretation

The interpretation of the MFI is as follows:

- Look for divergence (see page 36) between the indicator and prices. If the price trends higher and the MFI trends lower (or vice versa), a reversal may be imminent.
- Look for market tops to occur when the MFI is above 80. Look for market bottoms to occur when the MFI is below 20.

Example

Figure 115 shows Intel and a 14-day Money Flow Index. Divergences at points A and B provided leading indications of the reversals that followed.

Calculation

First, the period's Typical Price is calculated.

$$Typical\ Price = \frac{High + Low + Close}{3}$$

Next, Money Flow (not the MFI) is calculated by multiplying the period's Typical Price by the volume.

$$Money\ Flow = Typical\ Price * Volume$$

If today's Typical Price is greater than yesterday's Typical Price, it is considered Positive Money. If today's price is less, it is considered Negative Money.

Positive Money Flow is the sum of the Positive Money over the specified number of periods. Negative Money Flow is the sum of the Negative Money

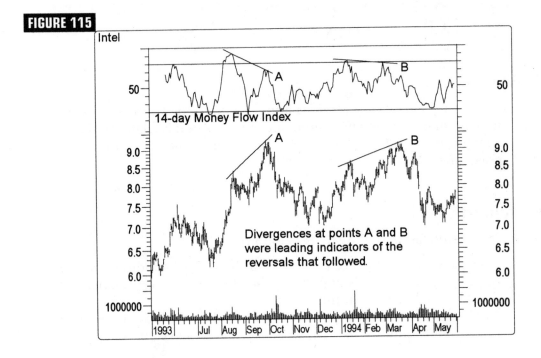

FIGURE 115

Intel

14-day Money Flow Index

Divergences at points A and B were leading indicators of the reversals that followed.

over the specified number of periods. The Money Ratio is then calculated by dividing the Positive Money Flow by the Negative Money Flow.

$$Money\ Ratio = \frac{Positive\ Money\ Flow}{Negative\ Money\ Flow}$$

Finally, the MFI is calculated using the Money Ratio.

$$Money\ Flow\ Index = 100 - \left[\frac{100}{1 + Money\ Ratio}\right]$$

The table for the Money Flow Index is too complex to present in this book. The A-to-Z Companion Spreadsheet (see page xvii) contains the full calculations.

MOVING AVERAGE CONVERGENCE/DIVERGENCE

Overview

The Moving Average Convergence/Divergence (MACD) is a trend-following momentum indicator that shows the relationship between two moving averages of prices. The MACD was developed by Gerald Appel, publisher of *Systems and Forecasts*.

The MACD is the difference between a 26-day and a 12-day exponential moving average. A 9-day exponential moving average, called the "signal" (or "trigger") line, is plotted on top of the MACD to show buy/sell opportunities. (Appel specifies exponential moving averages as percentages, as explained on page 208. Thus, he refers to these three moving averages as 7.5 percent, 15 percent, and 20 percent, respectively.)

Interpretation

There are three popular ways to use the MACD: crossovers, overbought/oversold conditions, and divergences.

Crossovers. The basic MACD trading rule is to sell when the MACD falls below its signal line. Similarly, a buy signal occurs when the MACD rises above its signal line. It is also popular to buy/sell when the MACD goes above/below zero.

Overbought/Oversold Conditions. The MACD is also useful as an over-bought/oversold indicator. When the shorter moving average pulls away dramatically from the longer moving average (i.e., the MACD rises), it is likely that the security price is overextending and will soon return to more realistic levels. MACD overbought and oversold conditions vary from security to security.

Divergences.   An indication that an end to the current trend may be near occurs when the MACD diverges from the security (see page 36). A bearish divergence occurs when the MACD is making new lows while prices fail to reach new lows. A bullish divergence occurs when the MACD is making new highs while prices fail to reach new highs. Both of these divergences are most significant when they occur at relatively overbought/oversold levels.

Example

Figure 116 shows Whirlpool and its MACD. "Buy" arrows indicate when the MACD rose above its signal line and "sell" arrows indicate when the MACD fell below its signal line.

FIGURE 116

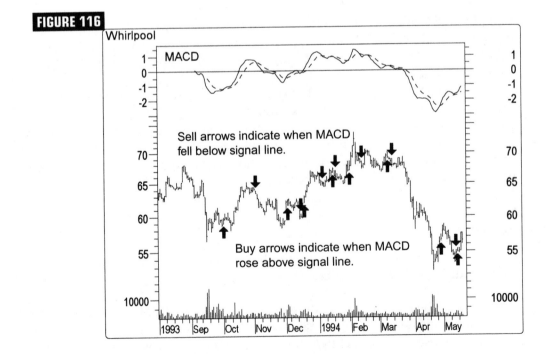

This chart shows that the MACD is truly a trend-following indicator— sacrificing early signals in exchange for keeping you on the right side of the market. When a significant trend developed, such as in October 1993 and again beginning in February 1994, the MACD was able to capture the majority of the move. When the trend was short-lived, such as in January 1994, the MACD proved unprofitable.

Calculation

The calculation of the MACD is usually described as "subtracting the value of a 26-day exponential moving average from a 12-day exponential moving average." That description is very close and it is how I usually describe the calculation of the MACD, but it isn't precise.

As explained on page 208, exponential moving averages are calculated by adding a percentage of today's price to a percentage of the previous day's exponential moving average. The percentages are determined from the number of periods (e.g., days) using the following formula:

exponential percentage = 2 / (number of periods + 1)

Given this formula, the percentage for a 12-day exponential moving average is 15.3846 percent and the percentage for a 26-day moving average is 7.4074 percent (these numbers actually have more digits, but I truncated them at 4 decimal places in this sentence). However, Appel originally defined the MACD as 15 percent and 7.5 percent exponential moving averages— slightly different from the percentage calculated using the above formula. Yes, the numbers are extremely close to those obtained by subtracting a 26-day exponential moving average from a 12-day exponential moving average, but the true MACD is calculated by subtracting a 15 percent exponential moving average from a 7.5 percent exponential moving average. Table 37 illustrates the calculation of the MACD.

- Column C is a 15 percent exponential moving average of the close. (See page 208 for details on calculating exponential moving averages.) Briefly, the first row of Column C is seeded with the closing value (i.e., 63.750). Subsequent rows in Column C are calculated by multiplying the close by 0.15, then multiplying the previous day's value in Column C by 0.85, and finally adding these two values together. (The value 0.85 was calculated as "1.0 − 0.15" as explained on page 208.) Note that this "12-period" moving average is not valid until the twelfth day (i.e., 08/17/93).
- Column D is a 7.5 percent exponential moving average of the close. The first row of Column D is seeded with the closing value (i.e.,

TABLE 37

A	B	MACD C	D	E
Date	Close	15% EMA	7.5% EMA	Column C minus Column D
08/02/93	63.750	63.750	63.750	
08/03/93	63.625	63.731	63.741	
08/04/93	63.000	63.622	63.685	
08/05/93	62.750	63.491	63.615	
08/06/93	63.250	63.455	63.588	
08/09/93	65.375	63.743	63.722	
08/10/93	66.000	64.081	63.893	
08/11/93	65.000	64.219	63.976	
08/12/93	64.875	64.318	64.043	
08/13/93	64.750	64.382	64.096	
08/16/93	64.375	64.381	64.117	
08/17/93	64.375	64.380	64.136	
08/18/93	64.625	64.417	64.173	
08/19/93	64.375	64.411	64.188	
08/20/93	64.500	64.424	64.212	
08/23/93	65.250	64.548	64.289	
08/24/93	67.875	65.047	64.558	
08/25/93	68.000	65.490	64.816	
08/26/93	66.875	65.698	64.971	
08/27/93	66.250	65.781	65.067	
08/30/93	65.875	65.795	65.127	
08/31/93	66.000	65.826	65.193	
09/01/93	65.875	65.833	65.244	
09/02/93	64.750	65.671	65.207	
09/03/93	63.000	65.270	65.041	
09/07/93	63.375	64.986	64.916	0.069
09/08/93	63.375	64.744	64.801	−0.057
09/09/93	63.375	64.539	64.694	−0.155

63.750). Subsequent rows in Column D are calculated by multiplying the close by 0.075, then multiplying the previous day's value in Column D by 0.925, and finally adding these two values together. (The value 0.925 was calculated as "1.0 − 0.075" as explained on page 208.) Note that this "26-period" moving average is not valid until the twenty-sixth day (i.e., 09/07/93).

- Column E is the value in Column C minus the value in Column D. This calculation does not begin until both moving averages are valid (i.e., the twenty-sixth day).

MOVING AVERAGES

Overview

A moving average is an indicator that shows the average value of a security's price over a period of time. When calculating a moving average, a mathematical analysis of the security's average value over a predetermined time period is made. As the security's price changes, its average price moves up or down.

There are seven popular types of moving averages: simple (also referred to as arithmetic), exponential, time series, triangular, variable, volume-adjusted, and weighted. Moving averages can be calculated on any data series, including a security's open, high, low, close, volume, or another indicator. A moving average of another moving average is also common. Explanations on the calculations of the various types of moving averages begin on page 207.

The only significant difference between the various types of moving averages is the weight assigned to the most recent data (except for the time-series moving average). Simple moving averages apply equal weight to the prices. Exponential and weighted averages apply more weight to recent prices. Triangular averages apply more weight to prices in the middle of the time period. Variable moving averages change the weighting based on the volatility of prices. Volume-adjusted moving averages change the weighting based on each period's volume.

Interpretation

The most popular method of interpreting a moving average is to compare the relationship between a moving average of the security's price with the security's price itself. A buy signal is generated when the security's price rises above its moving average, and a sell signal is generated when the security's price falls below its moving average.

Figure 117 shows the Dow Jones Industrial Average (DJIA) from 1970 through late 1999. It also displays a 15-month simple moving average. "Buy" arrows indicate when the DJIA's close rose above its moving average; "sell" arrows indicate when it closed below its moving average.

This type of moving average trading system is not intended to get you in at the exact bottom or out at the exact top. Rather, it is designed to keep you in line with the security's price trend by buying shortly after the security's price bottoms and selling shortly after it tops.

M

FIGURE 117

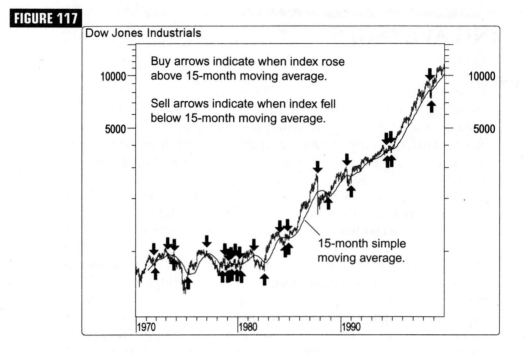

Dow Jones Industrials

Buy arrows indicate when index rose
above 15-month moving average.

Sell arrows indicate when index fell
below 15-month moving average.

10000

5000

15-month simple
moving average.

1970   1980   1990

M

The critical element in a moving average is the number of time periods used in calculating the average. With hindsight, you can always find a moving average that would have been profitable (using a computer, I found that the optimum number of months in the preceding chart would have been 43 months). The key is to find a moving average that will be consistently profitable. The most popular moving average is the 39-week (or 200-day) moving average. It has an excellent track record in timing the major (long-term) market cycles.

As shown in Table 38, the length of a moving average should fit the market cycle you wish to follow. For example, if you determine that a security has a 40-period peak-to-peak cycle, the ideal moving average length would be 21 periods calculated using the following formula:

$$\textit{Ideal Moving Average Length} = \frac{\textit{Cycle Length}}{2} + 1$$

You can convert the number of periods in a daily moving average into a weekly moving average by dividing the number of days by 5 (e.g., a 200-day

TABLE 38

Trend	Moving Average
Very Short Term	5–13 days
Short Term	14–25 days
Minor Intermediate	26–49 days
Intermediate	50–100 days
Long Term	100–200 days

moving average is almost identical to a 40-week moving average). To convert the number of periods in a daily moving average into a monthly moving average, divide the number of days by 21 (e.g., a 200-day moving average is very similar to a 9-month moving average because there are approximately 21 trading days in a month).

Moving averages can also be calculated and plotted on indicators. The interpretation of an indicator's moving average is similar to the interpretation of a security's moving average: When the indicator rises above its moving average, it signifies a continued upward movement by the indicator; when the indicator falls below its moving average, it signifies a continued downward movement by the indicator.

Indicators that are especially well-suited for use with moving average penetration systems include the MACD, Price ROC, Momentum, and Stochastic Oscillator.

Some indicators, such as short-term Stochastics, fluctuate so erratically that it is difficult to tell what their trend really is. By erasing the indicator and then plotting a moving average of the indicator, you can see the general trend of the indicator rather than its period-to-period fluctuations.

Whipsaws can be reduced, at the expense of slightly later signals, by plotting a short-term moving average (e.g., 2–10 period) of oscillating indicators such as the 12-period ROC, Stochastics, or RSI. For example, rather than selling when the Stochastic Oscillator falls below 80, you might sell only when a 5-period moving average of the Stochastic Oscillator falls below 80.

Example

Figure 118 shows Immunex and its 39-week exponential moving average. Although the moving average does not pinpoint the tops and bottoms perfectly, it does provide a good indication of the direction prices are trending.

FIGURE 118

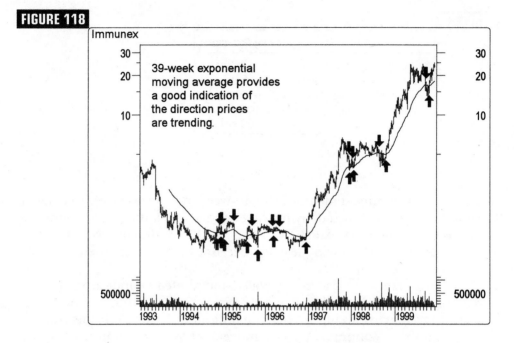

Immunex

39-week exponential moving average provides a good indication of the direction prices are trending.

M

Figure 119 displays 25-day moving averages using the simple, exponential, weighted, time series, triangular, variable, and volume-adjusted methods of calculation.

FIGURE 119

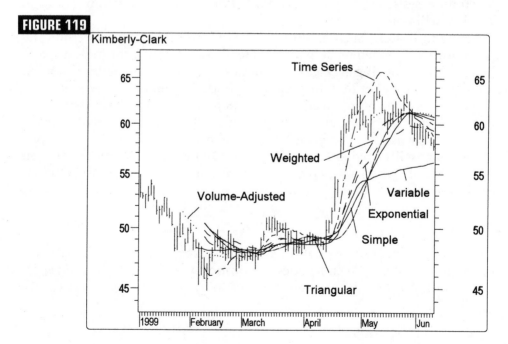

Kimberly-Clark

Calculation, Simple Moving Average

A simple (or "arithmetic") moving average is calculated by adding the closing price of the security for a number of time periods (e.g., 12 days) and then dividing this total by the number of time periods. The result is the average price of the security over the time period. Simple moving averages give equal weight to each daily price.

For example, to calculate a 21-day moving average of the closing prices, first add the closing prices for the most recent 21 days. Next, divide that sum by 21; this would give you the average price of closing prices over the preceding 21 days. You would plot this average price on the chart. You would perform the same calculation tomorrow: add up the most recent 21 days' closing prices, divide by 21, and plot the resulting figure on the chart.

The mathematic expression follows:

$$\frac{\sum_{1}^{n} closing\ price}{n}$$

Where:

- n = The number of time periods in the moving average

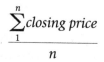

Table 39 illustrates the calculation of a 5-day simple moving average.

- Column C is the sum of the closing price for the previous 5 days.
- Column D is the value in Column C divided by 5. This is the 5-day simple moving average.

TABLE 39

	SIMPLE MOVING AVERAGE		
A	B	C	D
		5-day Sum of	Column C divided by
Date	Close	Closing Prices	5
08/22/97	25.000		
08/25/97	24.875		
08/26/97	24.781		
08/27/97	24.594		
08/28/97	24.500	123.750	24.750
08/29/97	24.625	123.375	24.675
09/02/97	25.219	123.719	24.744
09/03/97	27.250	126.188	25.238

Calculation, Exponential Moving Average

An exponential (or exponentially weighted) moving average is calculated by applying a percentage of today's closing price to a percentage of yesterday's moving average value. Exponential moving averages place more weight on recent prices.

For example, to calculate a 20-percent exponential moving average, first take today's closing price and multiply it by 20 percent. Next, add this product to the value of yesterday's moving average multiplied by 80 percent. The 80 percent was calculated by subtracting the percentage used in the moving average, in this case 20 percent, from 100 percent (i.e., 0.80 = 1.0− 0.2). In this example, we are adding 20 percent of today's closing price to 80 percent of the average price (i.e., yesterday's moving average).

*(Today's Close * 0.20) + (Yesterday's Moving Average * 0.80)*

Because most investors feel more comfortable working with time periods rather than with percentages, the exponential percentage can be calculated from a specific number of days using the following formula:

$$Exponential\ Percentage = \frac{2}{Time\ Periods + 1}$$

For example, you can use the above formula to determine that a 9-day exponential moving average is the same as a 20-percent exponential moving average:

$$0.20 = \frac{2}{9 + 1}$$

You can use the following formula to convert an exponential percentage into a number of time periods (e.g., days).

$$Time\ Periods = \left(\frac{2}{Percentage}\right) - 1$$

Using the above formula, you can see that a 20-percent moving average is the same as a 9-period exponential moving average:

$$9\ periods = \left(\frac{2}{0.20}\right) - 1$$

Note that most exponential percentages won't convert to an exact number of time periods. For example, as shown in the following formula, a 15-percent exponential moving average equates to 15.333... periods.

$$15.333...periods = \left(\frac{2}{0.15}\right) - 1$$

Some indicator calculations state an exponential percentage rather than a number of time periods. For example, the MACD calculation (see page 199) specifies 15-percent and 7.5-percent exponential moving averages. Although people (including me) often refer to these as 12- and 26-day exponential moving averages, they are really closer to 12.333- and 25.666-day moving averages.

TABLE 40

		EXPONENTIAL MOVING AVERAGE		
A	**B**	**C**	**D**	**E**
Date	Close	Close multiplied by 33.333%	Yesterday's Column E multiplied by 66.666%	Column C plus Column D
08/22/97	25.000			25.000
08/25/97	24.875	8.292	16.667	24.958
08/26/97	24.781	8.260	16.639	24.899
08/27/97	24.594	8.198	16.600	24.797
08/28/97	24.500	8.167	16.532	24.698
08/29/97	24.625	8.208	16.466	24.674
09/02/97	25.219	8.406	16.449	24.856
09/03/97	27.250	9.083	16.570	25.654

Table 40 illustrates the calculation of a 5-day exponential moving average.

- On the first day, Column E is "seeded" with the closing price (Column B).
- Column C is the closing price multiplied by 33.333... percent. Using the formula on page 208, the 33.333... percent was calculated as "2 / (n + 1)" where "n" is 5, because this is a 5-period exponential moving average.
- Column D is the value of the moving average (Column E) on the previous day multiplied by 66.666... percent. The 66.666... percent was calculated as "100% − 33.333%." Note that since there isn't a "previous day" on the *first* day, this value is not available on the first day (i.e., 08/22/97).
- Column E is the sum of Column C and Column D. (Remember that on the *first* day Column C was set to the closing price.) Although there are values for this moving average beginning on the first day, the indicator isn't "up to speed" (i.e., valid) until the fifth day since this is a 5-day moving average.

Calculation, Time Series Moving Average

A Time Series moving average is the same as a Time Series Forecast (see page 333). It is sometimes referred to as a "moving linear regression" study.

Calculation, Triangular Moving Average

Triangular moving averages place the majority of the weight on the middle portion of the price series. Triangular moving averages are actually double-smoothed simple moving averages (i.e., a moving average of a moving average). The periods used in the simple moving averages vary, depending on whether or not you specify an odd or even number of time periods.

To determine the number of periods to use in the two simple moving averages, do the following:

1. Add 1 to the number of periods in the triangular moving average. For example, if you are calculating a 12-period triangular moving average, 12 plus 1 is 13.
2. Divide the sum from step 1 by 2. For example, if the sum of the previous step was 13, then 13 divided by 2 is 6.5.
3. If the result of step 2 contains a fractional portion, round the result *up* to the nearest integer. For example, if the result of step 2 was 6.5, round up to 7. This is the number of periods you will use in the two simple moving averages.

Table 41 illustrates the calculation of a 5-day triangular moving average.

- Using the preceding instructions, you can determine that a 5-period triangular moving average contains 3-period simple moving averages (i.e., 5 plus 1 is 6; 6 divided by 2 is 3; 3 doesn't contain a fractional portion).
- Column C is a 3-period simple moving average of the close. It was calculated by summing the preceding 3 days of closing prices and dividing by 3.
- Column D is a 3-period simple moving average of Column C. It was calculated by summing the preceding 3 days of Column C and dividing by 3. This is the triangular moving average.

Calculation, Variable Moving Average

The variable moving average was defined by Tushar Chande in an article that appeared in *Technical Analysis of Stocks and Commodities* in March 1992. He also discusses it in his book *The New Technical Trader*. Chande mentions several variations of the calculations—there isn't one "right" method. I summarize the methodology here.

TABLE 41

	TRIANGULAR MOVING AVERAGE		
A	B	C	D
Date	Close	3-Period Simple MA of Close	3-Period Simple MA of Column C
08/22/97	25.0000		
08/25/97	24.8750		
08/26/97	24.7813	24.8854	
08/27/97	24.5938	24.7500	
08/28/97	24.5000	24.6250	24.7535
08/29/97	24.6250	24.5729	24.6493
09/02/97	25.2188	24.7813	24.6597
09/03/97	27.2500	25.6979	25.0174
09/04/97	26.2500	26.2396	25.5729
09/05/97	26.5938	26.6979	26.2118
09/08/97	27.5938	26.8125	26.5834
09/09/97	27.8750	27.3542	26.9549
09/10/97	27.5313	27.6667	27.2778
09/11/97	27.2188	27.5417	27.5209
09/12/97	26.9688	27.2396	27.4827
09/15/97	26.7500	26.9792	27.2535

M

A variable moving average is an exponential moving average (see page 208) that automatically adjusts the smoothing percentage based on the volatility of the data series. The more volatile the data, the more weight given to the current data.

Most moving average calculation methods are unable to compensate for trading range versus trending markets. During trading ranges (when prices move sideways in a narrow range), shorter-term moving averages tend to produce numerous false signals. In trending markets (when prices move up or down over an extended period), longer-term moving averages are slow to react to reversals in trend. By automatically adjusting the smoothing constant, a variable moving average is able to adjust its sensitivity, allowing it to perform better in both types of markets.

A variable moving average is calculated as follows:

$$((SM * VR) * Close) + ((1 - (SM * VR)) * Yesterday's\ MA)$$

Where:

- SM = The Scaling Multiplier
- VR = The Volatility Ratio

Different indicators can be used for the Volatility Ratio. I use the absolute value of a 9-day Chande Momentum Oscillator divided by 100. The higher this ratio, the "trendier" the market, thereby increasing the sensitivity of the moving average.

You can also choose the scaling multiplier. I use the following equation:

$$SM = \frac{2}{Times\ Periods\ +\ 1}$$

Calculation, Volume-Adjusted Moving Average

Volume-adjusted moving averages, developed by Dick Arms, incorporate a volume weighting into the moving average.

The calculation for a volume-adjusted moving average is somewhat complex; however, it is conceptually easy to understand. Thus, I have explained the steps to calculate the average but have not included a table.

All moving averages (even volume-adjusted) use some type of weighting scheme to "average" the data. As its name implies, volume-adjusted moving averages assign the majority of weight to the day's with the most volume.

A volume-adjusted moving average is calculated as follows:

1. Calculate the average volume using every time period in the entire price series being studied (note that this means that the exact value of the moving average will vary depending on which periods you use).
2. Calculate the volume increment by multiplying the average volume by 0.67.
3. Calculate each period's volume ratio by dividing each period's actual volume by the volume increment.
4. Starting at the most recent time period and working backward, multiply each period's price by the period's volume ratio, and cumulatively sum these values until the user-specified number of volume increments is reached. Note that only a fraction of the last period's volume will likely be used.

Calculation, Weighted Moving Average

A weighted moving average is designed to put more weight on recent data and less weight on past data. A weighted moving average is calculated by multiplying each of the previous day's data by a weighting factor.

The weighting factor is based on the number of days in the moving average. For example, a 5-day weighted moving average assigns 5 times more weight to today's price than the price 5 days ago.

Table 42 shows the values of a 5-day weighted moving average.

TABLE 42

WEIGHTED MOVING AVERAGE		
Date	Close	5-day Weighted Moving Average
08/22/97	25.0000	
08/25/97	24.8750	
08/26/97	24.7813	
08/27/97	24.5938	
08/28/97	24.5000	24.6646
08/29/97	24.6250	24.6229
09/02/97	25.2188	24.8042
09/03/97	27.2500	25.6396

TABLE 43

WEIGHTED MOVING AVERAGE						
A	B	C	D	E	F	G
Date	Close	Day #	Column C multiplied by Close	Sum of Last 5 Days of Column D	Sum of Last 5 Days of Column C	Column E divided by Column F
08/22/97	25.0000	1	25.0000			
08/25/97	24.8750	2	49.7500			
08/26/97	24.7813	3	74.3439			
08/27/97	24.5938	4	98.3752			
08/28/97	24.5000	5	122.5000	369.9691	15	24.6646

Table 43 shows the detailed calculation of the above 5-day weighted moving average for 1 day, 08/28/97.

- Column C is the "day number." This value is calculated by counting backward from the current day (i.e., 08/28/97) beginning with the number of periods in the moving average (i.e., 5). Remember, this table only illustrates the calculation for 08/28/97.
- Column D is the closing price (Column B) multiplied by Column C. As you can see, this column gives progressively more weight for each day.
- Column E is the sum of the preceding 5 days of Column D.
- Column F is the sum of the preceding 5 days of Column C (i.e., 1 plus 2 plus 3 plus 4 plus 5).
- Column G is Column E divided by Column F. This is the 5-day weighted moving average.

NEGATIVE VOLUME INDEX

Overview

The Negative Volume Index (NVI) focuses on days when the volume decreases from the previous day, the premise being that the "smart money" takes positions on days when volume decreases.

Interpretation

The interpretation of the NVI assumes that on days when volume increases, the crowd-following "uninformed" investors are in the market. Conversely, on days with decreased volume, the "smart money" is quietly taking positions. Thus, the NVI displays what the "smart money" is doing.

Because falling prices are usually associated with falling volume, the NVI usually trends downward.

In *Stock Market Logic*, Norman Fosback points out that the odds of a bull market are 95 out of 100 when the NVI rises above its 1-year moving average. The odds of a bull market are roughly 50/50 when the NVI is below its 1-year average. Therefore, the NVI is most useful as a bull market indicator.

Example

Figure 120 shows an NVI for Avon. "Buy" arrows indicate whenever the NVI crossed above its 1-year (255-trading-day) moving average. The arrows indicate when the NVI fell below the moving average. You can see that the NVI did a decent job of identifying profitable opportunities.

Calculation

The calculation of the NVI varies based on whether the current period's volume is greater than, or less than, the previous period's volume.

If the current volume is less than the previous period's volume then:

$$NVI = Previous\ NVI + \left(\frac{Close - Previous\ Close}{Previous\ Close} * Previous\ NVI \right)$$

If the current volume is greater than or equal to the previous period's volume then:

$$NVI = Previous\ NVI$$

FIGURE 120

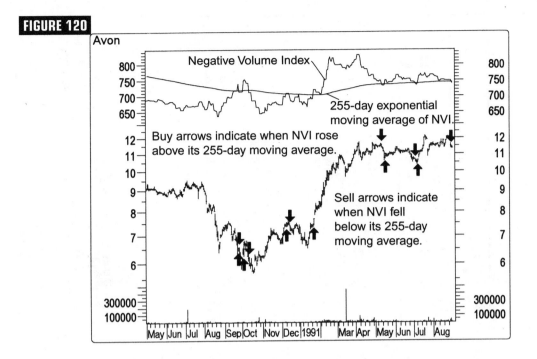

Table 44 illustrates the calculation of the NVI.

- On the first day, Column G is "seeded" with 1,000. This gives an initial NVI. (The value of the "seed" isn't important, as long as it isn't zero.)
- Column D is the change in price from the previous period. It is calculated by subtracting the previous close from the current close.
- Column E is the percent change in price. It is calculated by dividing Column D (the change in price) by the previous close (Column B).
- Column F is Column E (i.e., the 1-period percent change) multiplied by the previous value in Column G (i.e., the previous NVI).
- The calculation of Column G varies depending on whether volume increased or decreased. If the volume decreased from the previous period (as first occurred on 01/05/88), then Column G is Column F plus the previous value in Column G. If the volume is equal to or greater than the previous period's volume (as first occurred on 01/06/88), then Column G is equal to the previous value in Column G (i.e., it remains unchanged). You can see that Column G only changes when the volume decreases, and then Column G changes by the amount in Column F.

TABLE 44

NEGATIVE VOLUME INDEX

A	B	C	D	E	F	G
Date	Close	Volume	Close minus Previous Close	Column D divided by Previous Close	Column E multiplied by Previous Col G	NVI (see text)
01/04/88	6.5313	10,500				1000.0000
01/05/88	6.5625	6,492	0.0312	0.0048	4.7770	1004.7770
01/06/88	6.4688	6,540	−0.0937	−0.0143	−14.3463	1004.7770
01/07/88	6.4375	8,924	−0.0313	−0.0048	−4.8617	1004.7770
01/08/88	6.2188	5,416	−0.2187	−0.0340	−34.1351	970.6419
01/11/88	6.2500	4,588	0.0312	0.0050	4.8698	975.5116
01/12/88	6.1250	16,236	−0.1250	−0.0200	−19.5102	975.5116
01/13/88	6.1563	2,864	0.0313	0.0051	4.9851	980.4967
01/14/88	6.2500	3,080	0.0937	0.0152	14.9233	980.4967
01/15/88	6.3125	5,312	0.0625	0.0100	9.8050	980.4967
01/18/88	6.4688	12,456	0.1563	0.0248	24.2775	980.4967
01/19/88	6.2813	3,020	−0.1875	−0.0290	−28.4200	952.0767
01/20/88	6.1250	12,228	−0.1563	−0.0249	−23.6909	952.0767
01/21/88	6.1875	5,248	0.0625	0.0102	9.7151	961.7918
01/22/88	6.1563	6,632	−0.0312	−0.0050	−4.8498	961.7918
01/25/88	6.2813	4,104	0.1250	0.0203	19.5286	981.3204
01/26/88	6.2188	4,464	−0.0625	−0.0100	−9.7643	981.3204
01/27/88	6.1563	6,212	−0.0625	−0.0101	−9.8624	981.3204
01/28/88	6.1875	3,836	0.0312	0.0051	4.9733	986.2937
01/29/88	6.3750	7,640	0.1875	0.0303	29.8877	986.2937
02/01/88	6.2813	3,544	−0.0937	−0.0147	−14.4966	971.7971
02/02/88	6.2813	4,660	0.0000	0.0000	0.0000	971.7971

NEW HIGHS-LOWS CUMULATIVE

Overview

The New Highs-Lows Cumulative indicator is a long-term market momentum indicator. It is a cumulative total of the difference between the number of stocks reaching new 52-week highs and the number of stocks reaching new 52-week lows.

Interpretation

The New Highs-Lows Cumulative indicator provides a confirmation of the current trend. Most of the time, the indicator will move in the same direction as major market indices. However, when the indicator and market move in opposite directions, it is likely that the market will reverse.

   The interpretation of the New Highs-Lows Cumulative indicator is similar to the Advance/Decline Line in that divergences occur when the indicator fails to confirm the market index's high or low. Divergences (see page 36) during an uptrending market indicate potential weakness, while divergences in a downtrending market indicate potential strength.

N

Example

Figure 121 shows the Dow Jones Industrials and the New Highs-Lows Cumulative indicator. A classic divergence occurred during 1998, when the Dow made a new high but the New Highs-Lows Cumulative indicator was failing to surpass its previous high. This was followed by a 20+-percent correction.

Calculation

The New Highs-Lows Cumulative indicator is simply a cumulative total of the number of stocks making new 52-week highs minus the number of stocks making new 52-week lows.

(New Highs − New Lows) + Yesterday's Indicator Value

   Table 45 illustrates the calculation of the New Highs-New Lows Cumulative indicator.

- Column D is the number of new highs (Column B) minus the number of new lows (Column C).
- Column E is a cumulative total of Column D. It is calculated by adding the value in Column D to the previous value in Column E.

FIGURE 121

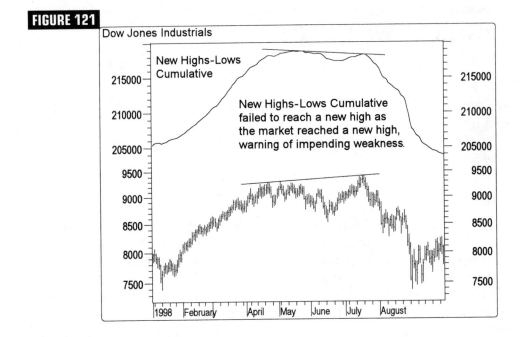

Dow Jones Industrials

New Highs-Lows Cumulative

New Highs-Lows Cumulative failed to reach a new high as the market reached a new high, warning of impending weakness.

TABLE 45

	NEW HIGHS—NEW LOWS CUMULATIVE			
A	**B**	**C**	**D**	**E**
Date	New Highs	New Lows	New Highs minus New Lows	Cumulative Total of Column D
12/07/98	98	43	55	55
12/08/98	100	42	58	113
12/09/98	87	49	38	151
12/10/98	72	76	−4	147
12/11/98	39	83	−44	103
12/14/98	29	109	−80	23

NEW HIGHS/LOWS RATIO

Overview

The New Highs/New Lows Ratio (NH/NL Ratio) displays the daily ratio between the number of stocks reaching new 52-week highs and the number of stocks reaching new 52-week lows.

Interpretation

The NH/NL Ratio is another useful method of visualizing the relationship of stocks that are making new highs and new lows. High readings indicate that a large number of stocks are making new highs (compared to the number of stocks making new lows). Readings less than 1 indicate that the number of stocks making new highs is less than the number of stocks making lows.

Refer to the New Highs-New Lows indicator (see page 220) for more information on interpreting the NH/NL Ratio.

Example

Figure 122 shows the S&P 500 and the NH/NL Ratio. As the S&P 500 rallied strongly in July 1998, the NH/NL Ratio barely budged, indicating that the advance was narrow and fragile. The market subsequently corrected.

Calculation

The calculation of the New Highs/New Lows Ratio is:

$$\frac{\textit{Number of New Highs}}{\textit{Number of New Lows}}$$

Table 46 illustrates the calculation of the New Highs/Lows Ratio.

- Column D is the number of new highs (Column B) divided by the number of new lows (Column C).

N

FIGURE 122

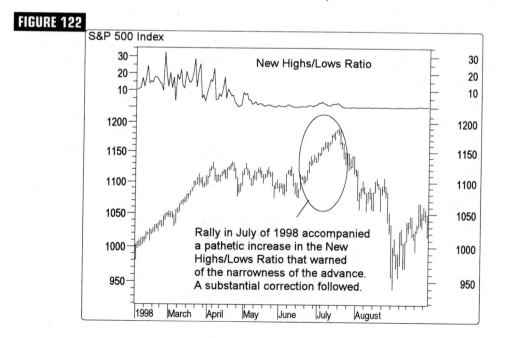

S&P 500 Index

New Highs/Lows Ratio

Rally in July of 1998 accompanied a pathetic increase in the New Highs/Lows Ratio that warned of the narrowness of the advance. A substantial correction followed.

TABLE 46

	NEW HIGHS/NEW LOWS RATIO		
A	B	C	D
Date	New Highs	New Lows	New Highs divided by New Lows
12/07/98	98	43	2.3
12/08/98	100	42	2.4
12/09/98	87	49	1.8
12/10/98	72	76	0.9
12/11/98	39	83	0.5
12/14/98	29	109	0.3

NEW HIGHS-NEW LOWS

Overview

The New Highs-New Lows (NH-NL) indicator displays the daily difference between the number of stocks reaching new 52-week highs and the number of stocks reaching new 52-week lows.

Interpretation

You can interpret the NH-NL indicator as a divergence indicator or as an oscillator. I usually plot a 10-day moving average of the NH-NL indicator to smooth the daily values.

Divergence. The NH-NL indicator generally reaches its extreme lows slightly before a major market bottom. As the market then turns up from the major bottom, the indicator jumps up rapidly. During this period, many new stocks are making new highs because it's easy to make a new high when prices have been depressed for a long time.

As the cycle matures, a divergence often occurs as fewer and fewer stocks are making new highs (the indicator falls), yet the market indices continue to reach new highs. This is a classic bearish divergence that indicates that the current upward trend is weak and may reverse.

Oscillator. The NH-NL indicator oscillates around zero. If the indicator is positive, the bulls are in control. If it is negative, the bears are in control. You can trade the NH-NL indicator by buying and selling as the indicator passes

FIGURE 123

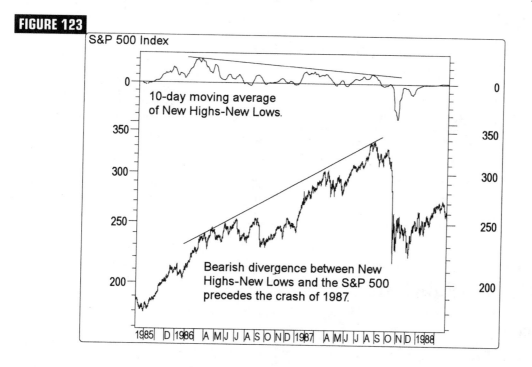

S&P 500 Index

10-day moving average of New Highs-New Lows.

Bearish divergence between New Highs-New Lows and the S&P 500 precedes the crash of 1987.

through zero. This won't always keep you on the right side of the market, but it is helpful to confirm the current trend.

Example

Figure 123 shows the S&P 500 and a 10-day moving average of the NH-NL indicator. A bearish divergence between the S&P 500 and the moving average of NH-NL preceded the crash of 1987.

Calculation

The New Highs-New Lows is the difference between the number of stocks that made new 52-week highs and the number of stocks that made new 52-week lows. I usually plot a moving average of this value.

New Highs — New Lows

Table 47 illustrates the calculation of the New Highs-New Lows indicator.

- Column D is the number of new highs (Column B) minus the number of new lows (Column C).

TABLE 47

	NEW HIGHS—NEW LOWS		
A	B	C	D
Date	New Highs	New Lows	New Highs minus New Lows
12/07/98	98	43	55
12/08/98	100	42	58
12/09/98	87	49	38
12/10/98	72	76	−4
12/11/98	39	83	−44
12/14/98	29	109	−80

ODD LOT BALANCE INDEX

Overview

The Odd Lot Balance Index (OLBI) is a market sentiment indicator that shows the ratio of odd-lot sales to purchases (an "odd lot" is a stock transaction of less than 100 shares). The assumption is that the "odd lotters," the market's smallest traders, don't know what they are doing.

Interpretation

When the Odd Lot Balance Index is high, odd lotters are selling more than they are buying and are therefore bearish on the market. To trade contrarily to the odd lotters, you should buy when they are selling (as indicated by a high OLBI) and sell when the odd lotters are bullish and buying (as indicated by a low OLBI).

You can smooth day-to-day fluctuations of the Odd Lot Balance Index by plotting a 10-day moving average of the Index.

Unfortunately, the trading of 99-share lots in an effort to skirt the "up-tick" rule, which requires that specialists take short positions only when prices move upward, has rendered odd-lot indicators less reliable. See the discussion on the increase in the number of odd-lot trades in the Interpretation section of the Odd Lot Short Ratio on page 225.

Example

Figure 124 shows the S&P 500 and a 10-day moving average of the OLBI. A vertical line indicates when the odd lotters were excessively pessimistic—which turned out to be a good time to buy.

FIGURE 124

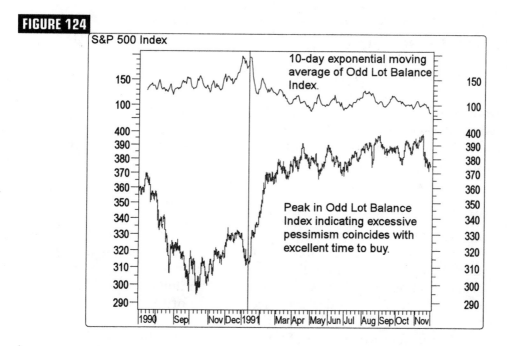

S&P 500 Index

10-day exponential moving average of Odd Lot Balance Index.

Peak in Odd Lot Balance Index indicating excessive pessimism coincides with excellent time to buy.

Calculation

The OLBI is calculated by dividing the number of odd-lot sales by the number of odd-lot purchases.

$$\left(\frac{Odd\text{-}Lot\ Sales}{Odd\text{-}Lot\ Purchases} \right) * 100$$

Table 48 illustrates the calculation of the OLBI.

- Column D is the number of odd-lot sales (Column B) divided by the number of odd-lot purchases (Column C), multiplied by 100.

TABLE 48

| | ODD LOT BALANCE INDEX | | |
A	B	C	D
Date	Odd Lot Sales	Odd Lot Purchases	Col B / Col C multiplied by 100
06/02/99	4,665	3,742	124.7
06/03/99	4,377	3,187	137.3
06/04/99	4,113	3,883	105.9
06/07/99	3,774	3,375	111.8
06/08/99	5,382	3,192	168.6
06/09/99	3,663	3,245	112.9
06/10/99	5,285	3,514	150.4
06/11/99	5,420	3,319	163.3

ODD LOT PURCHASES/SALES

Overview

Both of these indicators, Odd Lot Purchases and Odd Lot Sales, display what their names imply: the number of shares (in thousands) purchased or sold in odd lots. An "odd lot" is a stock transaction of less than 100 shares.

Interpretation

The odd-lot trade numbers are used in several different ratios and indicators. By themselves, they show the investment activities of the odd-lot traders. Being a contrarian indicator, a high number of Odd Lot Purchases is generally considered bearish, whereas a high number of Odd Lot Sales is considered bullish. The idea is to act opposite of the small, uninformed odd-lot traders.

Unfortunately, the trading of 99-share lots in an effort to skirt the "up-tick" rule, which requires that specialists take short positions only when prices move upward, has rendered odd-lot indicators less reliable. See the dis-

FIGURE 125

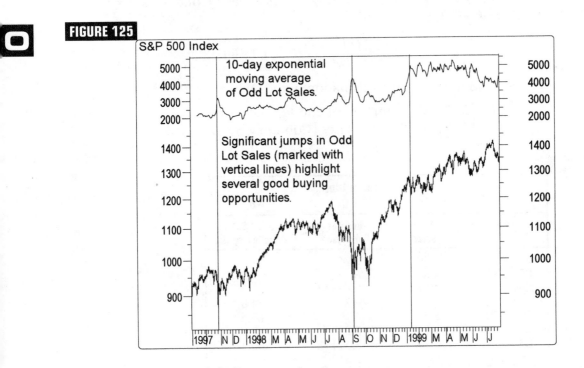

S&P 500 Index

10-day exponential moving average of Odd Lot Sales.

Significant jumps in Odd Lot Sales (marked with vertical lines) highlight several good buying opportunities.

cussion on the increase in the number of odd lot trades in the Interpretation section of the Odd Lot Short Ratio (below).

Example

Figure 125 shows the S&P 500 and a 10-day moving average of Odd Lot Sales. Vertical lines indicate when the number of odd lot sales jumped significantly (as identified by relatively high moving average values). These proved to be good buying points.

ODD LOT SHORT RATIO

Overview

The Odd Lot Short Ratio (OLSR) is a market sentiment indicator that displays the daily ratio of odd-lot short sales compared to odd-lot buy/sell transactions.

Investors "short" a stock in anticipation of the stock's price falling. Instead of the traditional transaction of buying at a lower price and profiting by selling at a higher price, the short-sale transaction is just the opposite. To profit from a short sale, the stock must be sold at a higher price and bought (covered) at a lower price. An "odd-lot" short is a short-sale transaction involving fewer than 100 shares.

Interpretation

If we could find investors who were always wrong and do the exact opposite of them, we would always be right! Odd-lot indicators strive to do just that. If we assume that small investors ("odd lotters") are inexperienced (and thus usually wrong), then trading contrarily to the odd-lot traders should be profitable.

The higher the OLSR indicator, the higher the percentage of odd-lot shorts and the more likely it is that the market will rise (proving the odd lotters wrong). Similarly, the lower the OLSR, the more likely it is that a market decline will occur.

Generally, this rule (invest contrarily to the odd lotters) has held true. Odd lotters tend to be reactive rather than proactive. High OLSRs tend to come after major market declines (when investors should be buying, not selling), and low readings usually come after long market advances.

In 1986, the number of odd-lot shorts reached levels that were unheard of. The explanation I have heard is that specialists are placing multiple odd-lot short orders to avoid the up-tick rule, which states that a short order must be processed on an up-tick. They do this on days with major declines in prices.

If this explanation is true, it drastically complicates the interpretation of all odd-lot indicators. It would mean that the odd-lot indicators show what the "littlest" guys are doing, except when it reaches extreme readings, in which case it would show what the "biggest" guys (the Members) are doing.

Example

Refer to the examples on pages 222 and 225.

Calculation

The OLSR is calculated by dividing the number of odd-lot short sales by the average number of odd-lot transactions for the day.

Because odd lots do not necessarily have a buyer and a seller for every transaction, the average number of transactions is calculated by adding the number of odd-lot buy orders to the number of odd-lot sell orders and then dividing by 2.

$$\left(\frac{Odd\ Lot\ Shorts}{\left(\dfrac{Odd\ Lot\ Purchases\ +\ Odd\ Lot\ Sales}{2} \right)} \right) * 100$$

Table 49 illustrates the calculation of the OLSR.

TABLE 49

			Odd Lot Short Ratio			
A	B	C	D	E	F	G
Date	Odd Lot Shorts	Odd Lot Purchases	Odd Lot Sales	Column C plus Column D	Column E divided by 2	Col B / Col F multiplied by 100
06/02/99	203	3,742	4,665	8,407	4,203.5	4.829
06/03/99	195	3,187	4,377	7,564	3,782.0	5.156
06/04/99	189	3,883	4,113	7,996	3,998.0	4.727
06/07/99	193	3,375	3,774	7,149	3,574.5	5.399
06/08/99	176	3,192	5,382	8,574	4,287.0	4.105
06/09/99	126	3,245	3,663	6,908	3,454.0	3.648

- Columns B, C, and D are the number of odd-lot transactions.
- Column E is the sum of odd-lot purchases (Column C) and odd-lot sales (Column D).
- Column F is the value in Column E divided by 2. This is the average number of odd-lot transactions.
- Column G is the number of odd-lot short sales (Column B) divided by the value in Column F, multiplied by 100. This is the OLSR.

ODDS™ PROBABILITY CONES

Overview

ODDS™ Probability Cones, developed by Don Fishback, are designed to graphically display the probability of a specified price movement based on a security's historical volatility. The ODDS methodology is based on the assumptions made in every commonly used option pricing model. If you use an option pricing model to value options, you are making the probability assumptions used by ODDS, whether you realize it or not.

The assumption is that the financial markets are random and that prices exhibit a normal distribution. That means if you plotted a security's price changes over an extended period of time, with price change across the bottom of the graph and number of occurrences on the side, the shape of the price distribution would look like a bell curve. A bell curve represents a "normal distribution." A normal distribution assumption has some very useful properties, including the one that is the most important to us—probability is equal to the area under the curve.

Volatility provides us with a value that can be used to measure the likelihood of a significant price change. The higher the volatility, the greater the likelihood of a significant price move.

Interpretation

ODDS Probability Cones provide a visual guide to the most probable range of future prices. This range (i.e. the cone's width) is determined by recent volatility in prices, the number of time periods projected, and the probability percentage (e.g., 68 percent confidence, 90 percent confidence, etc.). The more volatile the security prices, the wider the expected range of future prices, and hence the wider the cones. The cones always widen from the apex even if recent volatility is very low, because as time increases, the better the odds of a significant price move.

This type of analysis was intended originally to help option traders determine the best strategy to implement. From a probability standpoint, an option trader would prefer to sell options with strikes that lie outside the cones and buy options with strikes that lie within the cones.

The cones also have merit in the analysis of regular long and short positions. All else being equal, and assuming you are confident in your price directional forecast, you would prefer to establish a long or short position in a security with wide cones rather than one with narrow cones. Of course, this assumes that the recent calculated volatility will continue or rise. If you expect volatility to drop, then you should reconsider.

Example

Figure 126 of Exxon shows an ODDS probability cone with a 60-percent setting (i.e., the odds are 60 percent that the price will remain within the cone during the specified time period based on historical volatility).

FIGURE 126

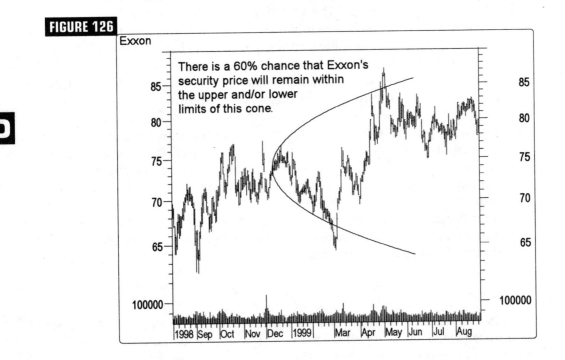

Calculation

The calculation of the ODDS Probability Cones are beyond the scope of this book. Basically, the calculations are based on standard probability calculations. First, a volatility calculation is done using the Option Volatility indicator (see page 236). Then, the estimated price range, given the volatility, is calculated for each period. Half of this value is added to the current period's price to get the upper cone, and half is subtracted from the current period's price to get the lower cone.

ON BALANCE VOLUME

Overview

On Balance Volume (OBV) is a momentum indicator that relates volume to price change. It was developed by Joe Granville and originally presented in his book *New Strategy of Daily Stock Market Timing for Maximum Profits.*

Interpretation

OBV is a running total of volume. It shows if volume is flowing into or out of a security. When the security closes higher than the previous close, all of the day's volume is considered up-volume. When the security closes lower than the previous close, all of the day's volume is considered down-volume.

A full explanation of OBV is beyond the scope of this book. If you would like further information on OBV analysis, I recommend that you read Granville's book.

The basic assumption regarding OBV analysis is that OBV changes precede price changes. The theory is that "smart money" can be seen flowing into the security by a rising OBV. When the public then moves into the security, both the security and the OBV will surge ahead.

If the security's price movement precedes OBV movement, a "nonconfirmation" has occurred. Nonconfirmations can occur at bull-market tops (when the security rises without, or before, the OBV) or at bear-market bottoms (when the security falls without, or before, the OBV).

The OBV is in a rising trend when each new peak is higher than the previous peak and each new trough is higher than the previous trough. Likewise, the OBV is in a falling trend when each successive peak is lower than the previous peak and each successive trough is lower than the previous trough. When the OBV is moving sideways and is not making successive highs and lows, it is in a doubtful trend. Figure 127 shows the three OBV trends.

Once a trend is established, it remains in force until it is broken. The OBV trend can be broken in two ways. The first occurs when the trend changes from a rising trend to a falling trend or from a falling trend to a rising trend.

FIGURE 127

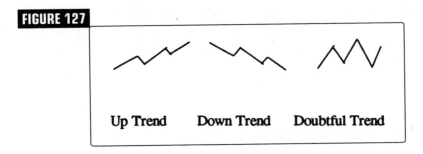

Up Trend   Down Trend   Doubtful Trend

The second way the OBV trend can be broken is if the trend changes to a doubtful trend and remains doubtful for more than 3 days. Thus, if the security changes from a rising trend to a doubtful trend and remains doubtful for only 2 days before changing back to a rising trend, the OBV is considered to have always been in a rising trend.

When the OBV changes to a rising or falling trend, a "breakout" has occurred. Since OBV breakouts normally precede price breakouts, investors should buy long on OBV upside breakouts. Likewise, investors should sell short when the OBV makes a downside breakout. Positions should be held until the trend changes (as explained in the preceding paragraph).

This method of analyzing OBV is designed for trading short-term cycles. According to Granville, investors must act quickly and decisively if they wish to profit from short-term OBV analysis.

Example

Figure 128 shows PepsiCo and the OBV indicator. I have labeled the up, down, and doubtful trends.

A falling trend, as you will recall, is defined by lower peaks and lower troughs. Conversely, a rising trend is defined by higher peaks and higher troughs.

Calculation

OBV is calculated by adding the period's volume to a cumulative total when the security's price closes up, and subtracting the volume when the security's price closes down. The logic is as follows:

If the close is greater than the previous close, then:

$$OBV = Previous\ OBV + Volume$$

If the close is less than the previous close, then:

$$OBV = Previous\ OBV - Volume$$

FIGURE 128

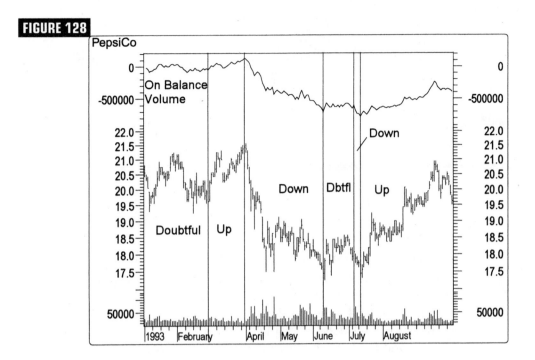

If the close is equal to the previous close, then:

$$OBV = Previous\ OBV$$

Table 50 illustrates the calculation of OBV.

- On the first day (01/04/93), the OBV (Column D) is zero because we don't know if prices increased or decreased.

TABLE 50

On Balance Volume			
A	B	C	D
Date	Close	Volume	OBV
01/04/93	20.5625	27,802	0
01/05/93	20.3750	16,178	−16,178
01/06/93	20.0625	22,766	−38,944
01/07/93	19.5000	46,074	−85,018
01/08/93	19.8125	22,904	−62,114
01/11/93	19.8125	20,428	−62,114
01/12/93	20.0625	29,260	−32,854
01/13/93	20.0625	30,652	−32,854
01/14/93	20.3750	38,332	5,478
01/15/93	20.7500	40,054	45,532

- On the second day (01/05/94), prices decreased, so we subtract the volume from the previous day's OBV and get $-16,178$.
- On the fifth day (01/08/93), prices increased so the volume was added to the OBV.
- On the sixth day (01/11/93), prices were unchanged so the OBV remained unchanged.

OPEN INTEREST

Overview

Open Interest is the number of open contracts of a given future or option contract. An open contract can be a long or short contract that has not been exercised, closed out, or allowed to expire. Open interest is really more of a data field (see page 6) than an indicator.

A fact that is sometimes overlooked is that a futures contract always involves a buyer and a seller. This means that one unit of open interest always represents two people, a buyer and a seller.

Open interest increases when a buyer and seller create a new contract. This happens when the buyer initiates a long position and the seller initiates a short position. Open interest decreases when the buyer and seller liquidate existing contracts. This happens when the buyer is selling an existing long position and the seller is covering an existing short position.

Interpretation

By itself, open interest shows only the liquidity of a specific contract or market. However, combining volume analysis with open interest sometimes provides subtle clues to the flow of money in and out of the market:

- Rising volume and rising open interest confirm the direction of the current trend.
- Falling volume and falling open interest signal that an end to the current trend may be imminent.

Example

Figure 129 shows Copper, open interest (the solid line), and a 5-day moving average of the volume (the dotted line). The open interest is for all copper contracts, not just the current contract.

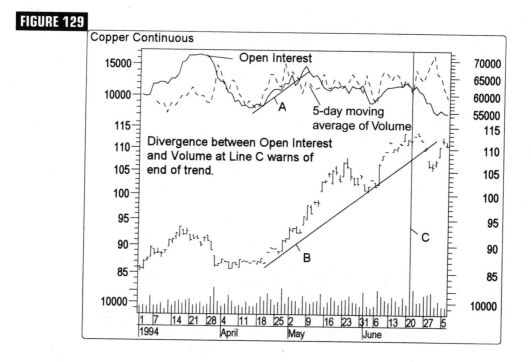

FIGURE 129

Copper Continuous

I drew a trendline (A) when both open interest and volume were increasing. This confirmed the upward trend of prices as shown by the trendline (B).

I then drew a vertical line (C) when open interest and volume began to diverge. From this point, volume continued to increase while open interest decreased sharply. This warned of an end to the rising trend.

OPEN-10 TRIN

Overview

The Open-10 TRIN is a smoothed variation of the Arms Index (see page 61). It is a market breadth indicator that uses advancing/declining volume and advancing/declining issues to measure the strength of the market.

Interpretation

The interpretation of Open-10 TRIN (also called the Open Trading Index) is similar to the interpretation of the "normal" TRIN.

Readings above 0.90 are generally considered bearish, and readings below 0.90 are considered bullish.

TABLE 51

1st Reading > 1.0	Days to Final Low	Next Market Move
May 23, 1984	3	60-point rally
June 15, 1984	1	63-point rally
July 20, 1984	3	165-point rally
October 10, 1984	0	88-point rally
November 16, 1984	1	45-point rally
December 5, 1984	3	69-point rally
January 3, 1985	1	130-point rally
March 15, 1985	1	48-point rally
April 30, 1985	2	96-point rally
June 19, 1985	3	78-point rally

Table 51 was reprinted from Peter Eliades' *Stock Market Cycles.* It shows what the DJIA did after the 10-day TRIN rose above the level of 1. Remember, in those days a 60-point rally was significant!

I created a similar table for the period 1985 through 1998. The average gain in the 79 additional trades generated an average gain of 301 points. You can see this table at AtoZbook.com/opentrin.htm.

Calculation

The Open-10 TRIN is calculated by keeping a 10-day total of each of the TRIN's components before performing the TRIN calculation (see page 61).

$$\frac{\left(\dfrac{10\text{-}Period\ Total\ of\ Advancing\ Issues}{10\text{-}Period\ Total\ of\ Declining\ Issues}\right)}{\left(\dfrac{10\text{-}Period\ Total\ of\ Advancing\ Volume}{10\text{-}Period\ Total\ of\ Declining\ Volume}\right)}$$

Table 52 illustrates the calculation of Open-10 TRIN.

- Column F is the sum of the preceding 10 days of advancing issues (Column B).
- Column G is the sum of the preceding 10 days of declining issues (Column C).
- Column H is the sum of the preceding 10 days of advancing volume (Column D).
- Column I is the sum of the preceding 10 days of declining volume (Column E).
- Column J is Column F divided by Column G.
- Column K is Column H divided by Column I.
- Column L is Column J divided by Column K. This is the Open-10 TRIN.

TABLE 52

OPEN-10 TRIN

A	B	C	D	E	F	G	H	I	J	K	L
Date	Advancing Issues	Declining Issues	Advancing Volume	Declining Volume	10-period sum of Advancing Issues	10-period sum of Declining Issues	10-period sum of Advancing Volume	10-period sum of Declining Volume	Column F divided by Column G	Column H divided by Column I	Column J divided by Column K
04/25/97	789	1,662	1,097,590	2,685,030							
04/28/97	1,348	1,085	2,247,369	1,430,582							
04/29/97	2,085	531	4,617,426	527,996							
04/30/97	1,599	941	4,000,088	1,163,730							
05/01/97	1,450	1,021	2,176,503	1,856,353							
05/02/97	2,119	476	3,918,818	749,109							
05/05/97	1,958	677	4,554,564	665,109							
05/06/97	1,258	1,270	2,774,558	2,762,761							
05/07/97	842	1,660	1,518,034	3,128,769							
05/08/97	1,398	1,097	3,072,179	1,743,590	14,846	10,420	29,977,129	16,713,029	1.4248	1.7936	0.7943
05/09/97	1,526	932	2,792,524	1,218,892	15,583	9,690	31,672,063	15,246,891	1.6082	2.0773	0.7742
05/12/97	1,766	761	3,387,345	850,940	16,001	9,366	32,812,039	14,667,249	1.7084	2.2371	0.7637
05/13/97	1,133	1,322	1,991,714	2,512,359	15,049	10,157	30,186,327	16,651,612	1.4816	1.8128	0.8173
05/14/97	1,472	992	2,877,362	1,616,582	14,922	10,208	29,063,601	17,104,464	1.4618	1.6992	0.8603
05/15/97	1,282	1,164	2,658,199	1,502,646	14,754	10,351	29,545,297	16,750,757	1.4254	1.7638	0.8081
05/16/97	973	1,431	1,325,087	3,133,338	13,608	11,306	26,951,566	19,134,986	1.2036	1.4085	0.8545
05/19/97	1,390	1,056	1,825,068	1,290,328	13,040	11,685	24,222,070	19,760,205	1.1160	1.2258	0.9104
05/20/97	1,411	1,040	2,707,087	1,284,888	13,193	11,455	24,154,599	18,282,332	1.1517	1.3212	0.8717
05/21/97	1,421	1,107	2,377,201	2,563,639	13,772	10,902	25,013,766	17,717,202	1.2633	1.4118	0.8948
05/22/97	1,270	1,176	1,873,511	1,901,396	13,644	10,981	23,815,098	17,875,008	1.2425	1.3323	0.9326

OPTION ANALYSIS

Overview

The most widely used option pricing model is the Black-Scholes option valuation model, which was developed by Fisher Black and Myron Scholes in 1973.

The Black-Scholes model helps determine the fair market value of an option based on the security's price and volatility, time until expiration, and the current market interest rate. The following assumptions were made by Black and Scholes when the model was developed:

1. Markets are "frictionless." In other words, there are no transaction costs or taxes; all market participants may borrow and lend at the "riskless" rate of interest; there are no penalties for short selling; and all securities are infinitely divisible (i.e., fractional shares can be purchased).
2. Stock prices are lognormally distributed (i.e., they follow a bell curve). This means that a stock can double in price as easily as it can drop to half its price.
3. Stocks do not pay dividends or make any distributions. (The model is often modified to allow for dividend adjustments.)
4. The option can be exercised only on the expiration date.

The components of the Black-Scholes option model are security price, volatility, option life, market interest rate, and dividend (if any).

The formula for the Black-Scholes option pricing model is widely available in many books and publications. The original work by Black and Scholes was done only on equity call options. Since their work was originally published, extensions of their model have been developed, such as models for put options and options on futures. Gamma, Theta, and Vega calculations are all extensions of the original Black-Scholes model.

Adjusting the model for dividends provides a more accurate calculation of an option's fair market value. A popular adjustment method assumes that dividend payments are paid out continuously.

The calculations for these option indicators are beyond the scope of this book. For more information on calculations and strategies using the Black-Scholes model, I suggest the book *Option Volatility and Pricing Strategies* by Sheldon Natenberg.

Interpretation

Put/Call Price. The Put/Call Price is the main output of the Black-Scholes model. It shows how much an option should sell for based on the various components that make up the model (e.g., volatility, option life, security price). It helps answer the question "Is the option overpriced or under-priced?"

The usefulness of the Put/Call Price is basically twofold:

1. It helps you locate miss-priced options. The option purchaser can use the model to find options that are underpriced. The option writer can use the model to find options that are overpriced.
2. It helps you form a riskless hedge to earn arbitrage profits. For example, you could buy undervalued calls and then short the underlying stock. This creates a riskless hedge because regardless of whether the security's price goes up or down, the two positions will exactly offset each other. You would then wait for the option to return to its fair market value to earn arbitrage profits.

Delta (see below) is used to determine the number of shares to purchase in order to form a riskless hedge.

Delta. Delta shows the amount that the option's price will change if the underlying security's price changes by $1.00.

For example, if XYZ is selling for $25.00/share, a call option on XYZ is selling for $2.00 and the Delta is 75 percent, then the option's price should increase $0.75 (to $2.75) if the price of XYZ increases to $26.00/share. In other words, the option should go up $0.75 for each $1.00 that XYZ goes up.

If an option is deep in the money (e.g., where the security's price is significantly above the call's strike price), then it will have a high Delta, because almost all of the gain/loss in the security will be reflected in the option price. Conversely, deep out-of-the-money options will have a low Delta, because very little of the gain/loss in the security is reflected in the option price.

If you don't have a computer, the rough rule of thumb for calculating Delta is this: 75 percent for an option $5.00 in the money (e.g., where the security's price is above the call's strike price), 50 percent for an option at the money (e.g., where the security's price is equal to the option's strike price), and 25 percent for an option $5.00 out of the money (e.g., where the security's price is below the call's strike price).

As an in-the-money option nears expiration, the Delta will approach 100 percent because the amount of time remaining for the option to move out of the money is small.

Delta is also used to determine the correct number of shares to buy/short to form a "riskless hedge." For example, suppose the Delta on a put option is 66 percent. A riskless hedge would result from owning a ratio of two-thirds (66 percent) of a position in stock (i.e., 66 shares) to every one long position in a put option contract. If the stock price goes up 1 point, then the stock position will increase $66.00. This $66.00 increase should be exactly offset by a $66.00 decrease in the value of the put option contract.

Forming a riskless hedge gives the investor the potential of earning arbitrage profits by profiting from the undervalued option's return to its fair market value (i.e., the price at which the option is neither overpriced nor underpriced). Theoretically, the market will eventually value underpriced options at their fair market value. However, it should be noted that high transaction costs may undermine this theory.

Gamma.   Gamma shows the anticipated change in Delta, given a 1-point increase in the underlying security. Thus, it shows how responsive Delta is to a change in the underlying security's price. For example, a Gamma of 4 indicates that the Delta will increase 4 points (e.g., from 50 percent to 54 percent) for each 1-point increase in the underlying security's price.

Gamma indicates the amount of risk involved with an option position. A large Gamma indicates higher risk because the value of the option can change more quickly. However, a trader may desire higher risk depending on the strategy employed.

Option Life.   Option Life shows the number of days until expiration. Generally speaking, the longer the time until expiration, the more valuable the option.

A graph of Option Life (Figure 130) appears as a stepped line from the upper-left to the lower-right side of the screen. The reason the line is stepped is because of weekends and holidays. For example, on Friday there may be 146 days to expiration and on the following Monday only 143 days remaining.

Theta.   Theta shows the change in the option's price (in points) due to the effect of time alone. The longer the time until expiration, the less effect that time has on the price of the option. However, as the option nears expiration, the effect can be great, particularly on out-of-the-money options. Theta is also referred to as "time decay."

For example, a Theta value of -0.0025 means that the option lost 1/4 of 1 cent due to the passage of time alone.

The effect of time on the option price is almost always positive. The more time until expiration, the better chance the option has of being in the money at expiration. The only exception to this positive relationship is deep in-the-money put options with an expiration date far into the future.

FIGURE 130

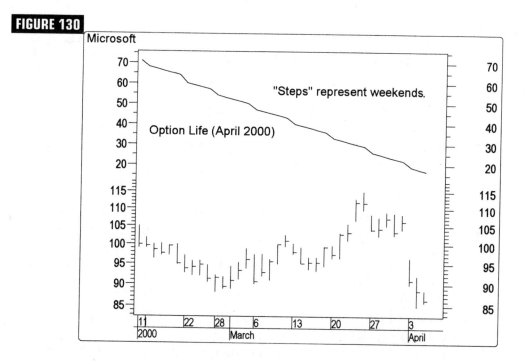

Microsoft. "Steps" represent weekends. Option Life (April 2000).

All other things being equal, options with low Thetas are more preferable (for purchase) than are those with high Thetas.

Vega.   Vega shows the change in the option price due to an assumed 1-percent increase in the underlying security's volatility. Vega shows the dollar amount of gain that should be expected if the volatility goes up 1 point (all else being equal).

The effect of volatility on the option price is always positive. The greater the volatility of the underlying security, the better chance the option has of being in the money at expiration. Therefore, options with higher volatilities will cost more than those with lower volatilities.

Since Vega measures the sensitivity of an option to a change in volatility, options with higher Vegas are more preferable (for purchase) than those with low Vegas.

Volatility.   Volatility is a measurement that shows the degree of fluctuation that a security experiences over a given time frame. Wide price movements over a short time frame are characteristic of high volatility stocks.

Volatility is the only input parameter of the Black-Scholes model (e.g., security price, volatility, option life, market interest rate) that is calculated, yet the accuracy of the model is highly dependent on a good volatility figure. The best measurement of volatility is the one that captures future price movements, but if we knew what future price movements would be, we wouldn't need the Black-Scholes model—we'd be trading! However, reality forces us to estimate volatility. There are two ways to estimate volatility for use with the Black-Scholes model: Historical Volatility and Implied Volatility.

Historical Volatility measures the actual volatility of the security's prices using a standard-deviation-based formula. It shows how volatile prices have been over the last *x* time periods. The advantage of Historical Volatility is that it can be calculated using only historical security prices. When you calculate the Black-Scholes put/call price using Historical Volatility, most options appear overpriced.

Implied Volatility is a more widely used measure of option volatility. Implied Volatility is the amount of volatility that the option market is assuming (i.e., implying) for the option. To calculate implied volatility, the actual option price, security price, strike price, and the option expiration date are plugged into the Black-Scholes formula. The formula then solves for the implied volatility.

Options of high-volatility stocks are worth more (i.e., carry higher premiums) than those with low volatility because of the greater chance the option has of moving in the money by expiration. Option purchasers normally prefer options with high volatilities and option writers normally prefer options with low volatilities (all else being equal).

OVERBOUGHT/OVERSOLD

Overview

The Overbought/Oversold (OB/OS) indicator is a market breadth indicator based on the smoothed difference between advancing and declining issues.

Interpretation

The OB/OS indicator shows when the stock market is overbought (and a correction is due) and when it is oversold (and a rally is due).

Readings above +200 are generally considered bearish and readings below −200 are generally considered bullish. When the OB/OS indicator falls below +200, a sell signal is generated. Similarly, a buy signal is generated when the OB/OS indicator rises above −200.

As with all OB/OS-type indicators, extreme readings may be a sign of a change in investor expectations and may not be followed by the expected correction. (Refer to the discussion on the Advance/Decline Ratio, page 55, and the McClellan Oscillator, page 183, for additional comments on extremely overbought/oversold conditions.)

Example

Figure 131 shows the DJIA and the Overbought/Oversold indicator. "Buy" and "sell" arrows identify when the indicator penetrated and then crossed back over the +200/–200 levels. The OB/OS indicator works very well in this type of trading-range market.

FIGURE 131

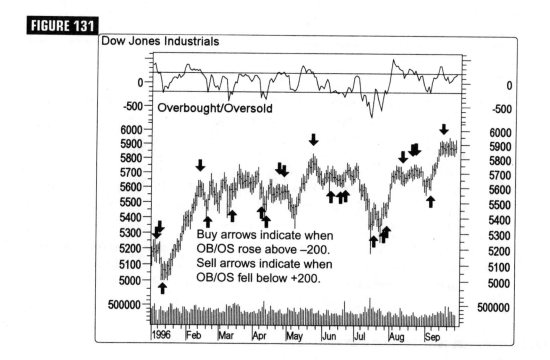

Calculation

The Overbought/Oversold indicator is a 10-period exponential moving average of the difference between the number of advancing and declining issues.

10-period moving average of (Advancing Issues − Declining Issues)

Table 53 illustrates the calculation of the Overbought/Oversold indicator.

TABLE 53

A	B	C	D	E
		OVERBOUGHT/OVERSOLD		
Date	Advancing Issues	Declining Issues	Column B minus Column C	10-day EMA
04/25/97	789	1,662	−873	−873
04/28/97	1,348	1,085	263	−666
04/29/97	2,085	531	1,554	−263
04/30/97	1,599	941	658	−95
05/01/97	1,450	1,021	429	0
05/02/97	2,119	476	1,643	299
05/05/97	1,958	677	1,281	477
05/06/97	1,258	1,270	−12	388
05/07/97	842	1,660	−818	169
05/08/97	1,398	1,097	301	193

- Column D is the number of advancing issues (Column B) minus the number of declining issues (Column C).
- Column E is a 10-day exponential moving average of Column D. The first row of Column E is seeded with the first value in Column D (i.e., −873). Subsequent rows in Column E are calculated by multiplying the value in Column D by 0.1818..., then multiplying the previous day's value in Column E by 0.8181..., and finally adding these two values together.

The value 0.1818 was calculated as "2 / (10+1)," as explained on page 208. The value 0.8181 was calculated as "1 − 0.1818," as explained on page 208. Note that this 10-period moving average is not valid until the tenth day.

PARABOLIC SAR

Overview

The Parabolic Time/Price System, developed by Welles Wilder, is used to set trailing price stops and is usually referred to as the Parabolic SAR (Stop and Reversal). This indicator is explained thoroughly in Wilder's book *New Concepts in Technical Trading Systems*.

Interpretation

The Parabolic SAR provides excellent exit points. You should close long positions when the price falls below the SAR and close short positions when the price rises above the SAR.

If you are long (i.e., the price is above the SAR), the SAR will move up every day, regardless of the direction the price is moving. The amount the SAR moves up depends on the amount that prices move.

Example

Figure 132 shows Compaq and its Parabolic SAR. You should be long when the SAR is below prices and short when it is above prices.

The Parabolic SAR in Figure 132 is plotted as shown in Wilder's book. Each SAR stop-level point is displayed on the day on which it is in effect. Note that the SAR value is today's, not tomorrow's, stop level.

FIGURE 132

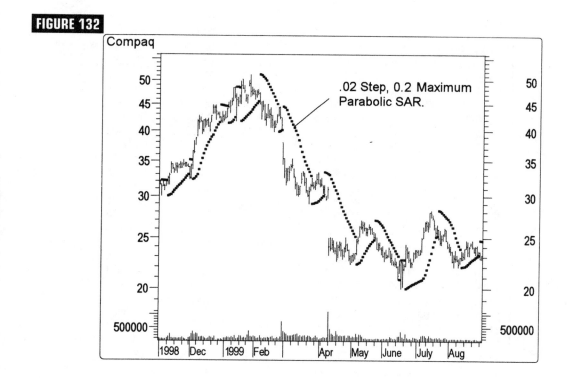

Calculation

Table 54 explains how to calculate the Parabolic SAR with a 0.02 Acceleration Factor Increase and an Acceleration Factor Maximum of 0.2. This is a difficult calculation to understand.

An oddity in the calculation is that the SAR can't start until a new position (i.e., long or short) occurs, yet we don't know what position we are in at the start of the data. In this example, I assume we are in a long trade since prices are moving up.

- Column D is the Acceleration Factor.
  - Column D is first initialized to the Acceleration Factor Maximum (0.2 in this example) because we don't know when this trade began.
  - Column G (below) states the conditions that cause the position to change from long to short (and vice versa). Whenever Column G

TABLE 54

	PARABOLIC SAR					
A	B	C	D	E	F	G
Date	High	Low	Acceleration Factor	Extreme Price	SAR	Position
10/01/99	90.6250	88.3125	0.20	90.6250	88.3125	Long
10/04/99	92.6250	90.2500	0.20	92.6250	88.7750	
10/05/99	93.8750	89.5000	0.20	93.8750	89.5450	
10/06/99	94.0000	92.0625	0.20	94.0000	90.4110	
10/07/99	95.0625	92.6875	0.20	95.0625	91.1288	
10/08/99	95.1875	92.1250	0.20	95.1875	91.9155	
10/11/99	95.0000	94.1250	0.20	95.1875	92.5699	
10/12/99	94.3125	92.3750	0.20	95.1875	93.0934	
10/13/99	93.1250	90.3125	0.02	90.3125	95.1875	Short
10/14/99	92.2344	89.6875	0.04	89.6875	95.0900	
10/15/99	89.8125	87.3125	0.06	87.3125	94.8739	
10/18/99	88.0000	85.0625	0.08	85.0625	94.4202	
10/19/99	89.2500	85.2500	0.08	85.0625	93.6716	
10/20/99	92.3750	90.2500	0.08	85.0625	92.9829	
10/21/99	93.1250	90.5000	0.02	93.1250	85.0625	Long
10/22/99	93.8750	91.7500	0.04	93.8750	85.2238	
10/25/99	93.5625	91.1250	0.04	93.8750	85.5698	
10/26/99	95.2500	92.2656	0.06	95.2500	85.9020	
10/27/99	91.6250	89.6875	0.06	95.2500	86.4629	
10/28/99	90.8750	89.3125	0.06	95.2500	86.9901	
10/29/99	94.0000	91.2500	0.06	95.2500	87.4857	
11/01/99	94.1875	92.1250	0.06	95.2500	87.9516	
11/02/99	94.5000	91.9375	0.06	95.2500	88.3895	
11/03/99	93.5000	91.5000	0.06	95.2500	88.8011	
11/04/99	92.7500	90.3125	0.06	95.2500	89.1880	
11/05/99	92.8750	90.5000	0.06	95.2500	89.5518	
11/08/99	90.7500	84.3750	0.02	84.3750	95.2500	Short

changes, Column D is reset to the Acceleration Factor Increase (i.e., 0.02 in this example). This first occurred on 10/13/99.

- The value in Column D increases by the Acceleration Factor Increase (e.g., 0.02) when we are in a long position (as defined by Column G) and a new high price is reached or when we are in a short position (as defined by Column G) and a new low is reached. If neither of the preceding two conditions are met (and Column G hasn't changed), Column D remains unchanged.
- The value in Column D may not exceed the Acceleration Factor Maximum (i.e., 0.2).

- Column E is the Extreme Price. When in a long position (as defined by Column G), the Extreme Price is the highest price reached while in the current position. When in a short position, the Extreme Price is the lowest price reached while in the current position.
- Column F is the Parabolic SAR (Stop and Reversal).
  - When the position changes (as defined by Column G), Column F is set to a new value based on the new position. If the new position is long, Column F is set to the lowest low during the previous position. If the new position is short, Column F is set to the highest high during the previous position.
  - In the days following a change in position, Column F is modified as follows: (1) subtract the previous Column F from the previous Column E, (2) multiply this value by the previous Column D, (3) add this to the previous Column F.
- Column G is the current position. It changes from a short to a long when the high (Column B) is greater than the SAR (Column F). It changes from a long to a short when the low (Column C) falls below the SAR (Column F).

It is important to note that the new position in Column G is entered in the following row. For example, when the low fell below the SAR on 10/12/99, the term "Short" was entered on the following row (10/13/99).

PATTERNS

Overview

A basic principle of technical analysis is that security prices move in trends. We also know that trends do not last forever. They eventually change direction, and when they do, they rarely do so on a dime. Instead, prices typically decelerate, pause, and then reverse. These phases occur as investors form new expectations, and by doing so they shift the security's supply/demand lines.

The changing of expectations often causes price patterns to emerge. Although no two markets are identical, their price patterns are often very similar. Predictable price behavior often follows these price patterns.

Chart patterns can last from a few days to many months or even years. Generally speaking, the longer a pattern takes to form, the more dramatic the ensuing price move.

Interpretation

The following sections explain some of the more common price patterns. For more information on chart patterns, I suggest the book *Technical Analysis of Stock Trends* by Robert Edwards and John Magee.

Head-and-Shoulders.   The Head-and-Shoulders price pattern is the most reliable and well-known chart pattern. It gets its name from its resemblance to a head with two shoulders on either side. The reason this reversal pattern is so common is due to the manner in which trends typically reverse.

An uptrend is formed as prices make higher highs and higher lows in a stair-step fashion. The trend is broken when this upward climb ends. As you can see in Figure 133, the "left shoulder" and the "head" are the last two higher highs. The right shoulder is created as the bulls try to push prices higher but are unable to do so. This signifies the end of the uptrend. Confirmation of a new downtrend occurs when the "neckline" is penetrated.

FIGURE 133

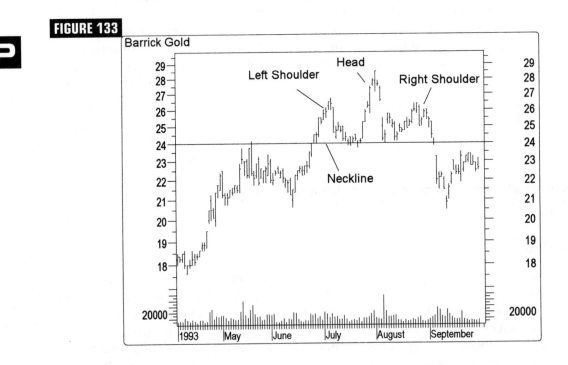

During a healthy uptrend, volume should increase during each rally. A sign that the trend is weakening occurs when the volume accompanying rallies is less than the volume accompanying the preceding rally. In a typical Head-and-Shoulders pattern, volume decreases on the head and is especially light on the right shoulder.

Following the penetration of the neckline, it is very common for prices to return to the neckline in a last effort to continue the uptrend (as shown in Figure 133). If prices are then unable to rise above the neckline, they usually decline rapidly on increased volume.

An inverse (or upside-down) Head-and-Shoulders pattern often coincides with market bottoms. As with a normal Head-and-Shoulders pattern, volume usually decreases as the pattern is formed and then increases as prices rise above the neckline.

Rounding Tops and Bottoms.   Rounding Tops occur as expectations gradually shift from bullish to bearish. The gradual, yet steady shift forms a rounded top. Rounding Bottoms occur as expectations gradually shift from bearish to bullish.

Volume during both Rounding Tops and Rounding Bottoms often mirrors the bowl-like shape of prices during a Rounding Bottom. Volume, which was high during the previous trend, decreases as expectations shift and traders become indecisive. Volume then increases as the new trend is established.

Figure 134 shows Goodyear Tire and a classic Rounding Bottom formation.

FIGURE 134

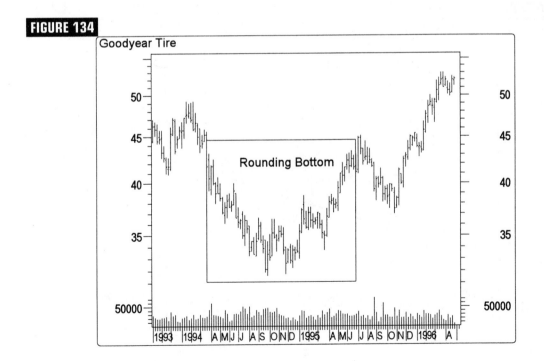

Goodyear Tire

Rounding Bottom

Triangles.   A Triangle occurs as the range between peaks and troughs narrows. Triangles typically occur as prices encounter a support or resistance level that constricts the prices.

A Symmetrical Triangle occurs when prices are making both lower highs and higher lows. An Ascending Triangle occurs when there are higher lows (as with a Symmetrical Triangle), but the highs are occurring at the same price level due to resistance. The odds favor an upside breakout from an Ascending Triangle. A Descending Triangle occurs when there are lower highs (as with a Symmetrical Triangle), but the lows are occurring at the same price level due to support. The odds favor a downside breakout from a Descending Triangle.

Just as pressure increases when water is forced through a narrow opening, the "pressure" of prices increases as the Triangle pattern forms. Prices will usually break out rapidly from a Triangle. Breakouts are confirmed when they are accompanied by an increase in volume.

The most reliable breakouts occur somewhere between half and three-quarters of the distance between the beginning and end (apex) of the Triangle. There are seldom many clues as to the direction prices will break out of a Symmetrical Triangle. If prices move all the way through the Triangle to the apex, a breakout is unlikely.

Figure 135 shows General Electric and an ascending triangle.

FIGURE 135

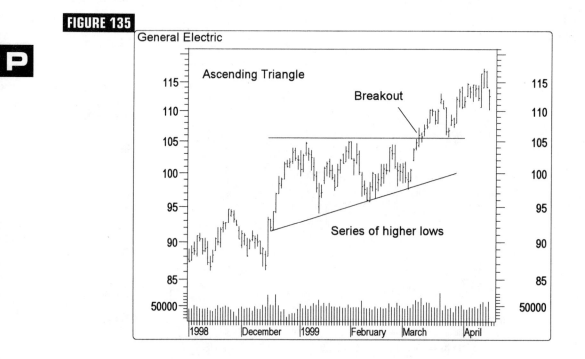

Double Tops and Bottoms.   A Double Top occurs when prices rise to a resistance level on significant volume, retreat, and subsequently return to the resistance level on decreased volume. Prices then decline, marking the beginning of a new downtrend.

A Double Bottom has the same characteristics as a Double Top except that it is upside-down.

Figure 136 shows Caterpillar and a Double Bottom pattern.

FIGURE 136

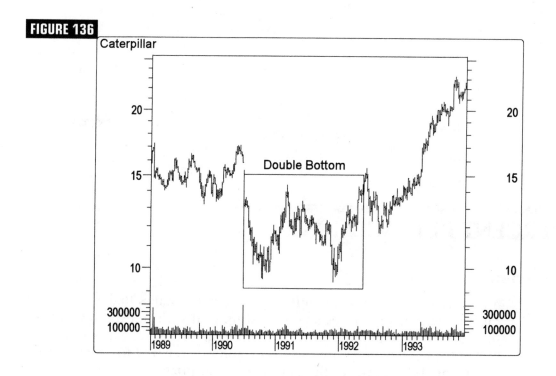

Gaps.   A Gap occurs when a security's price opens above/below the previous period's high-low trading range and stays above/below the range. This creates a "gap" on the chart. Gaps are usually the result of exceptional news about a security.

Figure 137 shows Qualcomm and two Gaps up, followed by strong rallies.

FIGURE 137

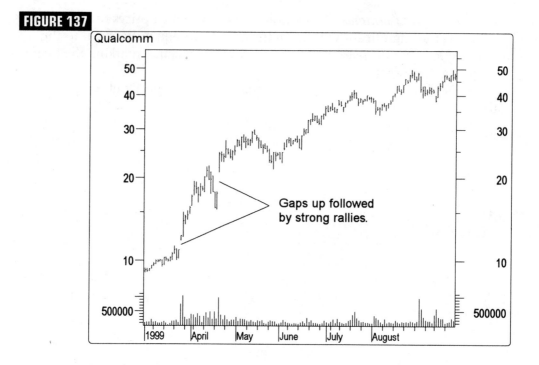

Qualcomm

Gaps up followed by strong rallies.

PERCENT RETRACEMENT

Overview

A characteristic of a healthy bull market is that it makes higher highs and higher lows. This indicates a continual upward shift in expectations and the supply/demand lines. The amount that prices retreat following a higher high can be measured using a technique referred to as Percent Retracement. This measures the percentage that prices "retraced" from the previous high.

For example, if a stock moves from a low of 50 to a high of 100 and then retraces to 75, the move from 100 to 75 (25 points) retraced 50 percent of the original move from 50 to 100.

Interpretation

Measuring the Percent Retracement can be helpful when determining the price levels at which prices will reverse and continue upward. During a vigorous bull market, prices often retrace up to 33 percent of the original move.

It is not uncommon for prices to retrace up to 50 percent. Retracements of more than 66 percent almost always signify an end to the bull market.

Some investors feel that the similarities between 33 percent, 50 percent, and 66 percent and the Fibonacci numbers of 38.2 percent, 50 percent, and 61.8 percent are significant. These investors will use Fibonacci Levels (see page 141) to view retracement levels.

Example

I labeled Figure 138 of Ann Taylor Stores at three points (labeled A, B, and C). These points define the price before the price move (A), at the end of the price move (B), and at the retraced price (C). In this example, prices retraced 61 percent of the original price move.

FIGURE 138

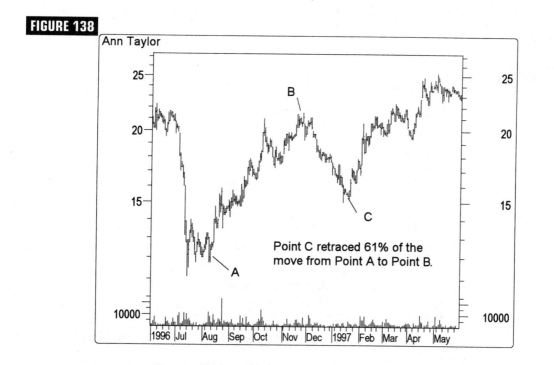

Ann Taylor

Point C retraced 61% of the move from Point A to Point B.

PERFORMANCE

Overview

The Performance indicator displays a security's price performance as a percentage. This is sometimes called a "normalized" chart.

Interpretation

The Performance indicator displays the percentage that the security has increased since the first period displayed. For example, if the Performance indicator is 10, it means that the security's price has increased 10 percent since the first period displayed on the left side of the chart. Similarly, a value of −10 means that the security's price has fallen by 10 percent since the first period displayed.

Performance charts are helpful for comparing the price movements of different securities because the prices are all normalized into percentages.

Example

Figure 139 shows Qwest Communications and its Performance indicator. The indicator shows that Qwest's price has increased 6 percent since the beginning of 1999.

FIGURE 139

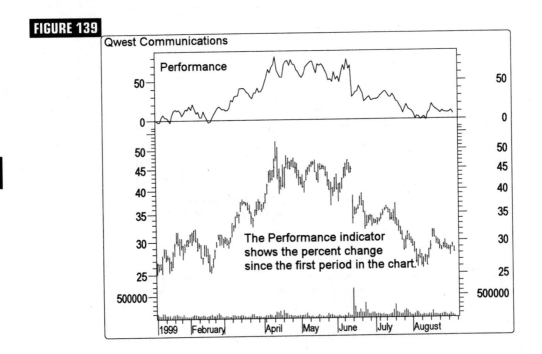

Calculation

The Performance indicator is calculated by dividing the change in prices by the first price displayed.

$$\left(\frac{Current\ Close - First\ Close}{First\ Close}\right) * 100$$

Table 55 illustrates the calculation of the Performance indicator.

- Column C is the close (Column B) minus the first closing price. For example, on 01/13/99 Column C is the close (26.7500) minus the first close (26.5625).
- Column D is the value in Column C divided by the *first* value in Column B and multiplied by 100. This is the Performance indicator.

TABLE 55

| | | PERFORMANCE | |
| A | B | C | D |
Date	Close	Col B minus first value in Col B	Col C divided by First value in Col B times 100
01/04/99	26.5625		
01/05/99	25.8125	−0.7500	−2.82%
01/06/99	25.8750	−0.6875	−2.59%
01/07/99	27.5000	0.9375	3.53%
01/08/99	28.4062	1.8437	6.94%
01/11/99	27.5312	0.9687	3.65%
01/12/99	27.4688	0.9063	3.41%
01/13/99	26.7500	0.1875	0.71%
01/14/99	25.6875	−0.8750	−3.29%
01/15/99	28.1562	1.5937	6.00%

POINT AND FIGURE

Overview

Point and Figure (P&F) charts differ from traditional price charts in that they completely disregard the passage of time and display only changes in prices. Rather than having price on the y-axis and time on the x-axis, P&F charts display price changes on both axes. This is similar to Kagi (see page 164), Renko (see page 302), and Three Line Break (see page 330) charts.

Interpretation

P&F charts display the underlying supply and demand of prices. A column of X's shows that demand is exceeding supply (a rally); a column of O's shows that supply is exceeding demand (a decline); and a series of short columns shows that supply and demand are relatively equal.

Several chart patterns (see page 245) regularly appear in P&F charts. These include Double Tops and Bottoms, Bullish and Bearish Signal Formations, Bullish and Bearish Symmetrical Triangles, Triple Tops and Bottoms, etc. It is beyond the scope of this book to fully explain all of these patterns.

Example

P&F charts focus only on price action. Looking at the P&F chart in Figure 140, you can see that prices were initially contained between a support level at 56.50 and a resistance level at 60.50. When prices broke above the resistance level at 60.50 (the long column of X's), that level became the new support level. This new support level eventually failed (the long column of O's), prices retested the support at 56.50, made a small rally, and then fell below the 56.50 support level.

FIGURE 140

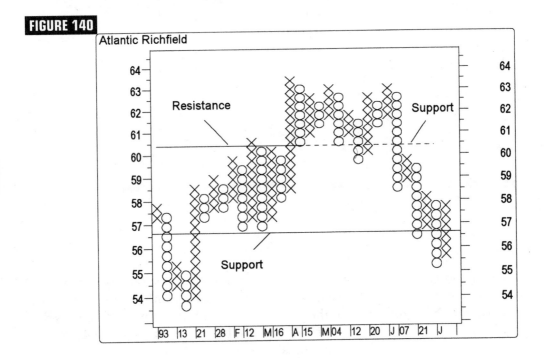

Figure 141 shows the same pricing information as the preceding P&F chart. You can see that the support and resistance levels are also identifiable in this bar chart, but the P&F chart made it much easier to identify them.

FIGURE 141

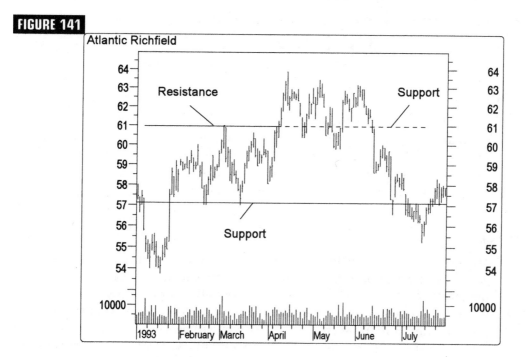

Atlantic Richfield

Calculation

P&F charts display an "X" when prices rise by the "box size" (a value you specify) and display an "O" when prices fall by the box size. Note that no X's or O's are drawn if prices rise or fall by an amount that is less than the box size.

Each column can contain either X's or O's, but never both. In order to change columns (e.g., from an X column to an O column), prices must reverse by the "reversal amount" (another value you specify) multiplied by the box size. For example, if the box size is 3 points and the reversal amount is 2 boxes, then prices must reverse direction 6 points (3 multiplied by 2) in order to change columns. If you are in a column of X's, the price must fall 6 points to change to a column of O's. If you are in a column of O's, the price must rise 6 points to change to a column of X's.

The changing of columns identifies a change in the trend of prices. When a new column of X's appears, it shows that prices are rallying higher. When a new column of O's appears, it shows that prices are moving lower.

Because prices must reverse direction by the reversal amount, the minimum number of X's or O's that can appear in a column is equal to the "reversal amount."

The common practice is to use the high and low prices (not just the close) to decide if prices have changed enough to display a new box.

POLARIZED FRACTAL EFFICIENCY

Overview

The Polarized Fractal Efficiency (PFE) indicator, developed by Hans Hannula, applies the laws of fractal geometry and chaos theory to the markets. PFE uses mathematics to determine how efficiently a price travels between two points. The more linear and efficient the price movement, the shorter the distance the prices must travel between two points.

Interpretation

The primary use of the PFE indicator is as a measure of how trendy or congested price action is. PFE readings above zero mean that the trend is up. The higher the reading, the "trendier" and more efficient the upward movement. PFE readings below zero mean that the trend is down. The lower the reading, the "trendier" and more efficient the downward movement. Readings around zero indicate choppy, less efficient movement, with a balance between the forces of supply and demand.

Several interesting phenomenon have been observed by Mr. Hannula:

- Indexes (particularly the OEX) tend to have a maximum PFE (both plus and minus) of about 43 percent.
- The middle region (around zero) is a balance between supply and demand and therefore a congestion point.
- A hooking pattern often occurs right before the end of an efficient period. This pattern occurs when the PFE appears to have reached its maximum, it turns in the opposite direction towards zero, and then makes one last attempt at maximum efficiency. Trades can be entered in the opposite direction, with a stop just beyond the extreme of the hook. Stay with the trade all the way to the other extreme, unless it slows around the zero line. If it slows around zero, exit the trade and wait for a new maximum efficiency entry.

Example

Figure 142 of Chevron shows a 14-day PFE with three smoothing periods. This chart shows the "hooking" pattern described previously. Prices were trending up during an efficient period, then the PFE made a run towards zero, then made a last attempt at maximum efficiency, then turned down for good, marking a turning point in Chevron's price.

FIGURE 142

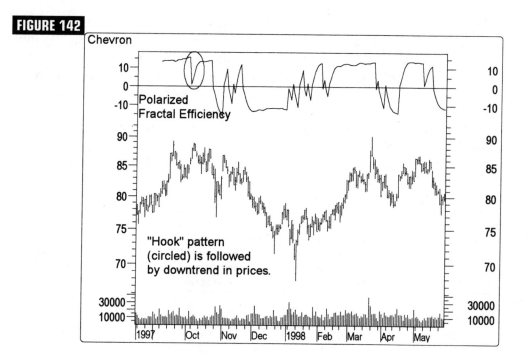

Chevron

Polarized Fractal Efficiency

"Hook" pattern (circled) is followed by downtrend in prices.

Calculation

The calculations for the Polarized Fractal Efficiency are quite complex and beyond the scope of this book. For further information, refer to the January 1994 issue of *Technical Analysis of Stocks and Commodities*.

POSITIVE VOLUME INDEX

Overview

The Positive Volume Index (PVI) focuses on days when the volume increased from the previous day. The premise is that the "crowd" takes positions on days when volume increases.

Interpretation

Interpretation of the PVI assumes that on days when volume increases, the crowd-following, "uninformed" investors are in the market. Conversely, on days with decreased volume, the "smart money" is quietly taking positions. Thus, the PVI displays what the not-so-smart money is doing. (The Negative Volume Index, page 214, displays what the smart money is doing.) Note, however, that the PVI is not a contrarian indicator. Even though the PVI is supposed to show what the not-so-smart money is doing, it still trends in the same direction as prices.

Because rising prices are usually associated with rising volume, the PVI usually trends upward.

Table 56 summarizes NVI and PVI data from 1941 through 1975 as explained in *Stock Market Logic* by Norman Fosback.

TABLE 56

Indicator	Indicator relative to 1-year moving average	Probability that bull market is in progress	Probability that bear market is in progress
NVI	Above	96%	4%
PVI	Above	79%	21%
NVI	Below	47%	53%
PVI	Below	33%	67%

As you can see, the NVI is excellent at identifying bull markets (i.e., when the NVI is above its 1-year moving average) and the PVI is pretty good at identifying bull markets (when the PVI is above its moving average) and bear markets (i.e., when the PVI is below its moving average).

Example

Figure 143 shows the NVI, the PVI, and the Dow Jones Industrial Average over a 4-year period (weekly data). The NVI and PVI indicators are labeled bullish or bearish, depending on if they were above or below their 52-week moving averages.

The Dow Jones Industrial Average is labeled as bullish when either the NVI or PVI was above its moving average, and as very bullish when both the indicators were both above their moving averages.

Calculation

The calculation of the PVI is based on whether the current period's volume is greater than, or less than, the previous period's volume.

FIGURE 143

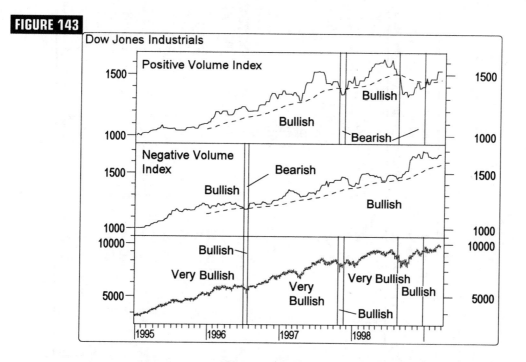

If the current volume is greater than the previous period's volume, then:

$$PVI = Previous\ PVI + \left(\frac{Close - Previous\ Close}{Previous\ Close} * Previous\ PVI\right)$$

However, if the current volume is less than or equal to the previous period's volume, then:

$$PVI = Previous\ PVI$$

Table 57 illustrates the calculation of the PVI.

- On the first day, Column G is "seeded" with 1,000. This gives us an initial PVI. (The value of the "seed" isn't important, as long as it isn't zero.)
- Column D is the change in price from the previous period. It is calculated by subtracting the previous close (Column B) from the current close.
- Column E is the percent change in price. It is calculated by dividing Column D (the change in price) by the previous close (the previous row in Column B).
- Column F is the value in Column E (i.e., the 1-period percent change) multiplied by the previous value in Column G (i.e., the previous PVI).

TABLE 57

POSITIVE VOLUME INDEX

A	B	C	D	E	F	G
Date	Close	Volume	Close minus Previous Close	Column D divided by Previous Close	Column E multiplied by Previous Col G	PVI (see text)
01/04/88	6.5313	10,500				1,000.0000
01/05/88	6.5625	6,492	0.0312	0.0048	4.7770	1,000.0000
01/06/88	6.4688	6,540	-0.0937	-0.0143	-14.2781	985.7219
01/07/88	6.4375	8,924	-0.0313	-0.0048	-4.7695	980.9524
01/08/88	6.2188	5,416	-0.2187	-0.0340	-33.3257	980.9524
01/11/88	6.2500	4,588	0.0312	0.0050	4.9215	980.9524
01/12/88	6.1250	16,236	-0.1250	-0.0200	-19.6190	961.3333
01/13/88	6.1563	2,864	0.0313	0.0051	4.9126	961.3333
01/14/88	6.2500	3,080	0.0937	0.0152	14.6317	975.9650
01/15/88	6.3125	5,312	0.0625	0.0100	9.7597	985.7247
01/18/88	6.4688	12,456	0.1563	0.0248	24.4069	1,010.1316
01/19/88	6.2813	3,020	-0.1875	-0.0290	-29.2790	1,010.1316
01/20/88	6.1250	12,228	-0.1563	-0.0249	-25.1355	984.9961
01/21/88	6.1875	5,248	0.0625	0.0102	10.0510	984.9961
01/22/88	6.1563	6,632	-0.0312	-0.0050	-4.9668	980.0293
01/25/88	6.2813	4,104	0.1250	0.0203	19.8989	980.0293
01/26/88	6.2188	4,464	-0.0625	-0.0100	-9.7515	970.2779
01/27/88	6.1563	6,212	-0.0625	-0.0101	-9.7515	960.5264
01/28/88	6.1875	3,836	0.0312	0.0051	4.8679	960.5264
01/29/88	6.3750	7,640	0.1875	0.0303	29.1069	989.6333
02/01/88	6.2813	3,544	-0.0937	-0.0147	-14.5457	989.6333
02/02/88	6.2813	4,660	0.0000	0.0000	0.0000	989.6333

- The calculation of Column G varies depending on whether volume increased or decreased. If the volume increased from the previous period (as first occurred on 01/06/88), then Column G is Column F *plus* the previous value in Column G. If the volume is equal to or less than the previous period's volume (as first occurred on 01/05/88), then Column G is the previous value in Column G (i.e., the PVI remains unchanged). You can see that Column G only changes when the volume increases, and then Column G changes by the amount in Column F.

PRICE AND VOLUME TREND

Overview

The Price and Volume Trend (PVT) is similar to On Balance Volume (OBV, page 229) in that it is a cumulative total of volume that is adjusted depending on changes in closing prices. However, where OBV adds all volume on days when prices close higher and subtracts all volume on days when prices close lower, the PVT adds/subtracts only a portion of the daily volume. The amount of volume added to the PVT is determined by the amount that prices rose or fell relative to the previous day's close.

Interpretation

The interpretation of the PVT is similar to the interpretation of On Balance Volume (see page 229) and the Volume Accumulation/Distribution Line (see page 48).

Many investors feel that the PVT more accurately illustrates the flow of money into and out of a security than does OBV. This is because OBV adds the same amount of volume to the indicator regardless of whether the security closes up a fraction of a point or doubles in price, whereas the PVT adds only a small portion of volume to the indicator when the price changes by a small percentage and adds a large portion of volume to the indicator when the price changes by a large percentage.

Example

Figure 144 shows Photon Dynamics and the PVT. The bullish divergence (the PVT was trending higher while prices trended lower) was followed by a strong price increase.

FIGURE 144

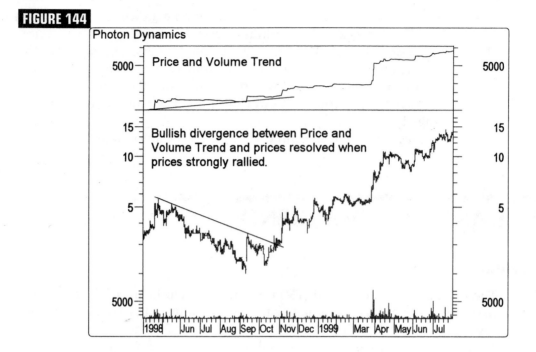

Calculation

The PVT is calculated by multiplying the current period's volume by the percent that the security's price changed, and adding this value to a cumulative total.

$$\left(\left(\frac{Close - Previous\ Close}{Previous\ Close}\right) * Volume\right) + Previous\ PVT$$

For example, if the security's price increased 0.5 percent on volume of 10,000 shares, you would add 50 (i.e., 0.005 * 10,000) to the PVT. If the security's price had closed down 0.5 percent, you would have subtracted 50 from the PVT.

Table 58 illustrates the calculation of the PVT.

- Column D is the close minus the previous close (i.e., the change since the previous close).
- Column E is the value in Column D divided by the previous close (i.e., the percent change since the previous close).
- Column F is the value in Column E multiplied by the volume.
- Column G is the value in Column F plus the previous value in Column G. This is the PVT.

TABLE 58

			PRICE AND VOLUME TREND			
A	B	C	D	E	F	G
Date	Close	Volume	Close minus Previous Close	Column D divided by Previous Close	Column E multiplied by Volume	Column F plus Previous G
04/01/98	3.4375	3,785				
04/02/98	3.5000	4,980	0.0625	0.0182	90.545	90.545
04/03/98	3.4375	4,696	−0.0625	−0.0179	−83.857	6.688
04/06/98	3.5000	2,467	0.0625	0.0182	44.855	51.543
04/07/98	3.5000	3,942	0.0000	0.0000	0.000	51.543
04/08/98	3.6250	2,259	0.1250	0.0357	80.679	132.221

PRICE CHANNEL

Overview

Price Channels are, in essence, dynamic support and resistance levels. Price Channels consist of two lines: an upper channel showing the highest high over the specified number of time periods and a lower channel showing the lowest low during the period. They are constantly adjusted to reflect recent new highs and new lows.

Interpretation

Price Channels are used like other types of channels and bands—they help gauge the ebb and flow of optimism and pessimism. When prices are at or near the upper channel, extreme optimism is indicated—look for prices to meet resistance and to move down to more rational levels. Likewise, when prices are at or near the lower channel, extreme pessimism is indicated—look for prices to find support and move up to more rational levels.

Since Price Channels are calculated from absolute high and low price levels, they tend to provide traditional support and resistance. For example, if prices bounce two or more times off of the bottom channel near the same price level, strong support is indicated. Likewise, if prices rebound two or more times off the top channel near the same price level, strong resistance is indicated.

Interestingly, much like Bollinger Bands (see page 71), narrow Price Channels often precede significant price moves. Several interesting observations involving the combination of a 20-period Bollinger Band and 20-period Price Channel are noted below:

- Expect a significant upward price move when the Price Channel and Bollinger Bands are very narrow and the closing price exceeds the upper Price Channel. Place a protective stop just below the middle Bollinger Band.
- Expect a significant downward price move when the Price Channel and Bollinger Bands are very narrow and the closing price drops below the lower Price Channel. Place a protective stop just above the middle Bollinger Band.
- Expect a short-term pullback against the prevailing uptrend when the Price Channel and Bollinger Bands are wide and the closing price exceeds the upper Price Channel.
- Expect a short-term pullback against the prevailing downtrend when the Price Channel and Bollinger Bands are wide and the closing price exceeds the lower Price Channel.

Example

Figure 145 shows Philip Morris, along with the above-described buy signal of a narrow Bollinger Band and a close above the upper Price Channel.

FIGURE 145

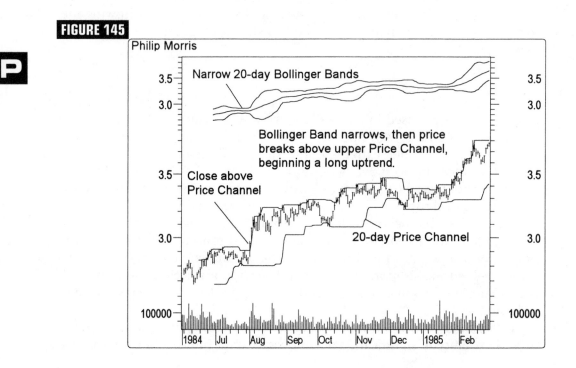

Calculation

The upper price channel is the highest high during the previous *n* periods (*excluding* the current period). The lower price channel is the lowest low during the previous *n* time periods (*excluding* the current period).

Table 59 illustrates the calculation of a 5-day Price Channel.

TABLE 59

| | | | PRICE CHANNEL | |
| A | B | C | D | E |
Date	High	Low	Highest High in last 5 Periods (excluding today)	Lowest Low in last 5 Periods (excluding today)
07/26/84	2.8907	2.8437		
07/27/84	2.9063	2.8543		
07/30/84	2.8750	2.8333		
07/31/84	2.8543	2.8127		
08/01/84	2.9740	2.8647		
08/02/84	3.0730	2.9793	2.9740	2.8127
08/03/84	3.1563	3.0937	3.0730	2.8127
08/06/84	3.1617	3.0677	3.1563	2.8127
08/07/84	3.1147	3.0520	3.1617	2.8127

To better understand the terminology "excluding the current period," refer to 08/02/84. On this date the highest high and lowest low were based on the 5 days from 07/26/84 through 08/01/84 rather than the 5 days from 07/27/84 through 08/02/84 as you might expect.

PRICE OSCILLATOR

Overview

The Price Oscillator displays the difference between two moving averages of a security's price. The difference between the moving averages can be expressed in either points or percentages.

The Price Oscillator is almost identical to the MACD (see page 199), except that the Price Oscillator can use any two user-specified moving averages. (The MACD always uses 12- and 26-day moving averages and always expresses the difference in points.)

Interpretation

Moving average analysis typically generates buy signals when a short-term moving average (or the security's price) rises above a longer-term moving average. Conversely, sell signals are generated when a shorter-term moving average (or the security's price) falls below a longer-term moving average. The Price Oscillator illustrates the cyclical and often profitable signals generated by these one- or two-moving-average systems.

Example

Figure 146 shows Kellogg and a 10-day/30-day Price Oscillator. In this example, the Price Oscillator shows the difference between the moving averages as percentages.

"Buy" arrows indicate when the Price Oscillator rose above zero and "sell" arrows indicate when the indicator fell below zero. This example is typical of the Price Oscillator's effectiveness. Because the Price Oscillator is a trend-following indicator, it does an outstanding job of keeping you on the right side of the market during trending periods (as shown by the arrows labeled B, E, and F). However, during less decisive periods, the Price Oscillator produces small losses (as shown by the arrows labeled A, C, and D).

FIGURE 146

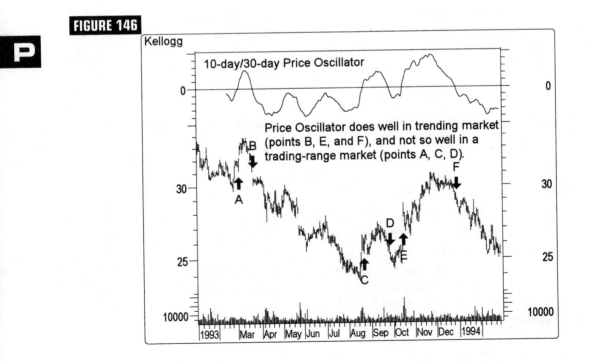

Price Oscillator does well in trending market (points B, E, and F), and not so well in a trading-range market (points A, C, D).

Calculation

The Price Oscillator displays the difference between two moving averages as either points or as percentages.

When the difference is displayed in points, the Price Oscillator is calculated simply by subtracting a longer-term moving average from a shorter-term average:

$$Shorter\ Moving\ Average - Longer\ Moving\ Average$$

When the Price Oscillator displays the difference between the moving averages in percentages, it divides the difference by the longer-term moving average:

$$\left(\frac{Shorter\ Moving\ Average - Longer\ Moving\ Average}{Longer\ Moving\ Average}\right) * 100$$

Table 60 illustrates the calculation of the Price Oscillator.

- Column D is the shorter-term moving average (Column B) minus the longer-term moving average (Column C). This is the Price Oscillator when expressed in points.
- Column E is Column D divided by Column C and multiplied by 100. This is the Price Oscillator when expressed in percentages.

TABLE 60

| | PRICE OSCILLATOR | | | |
| A | B | C | D | E |
Date	Short-Term Moving Average	Long-Term Moving Average	Column B minus Column C	Column D divided by Column C times 100
02/04/94	26.2500	27.7725	-1.5225	-5.4820
02/07/94	26.1250	27.6925	-1.5675	-5.6604
02/08/94	25.6875	27.5850	-1.8975	-6.8787
02/09/94	25.3125	27.4550	-2.1425	-7.8037
02/10/94	25.4375	27.3300	-1.8925	-6.9246
02/11/94	25.9375	27.2125	-1.2750	-4.6853

PRICE RATE-OF-CHANGE

Overview

The Price Rate-of-Change (ROC) indicator displays the difference between the current price and the price *n* time periods ago. The difference can be displayed either in points or as a percentage. The Momentum indicator (see page 195) displays the same information but as a ratio.

Interpretation

It is a well-recognized phenomenon that security prices surge ahead and retract in a cyclical, wavelike motion. This cyclical action is the result of the changing expectations as bulls and bears struggle to control prices.

The ROC displays the wavelike motion in an oscillator format by measuring the amount that prices have changed over a given time period. As prices increase, the ROC rises; as prices fall, the ROC falls. The greater the change in prices, the greater the change in the ROC.

The time period used to calculate the ROC may range from 1 day (which results in a volatile chart showing the daily price change) to 200 days (or longer). The most popular time periods are the 12- and 25-day ROC for short- to intermediate-term trading. These time periods were popularized by Gerald Appel and Fred Hitschler in their book *Stock Market Trading Systems.*

The 12-day ROC is an excellent short- to intermediate-term overbought/oversold indicator. The higher the ROC, the more overbought the security; the lower the ROC, the more likely a rally. However, as with all overbought/oversold indicators, it is prudent to wait for the market to begin to correct (i.e., turn up or down) before placing your trade. A market that appears overbought may remain overbought for some time. In fact, extremely overbought/oversold readings usually imply a *continuation* of the current trend.

The 12-day ROC tends to be very cyclical, oscillating back and forth in a fairly regular cycle. Often, price changes can be anticipated by studying the previous cycles of the ROC and relating the previous cycles to the current market.

Example

Figure 147 shows the 12-day ROC of Walgreen expressed as a percentage. "Buy" arrows indicate each time the ROC fell below, and then rose above, the oversold level of −6.5. "Sell" arrows indicate each time the ROC rose above, and then fell below, the overbought level of +6.5.

The optimum overbought/oversold levels (e.g., ±6.5) vary depending on the security being analyzed and overall market conditions. I selected ±6.5 by drawing a horizontal line on the chart that isolated previous "extreme" levels of Walgreen's 12-day ROC.

Calculation

The Price ROC displays the difference between two prices as either points or as percentages.

FIGURE 147

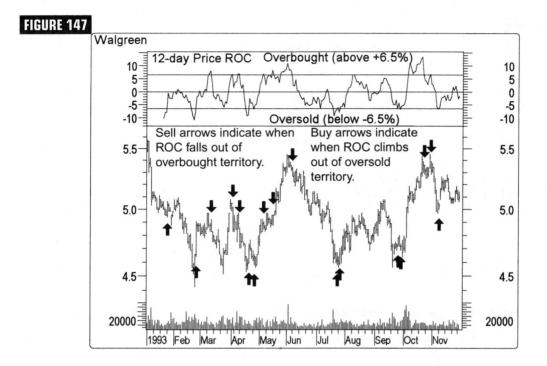

Walgreen

When the difference is displayed in points, the ROC is calculated simply by subtracting the price *n* time periods ago from the current price:

Current Close − Close n-periods ago

When the ROC displays the price change as percentages, it divides the price change by price *n* time periods ago:

$$\left(\frac{Today's\ Close\ -\ Close\ n\text{-}periods\ ago}{Close\ n\text{-}periods\ ago}\right) * 100$$

Table 61 illustrates the calculation of the 3-day Price ROC:

- Column C is the current closing minus the close 3 days ago. This is the 3-day ROC expressed in points.
- Column D is the value in Column C, divided by the close 3 days ago, multiplied by 100. This is the 3-day ROC expressed in percentages.

TABLE 61

| | PRICE RATE-OF-CHANGE | | |
A	B	C	D
Date	Close	Current Close minus Close 3 Days Ago	Column C divided by Close 3 Days Ago times 100
01/04/93	5.5625		
01/05/93	5.3750		
01/06/93	5.3750		
01/07/93	5.0625	-0.5000	-8.99
01/08/93	5.1094	-0.2656	-4.94
01/11/93	5.1094	-0.2656	-4.94
01/12/93	5.0938	0.0313	0.62
01/13/93	5.0000	-0.1094	-2.14

PROJECTION BANDS

Overview

Projection Bands, developed by Mel Widner, Ph.D., are plotted by finding the minimum and maximum prices over the specified number of periods and projecting these forward (parallel to a Linear Regression Trendline, see page 176). The resulting plot consists of two bands representing the minimum and maximum projected price boundaries.

Interpretation

Projections Bands are used much like other types of bands: when prices are at or near the upper band, extreme optimism is indicated—look for prices to move down to more rational levels. Likewise, when prices are at or near the lower band, extreme pessimism is indicated—look for prices to move up to more rational levels. Also, look for periods of narrowing of the bands, to be followed by a breakout (either to the upside or downside).

Example

Figure 148 shows 14-day Projection Bands for Yahoo. The bands narrowed until late February 1998, when prices broke to the upside.

FIGURE 148

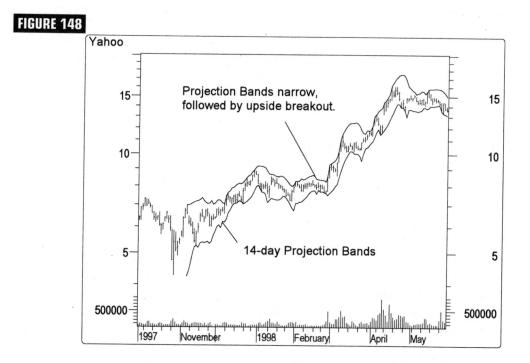

Yahoo

Projection Bands narrow, followed by upside breakout.

14-day Projection Bands

Calculation

Following is the calculation of the upper Projection Band:

$$Max_{i=1}^{n}(High_{-i+1} + (i - 1) * (n\text{-}period\ slope\ of\ high))$$

Following is the calculation of the lower Projection Band:

$$Max_{i=1}^{n}(Low_{-i+1} + (i - 1) * (n\text{-}period\ slope\ of\ low))$$

A table explaining the calculation of Projection Bands is too complex for this book. The A-to-Z Companion Spreadsheet (see page xvii) contains an example of the calculation.

PROJECTION OSCILLATOR

Overview

The Projection Oscillator is a further modification based on the Projection Bands (see page 270). Both were developed by Mel Widner, Ph.D. The Projection Oscillator shows where the current price is relative to the Projection Bands.

The Projection Oscillator is basically a slope-adjusted Stochastic Oscillator. Whereas the Stochastic Oscillator (see page 321) shows the relationship of the current price to its minimum and maximum prices over a recent time period, the Projection Oscillator shows the relationship of the current price to the upper and lower bands. This adjustment makes the Projection Oscillator more responsive to short-term price moves than the Stochastic Oscillator.

A value of 50 indicates that the current price is exactly in the middle of the bands. A value of 100 indicates that prices are touching the upper band. A value of 0 indicates that prices are touching the lower band.

Interpretation

The Projection Oscillator can be used as both a short- and intermediate-term trading oscillator depending on the number of time periods used when calculating the oscillator. When displaying a short-term Projection Oscillator (e.g., 10 to 20 periods), it is popular to use a 3-period moving average of the Projection Oscillator as a trigger line.

Overbought/Oversold.   Buy when the Projection Oscillator falls below a specific level (e.g., 20) and then rises above that level, and sell when the Projection Oscillator rises above a specific level (e.g., 80) and then falls below that level. High values (i.e., above 80) indicate excessive optimism. Low values (i.e., below 20) indicate excessive pessimism.

As with all overbought/oversold indicators, it is best to wait for the security's price to change direction before placing your trades. It is not unusual for overbought/oversold indicators to remain in an overbought/oversold condition for a long time period as the security's price continues to climb/fall.

Crossovers.   Buy when the Projection Oscillator crosses above its trigger line and sell when it crosses below its trigger line. You may want to qualify your trades by requiring that the Crossovers occur above the 70 level or below the 30 level.

Divergences.   Consider selling if prices are making a series of new highs and the Projection Oscillator is failing to surpass its previous highs. Consider buying if prices are making a series of new lows and the Projection Oscillator is failing to surpass its previous low. You may want to qualify your trades by requiring that the Divergence occur above the 70 level or below the 30 level.

FIGURE 149

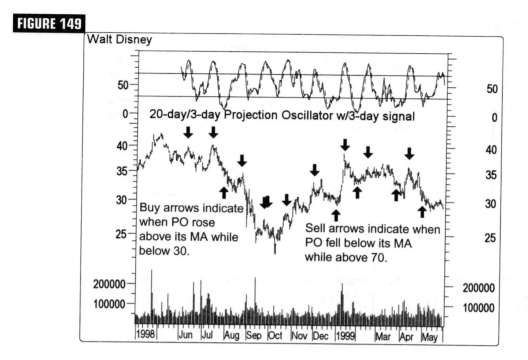

Walt Disney

20-day/3-day Projection Oscillator w/3-day signal

Buy arrows indicate when PO rose above its MA while below 30.

Sell arrows indicate when PO fell below its MA while above 70.

Example

Figure 149 shows a 20-day Projection Oscillator for Walt Disney, smoothed by 3 days, with a 3-day trigger line. Arrows indicate the crossovers that occur below 30 and above 70. As you can see, this indicator would be appropriate for short-term trading.

Calculation

Following is the formula for the Projection Oscillator:

$$\left(\frac{Close - Lower\ Projection\ Band}{Upper\ Projection\ band - Lower\ Project\ Band}\right) * 100$$

Table 62 illustrates the calculation of the Projection Oscillator:

- Columns C and D are Projection Bands, as explained on page 270.
- Column E is the close (Column B) minus the lower Projection Band (Column D).
- Column F is the upper Projection Band (Column C) minus the lower Projection Band (Column D).
- Column G is Column E divided by Column F, multiplied by 100. This is the Projection Oscillator.

TABLE 62

		PROJECTION OSCILLATOR				
A	B	C	D	E	F	G
Date	Close	Upper Band	Lower Band	Close minus Column D	Column C minus Column D	Column E/ Column F times 100
03/11/98	21.0625	23.6316	19.0438	2.0187	4.5878	44.0015
03/12/98	20.5000	24.1550	19.5494	0.9506	4.6056	20.6401
03/13/98	20.8438	24.5941	20.0179	0.8259	4.5762	18.0477
03/16/98	21.2500	24.9008	20.3877	0.8623	4.5131	19.1066

PUBLIC SHORT RATIO

Overview

The Public Short Ratio (PSR) shows the relationship between the number of public short sales and the total number of short sales. (The Public Short Ratio is sometimes referred to as the nonmember short ratio.)

Interpretation

The interpretation of the PSR assumes one premise: that of the short sellers, the public is the worst (well, except for the odd-lot traders, whose indicators begin on page 222). If this is true, then we should buy when the public is shorting and sell when the public is long. Historically, this premise has held true.

Generally speaking, the higher the PSR, the more bearish the public and the more likely prices will increase (given the above premise). Historically, it has been considered bullish when the 10-week moving average of the PSR is above 25 percent and bearish when the moving average is below 25 percent. The further the moving average is in the bullish or bearish territory, the more likely it is that a correction/rally will take place. Also, the longer the indicator is in the bullish/bearish territory, the better the chances of a market move. For more information on the PSR, I suggest reading the discussion on the nonmember short ratio in *Stock Market Logic* by Norman G. Fosback.

FIGURE 150

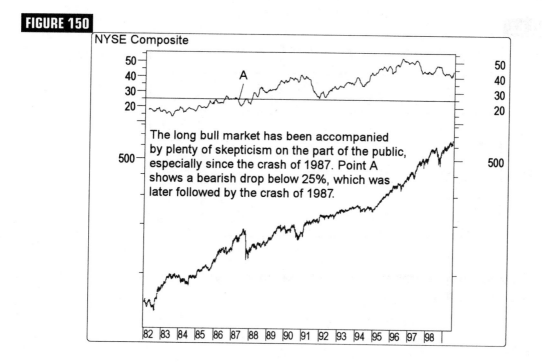

NYSE Composite

The long bull market has been accompanied by plenty of skepticism on the part of the public, especially since the crash of 1987. Point A shows a bearish drop below 25%, which was later followed by the crash of 1987.

Example

Figure 150 shows the New York Stock Exchange Composite Index and a 10-week moving average of the PSR.

The 10-week moving average of the PSR has been above the once-significant level of 25 percent since the crash of 1987, indicating that the public has doubted the strength of the bull market for the majority of its duration.

At the point labeled A, the PSR dropped below 25 percent into bearish territory (i.e., the public was too bullish). Over the next several months, the PSR continued to move lower as the public became more and more bullish. During this period, prices surged upward, adding to the bullish frenzy. The subsequent crash of 1987 gave the public a strong dose of reality.

Calculation

The PSR is calculated by dividing the number of public short sales by the total number of short sales. The result is the percentage of public shorts. This is shown in Table 63.

$$\frac{Total\ Public\ Short\ Sales}{Total\ Short\ Sales} * 100$$

TABLE 63

| | PUBLIC SHORT RATIO | | |
| A | B | C | D |
Date	Total Public Short Sales	Total Short Sales	Public Short Ratio
01/02/98	74.5	195	38.205
01/09/98	154.7	310	49.903
01/16/98	142.4	324	43.951
01/23/98	114.1	263	43.384
01/30/98	137.6	337	40.831
02/06/98	162.7	398	40.879
02/13/98	149.3	350	42.657
02/20/98	110.8	256	43.281

PUTS/CALLS RATIO

Overview

Developed by Martin Zweig, the Puts/Calls Ratio (P/C Ratio) is a market sentiment indicator that shows the relationship between the number of puts to calls traded on the Chicago Board Options Exchange (CBOE).

Traditionally, options are traded by unsophisticated, impatient investors who are lured by the potential for huge profits with a small capital outlay. Interestingly, the actions of these investors provide excellent signals for market tops and bottoms.

Interpretation

A call gives an investor the right to purchase 100 shares of stock at a predetermined price. Investors who purchase calls expect stock prices to rise in the coming months. Conversely, a put gives an investor the right to sell 100 shares of stock at a pre-set price. Investors purchasing puts expect stock prices to decline. (An exception to these general rules is that puts and calls can also be purchased to hedge other investments, even other options.)

Because investors who purchase calls expect the market to rise, and investors who purchase puts expect the market to decline, the relationship between the number of puts and calls illustrates the bullish/bearish expectations of these traditionally ineffective investors.

The higher the level of the P/C Ratio, the more bearish these investors are on the market. Conversely, lower readings indicate high call volume and thus bullish expectations.

TABLE 64

	10-Day Moving Average of P/C Ratio	4-Week Moving Average of P/C Ratio
Excessively Bearish (buy)	Greater than 80	Greater than 70
Excessively Bullish (sell)	Less than 45	Less than 40

The P/C Ratio is a contrarian indicator. When it reaches "excessive" levels, the market usually corrects by moving in the opposite direction. Table 64 defines general guidelines for interpreting the P/C Ratio. Keep in mind that the market does not have to correct itself just because investors are excessive in their bullish/bearish beliefs! As with all technical analysis tools, you should use the P/C Ratio in conjunction with other market indicators.

Example

Figure 151 shows the S&P 500 and a 4-week moving average of the P/C Ratio. Since the range of the P/C Ratio varies with time as it is affected by strategies other than naked option buying (such as institutional hedging), it is helpful to look for extreme levels relative to the recent range rather than absolute values. Thus, I drew a Standard Error Channel (see page 315) of the

FIGURE 151

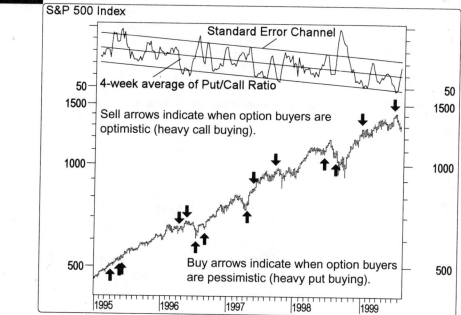

S&P 500 Index

Standard Error Channel

4-week average of Put/Call Ratio

Sell arrows indicate when option buyers are optimistic (heavy call buying).

Buy arrows indicate when option buyers are pessimistic (heavy put buying).

4-week moving average of the P/C Ratio to better see relatively high and low values. "Buy" arrows indicate when investors were excessively pessimistic (the P/C Ratio was above the upper band) and "sell" arrows indicate when they were excessively optimistic (the P/C Ratio was below the lower band). The arrows certainly show that investors are buying puts when they should be buying calls, and vice versa.

Calculation

The P/C Ratio is calculated by dividing the volume of puts by the volume of calls and then multiplying by 100. Table 65 illustrates the calculations.

$$\frac{Total\ CBOE\ Put\ Volume}{Total\ CBOE\ Call\ Volume} * 100$$

TABLE 65

| | PUTS/CALLS RATIO | | |
| A | B | C | D |
Date	Put Volume	Call Volume	Puts/Calls Ratio
01/02/98	183	239	76.5690
01/05/98	255	447	57.0470
01/06/98	245	413	59.3220
01/07/98	329	445	73.9326
01/08/98	340	464	73.2759
01/09/98	511	675	75.7037
01/12/98	467	543	86.0037
01/13/98	378	572	66.0839

QSTICK

Overview

The Qstick indicator, developed by Tushar Chande, provides a way to quantify the amount and size of black and white bars in a Candlestick chart (see page 79). Black Candlesticks represent a period when the price closed lower than it opened. White Candlesticks represent a period when the price closed higher than it opened. The Qstick indicator is simply a moving average of the difference between open and close prices.

Interpretation

Qstick values below zero indicate more black than white in the Candlesticks that cover the specified period, and therefore a bearish bias for the security. Values above zero indicate more white than black in the Candlesticks that cover the specified period, and therefore a bullish bias for the security.

Crossovers.   Buy when the indicator crosses above zero. Sell when it crosses below zero.

Extreme Levels.   Buy when the Qstick indicator is at an extremely low level and turning up. Sell when the Qstick indicator is at an extremely high level and turning down. You may want to plot a short-term moving average on the Qstick to serve as a trigger line.

Divergences.   Buy when the Qstick is moving up and prices are moving down. Sell when the Qstick is moving down and prices are moving up. You may want to consider waiting for the price to confirm the new direction before placing the trade.

Example

Figure 152 shows an 8-day Qstick of Hewlett-Packard. In May 1998, the Qstick reached its highest level in several years. This marked an extreme in

FIGURE 152

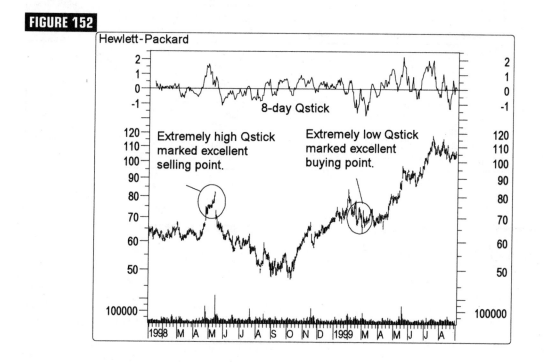

the indicator and a peak in the stock price, at which point the stock price fell from around 80 to a low near 47 just 5 months later. The extreme low Qstick value in March 1999 also marked an excellent buying point.

Calculation

The Qstick is the sum of the "close−open" over the last "*n*" days, divided by "*n*":

$$\frac{\sum_{1}^{n} (Close - Open)}{n}$$

Table 66 illustrates the calculation of the 4-day Qstick.

- Column D is the close (Column C) minus the open (Column B).
- Column E is the total of the last four periods in Column D.
- Column F is the value in Column E divided by 4 and is the Qstick indicator.

TABLE 66

			QSTICK		
A	**B**	**C**	**D**	**E**	**F**
Date	Open	Close	Column C minus Column B	4-Day sum of Column D	Column E divided by 4
01/02/98	62.5625	64.5625	2.0000		
01/05/98	64.6250	64.1250	-0.5000		
01/06/98	63.5625	64.3125	0.7500		
01/07/98	63.9375	64.8750	0.9375	3.1875	0.7969
01/08/98	64.5000	65.1875	0.6875	1.8750	0.4688
01/09/98	65.1875	62.0000	-3.1875	-0.8125	-0.2031
01/12/98	60.5625	62.1875	1.6250	0.0625	0.0156
01/13/98	62.2500	63.8750	1.6250	0.7500	0.1875

QUADRANT LINES

Overview

Quadrant Lines are a series of horizontal lines that divide the highest and lowest values (usually prices) into four equal sections.

Interpretation

Quadrant Lines are primarily intended to aid in the visual inspection of price movements. They help you see the highest, lowest, and average price during a specified period.

Example

An interesting technique is to display a Linear Regression Trendline (see page 176) and Quadrant Lines. This combination displays the highest, lowest, and average price, as well as the average slope of the prices. I used this technique on Figure 153 of General Mills.

FIGURE 153

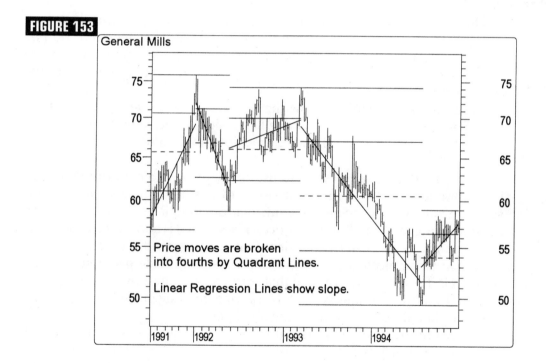

Calculation

Quadrant Lines are calculated by finding the highest high and the lowest low during the time period being analyzed. The top line is drawn at the highest price during the time period, and the bottom line is drawn at the lowest price during the time period. The remaining three lines are then drawn so that they divide the section between the highest high and the lowest low into four equal sections. The center line (the "mean") is usually displayed as a dotted line.

R-SQUARED

Overview

The r-Squared indicator measures how closely prices follow a Linear Regression Trendline (see page 176). This indicates the strength of the trend—the more closely prices move in a linear relationship with the passing of time, the stronger the trend.

Interpretation

It is helpful to consider r-Squared in relation to Linear Regression Slope (see page 174). While Linear Regression Slope gives you the general direction of the trend (positive or negative), r-Squared gives you the strength of the trend. A high r-Squared value can be associated with a high positive or negative Linear Regression Slope.

Although it is useful to know the r-Squared value, ideally, you should use r-Squared in tandem with Linear Regression Slope. High r-Squared values accompanied by a large Linear Regression Slope value are of most interest to traders.

One of the most useful ways to use r-Squared is as a confirming indicator. A momentum-based indicator (e.g., Stochastics, RSI, CCI, etc.) can be supplemented with an r-Squared confirmation. R-Squared provides a means of quantifying the "trendiness" of prices. If r-Squared is above its critical value and heading up, you can be confident that a strong trend is present.

When using momentum-based indicators, only trade overbought/oversold levels if you have determined that prices are trendless or weakening (i.e., a low or lowering r-Squared value). In a strong trending market, prices can remain overbought or oversold for extended periods.

To determine if the trend is statistically significant for a given n-period Linear Regression Trendline, plot the r-Squared indicator and refer to Table 67. This table shows the values of r-Squared required for a 95-percent confidence level at various time periods. If the r-Squared value is less than the critical values shown, you should assume that prices show no statistically significant trend.

You may even consider opening a short-term position opposite the prevailing trend when you observe r-Squared rounding off at extreme levels. For example, if the slope is positive and r-Squared is above 0.80 and begins to turn down, you may consider selling or opening a short position.

TABLE 67

Number of Periods	R-Squared Critical Value (95% confidence)
5	.77
10	.40
14	.27
20	.20
25	.16
30	.13
50	.08
60	.06
120	.03

Example

Figure 154 of Neiman Marcus shows a 14-day r-Squared and a 14-day Linear Regression Slope. In December 1997, the Linear Regression Slope crossed above 0 (indicating an uptrend) and the r-Squared crossed 0.27 (indicating that the trend was meaningful). This marked the start of a strong rally.

FIGURE 154

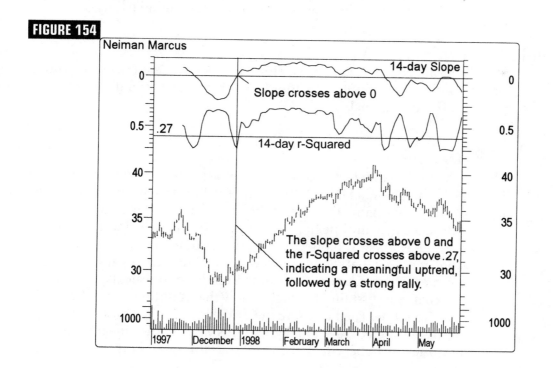

Calculation

The calculation of r-Squared is beyond the scope of this book. R-Squared can be calculated in a spreadsheet using the *rsq()* function (which calculates r-Squared). The A-to-Z Companion Spreadsheet (see page xvii) contains examples calculating r-Squared manually as well as using the *rsq()* function.

RAFF REGRESSION CHANNEL

Overview

The Raff Regression Channel, developed by Gilbert Raff, provides a precise quantitative way to define a price trend and its boundaries.

Interpretation

Raff Regression Channels contain price movement with the bottom channel line providing support and the top channel line providing resistance. Prices at either extreme should be expected to return to the middle line.

Example

Figure 155 illustrates a Raff Regression Channel of Caterpillar that shows prices continually returning to the Linear Regression Trendline after approaching either channel.

Calculation

The Regression Channel is constructed by plotting two parallel, equidistant lines above and below a Linear Regression Trendline (see page 176). The distance between the channel lines and the Linear Regression Trendline is the greatest distance that any one high or low price is from the Linear Regression Trendline. The channel is plotted at the farthest point away from the Linear Regression Trendline that the market has allowed the security to trade.

The center line is a Linear Regression Trendline. To calculate the upper and lower channels, first find the high or low that is furthest from the Linear Regression Trendline. Then measure the distance from the Linear Regression Trendline to this high or low. Finally, add this value to the Linear Regression Trendline to get the upper channel and subtract this value from the Linear Regression Trendline to get the lower channel.

FIGURE 155

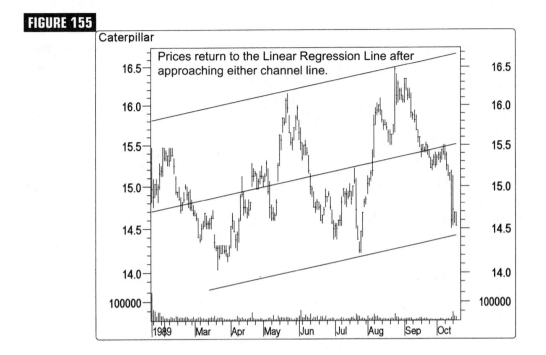

Caterpillar

Prices return to the Linear Regression Line after approaching either channel line.

Given that the upper and lower channels are set at the farthest point the security has traded from the Linear Regression Trendline, it's mathematically impossible for the security to trade outside of the channels.

RANDOM WALK INDEX

Overview

The Random Walk Index (RWI), developed by Michael Poulos, attempts to measure whether a security's price movement can be attributed to randomness or to a statistically significant trend.

The Random Walk Index is based on the geometric concept that the shortest distance between two points is a straight line. The farther prices stray from a straight line during a move between two points in time, the less efficient (and more random) the movement.

The RWI is separated into two plots: an RWI of high prices to measure uptrends and an RWI of low prices to measure downtrends.

Interpretation

Poulos found significant evidence during his research that the "dividing line" between short- and long-term time frames for most futures and stocks is near 8 to 10 periods. Therefore, he feels an effective trading system using the RWI can be devised using two different time frames—a short-term RWI (2 to 7 periods) for the market's frantic, random side and a long-term RWI (8 to 64 periods) for the market's steady, trending side.

Peaks in the short-term RWI of highs tend to coincide with price peaks. Peaks in the short-term RWI of lows tend to coincide with price troughs. Readings of the long-term RWI of highs above 1.0 provides a good indication of a sustainable uptrend. Readings of the long-term RWI of lows above 1.0 provide a good indication of a sustainable downtrend.

Therefore, Poulus feels that an effective trading system could be built that opens trades (after short-term pullbacks against the direction of the long-term trend) using the following guidelines:

- Enter long (or close short) when the long-term RWI of the highs is greater than 1.0 and the short-term RWI of lows peaks above 1.0.
- Enter short (or close long) when the long-term RWI of the lows is greater than 1.0 and the short-term RWI of highs peaks above 1.0.

FIGURE 156

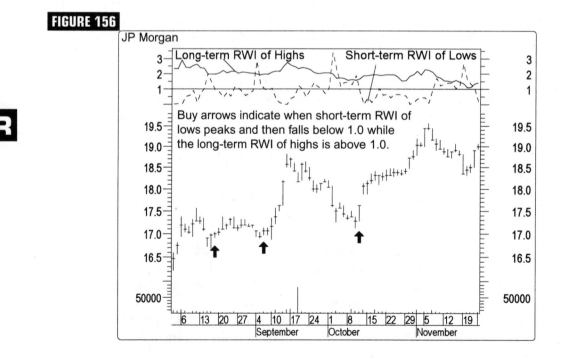

Example

Figure 156 shows JP Morgan with a short term RWI of the lows and a long-term RWI of the highs. An excellent buying opportunity occurred each time the short-term RWI of the lows peaked and then crossed below 1 as the long-term RWI was still above 1.

Calculation

The calculations for the RWI are beyond the scope of this book. Refer to the November 1993 issue of *Technical Analysis of Stocks and Commodities.*

RANGE INDICATOR

Overview

The Range Indicator, developed by Jack Weinberg, is based on his observation that changes in the average period's *intra*period range (high to low) as compared to the average period's *inter*period range (close to close) precede the start of a new trend or the end of the current trend.

For additional information on the Range Indicator, refer to the June 1995 issue of *Technical Analysis of Stocks and Commodities.*

Interpretation

The Range Indicator shows when the intraperiod high to low ranges exceed the interperiod close to close ranges.

This approach proves useful in identifying the start and end of trends. When the intraperiod ranges are dramatically higher than the interperiod ranges, the security is considered "out of balance" and the Range Indicator will be at a high level. When at a high level, look for the current trend to end. Conversely, when the Range Indicator is at a low level (e.g., below 20), look for the emergence of a new trend.

Weinberg found that the Range Indicator improves many momentum and trend-following trading systems. For example, he found that the results of a basic two moving averages crossover system (see page 203) on the four major currencies were dramatically improved by filtering the signals with the Range Indicator. Profits, number of trades, and risk were dramatically improved by waiting to enter a long position until the Range Indicator crossed above a defined low level and then waiting to exit until the indicator crossed above a defined high level.

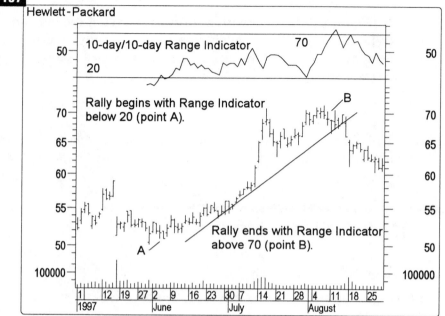

Example

Figure 157 shows a 10-day Range Indicator slowed by 10 days for Hewlett-Packard. Notice how a new trend began while the indicator was below 20. The Range Indicator also warned of the end of the trend, with a reading above 70 just before the upward trendline was broken.

Calculation

Table 68 illustrates the calculation of the Range Indicator where the Range periods ("r") are 5 and the Smoothing periods ("m") are 3:

- Column F is the True Range as explained on page 68. Note that the True Range cannot be calculated until the second day.
- If today's close (Column D) is greater than the previous close, then Column G is Column F divided by the change in the close; otherwise Column G is set to Column F.
- Column H is the minimum value of Column G over the last Range periods (e.g., 5 in this example).
- Column I is the maximum value of Column G over the last Range periods.

TABLE 68

A	B	C	D	E	F	G	H	I	J	K
Date	High	Low	Close	Volume	True Range	See Text	5-Day min of Column G	5-Day max of Column G	See Text	3-Day EMA of Column J
12/02/99	249.750	227.750	245.812	98,081						
12/03/99	258.750	248.938	253.000	100,081	12.9380	1.7999				
12/06/99	282.000	250.688	280.812	160,982	31.3120	1.1258				
12/07/99	353.000	286.125	348.000	663,351	72.1880	1.0744				
12/08/99	329.312	311.000	319.625	249,087	37.0000	37.0000				
12/09/99	341.250	312.062	340.000	114,180	29.1880	1.4325	1.0744	37.0000	0.9968	0.9968
12/10/99	357.500	334.250	353.500	95,457	23.2500	1.7222	1.0744	37.0000	1.8032	1.4000
12/13/99	356.250	344.500	351.062	56,966	11.7500	11.7500	1.0744	37.0000	29.7158	15.5579
12/14/99	350.500	333.000	333.125	72,000	18.0620	18.0620	1.4325	37.0000	46.7547	31.1563
12/15/99	334.750	315.500	327.500	82,831	19.2500	19.2500	1.4325	19.2500	100.0000	65.5782
12/16/99	341.875	332.375	341.000	49,703	14.3750	1.0648	1.0648	19.2500	0.0000	32.7891
12/17/99	352.125	337.000	350.000	51,630	15.1250	1.6806	1.0648	19.2500	3.3859	18.0875
12/20/99	369.875	346.000	369.500	68,821	23.8750	1.2244	1.0648	19.2500	0.8773	9.4824
12/21/99	408.312	364.812	405.562	101,076	43.5000	1.2063	1.0648	19.2500	0.7778	5.1301
12/22/99	421.188	394.750	419.312	86,393	26.4380	1.9228	1.0648	1.9228	100.0000	52.5651
12/23/99	426.250	400.000	402.625	46,171	26.2500	26.2500	1.2063	26.2500	100.0000	76.2825
12/27/99	428.062	377.875	415.000	95,395	50.1870	4.0555	1.2063	26.2500	11.3771	43.8298
12/28/99	420.000	390.000	390.250	52,241	30.0000	30.0000	1.2063	30.0000	100.0000	71.9149
12/29/99	410.000	394.000	403.688	29,408	19.7500	1.4697	1.4697	30.0000	0.0000	35.9575
12/30/99	448.000	406.750	416.062	62,431	44.3120	3.5811	1.4697	30.0000	7.4004	21.6789

R

- If Column I minus Column H is greater than zero, then Column J is set using the following stochastic-like equation:

$$Column\ J = \frac{Column\ G - Column\ H}{Column\ I - Column\ H} * 100$$

Otherwise Column J is set as follows:

$$Column\ J = (Column\ G - Column\ H) * 100$$

- Column K is a 3-day exponential moving average of Column J. When Column J is valid (i.e., 12/09/99), Column K is seeded with Column J (i.e., 0.9968). Subsequent rows in Column K are calculated by multiplying the value in Column J by 0.5, then multiplying the previous day's value in Column K by 0.5, and finally adding these two values together.

    (The first 0.5 was calculated as "2 / (3+1)" as explained on page 208. The second 0.5 was calculated as "1–0.5" as explained on page 208.)

RECTANGLE

Overview

A Rectangle, as the name implies, is simply a rectangular box containing the price action. It is another way of showing support and resistance (see page 14).

Interpretation

The top of the rectangle can be considered support, while the bottom is resistance. Look for breakouts above or below these levels.

Example

Figure 158 shows several Rectangles enclosing sideways trading action for Wal-Mart. When each Rectangle was exceeded, a strong move ensued.

FIGURE 158

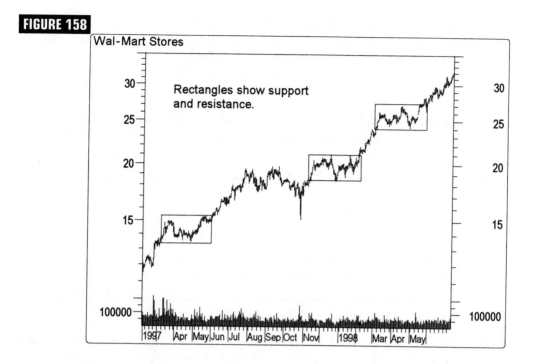

Rectangles show support and resistance.

RELATIVE MOMENTUM INDEX

Overview

The Relative Momentum Index (RMI), developed by Roger Altman, is a variation on the Relative Strength Index (RSI) (see page 297) that adds a momentum component.

Instead of counting up and down days from close to close as the RSI does, the RMI counts up and down days from the close relative to the close n periods ago (this is the momentum parameter, which is not necessarily 1 as required by the RSI). So as the name of the indicator reflects, "momentum" is substituted for "strength."

Interpretation

As an oscillator, the RMI exhibits the same strengths and weaknesses of other overbought/oversold indicators. During strong trending markets, the RMI will remain at overbought or oversold levels for an extended period.

However, during non-trending markets, the RMI tends to oscillate predictably between an overbought level of 70 to 90 and an oversold level of 10 to 30.

Since the RMI is based on the RSI, many of the same interpretation methods can be applied. In fact, many of these "situations" are more clearly manifested with the RMI than with the RSI.

Tops and Bottoms.   The RMI usually tops above 70 and bottoms below 30. The RMI usually forms these tops and bottoms before the underlying price chart.

Chart Formations.   The RMI often forms chart patterns (such as the Head-and-Shoulders price pattern or Triangles) that may or may not be visible on the price chart.

Failure Swings.   Failure Swings are also known as support or resistance penetrations or breakouts. A Failure Swing is where the RMI surpasses a previous high (peak) or falls below a recent low (trough).

Support and Resistance,   The RMI shows, sometimes more clearly than the price chart, levels of support and resistance.

Divergence.   As discussed above, this occurs when the price makes a new high (or low) that is not confirmed by a new RMI high (or low).

FIGURE 159

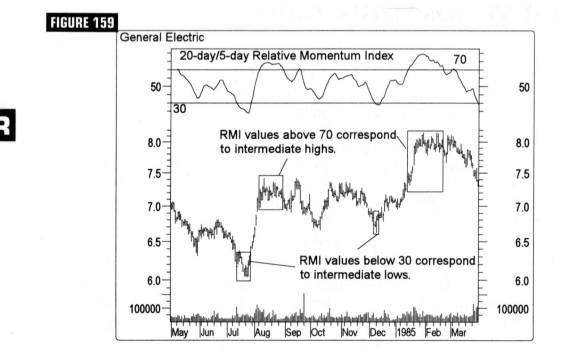

RELATIVE MOMENTUM INDEX

A	B	C	D	E	F	G	H
		If 4-day price change > 0 4-day price change	If 4-day price change < 0 absolute value of 4-day price change	Smoothed Column C	Smoothed Column D	Column E divided by Column F	Column G divided by Column G+1 multiplied by 100
Date	Close						
02/01/84	6.8750						
02/02/84	6.9375						
02/03/84	6.8125						
02/06/84	6.6095						
02/07/84	6.7345	0.0000	0.1405				
02/08/84	6.6720	0.0000	0.2655				
02/09/84	6.6250	0.0000	0.1875				
02/10/84	6.6875	0.0780	0.0000				
02/13/84	6.5470	0.0000	0.1875				
02/14/84	6.6563	0.0000	0.0157				
02/15/84	6.6720	0.0470	0.0000				
02/16/84	6.6563	0.0000	0.0312	0.0156	0.1035	0.1510	13.1179
02/17/84	6.5938	0.0468	0.0000	0.0195	0.0906	0.2156	17.7353
02/21/84	6.4845	0.0000	0.1718	0.0171	0.1007	0.1696	14.5019
02/22/84	6.5000	0.0000	0.1720	0.0149	0.1096	0.1363	11.9988
02/23/84	6.5000	0.0000	0.1563	0.0131	0.1155	0.1133	10.1750
02/24/84	6.7188	0.1250	0.0000	0.0271	0.1010	0.2679	21.1322
02/27/84	6.6407	0.1562	0.0000	0.0432	0.0884	0.4888	32.8331

TABLE 69

R

Example

Figure 159 on page 292 shows General Electric and a 20-day RMI with 5 momentum days. Notice that when the RMI peaks above 70 and bottoms below 30, it corresponds to intermediate high and low prices.

Calculation

The calculation of the RMI is the same as for the RSI, except that the RMI uses a variable number of momentum periods in calculating the price change, whereas the RSI always uses 1 for the momentum period. Thus, a 20-period RMI with a 1-period momentum is equivalent to a 20-period RSI. As the momentum parameter is increased, the oscillation range of the RMI becomes wider and the fluctuations become smoother.

Table 69 on page 293 illustrates the calculation of an 8-period RMI with 4 momentum periods.

- Column C varies, based on the close versus the close n periods ago (i.e., 4 periods). If the current close is greater than the close 4 periods ago, Column C is the 4-period change in the closing price. Otherwise, Column C is zero.
- Column D also varies based on the close versus the close n periods ago. If the current close is less than the close 4 periods ago, Column C is the absolute value of the 4-period change in the closing price. (The term "absolute value" means "regardless of sign." For example, the absolute value of -3 is 3.)
- Column E is an 8-period Wilder's Smoothing (see page 364) of Column C.
- Column F is an 8-period Wilder's Smoothing of Column D.
- Column G is Column C (the smoothed upward price change) divided by Column F (the smoothed downward price change).
- Column H is Column G divided by "Column G plus 1." It is then multiplied by 100. This is the RMI.

RELATIVE STRENGTH, COMPARATIVE

Overview

Comparative Relative Strength compares two securities to show how the securities are performing relative to each other. Be careful not to confuse Comparative Relative Strength with the Relative Strength Index (see page 297).

Interpretation

Comparative Relative Strength compares a security's price change with that of a "base" security. When the Comparative Relative Strength indicator is moving up, it shows that the security is performing better than the base security. When the indicator is moving sideways, it shows that both securities are performing the same (i.e., rising and falling by the same percentages). When the indicator is moving down, it shows that the security is performing worse than the base security (i.e., not rising as fast or falling faster).

Comparative Relative Strength is often used to compare a security's performance with a market index. It is also useful in developing spreads (i.e., buy the best performer and short the weaker issue).

Usually the ratio on the first day is subtracted from all days to start the indicator at zero. Thus, if the indicator is less than zero, it shows that the security has underperformed the base security during the time period displayed.

Example

Figure 160 shows Compaq, Dell, and the Comparative Relative Strength of Dell compared to Compaq.

FIGURE 160

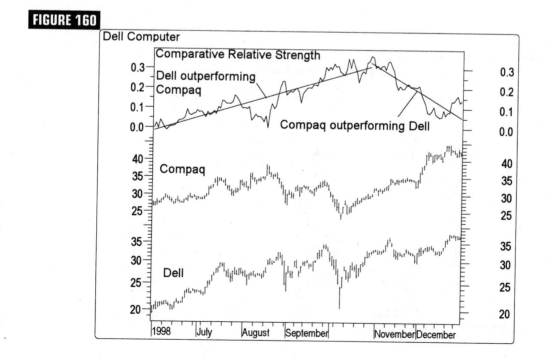

R

The Comparative Relative Strength indicator shows that Dell's price outperformed Compaq's price from June to October of 1998. It also shows that Dell's price then underperformed Compaq's price during November and December of 1998. (I drew the trendlines on the Comparative Relative Strength indicator using Linear Regression Trendlines, page 176.)

Calculation

The Comparative Relative Strength indicator is calculated by dividing one security's price by a second security's price (i.e., the "base" security). The result of this division is the ratio, or relationship, between the two securities.

Often the value of the ratio on the first day is subtracted from all days to "normalize" the indicator so it begins at zero.

Table 70 illustrates the calculation of the Comparative Relative Strength indicator.

- Column D is the raw (i.e., not normalized) indicator. It is calculated by dividing Column B by Column C. Note that Column C is considered the "base" security.
- Column E is the normalized indicator. It is calculated by subtracting the *first* value in Column D (i.e., 0.3602) from all values in Column D.

TABLE 70

| | COMPARATIVE RELATIVE STRENGTH | | | |
A	B	C	D	E
Date	Dell	Compaq	Column B divided by Column C	Column D minus 1st Value in Column D
01/05/98	11.0312	30.6250	0.3602	0.0000
01/06/98	11.0547	30.3125	0.3647	0.0045
01/07/98	10.7812	29.7188	0.3628	0.0026
01/08/98	10.7734	29.6562	0.3633	0.0031
01/09/98	10.3984	28.4688	0.3653	0.0051
01/12/98	10.8828	28.0000	0.3887	0.0285
01/13/98	11.2109	29.5625	0.3792	0.0190
01/14/98	11.4219	29.1250	0.3922	0.0320
01/15/98	11.4531	29.0312	0.3945	0.0343
01/16/98	11.5938	29.5625	0.3922	0.0320

RELATIVE STRENGTH INDEX

Overview

The Relative Strength Index (RSI) is a popular oscillator. It was first introduced by Welles Wilder in an article in *Commodities* (now known as *Futures*) magazine in June 1978. Step-by-step instructions on calculating and interpreting the RSI are also provided in Wilder's book *New Concepts in Technical Trading Systems*.

The name "Relative Strength Index" is slightly misleading, as the RSI does not compare the relative strength of two securities but rather the internal strength of a single security. A more appropriate name might be "Internal Strength Index." Relative strength charts that compare two market indices, which are often referred to as "Comparative Relative Strength," are discussed beginning on page 294.

Interpretation

When Wilder introduced the RSI, he recommended using a 14-day RSI. Since then, the 9-day and 25-day RSIs have also gained popularity. Because you can vary the number of time periods in the RSI calculation, I suggest that you experiment to find the period that works best for you. (The fewer days used to calculate the RSI, the more volatile the indicator.)

The RSI is a price-following oscillator that ranges between 0 and 100. A popular method of analyzing the RSI is to look for a divergence (see page 36) in which the security is making a new high but the RSI is failing to surpass its previous high. This divergence is an indication of an impending reversal. When the RSI then turns down and falls below its most recent trough, it is said to have completed a "failure swing." The failure swing is considered a confirmation of the impending reversal.

In his book, Wilder discusses five uses of the RSI in analyzing commodity charts. These methods can be applied to other security types as well.

Tops and Bottoms.   The RSI usually tops above 70 and bottoms below 30. It usually forms these tops and bottoms before the underlying price chart.

Chart Formations.   The RSI often forms chart patterns such as Head-and-Shoulders (see page 246) or Triangles (see page 248) that may or may not be visible on the price chart.

Failure Swings. Failure Swings are also known as support or resistance penetrations or breakouts. A Failure Swing is where the RSI surpasses a previous high (peak) or falls below a recent low (trough).

Support and Resistance. The RSI shows, sometimes more clearly than prices themselves, levels of support and resistance.

Divergences. As discussed above, divergences occur when the price makes a new high (or low) that is not confirmed by a new high (or low) in the RSI. Prices usually correct and move in the direction of the RSI.

For additional information on the RSI, refer to Wilder's book.

Example

Figure 161 shows Black & Decker and its 14-day RSI. A bullish divergence occurred from August to December as prices were falling while the RSI was rising. Prices subsequently corrected and trended upward. The new highs throughout 1998 were confirmed by new highs in the RSI.

FIGURE 161

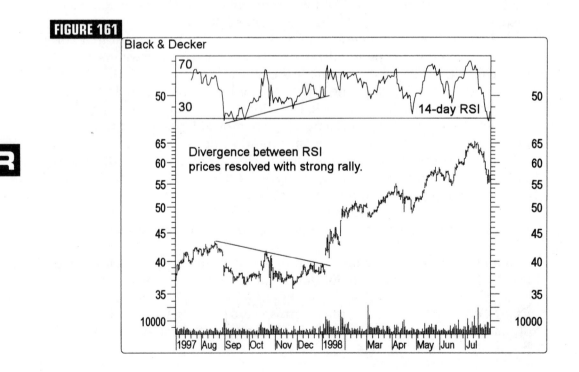

TABLE 71

RELATIVE STRENGTH INDEX

A	B	C	D	E	F	G	H	I	J
Date	Close	Upward Price Change	Smoothed Column C	Downward Price Change	Smoothed Column E	Column D divided by Column F	Column G plus 1.0	100 divided by Column G	100 minus Column I
07/01/97	37.8750								
07/02/97	39.5000	1.6250		0.0000					
07/03/97	38.7500	0.0000		0.7500					
07/07/97	39.8125	1.0625		0.0000					
07/08/97	40.0000	0.1875		0.0000					
07/09/97	39.8750	0.0000	0.5750	0.1250	0.1750	3.2857	4.2857	23.3333	76.6667
07/10/97	40.1875	0.3125	0.5225	0.0000	0.1400	3.7321	4.7321	21.1321	78.8679
07/11/97	41.2500	1.0625	0.6305	0.0000	0.1120	5.6295	6.6295	15.0842	84.9158
07/14/97	41.1250	0.0000	0.5044	0.1250	0.1146	4.4014	5.4014	18.5137	81.486
07/15/97	41.6250	0.5000	0.5035	0.0000	0.0917	5.4921	6.4921	15.4032	84.5968
07/16/97	41.2500	0.0000	0.4028	0.3750	0.1483	2.7154	3.7154	26.9149	73.0851
07/17/97	40.1875	0.0000	0.3223	1.0625	0.3312	0.9731	1.9731	50.6827	49.3173
07/18/97	39.9375	0.0000	0.2578	0.2500	0.3149	0.8186	1.8186	54.9881	45.0119
07/21/97	39.9375	0.0000	0.2062	0.0000	0.2520	0.8186	1.8186	54.9881	45.0119
07/22/97	40.5000	0.5625	0.2775	0.0000	0.2016	1.3767	2.3767	42.0748	57.9252
07/23/97	41.9375	1.4375	0.5095	0.0000	0.1612	3.1597	4.1597	24.0404	75.9596
07/24/97	42.2500	0.3125	0.4701	0.0000	0.1290	3.6442	4.6442	21.5324	78.4676
07/25/97	42.2500	0.0000	0.3761	0.0000	0.1032	3.6442	4.6442	21.5324	78.4676
07/28/97	41.8750	0.0000	0.3009	0.3750	0.1576	1.9095	2.9095	34.3701	65.6299
07/29/97	41.8750	0.0000	0.2407	0.0000	0.1260	1.9095	2.9095	34.3701	65.6299

Calculation

The basic formula of the RSI is as follows:

$$100 - \left(\frac{100}{1 + \left(\dfrac{U}{D}\right)} \right)$$

Where:

- U = An average of upward price change
- D = An average of downward price change
  (Table 71 on page 299 illustrates the calculation of the 5-day RSI.)
- Column C is the upward price change. If the price increased from the previous day, the increase is stored in Column C. If prices fell or were unchanged, Column C is set to zero.
- Column D is Column C smoothed using a 5-day Wilder's Smoothing (see page 364). Basically, the first value (on 07/09/97) is the average price over the last 5 days (i.e., 07/02/97 through 07/09/97). Subsequent days add 1/5 (because this is a 5-day smoothing) of the change in Column C to the previous value in Column D.
- Column E is the downward price change. If the price in column B decreased from the previous day, the decrease (without the minus sign) is stored in Column E. If prices rose or were unchanged, Column E is set to zero.
- Column F is Column E smoothed using a 5-day Wilder's Smoothing, as explained for Column D.
- Column G is Column D divided by Column F.
- Column H is column G plus 1.0.
- Column I is 100 divided by Column H.
- Column J is 100 minus Column I. This is the Relative Strength Index.

RELATIVE VOLATILITY INDEX

Overview

The Relative Volatility Index (RVI), developed by Donald Dorsey, is used to measure the direction of volatility. The calculation is identical to the Relative Strength Index (RSI) (see page 297), except that the RVI measures a 10-day standard deviation of high and low prices instead of measuring period-to-period price changes.

Interpretation

When developing the RVI, Dorsey was searching for a confirming indicator to use with traditional trend-following indicators (such as a dual moving average crossover system). He found that using a momentum-based indicator to confirm another "repackaged" momentum-based indicator was usually ineffective.

Dorsey states, "Technicians are tempted to use one set of indicators to confirm another. We may decide to use the MACD to confirm a signal in Stochastic. . . . Logic tells us that this form of diversification will enhance results, but too often the confirming indicator is just the original trading indicator repackaged, each using a theory similar to the other to measure market behavior. . . . Every trader should understand the indicators being applied to the markets to avoid duplicating information."

When testing the profitability of a basic moving average crossover system, Dorsey found that the results could be significantly enhanced by applying the following RVI rules for confirmation. Similar rules are likely to be effective for other momentum- or trend-following indicators:

- Only act on buy signals when RVI > 50.
- Only act on sell signals when RVI < 50.
- If a buy signal was ignored, enter long when RVI > 60.
- If a sell signal was ignored, enter short when RVI < 40.
- Close a long position if RVI falls below 40.
- Close a short position if RVI rises above 60.

Because the RVI measures a different set of market dynamics than other indicators, it is often superior as a confirming indicator. As Dorsey states, "There is no reason to expect the RVI to perform any better or worse than the RSI as an indicator in its own right. The RVI's advantage is as a confirming indicator because it provides a level of diversification missing in the RSI."

Example

Figure 162 shows the MACD and the RVI of United Technologies. During the time period shown, two MACD buy signals were generated. If we add the additional filter requiring the RVI to be above 50 for a buy signal, the first signal that occurred during the downtrend is ignored and the second, more profitable signal, is observed.

FIGURE 162

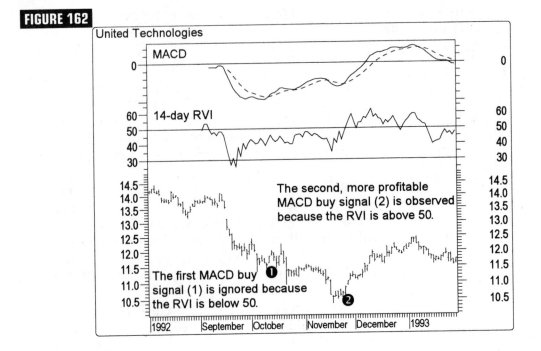

Calculation

The calculation of the RVI is similar to that for the RSI, except that where the RSI uses the average of up or down price changes, the RVI uses a 10-day standard deviation of high or low prices.

Due to the added steps, the table explaining the RVI requires 14 columns of data, which is beyond the scope of this book. The A-to-Z Companion Spreadsheet (see page xvii) contains the full calculations.

RENKO

Overview

Renko charts were first brought to the United States by Steven Nison when he published the book *Beyond Candlesticks*. The Renko charting method is thought to have acquired its name from *renga*, which is the Japanese word for "bricks." Renko charts are similar to Three Line Break charts (see page 330), except that in a Renko chart, a line (or "brick") is drawn in the direction of the prior move only if prices move by a minimum amount (i.e., the box size). The bricks are always equal in size. For example, in a 5-unit Renko chart, a 20-point rally is displayed as 4 Renko bricks, each 5 points tall.

Interpretation

Basic trend reversals are signaled with the emergence of a new white or black brick. A new white brick indicates the beginning of a new uptrend. A new black brick indicates the beginning of a new downtrend. Since the Renko chart is a trend-following technique, Renko charts tend to keep you on the right side of the market during strong trends and to produce whipsaws during short-lived trends.

Since a Renko chart isolates the underlying price trend by filtering out minor price changes, Renko charts can also be helpful in determining support and resistance levels.

Example

Figure 163 show Luby's as a classic high-low-close bar chart, and Figure 164 shows it as a 0.6-unit Renko chart. "Buy" and "sell" arrows on both charts indicate when trend reversals occurred in the Renko charts. You can see that

FIGURE 163

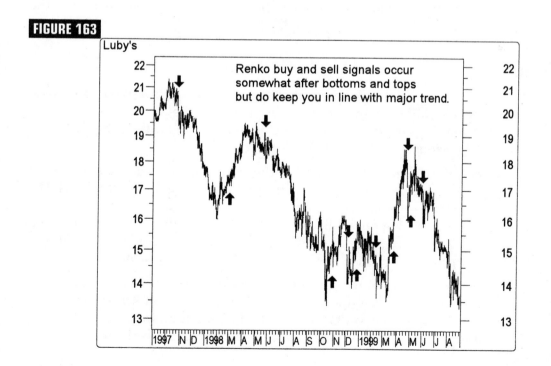

Renko buy and sell signals occur somewhat after bottoms and tops but do keep you in line with major trend.

FIGURE 164

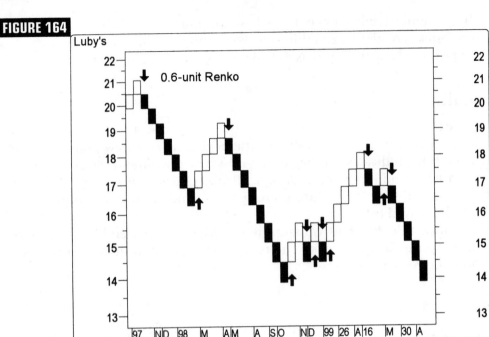

although the signals were late, they did ensure that you invested with the major trend.

Calculation

Renko charts are always based on closing prices. You specify a "box size," which determines the minimum price change to display.

In drawing Renko bricks, today's close is compared with the high and low of the previous brick (white or black):

- If the closing price rises above the top of the previous brick by at least the box size, one or more white bricks are drawn in new columns. The height of the bricks is always equal to the box size.
- If the closing price falls below the bottom of the previous brick by at least the box size, one or more black bricks are drawn in new columns. Again, the height of the bricks is always equal to the box size.

If prices move more than the box size, but not enough to create two bricks, only one brick is drawn. For example, in a two-unit Renko chart, if the prices move from 100 to 103, only one white brick is drawn, from 100 to 102. The rest of the move, from 102 to 103, is not shown on the Renko chart.

SPEED RESISTANCE LINES

Overview

Speed Resistance Lines (SRL), sometimes called 1/3-2/3 lines, are a series of trendlines that divide a price move into three equal sections. They are similar in construction and interpretation to Fibonacci Fan Lines (see page 143).

Interpretation

Speed Resistance Lines display three trendlines. The slope of each line defines a different rate at which pricing expectations are changing.

Prices should find support above the 2/3 line. When prices do fall below the 2/3 line, they should quickly drop to the 1/3 line, where they should then again find support.

Example

Figure 165 shows McDonald's price and Speed Resistance Lines. The initial trendline was drawn from the low point, labeled A, to the high point, labeled B. You can see that prices found support each time they fell to the 2/3 line.

FIGURE 165

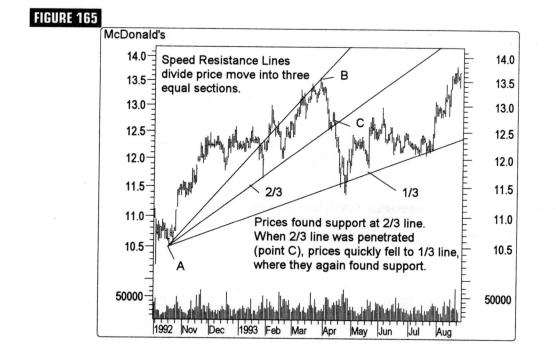

When prices finally penetrated the 2/3 line (at point C) they quickly fell to the 1/3 line, where they again found support.

Calculation

Figure 166 shows how to draw Speed Resistance Lines:

1. Draw a line from a major low to a major high.
2. Draw a vertical line on the day the major high occurred. Divide this vertical line into thirds.
3. Draw lines from the major low so that they intersect the vertical line at the 1/3 and 2/3 levels.

FIGURE 166

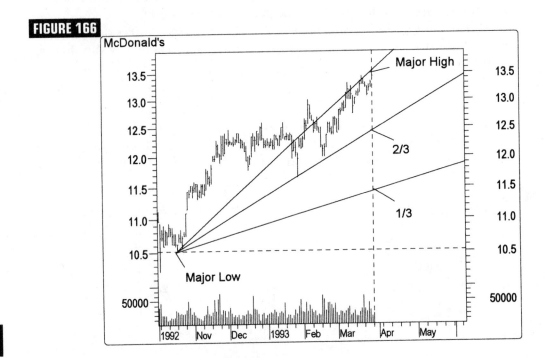

SPREADS

Overview

Spreads show the difference in price between two securities. Spreads are normally calculated using futures and are calculated simply subtracting the value of one security from another security.

Interpretation

A Spread involves buying one security and selling another with the goal of profiting from the narrowing or expanding of the difference between the two securities. For example, you might buy gold and short silver with the expectation that the price of gold will rise faster (or fall more slowly) than the price of silver.

You can also spread a single security by buying one contract and selling another. For example, buy an October contract and sell a December contract.

Example

Figure 167 shows live hogs (top plot), pork bellies (middle plot), and the spread between the hogs and bellies (bottom plot). This Spread involves buying the hogs and shorting the bellies with the anticipation that hogs will rise faster (or fall more slowly) than bellies.

You can see that during the time period shown, both hogs and bellies decreased in price. As desired, the price of hogs fell less than the price of bellies. This is shown by the spread increasing from 0.325 to 13.725, with a resulting profit of 13.40.

FIGURE 167

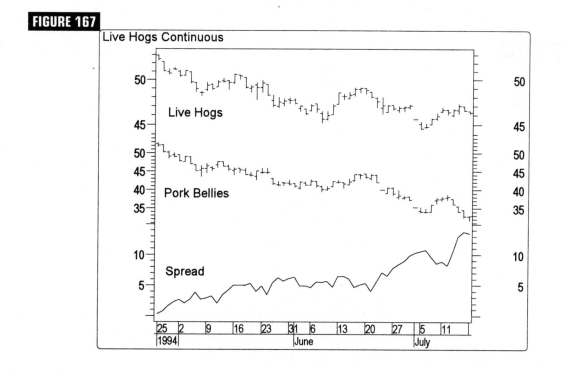

STANDARD DEVIATION

Overview

Standard Deviation is a statistical measure of volatility and is typically used as a component of other indicators, rather than as a stand-alone indicator. For example, Bollinger Bands (see page 71) are calculated by adding a security's Standard Deviation to a moving average.

Interpretation

High Standard Deviation values occur when the data item being analyzed (e.g., prices or an indicator) is changing dramatically. Similarly, low Standard Deviation values occur when prices are stable.

Many analysts feel that major tops are accompanied by high volatility as investors struggle with both euphoria and fear. Major bottoms are expected to be calmer, since investors have few expectations of profits.

Example

Figure 168 shows Procter & Gamble and its 10-week Standard Deviation. The extremely low Standard Deviation values at points A and B preceded significant rallies at points 1 and 2.

FIGURE 168

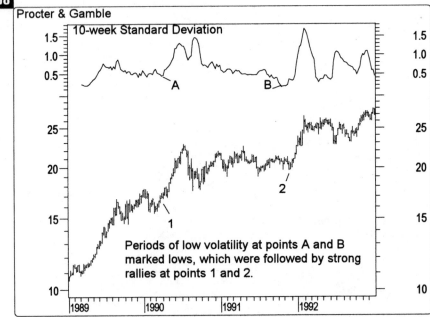

Procter & Gamble

10-week Standard Deviation

Periods of low volatility at points A and B marked lows, which were followed by strong rallies at points 1 and 2.

Calculation

The formula for Standard Deviation is as follows:

$$\sqrt{\frac{\sum_{j=1}^{n}(Close_j - n\text{-}period\ SMA\ of\ Close)^2}{n}}$$

Where:

- SMA = Simple Moving Average
- n = Number of time periods

Standard Deviation is derived by calculating an n-period simple moving average of the data item (i.e., the closing price or an indicator), summing the squares of the difference between the data item and its moving average over each of the preceding n time periods, dividing this sum by n, and then calculating the square root of this result.

The Standard Deviation can be calculated using the *stdvep()* spreadsheet function (which calculates the Standard Deviation) or manually as shown below in Table 72, which illustrates the calculation of the 5-period Standard Deviation of closing prices.

- Column C is a 5-day simple moving average of closing prices. It is calculated by adding the preceding 5 days of closing prices and dividing by 5.
- Column D subtracts each of the last 5 closes from today's simple moving average (e.g., the moving average minus the close 5 days ago, the moving average minus the close 4 days ago, etc.). Each of these 5 numbers is squared, and then the five squared values are summed.
- Column E divides Column D by the number of periods (e.g., 5). It then takes the square root of this result. This is the Standard Deviation.

TABLE 72

| | | STANDARD DEVIATION | | |
A	B	C	D	E
Date	Close	5-day SMA of Column B	Sum of squares of Col B — Col C last 5 periods (see text)	Square root of Column D divided by 5
01/04/99	21.4375			
01/05/99	21.6875			
01/06/99	22.1250			
01/07/99	21.5625			
01/08/99	21.8125	21.7250	0.2781	0.2358
01/11/99	21.4375	21.7250	0.2781	0.2358
01/12/99	21.5000	21.6875	0.3203	0.2531
01/13/99	21.1875	21.5000	0.2031	0.2016
01/14/99	20.6875	21.3250	0.7063	0.3758
01/15/99	20.9375	21.1500	0.4656	0.3052

STANDARD DEVIATION CHANNEL

Overview

Standard Deviation Channels are calculated by plotting two parallel lines above and below an *n*-period Linear Regression Trendline (see page 176). The lines are plotted a specified number of standard deviations away from the Linear Regression Trendline.

Interpretation

Statistical analysis states that approximately 67 percent of future price movement should be contained within one standard deviation and approximately 95 percent within two standard deviations. However, this assumes random, trendless data. Since most markets show overwhelming evidence of non-random, trending behavior, the 67-percent and 95-percent values tend to be low (i.e., prices are even more likely to be contained). In addition, Standard Deviation Channels incorporate the current trend (as shown by the middle Linear Regression Trendline), which makes prices even more likely to be contained by the channels.

As with other channels, price movement should be expected to return to the Linear Regression Trendline. Movement outside the upper or lower channel on heavy volume may indicate a change in trend.

Standard Deviation Channels can also be used in conjunction with other indicators. An effective combination would be a buy signal from another indicator combined with a price near the lower channel (and vice versa).

Example

The Standard Deviation Channels of Union Carbide in Figure 169 are placed two deviations away from the Linear Regression Trendline. We would expect 95 percent of future price movement to be contained within the bands. When the price breaks convincingly below the bottom band, a change in trend is indicated.

Calculation

The center line of the Standard Deviation Channel is a Linear Regression Trendline (see page 176). The upper channel is plotted the specified number of standard deviations (see page 308) above the center line. The lower channel is plotted the specified number of standard deviations below the center line.

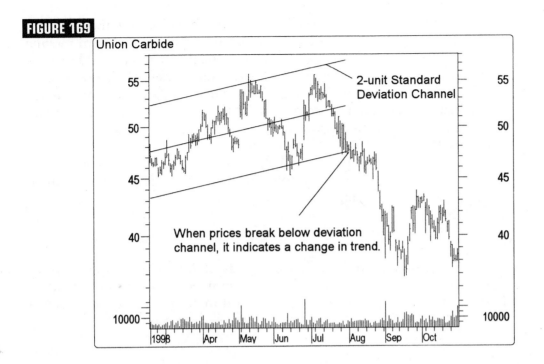

FIGURE 169

Union Carbide — 2-unit Standard Deviation Channel. When prices break below deviation channel, it indicates a change in trend.

STANDARD ERROR

Overview

Standard Error measures how closely prices congregate around a Linear Regression Trendline (see page 176). It quantifies how closely the actual prices are to the prices estimated by a Linear Regression Trendline. The closer prices are to the Linear Regression Trendline and the higher the r-Squared value (see page 282), the stronger the trend.

For example, if each day's closing price was equal to that day's Linear Regression Trendline value, then the Standard Error would be zero. The more variance around the Linear Regression Trendline, the larger the Standard Error and the less reliable the trend.

Interpretation

High Standard Error values indicate that the security's prices are very volatile around the Linear Regression Trendline. Changes in the prevailing trend are usually preceded by a rapidly increasing Standard Error.

S

Standard Error can be used effectively in combination with the r-Squared indicator. Changes in trend are often signaled by a high downward-moving r-Squared combined with a low upward-moving Standard Error indicating a weakening trend and increasing volatility around the trend, or a low upward-moving r-Squared and a high downward-moving Standard Error indicating a strengthening trend and decreasing volatility around the trend. In other words, when the two are at extreme levels and begin to converge, look for a change in trend.

Note that in this discussion a change in trend does not necessarily mean that an upward trend will reverse to a downward trend. Sideways movement is also considered a "change."

Example

Figure 170 shows America Online, a 14-day Standard Error, and a 14-day r-Squared. The rapidly falling r-Squared, combined with the rising Standard Error, indicated that a change in the upward trend was occurring. This was borne out as America Online corrected over the next two months.

FIGURE 170

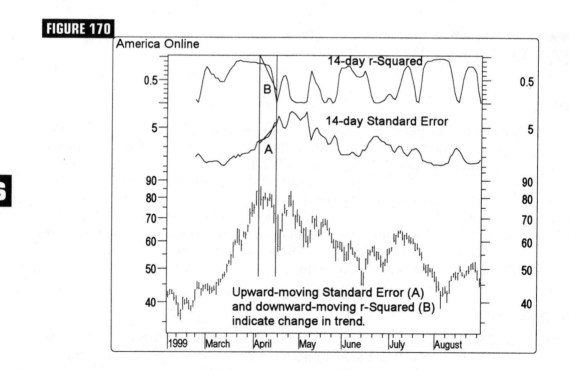

Calculation

The calculation for Standard Error is beyond the scope of this book. Standard Error can be calculated in a spreadsheet using the *steyx()* function. The A-to-Z Companion Spreadsheet (see page xvii) contains examples of both the brute force and the *steyx()* method.

STANDARD ERROR BANDS

Overview

Standard Error Bands, developed by Jon Anderson of Equis International, are a type of Envelope (see page 137) based on Standard Error (see page 311). They are similar in appearance to Bollinger Bands (see page 71), but they are calculated and interpreted quite differently. Where Bollinger Bands are plotted at Standard Deviation levels above and below a moving average, Standard Error Bands are plotted at Standard Error levels above and below the Linear Regression Indicator (see page 172).

The center line of the Standard Error Bands is simply the Linear Regression Indicator. The upper and lower bands are calculated by adding or subtracting the specified number of Standard Errors.

Interpretation

Because the spacing between Standard Error Bands is based on the Standard Error of the security, the bands widen when the volatility around the current trend (as defined by the Linear Regression Indicator) increases, and they contract when volatility around the current trend decreases.

Since Standard Error Bands are statistically based, other statistical indicators such as r-Squared, Standard Error, Linear Regression Indicator, etc., work well for trade confirmation.

Andersen notes the following characteristics of Standard Error Bands:

- Tight bands are an indication of a strong trend.
- Prices tend to bounce between the bands when the bands are wide.
- Tight bands followed by a widening of the bands may indicate the exhaustion of a trend and a possible reversal.

S

- When the bands reverse direction after an exhausted trend, prices tend to move in the direction of the bands.
- The r-Squared indicator works well in combination with Standard Error Bands. A high r-Squared value combined with tight bands confirms a strong trend. A low r-Squared value combined with wide bands confirms that prices are consolidating.

Example

Figure 171 of Dell Computer and 21-day Standard Error Standard Bands shows three of the five characteristics noted by Jon Anderson.

FIGURE 171

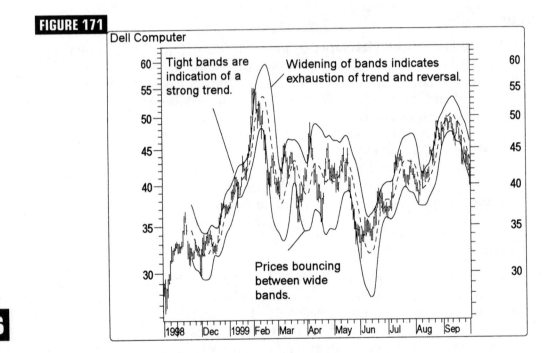

Calculation

The center line of the Standard Error Bands is a Linear Regression Indicator (see page 172). The upper band is calculated by adding the specified number of Standard Errors (see page 311) to the Linear Regression Indicator. The lower channel is calculated by subtracting the specified number of standard errors from the Linear Regression Indicator.

STANDARD ERROR CHANNEL

Overview

Standard Error Channels are calculated by plotting two parallel lines above and below an *n*-period Linear Regression Trendline (see page 176). The lines are plotted a specified number of Standard Errors (see page 311) away from the Linear Regression Trendline.

Interpretation

Standard Error Channels are similar to other channels (see Raff Regression Channels on page 284 and Standard Deviation Channels on page 310). The upper and lower bands should contain price movement. Extended moves outside of either band may indicate a change in trend.

Example

Figure 172 shows Delta Airlines and a 2-unit Standard Error Channel. The upper and lower channels acted as solid support and resistance for the 20 months displayed in the chart.

FIGURE 172

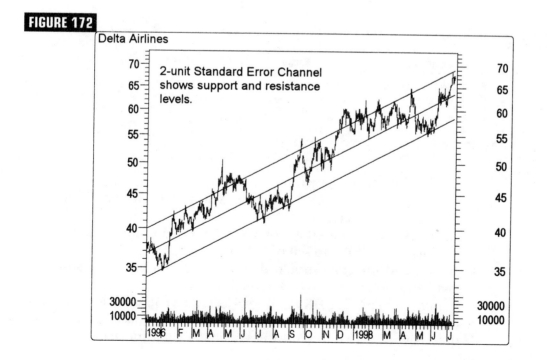

Calculation

The center line of the Standard Error Channel is a Linear Regression Trendline (see page 176). The upper channel is calculated by adding the requested number of Standard Errors to the Linear Regression Trendline. The lower channel is calculated by subtracting the requested number of Standard Errors from the Linear Regression Trendline.

STIX

Overview

STIX is a short-term trading oscillator that was published in *The Polymetric Report*. It compares the amount of volume flowing into advancing and declining stocks.

Interpretation

According to *The Polymetric Report* (see Table 73, also):

TABLE 73

Condition	Range
Extremely Overbought	greater than 58
Fairly Overbought	greater than 56
Fairly Oversold	less than 45
Extremely Oversold	less than 42

- STIX usually ranges between +42 and +58.
- If STIX gets as low as 45, the market is almost always a buy, except in a raging bear market.
- The market is fairly overbought if STIX rises to 56; and except in a new bull market, it's wise to sell if STIX goes over 58.
- Traders and investors should modify these rough rules to suit their own objectives.
- In normal markets, STIX rarely gets as high as 56 or as low as 45, so rigid use of these rules of thumb would keep you inactive most of the time. For active accounts, the rules might be made much less stringent.

Example

Figure 173 shows the S&P 500 and the STIX indicator. "Buy" arrows indicate when the STIX fell below, and then rose above, the oversold level of 45. "Sell" arrows indicate when the STIX rose above, and then fell below, the overbought level of 56.

FIGURE 173

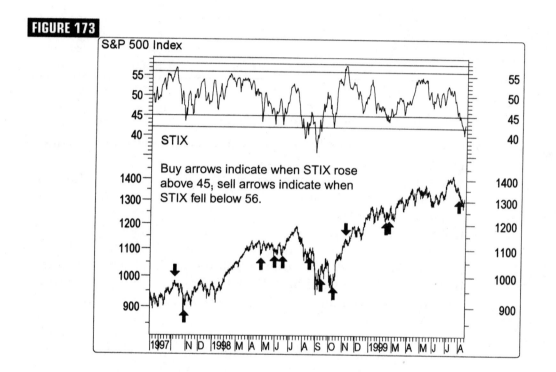

Calculation

STIX is based on a variation of the Advance/Decline Ratio (see page 55). Following is the Advance/Decline Ratio:

$$A/D \ Ratio = \left(\frac{Advancing \ Issues}{Advancing \ Issues \ + \ Declining \ Issues} \right) * 100$$

STIX is a 21-period (i.e., 9-percent) exponential moving average of the above Advance/Decline Ratio:

$$STIX = (A/D \ Ratio * 0.09) + (Yesterday's \ STIX * 0.91)$$

TABLE 74

			STIX		
A	**B**	**C**	**D**	**E**	**F**
Date	Advancing Issues	Declining Issues	Advancing plus Declining Issues	Col B / Col D muntiplied by 100	0.9 Exponential Average
04/25/97	789	1,662	2,451	32.19	32.191
04/28/97	1,348	1,085	2,433	55.40	34.280
04/29/97	2,085	531	2,616	79.70	38.368
04/30/97	1,599	941	2,540	62.95	40.581
05/01/97	1,450	1,021	2,471	58.68	42.210
05/02/97	2,119	476	2,595	81.66	45.760

Table 74 illustrates the calculation of STIX.

- Column D adds the Advancing Issues (Column B) and Declining Issues (Column C).
- Column E divides the number of Advancing Issues (Column B) by Column D. This value is then multiplied by 100 to create the Advance/Decline Ratio.
- Column F is a 9-percent exponential moving average of Column E. The first row of Column F is seeded with the first value in Column E (i.e., 32.191). Subsequent rows in Column F are calculated by multiplying the value in Column E by 0.9, then multiplying the previous day's value in Column F by 0.91, and finally adding these two values together.
- The value 0.9 was specified by the author of STIX. The value 0.91 was calculated as "1 − 0.9" as explained on page 208. Note that this "21-period" moving average is not valid until the twenty-first day (which is not displayed in this abbreviated table).

STOCHASTIC MOMENTUM INDEX

Overview

The Stochastic Momentum Index (SMI), developed by William Blau, incorporates an interesting twist on the popular Stochastic Oscillator (see page 321). While the Stochastic Oscillator provides a value showing the position of the close relative to the recent high/low range, the SMI shows you where the close is relative to the *midpoint* of the recent high/low range. The SMI is smoothed twice by exponential moving averages. The result is an oscillator that ranges between ±100 and is a bit less erratic than an equal-period Stochastic Oscillator.

Interpretation

When the close is greater than the midpoint of the high/low range over the specified number of time periods, the SMI is positive. When the close is less than the midpoint of the range, it is negative.

The interpretation of the SMI is virtually identical to the Stochastic Oscillator. Four popular methods include the following:

1. Buy when the SMI falls below a specific level (e.g., −40) and then rises above that level, and sell when it rises above a specific level (e.g., +40) and then falls below that level. However, before basing any trade on strict overbought/oversold levels, first qualify the trendiness of the market using indicators such as r-Squared (see page 282) or the Chande Momentum Oscillator (see page 100). If these indicators suggest a non-trending market, then trades based on strict overbought/oversold levels should produce the best results. If a trending market is suggested, use the oscillator to enter trades in the direction of the trend.
2. Buy when the SMI rises above its signal line (e.g., a 3-period moving average) and sell when it falls below the signal line.
3. Look for divergences. For example, where prices are making a series of new highs and the SMI is failing to surpass its previous highs.
4. Blau also notes that a 1-day SMI (with large smoothing periods, such as 100) is very sensitive to the closing price relative to the high and low of the day. These types of parameters make the RMI useful as a sentiment, or trend-identification indicator, thereby providing a better sense of the overall direction of the market.

Example

Figure 174 shows a 5-day Stochastic Momentum Index of 3M smoothed by two 3-day moving averages. The SMI diverged from 3M's prices in early 1992 (the SMI trended up while prices trended down). Subsequently, 3M's share price rallied, confirming the strength of the SMI.

FIGURE 174

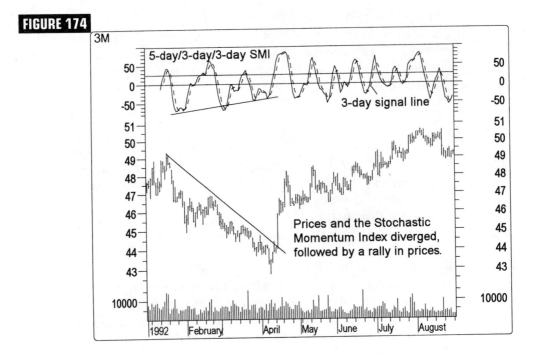

Prices and the Stochastic Momentum Index diverged, followed by a rally in prices.

Calculation

The table for the SMI is too large to present in this book. The A-to-Z Companion Spreadsheet (see page xvii) contains the full calculations.

The calculations are as follows:

1. Add the highest high to the lowest low over the desired time period.
2. Divide the value in step 1 by 2 to get the midpoint.
3. Subtract the midpoint in step 2 from the close, which gives you the distance of the close relative to the midpoint of the *n*-period high/low range.
4. Calculate an exponential moving average of the value obtained in step 3.
5. Calculate an exponential moving average of the value obtained in step 4.
6. Subtract the highest high from the lowest low over the desired time period.
7. Calculate an exponential moving average of the value obtained in step 6 (use the same number of periods as used in step 4).
8. Calculate an exponential moving average of the value obtained in step 7 (use the same number of periods as used in step 5).
9. Divide the value obtained in step 8 by 2.
10. Divide the value obtained in step 5 by the value obtained in step 9.
11. Multiply the value in step 10 by 100. This is the SMI.

STOCHASTIC OSCILLATOR

Overview

Stochastic (stōkas'tik) adj. . . . 2. Math. designating a process having an infinite progression of jointly distributed random variables. —*Webster's New World Dictionary*

The Stochastic Oscillator compares where a security's price closed relative to its price range over a given time period. It has four variables:

1. **%K Periods.** This is the number of time periods used in the stochastic calculation.
2. **%K Slowing Periods.** This value controls the internal smoothing of %K (above). A value of 1 is considered a fast stochastic; a value of 3 is considered a slow stochastic.
3. **%D Periods.** This is the number of time periods used when calculating a moving average of %K. The moving average is called %D and is usually displayed as a dotted line on top of %K.
4. **%D Method.** This is the method (i.e., Exponential, Simple, Time Series, Triangular, Variable, or Weighted) that is used to calculate %D.

Interpretation

The Stochastic Oscillator is displayed as two lines. The main line is called %K. The second line, called %D, is a moving average of %K. The %K line is usually displayed as a solid line, and the %D line is usually displayed as a dotted line.

There are several ways to interpret a Stochastic Oscillator. Three popular methods include the following:

1. Buy when the Stochastic Oscillator (either %K or %D) falls below a specific level (e.g., 20) and then rises above that level. Sell when it rises above a specific level (e.g., 80) and then falls below that level.
2. Buy when the %K line rises above the %D line, and sell when the %K line falls below the %D line.
3. Look for divergences (see page 36), for example, where prices are making a series of new highs and the Stochastic Oscillator is failing to surpass its previous highs.

S

FIGURE 175

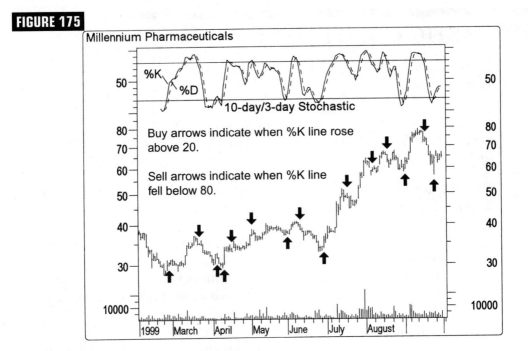

Example

Figure 175 shows Millennium Pharmaceuticals and its 10-day Stochastic. "Buy" arrows indicate when the %K line fell below, and then rose above, the level of 20. "Sell" arrows indicate when the %K line rose above, and then fell below, the level of 80.

Figure 176 also shows Millennium Pharmaceuticals. In this example, "buy" arrows indicate each time the %K line rose above the %D (dotted) line. "Sell" arrows indicate when the %K line fell below the %D line.

Figure 177 shows Polycom and the Stochastic Oscillator and a divergence between the Stochastic Oscillator and prices. This is a classic divergence where prices are headed lower but the underlying indicator (the Stochastic Oscillator) is moving higher. When a divergence occurs between an indicator and prices, the indicator typically provides the clue as to where prices will head.

Calculation

The Stochastic Oscillator has four variables:

1. **%K Periods.** This is the number of time periods used in the stochastic calculation.

FIGURE 176

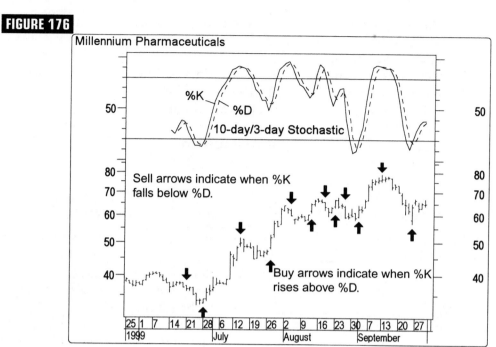

Millennium Pharmaceuticals

%K
%D
10-day/3-day Stochastic

Sell arrows indicate when %K falls below %D.

Buy arrows indicate when %K rises above %D.

FIGURE 177

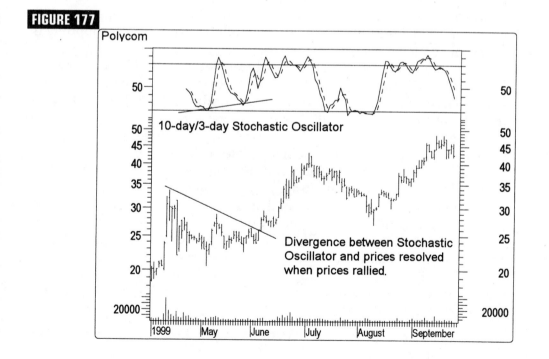

Polycom

10-day/3-day Stochastic Oscillator

Divergence between Stochastic Oscillator and prices resolved when prices rallied.

S

2. **%K Slowing Periods.** This value controls the internal smoothing of %K. A value of 1 is considered a fast stochastic; a value of 3 is considered a slow stochastic.
3. **%D Periods.** This is the number of time periods used when calculating a moving average of %K. The moving average is called %D and is usually displayed as a dotted line on top of %K.
4. **%D Method.** This method (i.e., Exponential, Simple, Time Series, Triangular, Variable, or Weighted) is used to calculate %D.

The formula for %K is as follows:

$$\left(\frac{Today's\ Close\ -\ Lowest\ Low\ in\ \%K\ Periods}{Highest\ High\ in\ \%K\ Periods\ -\ Lowest\ Low\ in\ \%K\ Periods} \right) * 100$$

For example, to calculate a 10-day %K, first find the security's highest high and lowest low over the last 10 days. Then run these numbers through the above equation. For example, assume that during the last 10 days the highest high was 46 and the lowest low was 38—a range of 8 points. If today's closing price was 41, %K would be calculated as the following:

$$37.5 = \left(\frac{41\ -\ 38}{46\ -\ 38} \right) * 100$$

The 37.5 percent in this example shows that today's close was at the level of 37.5 percent relative to the security's trading range over the last 10 days. If today's close was 42, the Stochastic Oscillator would be 50 percent. This would mean that the security closed today at 50 percent, or the midpoint, of its 10-day trading range.

The example above used a %K Slowing period of 1 day (i.e., no slowing). If you use a %K Slowing value that is greater than 1, the numerator is calculated each day for the number of slowing periods specified. These values are then summed. The same calculation is done for the denominator. This process has a smoothing effect. If you use 1, no smoothing is performed.

A moving average of %K is then calculated using the number of time periods specified in the %D periods. This moving average is called %D.

The Stochastic Oscillator always ranges between 0 percent and 100 percent. A reading of 0 percent shows that the security's close was the lowest price that the security has traded during the preceding n time periods. A reading of 100 percent shows that the security's close was the highest price that the security traded during the preceding n time periods.

Table 75 illustrates the calculation of the Stochastic Oscillator. In this example I used 5 %K periods, 3 %K Slowing periods, and 3 %D periods. The %D method is Simple.

- Column E is the lowest low (Column C) in the last %K periods (5 days in this example).

TABLE 75

STOCHASTIC OSCILLATOR

A	B	C	D	E	F	G	H	I	J	K	L
				Lowest Low in Last %K Periods	Highest High in Last %K Periods	Close minus Column E	Column F minus Column E	Sum of Column G for %K Slowing Periods	Sum of Column H for %K Slowing Periods	Col I / Col J times 100	%D Periods SMA
Date	High	Low	Close								
08/22/97	34.3750	33.5312	34.3125								
08/25/97	34.7500	33.9062	34.1250								
08/26/97	34.2188	33.6875	33.7500								
08/27/97	33.8281	33.2500	33.6406								
08/28/97	33.4375	33.0000	33.0156	33.0000	34.7500	0.0156	1.7500				
08/29/97	33.4688	32.9375	33.0469	32.9375	34.7500	0.1094	1.8125				
09/02/97	34.3750	33.2500	34.2969	32.9375	34.3750	1.3594	1.4375	1.4844	5.0000	29.6880	
09/03/97	34.7188	34.0469	34.1406	32.9375	34.7188	1.2031	1.7813	2.6719	5.0313	53.1056	
09/04/97	34.6250	33.9375	34.5469	32.9375	34.7188	1.6094	1.7813	4.1719	5.0001	83.4363	55.4100
09/05/97	34.9219	34.0625	34.3281	32.9375	34.9219	1.3906	1.9844	4.2031	5.5470	75.7725	70.7715
09/08/97	34.9531	34.4375	34.8281	33.2500	34.9531	1.5781	1.7031	4.5781	5.4688	83.7131	80.9740
09/09/97	35.0625	34.5938	34.8750	33.9375	35.0625	0.9375	1.1250	3.9062	4.8125	81.1678	80.2178
09/10/97	34.7812	33.7656	33.7812	33.7656	35.0625	0.0156	1.2969	2.5312	4.1250	61.3624	75.4144
09/11/97	34.3438	33.2188	34.2031	33.2188	35.0625	0.9843	1.8437	1.9374	4.2656	45.4192	62.6498
09/12/97	34.5938	33.9062	34.4844	33.2188	35.0625	1.2656	1.8437	2.2655	4.9843	45.4527	50.7448
09/15/97	34.3125	32.6562	22.6719	32.6562	35.0625	0.0157	2.4063	2.2656	6.0937	37.1794	42.6838
09/16/97	34.2500	32.7500	34.0938	32.6562	34.7812	1.4376	2.1250	2.7189	6.3750	42.6494	41.7605
09/17/97	34.1875	33.1562	33.2969	32.6562	34.5938	0.6407	1.9376	2.0940	6.4689	32.3703	37.3997
09/18/97	33.7812	32.8594	33.0625	32.6562	34.5938	0.4063	1.9376	2.4846	6.0002	41.4086	38.8094
09/19/97	33.8125	33.0000	33.7969	32.6562	34.3125	1.1407	1.6563	2.1877	5.5315	39.5499	37.7762
09/22/97	33.9688	33.2969	33.3281	32.7500	34.2500	0.5781	1.5000	2.1251	5.0939	41.7185	40.8923
09/23/97	33.8750	33.2812	33.8750	32.8594	34.1875	1.0156	1.3281	2.7344	4.4844	60.9758	47.4147
09/24/97	34.0156	33.0312	33.1094	32.8594	34.0156	0.2500	1.1562	1.8437	3.9843	46.2741	49.6562
09/25/97	33.5312	33.0156	33.1875	33.0000	34.0156	0.1875	1.0156	1.4531	3.4999	41.5183	49.5894

S

- Column F is the highest high (Column B) in the last %K periods.
- Column G is the current close (Column D) minus the lowest low (Column E).
- Column H is Column F minus Column E.
- Column I is the sum of Column G over the last %K Slowing periods (i.e., the last 3 periods in this example).
- Column J is the sum of Column H over the last %K Slowing periods (i.e., the last 3 periods in this example).
- Column K is Column I divided by Column J. This value is then multiplied by 100 to create the Stochastic Oscillator.
- Column L is a simple moving average of the Stochastic Oscillator (Column K) using "%D Periods" (i.e., 3 in this example). It is calculated by adding the preceding 3 days of Column K and dividing by 3. This is the %D Moving Average.

SWING INDEX

Overview

The Swing Index, developed by Welles Wilder, seeks to isolate the "real" price of a security by comparing the relationships between the current prices (i.e., open, high, low, and close) and the previous period's prices.

Interpretation

The Swing Index is primarily used as a component of the Accumulation Swing Index (see page 51).

Example

Figure 178 shows the British pound and the Swing Index. You can see that the Swing Index by itself is an erratic plot. The value of this indicator develops when it is accumulated into the Accumulation Swing Index (see page 51).

Table 76 lists the limit moves for several commodities. A "limit move" is the maximum amount that the price of a futures contract can change in one trading session. You can get a list of limit moves from your broker.

You may need to adjust the limit moves shown in Table 76, based on the position of the decimal in your data. For example, if the price of corn is quoted as $2.45, the limit move would be $0.10. However, if the price of corn is quoted as $245.00, the limit move would be $10.00.

FIGURE 178

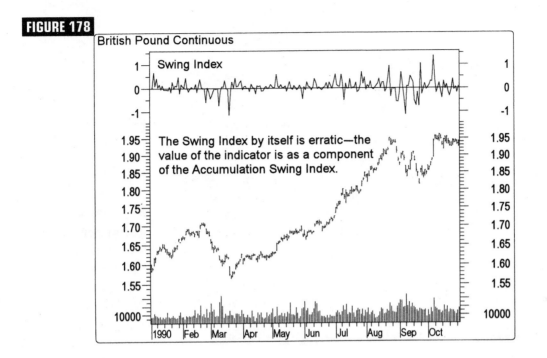

British Pound Continuous

Swing Index

The Swing Index by itself is erratic—the value of the indicator is as a component of the Accumulation Swing Index.

TABLE 76

Commodity	Limit Move
Coffee	$0.06
Gold	$75.00
Heating Oil	$0.04
Hogs	$0.015
Soybeans	$0.30
T-Bonds	$3.00

If the security does not have a limit move (e.g., a stock or some futures), use an extremely high value (e.g., $30,000).

Calculation

Although the full calculations for the Swing Index are beyond the scope of this book (they require 18 columns), the basic formula is shown below. The A-to-Z Companion Spreadsheet (see page xvii) contains the full calculations.

$$50 * \left(\frac{C\gamma - C + 0.5(C_\gamma - O\gamma) + 0.25(C - O)}{R} \right) * \frac{K}{T}$$

Where:

- C = Closing price
- $C\gamma$ = Previous period's closing price
- $H\gamma$ = Previous period's highest price
- K = The largest of: Hy-C and Ly-C
- L = Low price
- $L\gamma$ = Previous period's lowest price
- O = Opening price
- $O\gamma$ = Previous period's opening price
- R = A complex calculation based on the relationship between the current closing price and the previous period's high and low prices
- T = The value of a limit move

TEMA

Overview

The Triple Exponential Moving Average (TEMA) is a composite of a single exponential moving average, a double exponential moving average, and a triple exponential moving average that provides less lag time *when there is a trend* than either of the three components individually.

TEMA was developed by Patrick Mulloy. For additional information, refer to Mulloy's article in the February 1994 issue of *Technical Analysis of Stocks and Commodities*.

TEMA is an extension of DEMA (see page 121) which was also developed by Mulloy. As with DEMA, TEMA is a unique calculation, not simply an exponential moving average of an exponential moving average of an exponential moving average.

Interpretation

TEMA can be used in place of exponential moving averages (see page 203). You can use it to smooth price data or other indicators. Mulloy tested a TEMA-modified MACD and found it produced better results than the standard MACD, which is based on an exponential moving average.

FIGURE 179

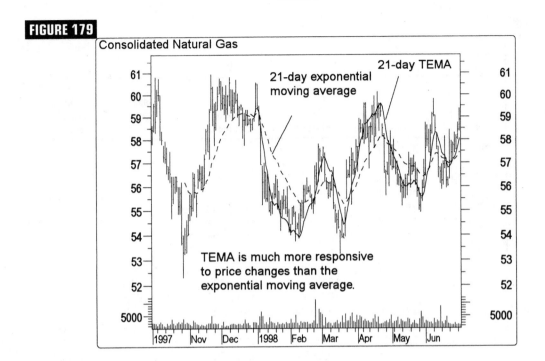

Consolidated Natural Gas

21-day exponential moving average

21-day TEMA

TEMA is much more responsive to price changes than the exponential moving average.

Example

Figure 179 shows a 21-day TEMA and a 21-day exponential moving average of Consolidated Natural Gas. The TEMA is much more responsive to price changes than exponential moving averages.

Calculation

Following is the formula for TEMA:

$$(3 * EMA) - (3 * EMA\ of\ EMA) + (EMA\ of\ EMA\ of\ EMA)$$

Where:

- EMA = n-day exponential moving average

Table 77 illustrates the calculation of a 5-day TEMA:

- Column C is a 5-day exponential moving average of the close as described on page 208.
- Column D is a 5-day exponential moving average of the exponential moving average calculated in Column C.

TABLE 77

		TEMA			
A	**B**	**C**	**D**	**E**	**F**
Date	Close	5-day EMA of Column B	5-day EMA of Column C	5-day EMA of Column D	(Col C * 3) minus (Col D * 3) plus Col E
12/02/99	122.906	122.9060			
12/03/99	126.500	124.1040			
12/06/99	140.406	129.5380			
12/07/99	174.000	144.3587			
12/08/99	159.812	149.5098	149.5098		
12/09/99	170.000	156.3399	151.7865		
12/10/99	176.750	163.1432	155.5721		
12/13/99	175.531	167.2725	159.4722		
12/14/99	166.562	167.0357	161.9934	161.9934	
12/15/99	163.750	165.9404	163.3090	162.4319	
12/16/99	170.500	167.4603	164.6928	163.1855	
12/17/99	175.000	169.9735	166.4530	164.2747	
12/20/99	184.750	174.8990	169.2684	165.9393	182.8312
12/21/99	202.781	184.1930	174.2432	168.7073	198.5565
12/22/99	209.656	192.6807	180.3891	172.6012	209.4760
12/23/99	201.312	195.5578	185.4453	176.8826	207.2200

- Column E is a 5-day exponential moving average of the exponential moving average calculated in Column D.
- Column F is Column C multiplied by 3, minus 3 times Column D, plus Column E. Note that this 5-day TEMA is not valid until the thirteenth day.

THREE LINE BREAK

Overview

Three Line Break charts display a series of vertical boxes ("lines") that are based on changes in prices. As with Kagi (see page 164), Point and Figure (see page 253), and Renko charts (see page 302), Three Line Break charts ignore the passage of time.

The Three Line Break charting method is so named because of the number of lines typically used. They were popularized in the United States by Steven Nison when he published the book *Beyond Candlesticks*.

Interpretation

The following are the basic trading rules for a Three Line Break chart:

- Buy when a white line emerges after three adjacent black lines (a "white turnaround line").
- Sell when a black line appears after three adjacent white lines (a "black turnaround line").
- Avoid trading in "trendless" markets where the lines alternate between black and white.

An advantage of Three Line Break charts is that there is no fixed reversal amount. It is the price action that gives the indication of a reversal. The disadvantage of Three Line Break charts is that the signals are generated after the new trend is well underway. However, many traders are willing to accept the late signals in exchange for calling major trends.

You can adjust the sensitivity of the reversal criteria by changing the number of lines in the break. For example, short-term traders might use 2-line breaks to get more reversals, while a longer-term investor might use 4-line or even 10-line breaks to reduce the number of reversals. The 3-line breaks (hence the name) are the most popular in Japan.

Nison recommends using Three Line Break charts in conjunction with Candlestick charts (see page 79). He suggests using the Three Line Break chart to determine the prevailing trend and then using candlestick patterns to time individual trades.

Example

Figure 180 shows a Three Line Break, and Figure 181 shows a bar chart of Du Pont. You can see that the number of break lines in a given month depends on the price change during the month. For example, January and May have many lines because the prices changed significantly, whereas February and March have only one line each because prices were relatively flat.

Calculation

Line Break charts are always based on closing prices. The general rules for calculating a Line Break chart are as follow:

- If the price exceeds the previous line's high price, a new *white* line is drawn.
- If the price falls below the previous line's low price, a new *black* line is drawn.
- If the price neither rises above nor falls below the previous line, *nothing* is drawn.

FIGURE 180

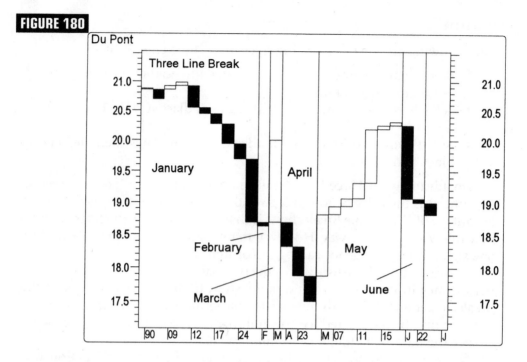

FIGURE 181

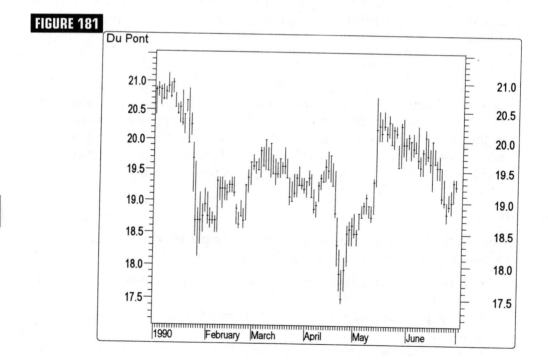

In a Three Line Break chart, if rallies are strong enough to display three consecutive lines of the same color, then prices must reverse by the extreme price of the last three lines in order to create a new line:

- If a rally is powerful enough to form three consecutive *white* lines, then prices must fall below the lowest point of the last three white lines before a new black line is drawn.
- If a sell-off is powerful enough to form three consecutive *black* lines, then prices must rise above the highest point of the last three black lines before a new white line is drawn.

TIME SERIES FORECAST

Overview

The Time Series Forecast indicator displays the statistical trend of a security's price over a specified time period. The trend is based on linear regression analysis. Rather than plotting a straight Linear Regression Trendline (see page 176), the Time Series Forecast plots the *next* point of multiple Linear Regression Trendlines. The resulting Time Series Forecast indicator is sometimes referred to as the "moving linear regression" indicator or the "regression oscillator."

Interpretation

The interpretation of a Time Series Forecast is identical to a moving average. However, the Time Series Forecast indicator has two advantages over classic moving averages.

Unlike a moving average, a Time Series Forecast does not exhibit as much delay when adjusting to price changes. Since the indicator is "fitting" itself to the data rather than averaging them, the Time Series Forecast is more responsive to price changes.

As the name suggests, you can use the Time Series Forecast to forecast the next period's price. This estimate is based on the trend of the security's prices over the period specified (e.g., 20 days). If the current trend continues, the value of the Time Series Forecast is a forecast of the next period's price.

FIGURE 182

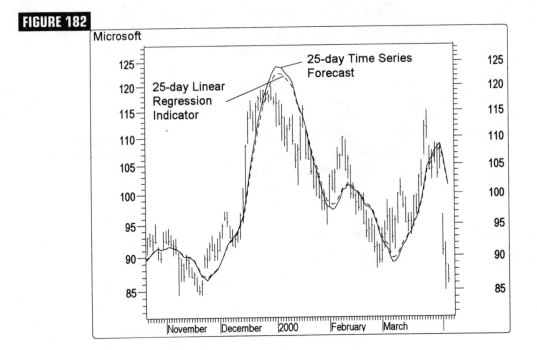

Example

Figure 182 shows a 25-day Time Series Forecast and 25-day Linear Regression Indicator (see page 172) of Microsoft's prices. The Linear Regression Indicator shows the endpoints of a series of 25-day Linear Regression Trendlines, while the Time Series Forecast projects these values one period into the future.

Calculation

The Time Series Forecast is calculated by adding the Linear Regression Slope (see page 174) to the Linear Regression Indicator (see page 172). Since each point on the Linear Regression Indicator is the ending point of a Linear Regression Trendline (see page 176), adding the Slope to the Indicator gives you the forecast value of the line on the following day (i.e., the Time Series Forecast).

The Time Series Forecast indicator can be calculated in a spreadsheet using the *forecast()* function (as can the Linear Regression Indicator).

TIRONE LEVELS

Overview

Tirone Levels are a series of horizontal lines that identify support and resistance levels. They were developed by John Tirone.

Interpretation

Tirone Levels can be drawn using either the Midpoint 1/3-2/3 method or the Mean method. Both methods are intended to help you identify potential support and resistance levels based on the range of prices over a given time period. The interpretation of Tirone Levels is similar to Quadrant Lines (see page 280).

Example

Figure 183 shows Midpoint Tirone Levels for Bristol-Myers Squibb. The dotted line shows the average price. The top and bottom lines divide the range between the highest and lowest prices into thirds.

FIGURE 183

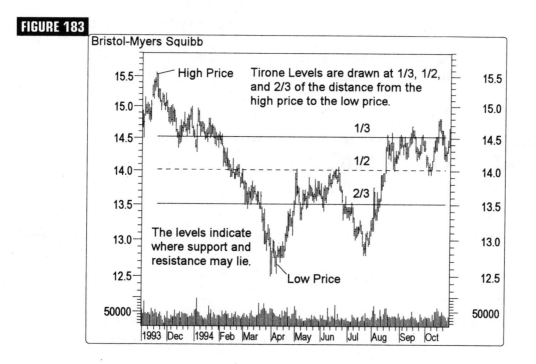

Calculation

Midpoint Method. Midpoint levels are calculated by finding the highest high and the lowest low during the time period being analyzed. The lines are then calculated as follows:

- **Top Line:** Subtract the lowest low from the highest high, divide this value by 3, and then subtract this result from the highest high.
- **Center Line:** Subtract the lowest low from the highest high, divide this value by 2, and then add this result to the lowest low.
- **Bottom Line:** Subtract the lowest low from the highest high, divide this value by 3, and then add this result to the lowest low.

Mean Method. Mean levels are displayed as five lines (the spacing between the lines is not necessarily symmetrical). The lines are calculated as follows:

- **Extreme High:** Subtract the lowest low from the highest high and add this value to the Adjusted Mean.
- **Regular High:** Subtract the lowest low from the value of the Adjusted Mean multiplied by 2.
- **Adjusted Mean:** This is the sum of the highest high, the lowest low, and the most recent closing price, divided by 3.
- **Regular Low:** Subtract the highest high from the value of the Adjusted Mean multiplied by 2.
- **Extreme Low:** Subtract the lowest low from the highest high and then subtract this value from the Adjusted Mean.

TOTAL SHORT RATIO

Overview

The Total Short Ratio (TSR) shows the percentage of short sales to the total volume on the New York Stock Exchange.

Interpretation

As with the Public Short Ratio (see page 274), the Total Short Ratio takes the contrarian view that short sellers are usually wrong. While the odd lotters are typically the worst of the short sellers, history has shown that even the specialists tend to over-short at market bottoms.

The TSR shows investor expectations. High values indicate bearish expectations and low values indicate bullish expectations. Taking a contrarian stance, when there are high levels of shorts (i.e., many investors expect a market decline), we would expect the market to rise. Likewise, extremely low levels of short sales should indicate excessive optimism and the increased likelihood of a market decline.

The interpretation of all of the short sale indicators has become more difficult recently due to option hedging and arbitrage. However, they are still helpful in determining overall market expectations.

Example

Figure 184 shows the New York Stock Exchange and a 10-week moving average of the TSR. "Buy" arrows indicate each time investors were excessively bearish. In hindsight, each of these turned out to be excellent times to enter the market.

FIGURE 184

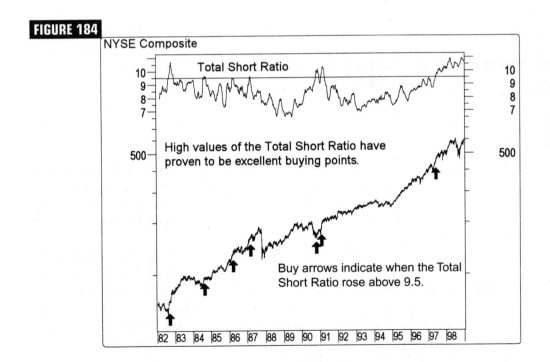

NYSE Composite

Total Short Ratio

High values of the Total Short Ratio have proven to be excellent buying points.

Buy arrows indicate when the Total Short Ratio rose above 9.5.

TABLE 78

| | TOTAL SHORT RATIO | | |
| A | B | C | D |
Date	Total Short Sales	Total Buy/Sell Orders	Col B / Col C times 100
01/02/98	195	1,789	10.90
01/09/98	310	3,328	9.31
01/16/98	324	3,201	10.12
01/23/98	263	2,551	10.31
01/30/98	337	3,322	10.15
02/06/98	398	3,413	11.66

Calculation

The TSR is calculated by dividing the total number of short sales by the total number of buy and sell orders and multiplying this result by 100 (see also Table 78).

$$\left(\frac{Total\ Short\ Sales}{Total\ Buy/Sell\ Orders} \right) * 100$$

TRADE VOLUME INDEX

Overview

The Trade Volume Index (TVI) shows whether a security is being accumulated (purchased) or distributed (sold). It was designed to be calculated using intraday "tick" price data. The TVI is based on the premise that trades taking place at higher "asking" prices are buy transactions and trades at lower "bid" prices are sell transactions.

The TVI is very similar to On Balance Volume (OBV) (see page 229). The OBV method works well with daily prices, but it doesn't work as well with intraday tick prices. Tick prices, especially stock prices, often trade at the bid or ask price for extended periods without changing. This creates a flat support or resistance level. During these periods of unchanging prices, the TVI continues to accumulate this volume on either the buy or sell side, depending on the direction of the last price change.

Interpretation

The TVI helps identify whether a security is being accumulated or distributed. When the TVI is trending up, it shows that trades are taking place at the asking price as buyers accumulate the security. When the TVI is trending down, it shows that trades are taking place at the bid price as sellers distribute the security.

When prices create a flat resistance level and the TVI is rising, look for prices to break out to the upside. When prices create a flat support level and the TVI is falling, look for prices to drop below the support level.

Example

Figure 185 shows Gateway's tick prices and the TVI. During the period labeled "A," prices remained at the same level while the TVI steadily increased. This indicated that more volume was occurring at the ask than at the bid. Also, there was a divergence between the TVI and Gateway's prices (Trendline B and Linear Regression Trendline C), which was resolved when the price moved up.

FIGURE 185

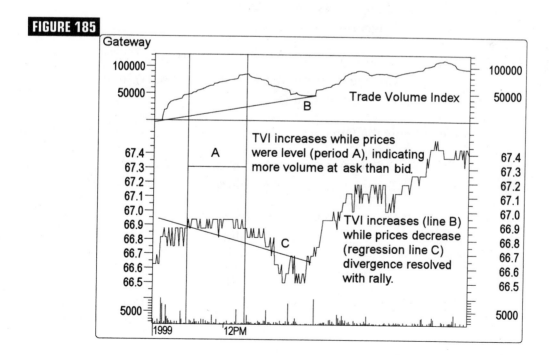

Calculation

The TVI is calculated by adding each trade's volume to a cumulative total when the price moves up by a specified amount and subtracting the trade's volume when the price moves down by a specified amount. The "specified" amount is called the Minimum Tick Value.

The calculations are very awkward in a spreadsheet, so I've skipped my customary table and explained the basic steps.

To calculate the TVI you must first determine if prices are being accumulated or distributed based on the Change and Minimum Tick Value:

MTV = Minimum Tick Value

Change = Price minus the extreme price since direction changed

If the Direction (defined below) is "Accumulate," the extreme price is the high since the direction changed to Accumulate. If the Direction is "Distribute," the extreme price is the low since the Direction changed to Distribute.

> If Change is greater than MTV, then
> Direction = Accumulate

> If Change is less than −MTV, then
> Direction = Distribute

> If Change is less than or equal to MTV and
> Change is greater than or equal to −MTV, then
> Direction = Last Direction

Once you know the Direction, you can then calculate the TVI:

> If Direction is Accumulate, then
> TVI = previous TVI + Volume

> If Direction is Distribute, then
> TVI = previous TVI − Volume

TRENDLINES

Overview

One of the basic tenets put forth by Charles Dow in the Dow Theory (see page 123) is that security prices do trend. Trends are often measured and identified by "trendlines." A trendline is a sloping line that is drawn between two or more prominent points on a chart.

- Rising trends are defined by a trendline that is drawn between two or more troughs (low points) to identify price support.
- Falling trends are defined by trendlines that are drawn between two or more peaks (high points) to identify price resistance.

Interpretation

A principle of technical analysis is that once a trend has been formed (two or more peaks/troughs have touched the trendline and reversed direction), it will remain intact until broken.

That sounds much more simplistic than it is! The goal is to analyze the current trend using trendlines and then either invest with the current trend until the trendline is broken or wait for the trendline to be broken and then invest with the new (opposing) trend.

The interpretation of trendlines is very similar to the interpretation of support and resistance concepts discussed earlier (see page 14).

One benefit of trendlines is that they help distinguish emotional decisions ("I think it's time to sell") from analytical decisions ("I will hold until the current rising trendline is broken"). Another benefit of trendlines is that they almost always keep you on the "right" side of the market. When using trendlines, it's difficult to hold a security for very long when prices are falling just as it's hard to be short when prices are rising—either way the trendline will be broken.

T

Example

Figure 186 shows Goodyear along with several trendlines. Trendlines A, C, and E are falling trendlines. Note how they were drawn between successive peaks. Trendlines B and D are rising trendlines. They were drawn between successive troughs in the price.

FIGURE 186

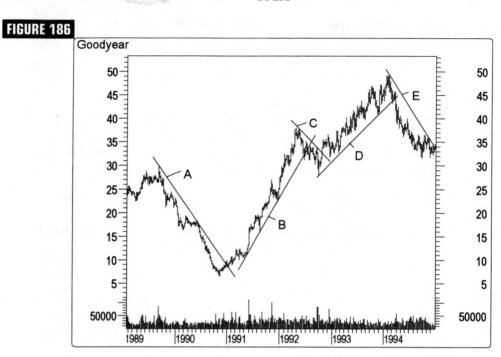

TRIX

Overview

TRIX is a momentum indicator that displays the percent rate-of-change of a triple exponentially smoothed moving average of a security's closing price. It is designed to keep you in trends equal to or shorter than the number of periods you specify.

Interpretation

The TRIX indicator oscillates around a zero line. Its triple exponential smoothing is designed to filter out "insignificant" cycles (i.e., those that are shorter than the number of periods you specify).

Trades should be placed when the indicator changes direction (i.e., buy when it turns up and sell when it turns down). You may want to plot a 9-period moving average of the TRIX to create a "signal" line (similar to the MACD indicator, page 199), and then buy when the TRIX rises above its signal and sell when it falls below its signal.

Divergences between the security and the TRIX can also help identify turning points.

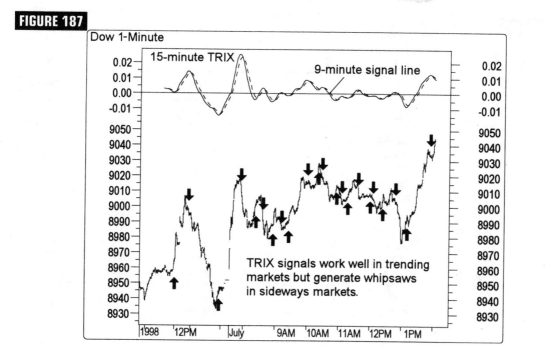

FIGURE 187

Dow 1-Minute

15-minute TRIX

9-minute signal line

TRIX signals work well in trending markets but generate whipsaws in sideways markets.

Example

Figure 187 shows a 1-minute chart of the Dow Industrials and a 15-minute TRIX (solid line) with a 9-minute "signal" moving average of the TRIX (dotted line). "Buy" arrows indicate when the TRIX rose above its signal line, and "sell" arrows indicate when it fell below its signal line. This method worked well when prices were trending, but it generated numerous false signals when prices were moving sideways.

Calculation

The TRIX is the 1-period percent rate-of-change (see page 267) of a triple exponentially smoothed moving average.

Table 79 illustrates the calculation of a 3-minute TRIX indicator:

- Column D is a 3-minute exponential moving average of the close. (See page 208 for details on calculating exponential moving averages.)
- Column E is a 3-minute exponential moving average of Column D.
- Column F is a 3-minute exponential moving average of Column E.
- To calculate Column G, first subtract the previous value in Column F from the current value in Column F. Next, divide this value by the current value in Column F. Finally, multiply this result by 100. This is the TRIX. Note that a 3-period TRIX isn't valid until the seventh period.

T

TABLE 79

			TRIX			
A	B	C	D	E	F	G
			3-period EMA of Close	3-period EMA of Col D	3-period EMA of Col E	1-period % change in Col F
Date	Time	Close				
06/30/98	7:35 AM	8,996.96				
06/30/98	7:36 AM	9,003.19				
06/30/98	7:37 AM	9,010.41	9,005.24			
06/30/98	7:38 AM	9,008.07	9,006.66			
06/30/98	7:39 AM	9,018.03	9,012.34	9,009.15		
06/30/98	7:40 AM	9,009.80	9,011.07	9,010.11		
06/30/98	7:41 AM	9,011.55	9,011.31	9,010.71	9,010.17	
06/30/98	7:42 AM	9,020.26	9,015.79	9,013.25	9,011.71	0.0171
06/30/98	7:43 AM	9,013.29	9,014.54	9,013.89	9,012.80	0.0121
06/30/98	7:44 AM	9,018.78	9,016.66	9,015.28	9,014.04	0.0137

TYPICAL PRICE

Overview

The Typical Price indicator is simply an average of each day's price. The Median Price (see page 190) and the Weighted Close (see page 362) are similar indicators.

Interpretation

The Typical Price indicator provides a simple, single-line plot of the day's average price. Some investors use the Typical Price, rather than the closing price, when creating moving average penetration systems.

The Typical Price is a building block of the Money Flow Index (see page 197).

Example

Figure 188 shows the Typical Price indicator on top of Imclone's bar chart.

FIGURE 188

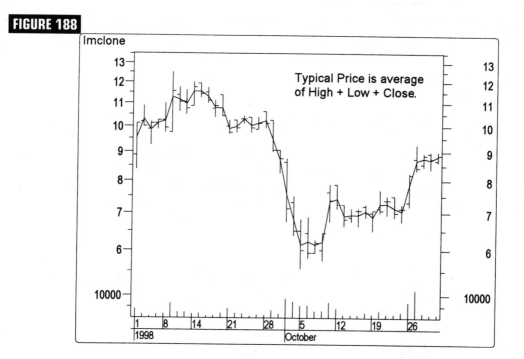

Imclone

Typical Price is average
of High + Low + Close.

Calculation

The Typical Price indicator is calculated by adding the high, low, and closing prices together and then dividing by 3, as illustrated in Table 80. The result is the average (or typical) price.

$$\frac{(High + Low + Close)}{3}$$

TABLE 80

| | | TYPICAL PRICE | | | |
| A | B | C | D | E | F |
Date	High	Low	Close	Column B plus Column C plus Column D	Column E divided by 3.0
09/01/98	10.1250	8.3750	10.1250	28.6250	9.5417
09/02/98	10.8750	10.0000	10.0000	30.8750	10.2917
09/03/98	10.1875	9.2500	10.1250	29.5625	9.8542
09/04/98	10.2500	9.8750	10.2500	30.3750	10.1250
09/08/98	11.0000	9.7500	9.9375	30.6875	10.2292
09/09/98	12.5000	9.7500	11.5625	33.8125	11.2708
09/10/98	11.7500	10.6250	11.0625	33.4375	11.1458
09/11/98	11.6250	10.5000	10.7500	32.8750	10.9583

T

ULTIMATE OSCILLATOR

Overview

Price oscillators typically compare a security's smoothed price with its price n periods ago. Larry Williams noted that the value of this type of oscillator can vary greatly depending on the number of time periods used during the calculation. So he developed the Ultimate Oscillator, which uses weighted sums of three oscillators, each of which uses a different time period. The three oscillators are based on Williams's definitions of buying and selling "pressure."

Interpretation

Williams recommended initiating a trade following a divergence (see page 36) and a breakout in the Ultimate Oscillator's trend. The following text summarizes these rules.

Buy when:

1. A bullish divergence occurs. This is when the security's price makes a lower low that is not confirmed by a lower low in the Ultimate Oscillator. (It is "bullish," because the indicator is forecasting higher prices.)
2. During the bullish divergence, the Ultimate Oscillator falls below 30.
3. The Ultimate Oscillator then rises above the highest point reached during the span of the bullish divergence. This is the point at which you buy.

Close long positions when:

1. The conditions are met to sell short (explained below), or
2. The Ultimate Oscillator rises above 50 and then falls below 45, or
3. The Ultimate Oscillator rises above 70. (I sometimes wait for it to then fall below 70.)

Sell short when:

1. A bearish divergence occurs. This is when the security's price makes a higher high that is not confirmed by a higher high in the Ultimate Oscillator.
2. During the bearish divergence, the Ultimate Oscillator rises above 50.
3. The Ultimate Oscillator then falls below the lowest point reached during the span of the bearish divergence. This is the point at which you sell short.

Close short positions when:

1. The conditions are met to buy long (explained above), or
2. The Ultimate Oscillator rises above 65, or
3. The Ultimate Oscillator falls below 30. (I will sometimes wait for it to then rise above 30.)

Example

Figure 189 shows Noble Drilling and its Ultimate Oscillator. The "buy" arrow indicates when the conditions for a buy signal were met:

- A bullish divergence occurred (trendlines) when prices made a new low that was not confirmed by the Ultimate Oscillator.
- The Ultimate Oscillator fell below 30 during the divergence.
- The Ultimate Oscillator rose above the highest point reached during the span of the divergence (line B).

Calculation

The calculations for the Ultimate Oscillator are too complex to present in this book. The A-to-Z Companion Spreadsheet (see page xvii) contains the full calculations.

FIGURE 189

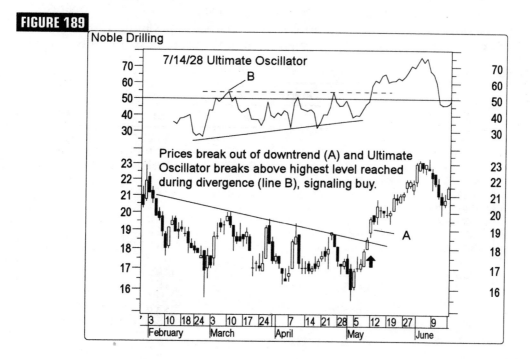

UPSIDE/DOWNSIDE RATIO

Overview

The Upside/Downside Ratio shows the relationship between up (advancing) and down (declining) volume on the New York Stock Exchange. Advancing, declining, and unchanged volume are discussed on page 58.

Interpretation

When the Upside/Downside Ratio is greater than 1.0, it is showing that there is more volume associated with stocks that are increasing in price than with stocks that are decreasing in price.

While discussing advancing/declining volume in his book *Winning on Wall Street*, Martin Zweig states, "Every bull market in history, and many good intermediate advances, have been launched with a buying stampede that included one or more 9-to-1 days" ("9-to-1" refers to a day were the Upside/Downside Ratio is greater than 9). He goes on to say, "The 9-to-1 up day is a most encouraging sign, and having two of them within a reasonably short span is very bullish. I call it a 'double 9-to-1' when two such days occur within three months of one another."

Table 81 shows all of the double 9-to-1 buy signals that occurred from 1962 to August 1999. As of this writing, no signals have occurred since the last one on June 8, 1988, although October 15, 1998, came within a whisker and was followed by a 25.1 percent gain in the ensuing six months.

TABLE 81

| Date | DHIA | PERCENT CHANGE AFTER | | |
		3 Months	6 Months	12 Months
11/12/62	624	+8.5	+15.9	+20.2
11/19/63	751	+6.9	+9.1	+16.5
10/12/66	778	+6.9	8.6	+17.4
05/27/70	663	+14.6	+17.8	+16.5
11/19/71	830	+11.8	+17.0	+22.8
09/19/75	830	+1.7	+18.1	+19.9
04/22/80	790	+17.3	+20.9	+27.5
03/22/82	820	−2.4	+13.2	+37.0
08/20/82	869	+15.1	+24.3	+38.4
01/06/83	1,071	+3.9	+14.0	+20.2
08/02/84	1,166	+4.4	+10.6	+16.0
11/23/84	1,220	+4.7	+6.2	+19.3
01/02/87	1,927	+20.4	+26.4	+4.6
10/29/87	1,938	+1.0	+4.9	+10.8
01/04/88	2,015	−1.7	+7.1	+8.0
06/08/88	2,102	−1.9	+1.9	+19.7
Average		+6.4	+12.5	+18.4

FIGURE 190

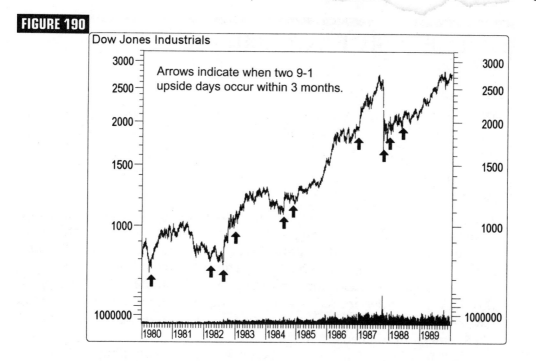

Dow Jones Industrials

Arrows indicate when two 9-1 upside days occur within 3 months.

Example

Figure 190 shows the Dow Jones Industrial Average during the 1980s. "Buy" arrows indicate where double 9-to-1 buy signals occurred.

Calculation

The Upside/Downside Ratio is calculated by dividing the daily volume of advancing stocks by the daily volume of declining stocks (see Table 82).

$$\frac{NYSE\ Advancing\ Volume}{NYSE\ Declining\ Volume}$$

TABLE 82

	UPSIDE/DOWNSIDE RATIO		
A	B	C	D
Date	Advancing Volume	Declining Volume	Column B divided by Column C
04/25/97	1,097,590	2,685,030	0.409
04/28/97	2,247,369	1,430,582	1.571
04/29/97	4,617,426	527,996	8.745
04/30/97	4,000,088	1,163,730	3.437

U

UPSIDE/DOWNSIDE VOLUME

Overview

The Upside/Downside Volume indicator shows the difference between up (advancing) and down (declining) volume on the New York Stock Exchange. Advancing, declining, and unchanged volume are discussed on page 58.

Interpretation

The Upside/Downside Volume indicator shows the net flow of volume into or out of the market. A reading of +40 would indicate that up volume exceeded down volume by 40 million shares. Likewise a reading of −40 would indicate that down volume exceeded up volume by 40 million shares.

The indicator is useful for comparing today's volume action with previous days. Currently, normal readings are in the area of ±150. Very active days exceed ±300 million shares (The October 1987 crash reached −602; the 1998 correction reached −836.)

The Cumulative Volume Index (see page 110) is a cumulative total of the Upside/Downside Volume indicator.

FIGURE 191

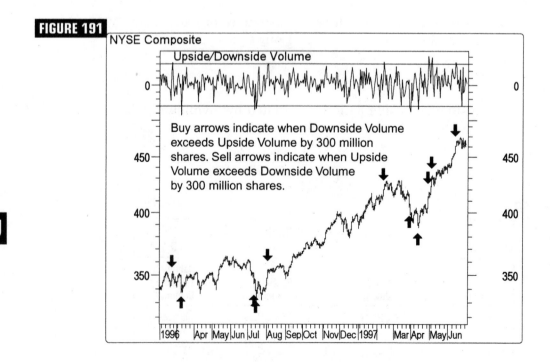

NYSE Composite

Upside/Downside Volume

Buy arrows indicate when Downside Volume exceeds Upside Volume by 300 million shares. Sell arrows indicate when Upside Volume exceeds Downside Volume by 300 million shares.

Example

Figure 191 shows the NYSE Composite and the Upside/Downside Volume indicator. "Buy" arrows indicate when the Upside/Downside Volume indicator was greater than 300, and "sell" arrows indicate when it was less than −300.

Calculation

The Upside/Downside Volume indicator is calculated by subtracting the daily volume of declining stocks from the daily volume of advancing stocks (see Table 83).

NYSE Advancing Volume − NYSE Declining Volume

TABLE 83

| | UPSIDE/DOWNSIDE VOLUME | | |
| A | B | C | D |
Date	Advancing Volume	Declining Volume	Column B minus Column C
04/25/97	1,097,590	2,685,030	−1,587,440
04/28/97	2,247,369	1,430,582	816,787
04/29/97	4,617,426	527,996	4,089,430
04/30/97	4,000,088	1,163,730	2,836,358

VERTICAL HORIZONTAL FILTER

Overview

The Vertical Horizontal Filter (VHF) determines whether prices are in a trending phase or a congestion phase. It was first presented by Adam White in an article published in the August 1991 issue of *Futures* magazine.

Interpretation

Probably the biggest dilemma in technical analysis is determining if prices are trending or are in a trading range. Trend-following indicators such as the MACD and moving averages are excellent in trending markets, but they usually generate multiple conflicting trades during trading-range (or "congestion") periods. On the other hand, oscillators such as the RSI and the

V

Stochastic Oscillators work well when prices fluctuate within a trading range, but they almost always close positions prematurely during trending markets. The VHF indicator attempts to determine the "trendiness" of prices to help you decide which indicators to use.

There are three ways to interpret the VHF indicator:

1. You can use the VHF values themselves to determine the degree to which prices are trending. The higher the VHF, the higher the degree of trending and the better trend-following indicators will work.
2. You can use the direction of the VHF to determine whether a trending or congestion phase is developing. A rising VHF indicates a developing trend; a falling VHF indicates that prices may be entering a congestion phase.
3. You can use the VHF as a contrarian indicator. Expect congestion periods to follow high VHF values; expect prices to trend following low VHF values.

Example

Figure 192 shows Motorola and the VHF indicator. The VHF indicator was relatively low from 1989 through most of 1992. These low values showed that prices were in a trading range. From late 1992 through 1993 the VHF was significantly higher. These higher values indicated that prices were trending.

FIGURE 192

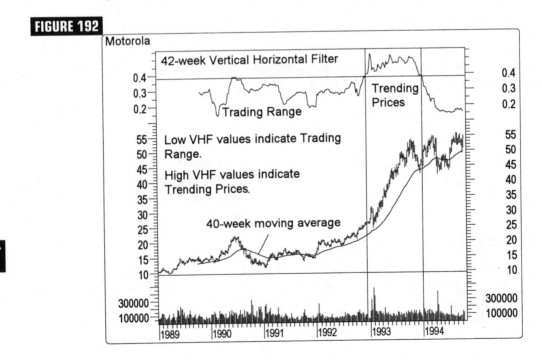

The 40-week (i.e., 200-day) moving average on Motorola's prices demonstrates the value of the VHF indicator. You can see that a classic moving average trading system (buy when prices rise above their moving average and sell when prices fall below their average) worked well in 1992 and 1993 but generated numerous whipsaws when prices were in a trading range.

Calculation

To calculate the VHF indicator, first determine the highest closing price (HCP) and the lowest closing price (LCP) over the specified time period.

$$HCP = \text{Highest closing price in } n \text{ periods}$$
$$LCP = \text{Lowest closing price in } n \text{ periods}$$

Next, subtract the lowest closing price from the highest closing price and take the absolute value of this difference. This value will be the numerator. (The term "absolute value" means "regardless of sign." For example, the absolute value of -3 is 3.)

$$Numerator = \text{Absolute value of } (HCP - LCP)$$

To determine the denominator, sum the absolute value of the difference between each day's price and the previous day's price over the specified time periods.

$$Denominator = \sum_{j=1}^{n} \text{Absolute value of } (Close_j - Close_{j-1})$$

The VHF is then calculated by dividing the previously defined numerator by the denominator.

$$VHF = \frac{Numerator}{Denominator}$$

Table 84 illustrates the calculation of a 5-day Vertical Horizontal Filter:

- Column C is the highest closing price (Column B) over the last n days (i.e., 5 in this example).
- Column D is the lowest closing price (Column B) over the last n days.
- Column E is the absolute value of Column C minus Column D.
- Column F is the change in the close. It is calculated by subtracting today's closing price (Column B) from the previous closing price.
- Column G is the absolute value of Column F.
- Column H is the n-day (i.e., 5) sum of Column G.
- Column I is Column E divided by Column H. This is the Vertical Horizontal Filter.

TABLE 84

		VERTICAL HORIZONTAL FILTER						
A	B	C	D	E	F	G	H	I
Date	Close	Highest Close in 5 days	Lowest Close in 5 days	Abs of C – D	1-period Change in Column B	Absolute value of Column F	5-day sum of Column G	Column E divided by Column H
01/03/94	44.3125							
01/04/94	44.1250				−0.1875	0.1875		
01/05/94	45.0625				0.9375	0.9375		
01/06/94	44.8125				−0.2500	0.2500		
01/07/94	44.8125	45.0625	44.1250	0.9375	0.0000	0.0000		
01/10/94	45.2500	45.2500	44.1250	1.1250	0.4375	0.4375	1.8125	0.6207
01/11/94	46.1250	46.1250	44.8125	1.3125	0.8750	0.8750	2.5000	0.5250
01/12/94	47.3750	47.3750	44.8125	2.5625	1.2500	1.2500	2.8125	0.9111
01/13/94	49.0000	49.0000	44.8125	4.1875	1.6250	1.6250	4.1875	1.0000

VOLATILITY, CHAIKIN'S

Overview

Chaikin's Volatility indicator compares the spread between a security's high and low prices. It quantifies volatility as a widening of the range between the high and the low price.

Interpretation

There are two ways to interpret this measure of volatility. One method assumes that market tops are generally accompanied by increased volatility (as investors get nervous and indecisive) and that the latter stages of a market bottom are generally accompanied by decreased volatility (as investors get bored).

Another method (Chaikin's) assumes that an increase in the Volatility indicator over a relatively short time period indicates that a bottom is near (e.g., a panic sell-off) and that a decrease in volatility over a longer time period indicates an approaching top (e.g., a mature bull market).

As with almost all experienced investors, Chaikin recommends that you do not rely on any one indicator. He suggests using a moving average penetration or trading band system to confirm this (or any) indicator.

V

FIGURE 193

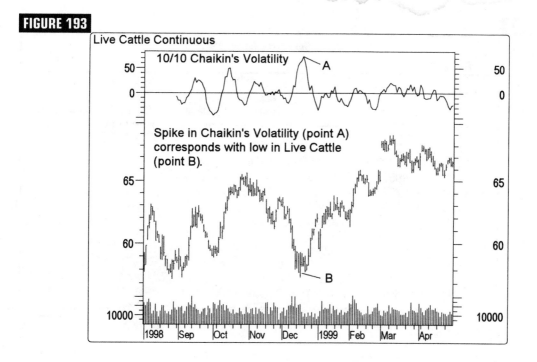

Live Cattle Continuous

10/10 Chaikin's Volatility — A

Spike in Chaikin's Volatility (point A) corresponds with low in Live Cattle (point B).

B

1998 Sep Oct Nov Dec 1999 Feb Mar Apr

Example

Figure 193 shows Live Cattle and Chaikin's Volatility indicator. The indicator reached a rapid peak following a panic sell-off (point A). This indicated that a bottom was near (point B).

Calculation

Chaikin's Volatility is calculated by first calculating an exponential moving average of the difference between the daily high and low prices. Chaikin recommends a 10-day moving average.

HL Average = Exponential moving average of (High − Low)

Next, calculate the percent that this moving average has changed over a specified time period. Chaikin again recommends 10 days.

$$\left(\frac{(HL\ Average) - (HL\ Average\ \textit{n-periods ago})}{HL\ Average\ \textit{n-periods ago}} \right) * 100$$

Table 85 illustrates the calculation of Chaikin's Volatility:

- Column D is the high (Column B) minus the low (Column C).

V

TABLE 85

			VOLATILITY, CHAIKIN'S			
A	**B**	**C**	**D**	**E**	**F**	**G**
Date	High	Low	High minus Low	5-day EMA of Column D	Column E minus Column E 5 days ago	Chaikin's Volatility
08/03/98	60.2476	58.4915	1.7561	1.7561		
08/04/98	60.5637	59.0323	1.5314	1.6812		
08/05/98	62.0859	60.8968	1.1891	1.5172		
08/06/98	62.7016	61.3758	1.3258	1.4534		
08/07/98	62.9355	61.7601	1.1754	1.3607		
08/10/98	62.8032	62.0952	0.7080	1.1431		
08/11/98	62.3419	61.6508	0.6911	0.9925		
08/12/98	61.8435	60.3919	1.4516	1.1455		
08/13/98	61.6278	60.8040	0.8238	1.0383		
08/14/98	61.3613	60.6952	0.6661	0.9142	−0.4465	−32.8138
08/17/98	60.5073	59.6734	0.8339	0.8874	−0.2557	−22.3683
08/18/98	61.4379	59.6702	1.7677	1.1809	0.1884	18.9829

- Column E is a 5-day exponential moving average of Column D. The first row in Column E is seeded with the first value in Column D (i.e., 1.7561). Subsequent rows in Column E are calculated by multiplying the value in Column D by 0.333..., then multiplying the previous day's value in Column E by 0.666..., and finally adding these two values together. (The value 0.333... was calculated as "2 / (5+1)" as explained on page 208. The value 0.666... was calculated as "1 − 0.333" as explained on page 208.)
- Column F is Column E minus the value in Column E 5 days ago.
- Column G is Column F divided by Column E 5 days ago. This value is then multiplied by 100. This is Chaikin's Volatility.

VOLUME

Overview

Volume is simply the number of shares (or contracts) traded during a specified time frame (e.g., hour, day, week, month, etc). The analysis of volume is a basic yet very important element of technical analysis. Volume provides clues as to the intensity of a given price move.

Interpretation

Low volume levels are characteristic of the indecisive expectations that typically occur during consolidation periods (i.e., periods where prices move sideways in a trading range). Low volume also often occurs within the indecisive period during market bottoms.

High volume levels are characteristic of market tops when there is a strong consensus that prices will move higher. High volume levels are also very common at the beginning of new trends (i.e., when prices break out of a trading range). Just before market bottoms, volume will often increase due to panic-driven selling.

Volume can help determine the health of an existing trend. A healthy uptrend should have higher volume on the upward legs of the trend and lower volume on the downward (corrective) legs. A healthy downtrend usually has higher volume on the downward legs of the trend and lower volume on the upward (corrective) legs.

Example

Figure 194 shows Merck and its volume. Notice how volume (trendline A2) was relatively high during the initial price decline (trendline A1). The increase in volume during the price decline showed that many investors would sell when prices declined. This was bearish.

FIGURE 194

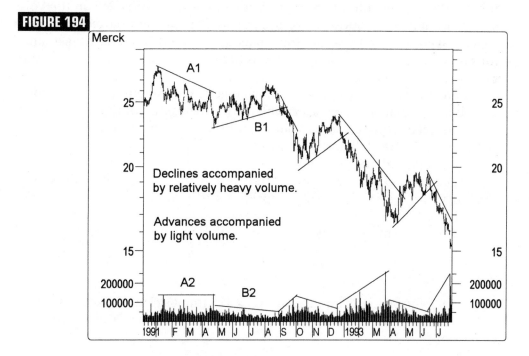

Prices then tried to rally (trendline B1). However, volume decreased dramatically during this rally (trendline B2). This showed that investors were not willing to buy, even when prices were rising. This too, was bearish.

This pattern continued throughout the decline in 1992 and 1993. When prices rallied, they did so on decreased volume. When prices declined, they did so on increased volume. This showed, again and again, that the bears were in control and that prices would continue to fall.

VOLUME OSCILLATOR

Overview

The Volume Oscillator displays the difference between two moving averages of a security's volume (see page 203). The difference between the moving averages can be expressed in either points or percentages.

Interpretation

You can use the difference between two moving averages of volume to determine if the overall volume trend is increasing or decreasing. When the Volume Oscillator rises above zero, it signifies that the shorter-term volume moving average has risen above the longer-term volume moving average, and thus that the short-term volume trend is higher (i.e., more volume) than the longer-term volume trend.

There are many ways to interpret changes in volume trends. One common belief is that rising prices coupled with increased volume, and falling prices coupled with decreased volume, is bullish. Conversely, if volume increases when prices fall and decreases when prices rise, the market is showing signs of underlying weakness.

The theory behind this is straightforward. Rising prices coupled with increased volume signify increased upside participation (more buyers) that should lead to a continued move. Conversely, falling prices coupled with increased volume (more sellers) signify decreased upside participation.

Example

Figure 195 shows Xerox and a 5/10-week Volume Oscillator. Linear Regression Trendlines (see page 176) are drawn for both the prices and the Volume Oscillator.

FIGURE 195

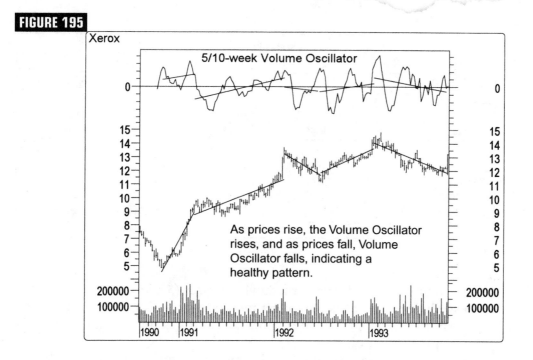

This chart shows a healthy pattern. When prices were moving higher, as shown by rising Linear Regression Trendlines, the Volume Oscillator was also rising. When prices were falling, the Volume Oscillator was also falling.

Calculation

The Volume Oscillator displays the difference between two moving averages of volume. The difference can be displayed as either points or percentages. To see the difference in points, subtract the longer-term moving average of volume from the shorter-term moving average of volume:

$$Shorter\ Moving\ Average - Longer\ Moving\ Average$$

To display the difference in percentages, divide the difference by the longer-term moving average:

$$\left(\frac{Shorter\ Moving\ Average - Longer\ Moving\ Average}{Longer\ Moving\ Average}\right) * 100$$

Table 86 illustrates the calculation of the Volume Oscillator:

- Column C is a short-term simple moving average of the volume (2 periods in this example).

TABLE 86

		VOLUME OSCILLATOR			
A	B	C	D	E	F
Date	Volume	Shorter M.A. (2-day)	Longer M.A. (5-day)	Column C minus Column D	Column E divided by Column D multiplied by 100
01/04/99	17,604				
01/05/99	18,918	18,261			
01/06/99	21,030	19,974			
01/07/99	13,854	17,442			
01/08/99	10,866	12,360	16,454.40	−4,094.40	−24.88
01/11/99	14,580	12,723	15,849.60	−3,126.60	−19.73

- Column D is the longer-term moving average (5 periods in this example).
- Column E subtracts the longer moving average (Column D) from the shorter moving average (Column C). This is the Volume Oscillator expressed in points.
- Column F divides Column C by the longer moving average and multiplies by 100. This is the Volume Oscillator expressed in percentages.

VOLUME RATE-OF-CHANGE

Overview

The Volume Rate-of-Change (ROC) is calculated identically as the Price ROC (see page 267), except that it displays the ROC of the security's volume rather than of its closing price.

Interpretation

Almost every significant chart formation (e.g., tops, bottoms, breakouts) is accompanied by a sharp increase in volume. The Volume ROC shows the speed at which volume is changing.

Additional information on the interpretation of volume trends can be found in the discussions on Volume (see page 356) and Volume Oscillator (see page 358).

V

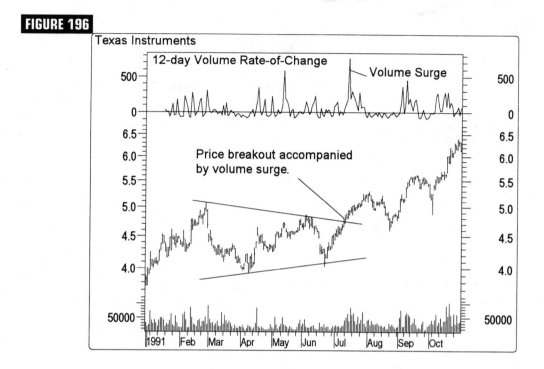

FIGURE 196

Texas Instruments

Example

Figure 196 shows Texas Instruments and its 12-day Volume ROC. When prices broke out of the triangular pattern, they were accompanied by a sharp increase in volume. The increase in volume confirmed the validity of the price breakout.

Calculation

The Volume Rate-of-Change indicator is calculated by dividing the amount that volume has changed over the last *n* periods by the volume *n* periods ago. The result is the percentage that the volume has changed in the last *n* periods.

If the volume is higher today than *n* periods ago, the ROC will be a positive number. If the volume is lower today than *n* periods ago, the ROC will be a negative number.

$$\left(\frac{Volume \ - \ Volume \ n\text{-}periods \ ago}{Volume \ n\text{-}periods \ ago}\right) * 100$$

TABLE 87

		VOLUME ROC		
A	B	C	D	E
Date	Volume	Volume 5 periods ago	Column B minus Column C	Col D / Col C multiplied by 100
01/02/92	9,996			
01/03/92	12,940			
01/06/92	37,524			
01/07/92	21,032			
01/08/92	14,880			
01/09/92	21,304	9,996	11,308	113.1253
01/10/92	15,776	12,940	2,836	21.9165
01/13/92	10,384	37,524	−27,140	−72.3270
01/14/92	20,896	21,032	−136	−0.6466
01/15/92	24,892	14,880	10,012	67.2849

Table 87 illustrates the calculation of the 5-day Volume ROC:

- Column C is the volume 5 periods ago.
- Column D is the current volume (Column B) minus the volume 5 periods ago (Column C). This is the Volume ROC expressed in points.
- Column E divides Column D by the volume *n* periods ago (Column C). This result is then multiplied by 100. This is the Volume ROC expressed in percentages.

WEIGHTED CLOSE

Overview

The Weighted Close indicator is simply an average of each day's price. It gets its name from the fact that extra weight is given to the closing price. The Median Price (see page 190) and Typical Price (see page 344) are similar indicators.

Interpretation

When plotting and back-testing moving averages, indicators, trendlines, etc., some investors like the simplicity that a line chart offers. However, line charts that show only the closing price can be misleading, since they ignore the high and low prices. By plotting a single point for each day that includes the high, low, and closing prices, a Weighted Close chart combines the simplicity of the line chart with the scope of a bar chart.

Example

Figure 197 shows the Weighted Close plotted on top of a normal high/low/close bar chart of Paychex.

FIGURE 197

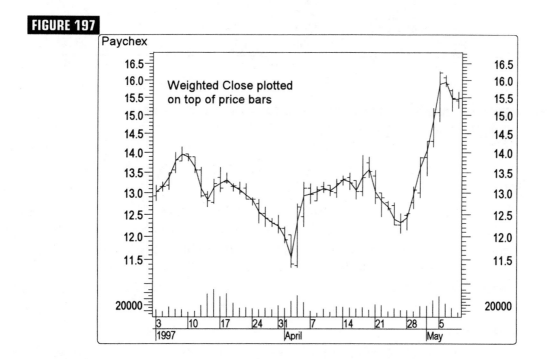

Calculation

The Weighted Close is calculated by multiplying the close by 2, adding the high and the low to this product, and dividing by 4. The result is the average price with extra weight given to the closing price.

$$\frac{(Close * 2) + High + Low}{4}$$

Table 88 illustrates the calculation of the Weighted Close:

- Column E adds the high, low, and 2 times the close.
- Column F divides Column E by 4 to get the Weighted Close.

TABLE 88

| | | | | WEIGHTED CLOSE | | |
	A	B	C	D	E	F
	Date	High	Low	Close	Close * 2 plus High plus Low	Column E divided by 4
	08/28/98	39.7500	38.2500	39.0000	156.0000	39.0000
	08/31/98	39.6250	37.8750	38.0000	153.5000	38.3750
	09/01/98	38.7500	36.5000	38.7500	152.7500	38.1875
	09/02/98	41.6250	38.5000	41.4375	163.0000	40.7500
	09/03/98	41.2500	40.5000	40.6875	163.1250	40.7813
	09/04/98	41.1250	40.5000	41.1250	163.8750	40.9688

WILDER'S SMOOTHING

Overview

Wilder's Smoothing is a moving average method similar to an exponential moving average in that it retains a decreasingly smaller percentage of all the historical data in its calculation. Welles Wilder, who uses it as a component of many of his other studies, most notably the Relative Strength Index (see page 297), developed it.

Interpretation

Wilder's Smoothing should be interpreted like other moving averages (see page 203). It is slower to respond to price changes than other moving averages. It can also be expressed as a $2n - 1$ exponential moving average (e.g., a 14-period Wilder's Smoothing is very similar to a 27-period exponential moving average, although the moving averages begin on different periods and have slightly different values for a short time period).

Example

Figure 198 shows a 14-day Wilder's Smoothing of Merck, along with a 14-day exponential moving average.

W

FIGURE 198

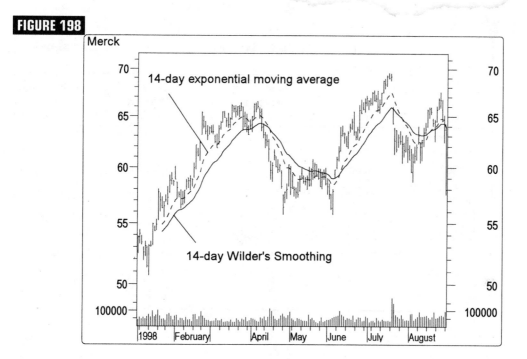

Calculation

The calculation of Wilder's Smoothing is as follows:

$$Previous\ M.A.\ +\ \frac{1}{Periods}(Close\ -\ Previous\ M.A.)$$

Table 89 illustrates the calculation of a 5-day Wilder's Smoothing:

- First, sum the first n days of data (5 in this example), divide by n, and enter the value in Column E the nth day. This "seeds" Wilder's Smoothing with an n-period simple moving average.
- Column C is the current close (Column B) minus the previous Wilder's Smoothing value.
- Column D multiplies Column C (the difference between today's close and yesterday's Wilder's Smoothing) $1/n$, which is $1/5$, or 0.2 in this example.
- Column E adds Column D to the previous value in Column E. This is Wilder's Smoothing.

TABLE 89

		WILDER'S SMOOTHING		
A	B	C	D	E
Date	Close	Close minus Previous M.A.	Column C multiplied by 1/n	Column D plus Previous Column E
02/18/98	62.1250			
02/19/98	61.1250			
02/20/98	62.3438			
02/23/98	65.3125			
02/24/98	63.9688			62.9750
02/25/98	63.4375	0.4625	0.0925	63.0675
02/26/98	63.0000	−0.0675	−0.0135	63.0540
02/27/98	63.7812	0.7272	0.1454	63.1995
03/02/98	63.4062	0.2067	0.0413	63.2408
03/03/98	63.4062	0.1654	0.0331	63.2739
03/04/98	62.4375	−0.8364	−0.1673	63.1066
03/05/98	61.8438	−1.2628	−0.2526	62.8540

WILLIAMS'S ACCUMULATION/DISTRIBUTION

Overview

"Accumulation" is a term used to describe a market controlled by buyers, whereas "distribution" is defined by a market controlled by sellers. This indicator was developed by Larry Williams.

Interpretation

Williams recommends trading this indicator based on divergences (see page 36):

- Distribution of the security is indicated when the security is making a new high and the Accumulation/Distribution indicator is failing to make a new high. Sell.
- Accumulation of the security is indicated when the security is making a new low and the Accumulation/Distribution indicator is failing to make a new low. Buy.

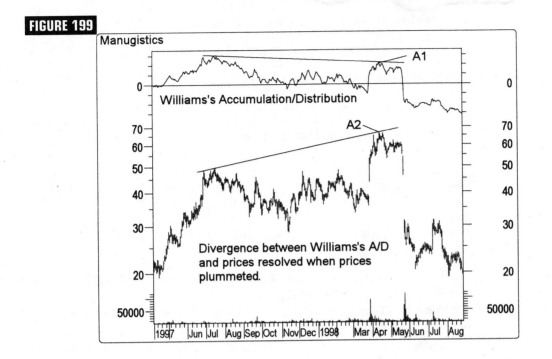

FIGURE 199

Manugistics

Williams's Accumulation/Distribution

Divergence between Williams's A/D
and prices resolved when prices
plummeted.

Example

Figure 199 shows Manugistics and Williams's Accumulation/Distribution
Line. A bearish divergence occurred when the prices were making a new high
(point A2) and the Accumulation/Distribution indicator was failing to make
a new high (point A1). This was the time to sell.

Calculation

To calculate Williams's Accumulation/Distribution Line, first determine the
True Range High (TRH) and the True Range Low (TRL).

$$TRH = \textit{Yesterday's close or today's high, whichever is greater}$$
$$TRL = \textit{Yesterday's close or today's low, whichever is less}$$

Today's Accumulation/Distribution is then determined by comparing today's closing price to yesterday's closing price.
If today's close is greater than yesterday's close:

$$\textit{Today's A/D} = \textit{today's close} - TRL$$

W

If today's close is less than yesterday's close:

$$Today's\ A/D = today's\ close - TRH$$

If today's close is equal to yesterday's close:

$$Today's\ A/D = 0$$

Williams's Accumulation/Distribution Line is a cumulative total of these daily values.

Williams's Accumulation/Distribution = Today's Accumulation/Distribution + Yesterday's Williams's Accumulation/Distribution

Table 90 illustrates the calculation of Williams's Accumulation/Distribution:

- Column E is yesterday's close or today's high, whichever is greater. This is the True Range High (TRH).
- Column F is yesterday's close or today's low, whichever is lesser. This is the True Range Low (TRL).
- Column G is "Today's Accumulation/Distribution" based on the above equation.
- Column H is a cumulative total of Column G.

TABLE 90

			WILLIAMS'S ACCUMULATION/DISTRIBUTION				
A	B	C	D	E	F	G	H
Date	High	Low	Close	TRH	TRL	Today's A/D	Cumulative total of Column G
04/18/97	21.5000	20.7500	21.2500				
04/21/97	21.6250	21.0000	21.0310	21.6250	21.0000	−0.5940	−0.5940
04/22/97	21.1250	20.5000	20.8750	21.1250	20.5000	−0.2500	−0.8440
04/23/97	22.4380	20.8750	22.0000	22.4380	20.8750	1.1250	0.2810
04/24/97	23.5000	22.4380	22.5000	23.5000	22.0000	0.5000	0.7810
04/25/97	23.2500	22.4380	23.0000	23.2500	22.4380	0.5620	1.3430
04/28/97	25.0000	22.8750	24.5630	25.0000	22.8750	1.6880	3.0310
04/29/97	25.6250	23.7500	25.3750	25.6250	23.7500	1.6250	4.6560
04/30/97	27.1250	24.9380	26.8750	27.1250	24.9380	1.9370	6.5930
05/01/97	28.7500	26.8750	27.3750	28.7500	26.8750	0.5000	7.0930
05/02/97	28.0000	26.2500	27.7500	28.0000	26.2500	1.5000	8.5930
05/05/97	30.3750	27.6250	29.5000	30.3750	27.6250	1.8750	10.4680

WILLIAMS'S %R

Overview

Williams's %R (pronounced "percent R") is a momentum indicator that measures overbought/oversold levels. It was developed by Larry Williams.

Interpretation

The interpretation of Williams's %R is very similar to that of the Stochastic Oscillator (see page 321), except that %R is plotted upside down and the Stochastic Oscillator has internal smoothing.

To display Williams's %R indicator on an upside-down scale, it is usually plotted using negative values (e.g., −20 percent). For the purpose of analysis and discussion, simply ignore the negative symbols.

Readings in the range of 80 to 100 percent indicate that the security is oversold, while readings in the range of 0 to 20 percent suggest that it is overbought.

As with all overbought/oversold indicators, it is best to wait for the security's price to change direction before placing your trades. For example, if an overbought/oversold indicator (such as the Stochastic Oscillator or Williams's %R) is showing an overbought condition, it is wise to wait for the security's price to turn down before selling the security. (The MACD—see page 199—is a good indicator for monitoring change in a security's price.) It is not unusual for overbought/oversold indicators to remain in an overbought/oversold condition for a long time period as the security's price continues to climb or fall. Selling simply because the security appears overbought may take you out of the security long before its price shows signs of deterioration.

An interesting phenomenon of the %R indicator is its uncanny ability to anticipate a reversal in the underlying security's price. The indicator almost always forms a peak and turns down a few days before the security's price peaks and turns down. Likewise, %R usually creates a trough and turns up a few days before the security's price turns up.

Example

Figure 200 shows the S&P 100 Index and its 14-day Williams's %R. "Buy" arrows indicate each time the %R formed a trough below 80 percent. In almost every case this occurred 1 or 2 days before the prices bottomed.

FIGURE 200

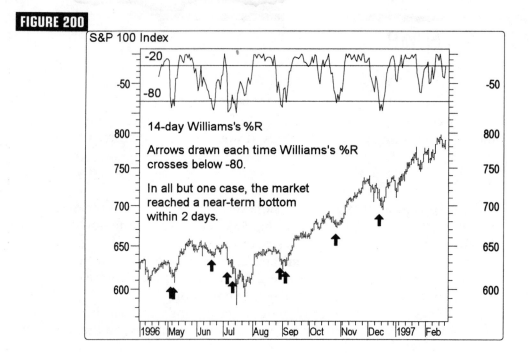

Calculation

The formula used to calculate Williams's %R is similar to the Stochastic Oscillator (see page 321):

$$\left(\frac{Highest\ High\ in\ n\ periods\ -\ Current\ Close}{Highest\ High\ in\ n\ periods\ -\ Lowest\ Low\ in\ n\ periods} \right) * -100$$

Table 91 illustrates the calculation of a 5-period Williams's %R:

- Column E is the highest high (Column B) in the last *n* periods (n being 5 in this example).
- Column F is the lowest low (Column C) in the last *n* periods.
- Column G is Column E minus the current close (Column D).
- Column H is Column E minus Column F. This is the trading range during the 5-day period.
- Column I divides Column G by Column H, and then multiplies by −100 (i.e., negative 100). This is Williams's %R.

TABLE 91

WILLIAMS'S %R

A	B	C	D	E	F	G	H	I
Date	High	Low	Close	Highest High in last 5 periods	Lowest Low in last 5 periods	Column E minus Close	Column E minus Column F	Col G / Col H times −100
03/27/96	631.34	624.81	626.01					
03/28/96	627.11	623.59	626.44					
03/29/96	628.49	621.33	622.20					
04/01/96	630.89	622.20	630.80					
04/02/96	632.85	630.21	632.85	632.85	621.33	0.00	11.52	0.00
04/03/96	633.26	629.64	633.06	633.26	621.33	0.20	11.93	−1.68
04/04/96	634.65	632.34	633.56	634.65	621.33	1.09	13.32	−8.18
04/08/96	633.56	616.31	622.11	634.65	616.31	12.54	18.34	−68.38
04/09/96	624.84	618.98	620.34	634.65	616.31	14.31	18.34	−78.03
04/10/96	621.62	609.84	611.60	634.65	609.84	23.05	24.81	−92.91
04/11/96	614.01	602.56	609.89	634.65	602.56	24.76	32.09	−77.16
04/12/96	615.36	609.71	615.36	633.56	602.56	18.20	31.00	−58.71
04/15/96	620.51	615.36	620.44	624.84	602.56	4.40	22.28	−19.75
04/16/96	624.33	620.21	623.66	624.33	602.56	0.67	21.77	−3.08

ZIG ZAG

Overview

The Zig Zag indicator filters out changes in an underlying plot (e.g., a security's price or another indicator) that are less than a specified amount. The Zig Zag indicator shows only significant changes. For additional information, refer to *Filtered Waves* by Arthur Merrill.

Interpretation

The Zig Zag indicator is used primarily to help you see changes by punctuating the most significant reversals.

It is very important to understand that the last "leg" displayed in a Zig Zag chart can change based on changes in the underlying plot (e.g., prices). This is the only indicator in this book where a change in the security's price can change a previous value of the indicator. Since the Zig Zag indicator can adjust its values based on subsequent changes in the underlying plot, it has perfect hindsight into what prices have done. Please don't try to create a trading system based on the Zig Zag indicator—its hindsight is much better than its foresight!

In addition to identifying significant prices reversals, the Zig Zag indicator is also useful when doing Elliott Wave counts (see page 134).

Example

Figure 201 shows the 8-percent Zig Zag indicator plotted on top of Mattel's bar chart. This Zig Zag indicator ignores changes in prices that are less than 8 percent.

Calculation

The Zig Zag indicator is calculated by placing imaginary points on the chart when prices reverse by at least the specified amount. Straight lines are then drawn to connect these imaginary points.

Z

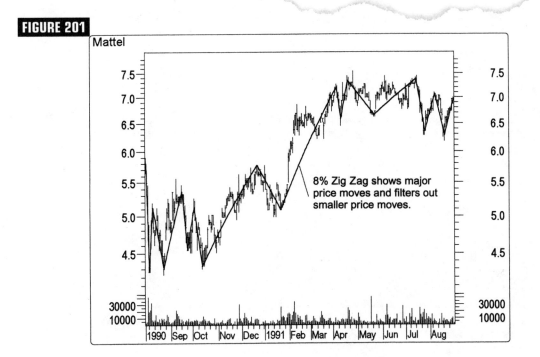

FIGURE 201

Mattel

8% Zig Zag shows major price moves and filters out smaller price moves.

Z

INDEX

A

A/D Line, 52–54, 57, 217
A/D Ratio, 55–56
ABI, 46–47, 57
Absolute Breadth Index, 46–47, 57
Accumulation/Distribution Line, 48–50
Accumulation Swing Index, 51–52, 326
Advance/Decline Line, 52–54, 57, 217
Advance/Decline Ratio, 55–56
Advancing, declining, unchanged volume, 58–60
Advancing-Declining Issues, 56–58
Altman, Roger, 291
Anderson, Jon, 313
Andrews, Alan, 60
Andrew's Pitchfork, 60–61
Appel, Gerald, 168, 199
Arithmetic moving average, 207
Arms, Richard W. Jr., 61, 131, 138
Arms Index, 61–64
Aroon, 64–68
Ascending triangle, 248
Ask price, 7
ATR, 68–70
Average True Range, 68–70

B

Bar charts, 8
    volume, 11
Bear trap, 20
Bid price, 7
Black, Fisher, 236
Black-Scholes option evaluation model, 236
Blau, William, 318

Bollinger, John, 71
Bollinger Bands, 71–74, 263, 264, 308, 313
Bolton, Hamilton, 134
Bond rates, 159–60
Book value per share, 152
Breadth Thrust, 57, 74–77
Bull/Bear Ratio, 78–79
Bull trap, 20

C

Candlestick charts, 79–90, 161, 162
    big candles, 83
    bodies, 83
    dark cloud cover, 89
    Doji's, 83–84
    engulfing lines, 84–85
    hanging man, 89
    Harami's, 85
    long shadows, 85–86
    on-neck line, 89
    piercing line, 89
    Qstick indicator, 278–80
    separating lines, 86
    shaven bottom/head, 86
    spinning top, 90
    stars, 86–87
    threesomes, 88
    tweezers, 88
    windows, 88–89
Candlevolume charts, 139
CANSLIM, 90–92
CCI, 103–6
Chaikin, Marc, 93, 96
Chaikin Money Flow, 93–95
Chaikin Oscillator, 96–100

Chaikin's Volatility, 354–56
Chande, Tushar, 64, 100, 128, 145, 161, 174, 278
Chande Momentum Oscillator, 100–103, 161
Chart types, 7–11. *(See specific headings throughout this index)*
Close price, 6
CMO, 100–103, 161
Collins, C. J., 134
Commodities and seasonal cycles, 112–13
Commodity Channel Index, 103–6
Commodity Selection Index, 106–7
Company analysis, 151–52
Comparative Relative Strength, 294–96
Computerized trading, 5–6
Confidence Index, 159
Contrarian investors, 38
Corporate bond rates, 159–60
Correlation analysis, 108–10
CSI, 106–7
Cumulative Volume Index, 59, 110–12
Current ratio, 152
CVI, 59, 110–12
Cycles, 112–15

D

Davis, Ned, 147
DeBry, Jon, xv, xvii
Debt ratio, 152
Declining value, 58–60
Definition of "technical analysis," 3, 4
Delta, 237–38
DEMA, 121–23, 329
Demand Index, 116–17
Descending triangle, 248
Detrended Price Oscillator, 117–19
Directional Movement, 119–20
Discount rate, 160
Divergences, 36–37
DMI, 128–30
Dobson, Edward, 141
Dorsey, Donald, 157, 181, 300
Dorsey's Relative Volatility Index, 157
Double Exponential Moving Average, 121–23, 329

Double Tops and Bottoms, 249
Dow, Charles, 2, 123
Dow Theory, 2, 123–28
DPO, 117–19
Dynamic Momentum Index, 128–30

E

Ease of Movement, 130–33
Economic analysis, 151
Edwards, Robert, 246
Efficient Market Theory, 3, 133–34
Eliades, Peter, 234
Elliott, Ralph Nelson, 134–36
Elliott Wave Theory, 134–36
Envelopes, 137–38
Equivolume, 138–41
Exponential moving average, 208-209

F

Fast Fourier Transform, 149–50
Fed Funds rate, 160
FFTs, 149–50
Fibonacci, Leonardo, 141
Fibonacci Arcs, 142
Fibonacci Fan Lines, 143, 305
Fibonacci numbers, 141
Fibonacci Retracements, 143–44
Fibonacci Time Zones, 144–45
Filtered waves, 372–73
Fishback, Don, 227
Forecast Oscillator, 145–47
Forecasting prices, 3–4
Fosback, Norman G., 46, 258, 274
Four Percent Model, 147–48
Fourier Transform, 149–50
Frost, A. J., 134
Fundamental analysis, 3, 151–53

G

Gambling analogy, 4–5, 40
Gamma, 238

Gann, W. D., 153–55
Gann angles, 153–55
Gaps, 249–50
Granville, Joseph, 96, 229

H

Hannula, Hans, 256
Head-and-Shoulders, 246–47
Herrick, John, 156
Herrick Payoff Index, 156–57
High price, 6
Historical price action, 3, 4
Historical Volatility, 240
Hitschler, Fred, 267
HPI, 156–57
Human emotions and expectations, 2–3

I

IMI, 161–64
Implied Volatility, 240
Indicators, 31–40. *(See specific headings throughout this index)*
Industry analysis, 151
Inertia, 157–58
Interest rates, 158–60
Intraday Momentum Index, 161–64
Inventory turnover, 153

J

January barometer, 114
January effect, 114
Japanese candlesticks, 79–90
Juglar, Clemant, 115
Juglar Wave, 115

K

Kagi charts, 164–66, 253, 330
Kitchin, Joseph, 114
Kitchin Wave, 114–15
Klinger, Stephen J., 167

Klinger Oscillator, 167–70
Kondratieff Wave, 115
Kroll, Stanley, 128
KVO, 167–70

L

Lagging indicators, 33–35
Lambert, Donald, 103, 104
Large Block Ratio, 171–72
Leading indicators, 35
Line Breaks, 330–33
Line charts, 8
Line studies, 41
Linear Regression Indicator, 172–73
Linear Regression Slope, 174–75
Linear Regression Trendlines, 176–77
Linear Scaling, 9–10
Linear versus semi-log scaling, 9–10
Low price, 6

M

MACD, 31–33, 199–202
Magee, John , 246
Market Facilitation Index, 178–80
Market indicators, 37–40
Mass Index, 181–83
McClellan, Marian, 183, 187
McClellan, Sherman, 187
McClellan Oscillator, 57, 183–86
McClellan Summation Index, 57, 187–90
Median Price, 190–91
Member Short Ratio, 192–93
Merrill, Arthur, 372
MESA Sine Wave, 193–94
MetaStock, 5–6, 149, 150
MFI
    Market Facilitation Index, 178–80
    Money Flow Index, 197–99, 344
MKDS, 61–64
Momentum, 267
Momentum indicators, 39–41, 195–97
Monetary indicators, 38, 40, 41

Money Flow Index, 197–99, 344

Moving Average Convergence Divergence, 31–33, 199–202

Moving averages, 27–30, 40, 203–13, 265, 266
    example, 205–6
    exponential average calculation, 208–9
    interpretation, 203–5
    overview, 203
    simple average calculation, 207
    time series average calculation, 210
    triangular average calculation, 210
    variable average calculation, 210–12
    volume-adjusted average calculation, 212
    weighted average calculation, 212–13

MSR, 192–93

MSW, 193–94

Mulloy, Patrick, 121, 328

N

Natenberg, Sheldon, 236

Negative Volume Index, 59, 214–16, 258

Net profit margin, 152

New Highs-Lows Cumulative, 217–18

New Highs/Lows Ratio, 218–20

New Highs-New Lows, 220–22

NH-NL, 220–22

NH/NL Ratio, 218–20

Nison, Steven, 79, 164, 302, 330

NVI, 59, 214–16, 258

O

OB/OS, 57, 161, 240–42, 272

OBV, 48, 110, 229–32, 261, 338

Odd Lot Balance Index, 222–23

Odd Lot Purchases/Sales, 224–25

Odd Lot Short Ratio, 225–27

ODDS™ Probability Cones, 227–29

OLBI, 222–23

On Balance Volume, 48, 110, 229–32, 261, 338

O'Neil, William, 90, 91

Open-10 TRIN, 233–35

Open Interest, 7, 232–33

Open price, 6

Open Trading Index, 233–35

Option analysis, 236–40

Option Life, 238

OSLR, 225–27

Overbrought/Oversold, 57, 161, 240–42, 272

P

P/C Ratio, 276–78

P/E ratio, 152

Parabolic SAR (Stop and Reversal), 242–45

Patterns, 245–50. *See* Price patterns

Percent Retracement, 250–51

Performance, 251–53

Periodicity, 12–13

P&F charts, 253–55, 330

PFE, 256–57

Point and Figure charts, 253–55, 330

Polarized Fractal Efficiency, 256–57

Positive Volume Index, 59, 257–61

Poulos, Michael, 285

Prechter, Robert, 134

Presidential cycle, 115

Price and Volume Trend, 261–63

Price Channels, 263–65

Price fields, 6–7

Price Oscillator, 265–67

Price patterns, 245–50
    Double Tops and Bottoms, 249
    Gaps, 249–50
    Head-and-Shoulders, 246–47
    Rounding Tops and Bottoms, 247
    Triangles, 248

Price Rate-of-Change, 195, 267–70

Prime rate, 160

Pring, Martin, 113

Projection Bands, 270–71

Projection Oscillator, 271–74

PSR, 192, 274–76, 336

Public Short Ratio, 192, 274–76, 336

Put/Call Price, 237

Puts/Calls Ratio, 276–78
PVI, 59, 257–61
PVT, 261–63

Q

Qstick, 278–80
Quadrant Lines, 280–81

R

R-Squared, 161, 282–84, 312
Raff, Gilbert, 284
Raff Regression Channel, 176, 284–85
Random Walk Index, 285–87
Range Indicator, 287–90
Rectangle, 290–91
Relative Momentum Index, 291–94
Relative Strength, Comparative, 294–96
Relative Strength Index, 297–300
Relative Volatility Index, 300–302
Renko charts, 302–4, 330
Resistance and support levels, 14–25
RMI, 291–94
ROC
    Price Rate-of-Change, 195, 267–70
    Volume Rate-of-Change, 360–62
"Roulette wheel" analogy, 4–5, 40
Rounding Tops and Bottoms, 247
RSI, 297–300
RVI, 157, 300–302
RWI, 285–87

S

Sample approach, 41–42
Scholes, Myron, 236
Semi-log *versus* linear scaling, 9–10
Sentiment indicators, 38
Short-Term Trading Index, 61–64
Sibbet, James, 116
Simple moving average, 207
Spectral analysis, 149

Speed Resistance Lines, 305–6
Spreads, 306–7
SRLs, 305–6
Standard Deviation, 308–9
Standard Deviation Channels, 310–11
Standard Error, 311–13
Standard Error Bands, 313–14
Standard Error Channels, 315–16
STIX, 316–18
STKS, 61–64
Stochastic Momentum Index, 318–20
Stochastic Oscillator, 113, 272, 321–26, 352, 369
Stock price valuation, 153
Supply and demand, 18–19
Support and resistance levels, 14–25
Swing Index, 326–28

T

TEMA, 328–30
Theta, 238–39
Three Line Break charts, 253, 302, 330–33
Time element, 13–14
Time Series Forecast, 333–34
Time Series moving average, 210
Tirone, John, 335
Tirone Levels, 335–36
Total Short Ratio, 336–38
Trade Volume Index, 338–40
Traders' remorse, 19–23
    moving averages, 30–31
Trading Bands, 137–38
TRading INdex, 61–64
Trading prices, 35–36
Treasury bill rates, 160
Treasury bond rates, 160
Trend-following indicators, 33–35
Trending prices, 35–36
Trendlines, 341–42
Trends, 25–27
Triangles, 248
Triangular moving average, 210
TRIN, 61–64
Triple Exponential Moving Average, 328–30

TRIX, 342–44
TSR, 336–38
TVI, 338–40
Typical Price, 190, 344–45

U

Ultimate Oscillator, 346–47
Unchanged volume, 58–60
Upside/Downside Ratio, 59, 348–49
Upside/Downside Volume, 350–51

V

Variable moving average, 210–12
Vega, 239
Vertical Horizontal Filter, 161, 351–54
VHF, 161, 351–54
Volatility, 239–40
    Chaikin's, 354–56
    Relative Volatility Index, 300–302
Volume, 356–58
    bar charts, 11
    defined, 7
Volume Accumulation/Distribution Line,
    261

Volume adjusted moving average, 212
Volume Oscillator, 358–60
Volume Rate-of-Change, 360–62

W

"Weatherman" analogy, 3–4, 40
Weekly cycle, 114
Weighted Close, 190, 362–64
Weighted moving average, 212–13
Weinberg, Jack, 287
White, Adam, 351
Widner, Mel, 270, 271
Wilder, Welles, 51, 68, 106, 119, 242, 297,
    326, 364
Wilder's Smoothing, 364–66
Williams, Larry, 96, 178, 346, 366, 369
Williams's Accumulation/Distribution,
    366–68
Williams's %R, 369–71

Z

Zig Zag, 372–73
Zweig, Martin, 74, 78, 147

ABOUT THE AUTHOR

Steven B. Achelis (pronounced "ə · kāy′· lĭss") is the founder and former president of Equis International, Inc. (equis.com). Equis is a leading provider of investment analysis software and services.

An experienced investment analyst and trader, Achelis has published a number of articles on stock market timing and is the author of *The Market Indicator Interpretation Guide*.

He is a gifted computer programmer and the author of many programs, including the best-selling MetaStock software.

Achelis has appeared on various national radio and television shows, including on CBS and CNBC. When not immersed in investing or technology, he likes spending time with his family and participating in active outdoor sports.

A companion spreadsheet, corrections, suggested books, and other supplemental information can be found at AtoZbook.com.